Scott Foresman
SCIENCE

Series Authors

Dr. Timothy Cooney
Professor of Earth Science and
Science Education
Earth Science Department
University of Northern Iowa
Cedar Falls, Iowa

Michael Anthony DiSpezio
Science Education Specialist
Cape Cod Children's Museum
Falmouth, Massachusetts

Barbara K. Foots
Science Education Consultant
Houston, Texas

Dr. Angie L. Matamoros
Science Curriculum Specialist
Broward County Schools
Ft. Lauderdale, Florida

Kate Boehm Nyquist
Science Writer and Curriculum Specialist
Mount Pleasant, South Carolina

Dr. Karen L. Ostlund
Professor
Science Education Center
The University of Texas at Austin
Austin, Texas

Contributing Authors

Dr. Anna Uhl Chamot
Associate Professor and
ESL Faculty Advisor
Department of Teacher Preparation
and Special Education
Graduate School of Education
and Human Development
The George Washington University
Washington, DC

Dr. Jim Cummins
Professor
Modern Language Centre and
Curriculum Department
Ontario Institute for Studies in Education
Toronto, Canada

Gale Philips Kahn
Lecturer, Science and Math Education
Elementary Education Department
California State University, Fullerton
Fullerton, California

Vincent Sipkovich
Teacher
Irvine Unified School District
Irvine, California

Steve Weinberg
Science Consultant
Connecticut State
Department of Education
Hartford, Connecticut

Scott Foresman

Editorial Offices: Glenview, Illinois · Parsippany, New Jersey · New York, New York
Sales Offices: Parsippany, New Jersey · Duluth, Georgia · Glenview, Illinois
Carrollton, Texas · Ontario, California
www.sfscience.com

Content Consultants

Dr. J. Scott Cairns
National Institutes of Health
Bethesda, Maryland

Jackie Cleveland
Elementary Resource Specialist
Mesa Public School District
Mesa, Arizona

Robert L. Kolenda
Science Lead Teacher, K-12
Neshaminy School District
Langhorne, Pennsylvania

David P. Lopath
Teacher
The Consolidated School District
of New Britain
New Britain, Connecticut

Sammantha Lane Magsino
Science Coordinator
Institute of Geophysics
University of Texas at Austin
Austin, Texas

Kathleen Middleton
Director, Health Education
ToucanEd
Soquel, California

Irwin Slesnick
Professor of Biology
Western Washington University
Bellingham, Washington

Dr. James C. Walters
Professor of Geology
University of Northern Iowa
Cedar Falls, Iowa

Multicultural Consultants

Dr. Shirley Gholston Key
Assistant Professor
University of Houston-Downtown
Houston, Texas

Damon L. Mitchell
Quality Auditor
Louisiana-Pacific Corporation
Conroe, Texas

Classroom Reviewers

Kathleen Avery
Teacher
Kellogg Science/Technology Magnet
Wichita, Kansas

Margaret S. Brown
Teacher
Cedar Grove Primary
Williamston, South Carolina

Deborah Browne
Teacher
Whitesville Elementary School
Moncks Corner, South Carolina

Wendy Capron
Teacher
Corlears School
New York, New York

Jiwon Choi
Teacher
Corlears School
New York, New York

John Cirrincione
Teacher
West Seneca Central Schools
West Seneca, New York

Jacqueline Colander
Teacher
Norfolk Public Schools
Norfolk, Virginia

Dr. Terry Contant
Teacher
Conroe Independent
School District
The Woodlands, Texas

Susan Crowley-Walsh
Teacher
Meadowbrook Elementary School
Gladstone, Missouri

Charlene K. Dindo
Teacher
Fairhope K-1 Center/Pelican's Nest
Science Lab
Fairhope, Alabama

Laurie Duffee
Teacher
Barnard Elementary
Tulsa, Oklahoma

Beth Anne Ebler
Teacher
Newark Public Schools
Newark, New Jersey

Karen P. Farrell
Teacher
Rondout Elementary School
District #72
Lake Forest, Illinois

Anna M. Gaiter
Teacher
Los Angeles Unified School District
Los Angeles Systemic Initiative
Los Angeles, California

Federica M. Gallegos
Teacher
Highland Park Elementary
Salt Lake School District
Salt Lake City, Utah

Janet E. Gray
Teacher
Anderson Elementary - Conroe ISD
Conroe, Texas

Karen Guinn
Teacher
Ehrhardt Elementary School - KISD
Spring, Texas

Denis John Hagerty
Teacher
Al Ittihad Private Schools
Dubai, United Arab Emirates

Judith Halpern
Teacher
Bannockburn School
Deerfield, Illinois

Debra D. Harper
Teacher
Community School District 9
Bronx, New York

Gretchen Harr
Teacher
Denver Public Schools - Doull School
Denver, Colorado

Bonnie L. Hawthorne
Teacher
Jim Darcy School
School Dist #1
Helena, Montana

Marselle Heywood-Julian
Teacher
Community School District 6
New York, New York

Scott Klene
Teacher
Bannockburn School 106
Bannockburn, Illinois

Thomas Kranz
Teacher
Livonia Primary School
Livonia, New York

Tom Leahy
Teacher
Coos Bay School District
Coos Bay, Oregon

Mary Littig
Teacher
Kellogg Science/Technology Magnet
Wichita, Kansas

Patricia Marin
Teacher
Corlears School
New York, New York

Susan Maki
Teacher
Cotton Creek CUSD 118
Island Lake, Illinois

Efraín Meléndez
Teacher
East LA Mathematics Science
Center LAUSD
Los Angeles, California

Becky Mojalid
Teacher
Manarat Jeddah Girls' School
Jeddah, Saudi Arabia

Susan Nations
Teacher
Sulphur Springs Elementary
Tampa, Florida

Brooke Palmer
Teacher
Whitesville Elementary
Moncks Corner, South Carolina

Jayne Pedersen
Teacher
Laura B. Sprague
School District 103
Lincolnshire, Illinois

Shirley Pfingston
Teacher
Orland School Dist 135
Orland Park, Illinois

Teresa Gayle Rountree
Teacher
Box Elder School District
Brigham City, Utah

Helen C. Smith
Teacher
Schultz Elementary
Klein Independent School District
Tomball, Texas

Denette Smith-Gibson
Teacher
Mitchell Intermediate, CISD
The Woodlands, Texas

Mary Jean Syrek
Teacher
Dr. Charles R. Drew Science
Magnet
Buffalo, New York

Rosemary Troxel
Teacher
Libertyville School District 70
Libertyville, Illinois

Susan D. Vani
Teacher
Laura B. Sprague School
School District 103
Lincolnshire, Illinois

Debra Worman
Teacher
Bryant Elementary
Tulsa, Oklahoma

Dr. Gayla Wright
Teacher
Edmond Public School
Edmond, Oklahoma

ISBN: 0-328-03425-8

 **Activity and Safety Consultants**

Laura Adams
Teacher
Holley-Navarre Intermediate
Navarre, Florida

Dr. Charlie Ashman
Teacher
Carl Sandburg Middle School
Mundelein District #75
Mundelein, Illinois

Christopher Atlee
Teacher
Horace Mann Elementary
Wichita Public Schools
Wichita, Kansas

David Bachman
Consultant
Chicago, Illinois

Sherry Baldwin
Teacher
Shady Brook
Bedford ISD
Euless, Texas

Pam Bazis
Teacher
Richardson ISD
  Classical Magnet School
Richardson, Texas

Angela Boese
Teacher
McCollom Elementary
Wichita Public Schools USD #259
Wichita, Kansas

Jan Buckelew
Teacher
Taylor Ranch Elementary
Venice, Florida

Shonie Castaneda
Teacher
Carman Elementary, PSJA
Pharr, Texas

Donna Coffey
Teacher
Melrose Elementary - Pinellas
St. Petersburg, Florida

Diamantina Contreras
Teacher
J.T. Brackenridge Elementary
San Antonio ISD
San Antonio, Texas

Susanna Curtis
Teacher
Lake Bluff Middle School
Lake Bluff, Illinois

Karen Farrell
Teacher
Rondout Elementary School,
  Dist. #72
Lake Forest, Illinois

Paul Gannon
Teacher
El Paso ISD
El Paso, Texas

Nancy Garman
Teacher
Jefferson Elementary School
Charleston, Illinois

Susan Graves
Teacher
Beech Elementary
Wichita Public Schools USD #259
Wichita, Kansas

Jo Anna Harrison
Teacher
Cornelius Elementary
Houston ISD
Houston, Texas

Monica Hartman
Teacher
Richard Elementary
Detroit Public Schools
Detroit, Michigan

Kelly Howard
Teacher
Sarasota, Florida

Kelly Kimborough
Teacher
Richardson ISD
  Classical Magnet School
Richardson, Texas

Mary Leveron
Teacher
Velasco Elementary
Brazosport ISD
Freeport, Texas

Becky McClendon
Teacher
A.P. Beutel Elementary
Brazosport ISD
Freeport, Texas

Suzanne Milstead
Teacher
Liestman Elementary
Alief ISD
Houston, Texas

Debbie Oliver
Teacher
School Board of Broward County
Ft. Lauderdale, Florida

Sharon Pearthree
Teacher
School Board of Broward County
Ft. Lauderdale, Florida

Jayne Pedersen
Teacher
Laura B. Sprague School
District 103
Lincolnshire, Illinois

Sharon Pedroja
Teacher
Riverside Cultural
  Arts/History Magnet
Wichita Public Schools USD #259
Wichita, Kansas

Marcia Percell
Teacher
Pharr, San Juan, Alamo ISD
Pharr, Texas

Shirley Pfingston
Teacher
Orland School Dist #135
Orland Park, Illinois

Sharon S. Placko
Teacher
District 26, Mt. Prospect
Mt. Prospect, IL

Glenda Rall
Teacher
Seltzer Elementary
USD #259
Wichita, Kansas

Nelda Requenez
Teacher
Canterbury Elementary
Edinburg, Texas

Dr. Beth Rice
Teacher
Loxahatchee Groves
  Elementary School
Loxahatchee, Florida

Martha Salom Romero
Teacher
El Paso ISD
El Paso, Texas

Paula Sanders
Teacher
Welleby Elementary School
Sunrise, Florida

Lynn Setchell
Teacher
Sigsbee Elementary School
Key West, Florida

Rhonda Shook
Teacher
Mueller Elementary
Wichita Public Schools USD #259
Wichita, Kansas

Anna Marie Smith
Teacher
Orland School Dist. #135
Orland Park, Illinois

Nancy Ann Varneke
Teacher
Seltzer Elementary
Wichita Public Schools USD #259
Wichita, Kansas

Aimee Walsh
Teacher
Rolling Meadows, Illinois

Ilene Wagner
Teacher
O.A. Thorp Scholastic Acacemy
Chicago Public Schools
Chicago, Illinois

Brian Warren
Teacher
Riley Community Consolidated
  School District 18
Marengo, Illinois

Tammie White
Teacher
Holley-Navarre
  Intermediate School
Navarre, Florida

Dr. Mychael Willon
Principal
Horace Mann Elementary
Wichita Public Schools
Wichita, Kansas

Inclusion Consultants

Dr. Eric J. Pyle, Ph.D.
Assistant Professor, Science Education
Department of Educational Theory
  and Practice
West Virginia University
Morgantown, West Virginia

Dr. Gretchen Butera, Ph.D.
Associate Professor, Special Education
Department of Education Theory
  and Practice
West Virginia University
Morgantown, West Virginia

Bilingual Consultant

Irma Gomez-Torres
Dalindo Elementary
Austin ISD
Austin, Texas

Bilingual Reviewers

Mary E. Morales
E.A. Jones Elementary
Fort Bend ISD
Missouri City, Texas

Gabriela T. Nolasco
Pebble Hills Elementary
Ysleta ISD
El Paso, Texas

Maribel B. Tanguma
Reed and Mock Elementary
San Juan, Texas

Yesenia Garza
Reed and Mock Elementary
San Juan, Texas

Teri Gallegos
St. Andrew's School
Austin, Texas

Unit B
Physical Science

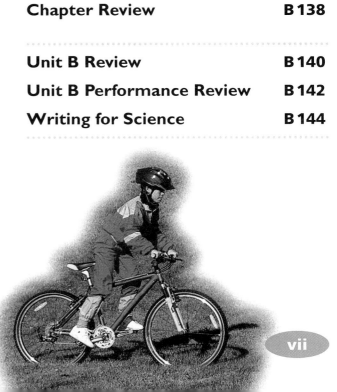

UNIT C
Earth Science

Unit D
Human Body

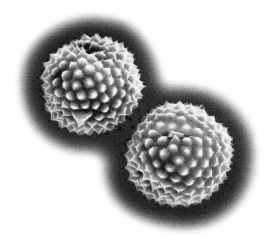

Using Scientific Methods for Science Inquiry

Scientists try to solve many problems. Scientists study problems in different ways, but they all use scientific methods to guide their work. Scientific methods are organized ways of finding answers and solving problems. Scientific methods include the steps shown on these pages. The order of the steps or the number of steps used may change. You can use these steps to organize your own scientific inquiries.

State the Problem

The problem is the question you want to answer. Curiosity and inquiry have resulted in many scientific discoveries. State your problem in the form of a question.

Formulate Your Hypothesis

Your hypothesis is a possible answer to your problem. Make sure your hypothesis can be tested. Your hypothesis should take the form of a statement.

▲ Sand heats up faster than water.

Identify and Control the Variables

For a fair test, you must select which variable to change and which variables to control. Choose one variable to change when you test your hypothesis. Control the other variables so they do not change.

Fill one pie pan with water and another with sand. Put a thermometer in each pan. Let them stand until they reach the same temperature. ▼

Test Your Hypothesis

Do experiments to test your hypothesis. You may need to repeat experiments to make sure your results remain consistent. Sometimes you conduct a scientific survey to test a hypothesis.

◀ *Direct a heat source on each pan.*

Collect Your Data

As you test your hypothesis, you will collect data about the problem you want to solve. You may need to record measurements. You might make drawings or diagrams. Or you may write lists or descriptions. Collect as much data as you can while testing your hypothesis.

Temperature of Water and Sand

Time (minutes)	0	1	2	3	4	5
Water	22°					
Sand	22°					

Interpret Your Data

By organizing your data into charts, tables, diagrams, and graphs, you may see patterns in the data. Then you can decide what the information from your data means.

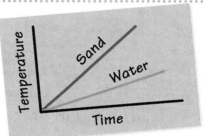

State Your Conclusion

Your conclusion is a decision you make based on evidence. Compare your results with your hypothesis. Based on whether or not your data supports your hypothesis, decide if your hypothesis is correct or incorrect. Then communicate your conclusion by stating or presenting your decision.

Sand heats faster than water.

🔍 Inquire Further

Use what you learn to solve other problems or to answer other questions that you might have. You may decide to repeat your experiment, or to change it based on what you learned.

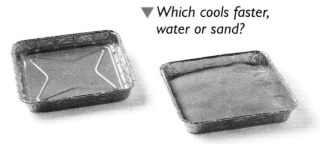
▼ *Which cools faster, water or sand?*

Using Process Skills for Science Inquiry

These 12 process skills are used by scientists when they do their research. You also use many of these skills every day. For example, when you think of a statement that you can test, you are using process skills. When you gather data to make a chart or graph, you are using process skills. As you do the activities in your book, you will use these same process skills.

Observing
Use one or more of your senses—seeing, hearing, smelling, touching, or tasting—to gather information about objects or events.

Tools can help in making observations

The Temperature of Water Affects How Much Sugar Dissolves in It

Communicating
Share information about what you learn using words, pictures, charts, graphs, and diagrams.

Classifying
Arrange or group objects according to their common properties.

◄ Objects that are attracted to a magnet.

Objects that are not attracted to a magnet. ▶

Estimating and Measuring
Make an estimate about an object's properties, then measure and describe the object in units.

An apple's mass is about 150 grams. Its diameter is 6.5 centimeters. ▶

Inferring
Draw a conclusion or make a reasonable guess based on what you observe, or from your past experiences.

I can infer that increasing the thickness of the paper or plastic decreases the effect of the magnetic force.

Predicting

Form an idea about what will happen based on evidence.

◀ Predict how five sheets of paper would affect the magnetic force.

A mold is an impression made by an object in a substance... ▶

Making Operational Definitions

Define or describe an object or event based on your experiences with it.

Making and Using Models

Make real or mental representations to explain ideas, objects, or events.

◀ The model is different from a molecule because...
It's like a molecule because...

If you plant a seed upside down, the root will grow toward... ▶

Formulating Questions and Hypotheses

Think of a statement that you can test to solve a problem or to answer a question about how something works.

Collecting and Interpreting Data

Gather observations and measurements into graphs, tables, charts, or diagrams. Then use the information to solve problems or answer questions.

Water evaporated faster in warm air than in cold air.

Variables	
Change	**Same**
✓ Temperature of water	✓ Kind of fish
	✓ Size and shape of bowl
	✓ Amount of water in bowl
	✓ Light
	✓ Food

Identifying and Controlling Variables

Change one factor that may affect the outcome of an event while holding other factors constant.

Experimenting

Design an investigation to test a hypothesis or to solve a problem. Then form a conclusion.

I'll plan an experiment and use scientific methods to test my hypothesis.

Science Inquiry

How fast will an ice cube melt at different temperatures?

Throughout your science book, you will ask questions, do investigations, answer your questions, and tell others what you have learned. Use the descriptions below to help you during your scientific inquiries.

1 **Ask questions that can be answered by scientific investigations.**
Direct your questions and inquiries toward objects and events that can be described, explained, or predicted by scientific investigations.

2 **Design and conduct a scientific investigation.**
Investigations can include using scientific methods to carry out science inquiry. As you conduct your investigations, you will relate your ideas to current scientific knowledge, suggest alternate explanations, and evaluate explanations and procedures.

3 **Use appropriate tools and methods to gather, analyze, and interpret data.**
The tools and methods you use will depend on the questions you ask and the investigations you design. A computer can be a useful tool for collecting, summarizing, and displaying your data.

4 **Use data to develop descriptions, suggest explanations, make predictions, and construct models.**
Base your explanations and descriptions on the information that you have gathered. In addition, understanding scientific subject matter will help you develop explanations, identify causes, and recognize relationships of events you observe with science content.

5 **Use logic to make relationships between data and explanations.**
Review and summarize the data you have gathered in your investigation. Use logic to determine the cause and effect relationships in the events and variables you observe.

6 **Analyze alternative explanations and predictions.**
Listen to, consider, and evaluate explanations offered by others. Asking questions and querying and evaluating explanations are part of scientific inquiry.

7 **Communicate procedures and explanations.**
Share your investigations with others by describing your methods, observations, results, and explanations.

8 **Use mathematics to analyze data and construct explanations.**
Use mathematics in your investigations to gather, organize, and collect data and to present explanations and results in a meaningful manner.

Unit A
Life Science

Science and Technology
In Your World!

Small Wonder

A tiny mosquito becomes frighteningly huge. Scientists used a scanning electron microscope, or SEM, to make this image. Using SEMs scientists can see some of the world's tiniest structures. Scientists use SEMs to study cells, tissues, and even small animals like this mosquito. You'll learn more about how scientists study the structures of living things in **Chapter 1 Comparing Living Things.**

A Human Road Map!

When you take a trip a map is helpful. A map of all the human genes would help doctors treat patients. That's because our genes carry information that affects how well our bodies use food and fight infection. The U.S. Human Genome Project seeks to find the location of all the 80,000 human genes. The new knowledge will help scientists find new ways to diagnose, treat, and prevent many diseases. You'll learn more about genetic information in **Chapter 2 Reproduction and Change.**

Suited for the Extreme!

Human bodies are not well adapted to survive Antarctica's bitter cold temperatures and high winds. Now, thanks to advanced robots, humans can safely explore places too extreme for humans. One type of robot is called a remotely operated vehicle, or ROV. ROVs have metal wheels and frames that adapt to different terrain. You'll read about the adaptations that living things need to survive in different environments in **Chapter 3 Adaptations.**

This Raft Sails on Treetops!

"Raft, away!" The brightly colored hot air blimp *Heartopia* gently lowers the giant "Raft of the Treetops" onto its 10-story-high perch on top of the tropical rain forest. Scientists can study the species that live in the top layer of rain forest up close. They peek and reach through—and even snooze on—the netting. You'll learn more about the rain-forest ecosystem in **Chapter 4 Ecology.**

What's That?

What would you see if you looked through a microscope? Everything would look very different. You might see tiny parts of a leaf.

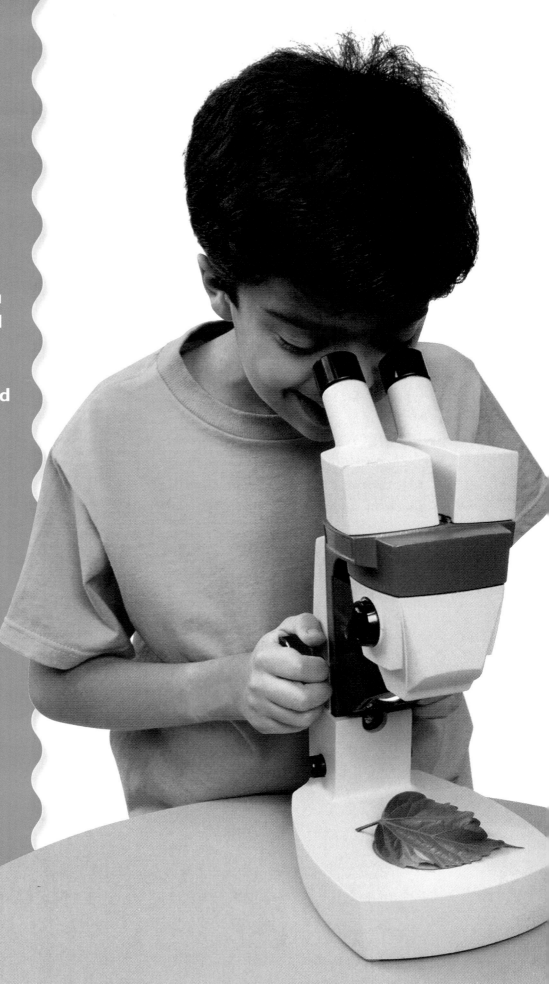

Chapter 1
Comparing Living Things

Inquiring about Comparing Living Things

Lesson 1
Is It Living or Nonliving?
- What are the processes of life?
- What are cells?
- What are tissues, organs, and systems?

Lesson 2
How Are Living Things Classified?
- How do scientists classify living things?
- What are the five kingdoms?
- How do scientists divide the kingdoms into smaller groups?
- How can ideas about classifying organisms change?

Lesson 3
How Are Animals Classified?
- What are invertebrates?
- What are vertebrates?

Lesson 4
How Are Plants Classified?
- How do scientists classify plants?
- What are mosses?
- What are ferns?
- What are conifers?
- What are flowering plants?

Copy the chapter graphic organizer onto your own paper. This organizer shows you what the whole chapter is all about. As you read the lessons and do the activities, look for answers to the questions and write them on your organizer.

Exploring Life Characteristics

Process Skills

- observing
- inferring

Materials

- graduated cup
- warm water
- 2 plastic bottles
- funnel
- plastic spoon
- dry sand
- sugar
- 2 balloons
- paper towel
- dry yeast
- clock

Explore

1 Measure 30 mL of warm water into the graduated cup. Pour it into a plastic bottle. Use the funnel to add a spoonful of dry sand and a spoonful of sugar to the bottle. Swirl the bottle to mix the contents. Stretch an uninflated balloon over the opening of the bottle.

2 Wipe off the spoon and the funnel with the paper towel. Repeat step 1, using a spoonful of yeast instead of sand.

3 Wait about 15 minutes. Look at the bottles and the balloons. Record your **observations** of the contents and of the balloons.

Reflect

1. Yeast is a fungus. Sugar acts as a food for many living things. Make an **inference.** Which shows signs of life, the yeast or the sand? Explain.

2. What signs of life did you observe in this activity?

? Inquire Further

What would happen to the yeast cells if you did not add sugar to the water? Make a plan to answer this or other questions you may have.

Comparing and Contrasting

In scientific investigations you often have to **compare** and **contrast** observations to reach a conclusion. The Explore Activity, *Exploring Life Characteristics*, focuses on the production of waste products, one of the six processes of life. The goal was to compare and contrast two bottles—one with yeast and one without yeast—to discover whether yeast are living things.

Reading Vocabulary

compare (kəm pâr′), to point out how things are alike and how they are different

contrast (kən trast), show differences

Example

In Lesson 1, *Is It Living or Not Living?*, you will discover that an object must carry out certain life processes to be considered living. A chart like the one below can help you conclude whether something is living or not. Select three objects and write the name of each in the left column. Write "yes" or "no" in each column to indicate if the object shows evidence of carrying out that life process.

Object	Gets Energy	Uses Energy	Gets Rid of Wastes	Reproduces	Grows	Responds to Changes

Talk About It!

Compare and contrast the objects you selected.

1. Does anything you selected show evidence of carrying out all six life processes?

2. Does anything you selected show evidence of carrying out no life processes?

3. Which objects seem to be living? Which objects seem to be nonliving?

4. How did the chart help you find out if an object is likely to be alive?

You will learn:
- **what the life processes are.**
- **what cells are.**
- **what tissues, organs, and systems are.**

Lesson 1

Is It Living or Nonliving?

WHOOSH! What is that flying through the air? Is it alive? It might be a bird or an airplane. They both fly. How are they alike? How are they different?

Life Processes

You know you need to eat and breathe to stay alive. Like the boy and the dog in the picture, all living things carry out activities called life processes. There are six life processes.

All organisms must **get energy.** Plants get energy from sunlight. Animals get energy and nutrients by eating other living things.

Living things **use energy** to do work. They break down food material and release the stored energy.

When they use energy, living things produce wastes. These wastes can be poisonous. Living things must **get rid of wastes.**

Living things make more of their own kind. **Reproducing** keeps groups of organisms alive. For example, not all lions reproduce, but some must reproduce or lions will become extinct.

Growing is a job that takes energy and nutrients. How much have you grown in the last year?

Living things **respond to changes** around them. You put on a coat when it gets cold. Dogs grow a thicker coat of hair as the weather gets colder.

All living things carry out life processes. ▼

Some nonliving things seem to carry out some of the life processes. Both a bird and a plane can use energy to fly, but which one carries out all the life processes you just learned about? Compare them on the chart and decide.

Life Process	Bird	Plane
Getting Energy	A bird gets energy from eating fruits, seeds, insects, fish, or other living things.	The engine burns fuel to release energy. A plane cannot get sources of energy on its own.
Using Energy	A bird uses energy to fly, to stay warm, and to carry out other life processes.	A plane uses energy to fly and to run the air conditioner and lights.
Getting Rid of Waste	Wastes leave a bird's body after food is broken down and energy is released.	Waste products are released as exhaust gas.
Reproducing	A bird lays eggs that hatch into baby birds.	A plane cannot reproduce.
Growing	A baby bird grows larger and develops into an adult.	A plane cannot grow.
Reacting to Change	A bird responds to what is around it. A bird will fly away if it hears a loud noise.	Instruments identify changes and direct the plane or its pilot to respond to them.

Glossary

virus (vī′rəs), a tiny particle that can reproduce only inside the cells of living things

bacteria (bak tir′ē ə), tiny one-celled organisms, some of which can cause diseases

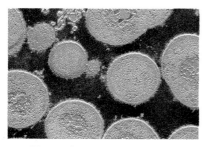

▲ These hepatitis B viruses are magnified 240,000 times.

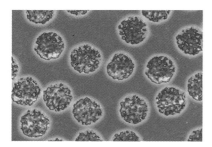

▲ These Streptococcus pneumoniae *bacteria are magnified 13,500 times.*

You know that a bird is a living thing and an airplane isn't. The chart on page A9 shows you that an airplane can't carry out all the life processes.

It's not always easy to tell if something is living. For example, most scientists think that viruses, such as the ones in the top picture, aren't living things because they can't carry out some of the life processes. A **virus** is a tiny particle that can reproduce only when it is inside a living cell, the basic unit of an organism's body. The virus uses the parts of the cell to produce more viruses. Viruses don't grow the way living things do, and they can't release and use energy. Whenever you have a cold or flu, you have viruses inside your body.

Unlike viruses, **bacteria** carry out all the life processes. Bacteria, such as the ones shown, are tiny living things, not much bigger than viruses. Most bacteria are harmless and many are helpful. However, some kinds can make you sick if they get into your body.

The pictures of the viruses and bacteria on this page were taken through an electron microscope, an instrument that magnifies objects, or makes them look bigger. This helps you see more detail. Look at the pictures of the pin below. How does the magnification affect what you can see?

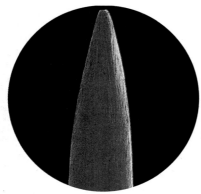

▲ This pin is magnified 18 times. It looks 18 times bigger than it really is.

▲ When the pin is magnified 400 times, its point looks flat. Find the bacteria on the pin.

▲ When the bacteria on the pin are magnified 18,375 times, you can see them easily.

Cells

A **cell** is the smallest unit of life. Living things are made up of cells. A row of 50 to 100 of most animal cells would fit inside the millimeter space on a ruler. You could not see one of them without a microscope. A few kinds of cells are much bigger. For example, a giraffe has nerve cells that stretch $2\frac{3}{4}$ meters from its backbone down its hind leg.

Each of the bacteria you saw on the pin on page A 10 is a single cell. So is the ameba in the picture. Each of these cells can carry out all the processes of life. The jellyfish below, like trees and monkeys and many other organisms, is made up of millions and millions of cells. Look for the different kinds of cells that work together as they carry out the jellyfish's life processes.

Glossary

cell (sel), the basic unit of a living organism

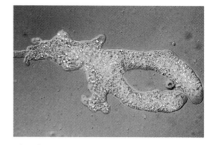

▲ *An ameba is a one-celled organism. It takes food into its body by changing its own shape and surrounding the food. (magnified 183×)*

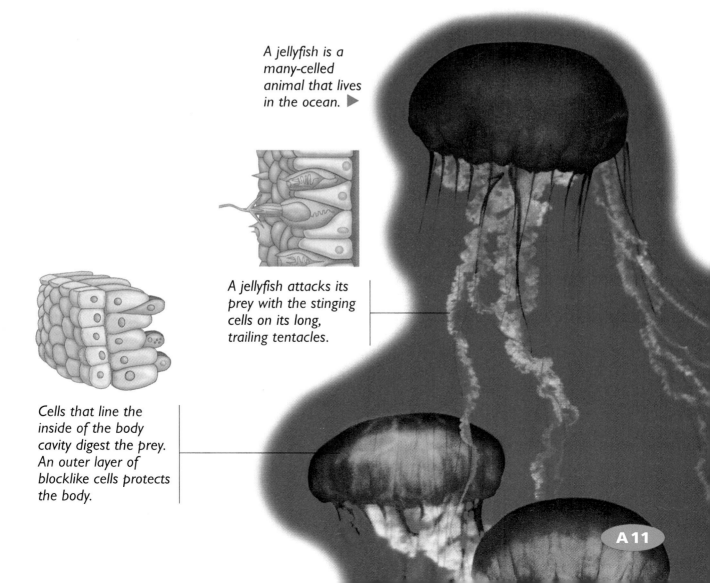

A jellyfish is a many-celled animal that lives in the ocean. ▶

A jellyfish attacks its prey with the stinging cells on its long, trailing tentacles.

Cells that line the inside of the body cavity digest the prey. An outer layer of blocklike cells protects the body.

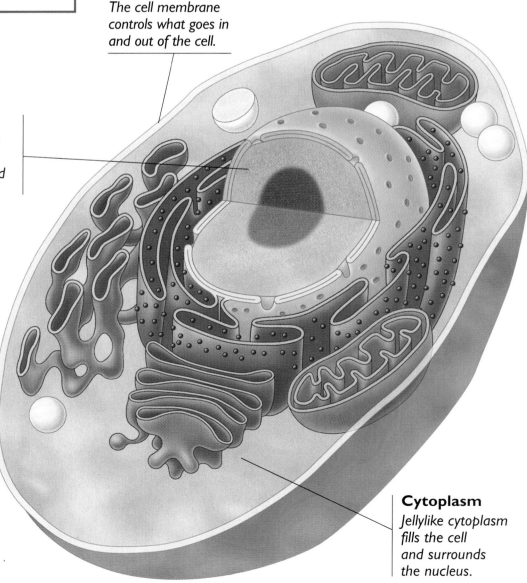

Glossary

cell membrane (mem′brān), a thin layer that makes up the outside of the cell and controls what enters and leaves it

nucleus (nü′klē əs), the cell part that controls the cell's activities

cytoplasm (sī′tə plaz′əm), jellylike material that fills most of a cell

You know that living things are made of cells. You also know that the cells aren't all alike. Cells of animals and plants are different in some ways and alike in others. First, look at the animal cell. Find the **cell membrane.** Nutrients, water, oxygen, and all the other things that enter and leave the cell pass through the cell membrane. Look for the **nucleus.** It controls what other cell parts do. The jellylike substance around the nucleus is the **cytoplasm.**

Animal Cell

Cell Membrane
The cell membrane controls what goes in and out of the cell.

Nucleus
The nucleus directs the way the cell grows, develops, and divides.

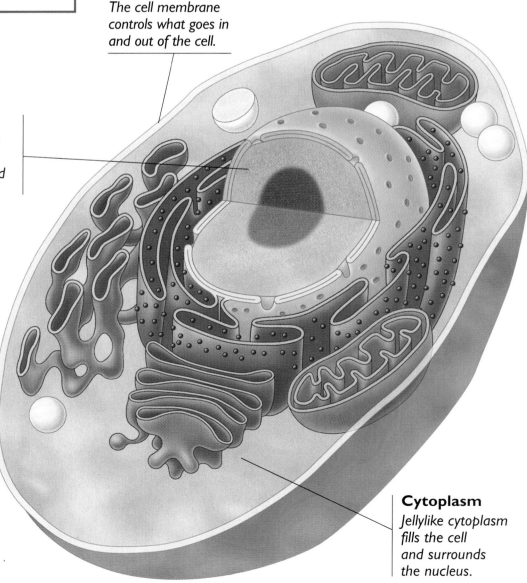

Cytoplasm
Jellylike cytoplasm fills the cell and surrounds the nucleus.

Now, look at the plant cell. What parts does it have that the animal cell doesn't have? If you said a cell wall and chloroplasts, you're right! The stiff **cell wall** surrounds a plant cell just outside the cell membrane. It helps the cell keep its shape. Find a green chloroplast. A **chloroplast** captures energy from the sun and uses it to make sugar from water and carbon dioxide.

Glossary

cell wall, a stiff outer layer that helps keep plant cells firm

chloroplast (klôr′ə plast), the green cell part in plant cells that traps and uses light energy

Plant Cell

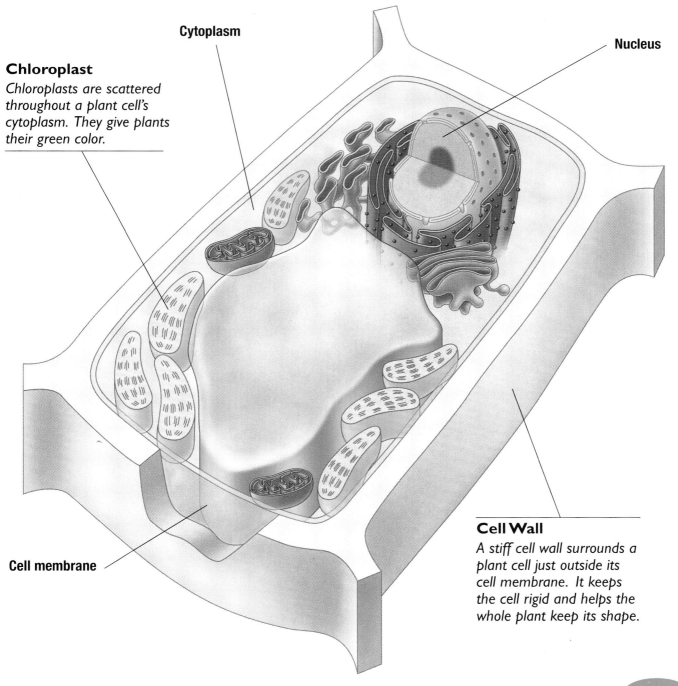

Cytoplasm

Nucleus

Chloroplast
Chloroplasts are scattered throughout a plant cell's cytoplasm. They give plants their green color.

Cell Wall
A stiff cell wall surrounds a plant cell just outside its cell membrane. It keeps the cell rigid and helps the whole plant keep its shape.

Cell membrane

Tissues, Organs, and Systems

Human Body

Cells of many shapes and sizes do different jobs in your body and in the bodies of most many-celled organisms. Their special shapes help them.

Compare the different cells shown. Nerve cells carry messages to and from different parts of your body. Short branches at one end of the cell receive a signal. They pass it to the main part of the cell. The signal moves through a long, thin branch to the next nerve cell.

Red blood cells can travel through blood vessels to every part of your body. They carry oxygen to all your cells. Red blood cells have a flat center and bulging edges. Their shape helps them carry a lot of oxygen. Mature red blood cells do not have a nucleus.

Squarish skin cells that fit together in flat sheets cover the surface of your body. They protect the cells beneath them from damage.

Groups of similar cells form tissues. They look alike and work together to do the same job. Heart muscle cells like the ones in the picture contract and relax regularly. The heart muscle tissue shown is made up of many heart muscle cells. They contract and relax together. This makes your heart beat.

▲ Nerve cell
(magnified 3,500×, false color)

Red blood cells
(magnified 900×,
color-enhanced) ▶

▲ Skin cells (magnified 385×)

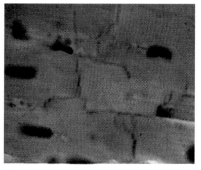

▲ Heart muscle cells
(magnified 683×)

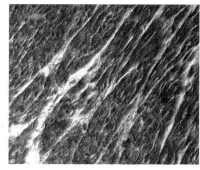

▲ Heart muscle tissue
(magnified 148×)

Organs are made up of different kinds of tissues that work together. Like the heart in the picture, your heart is an organ made of muscle, nerve, blood, and other tissues. When it beats, it pumps blood throughout your body.

Organs working together make up organ systems. Look at the picture of the heart and the blood vessels. They are organs in your circulatory system. They work together pumping blood and carrying it to all your body's cells.

Your heart pushes blood through your blood vessels. The blood brings nutrients and oxygen to all your cells and takes away wastes. ▶

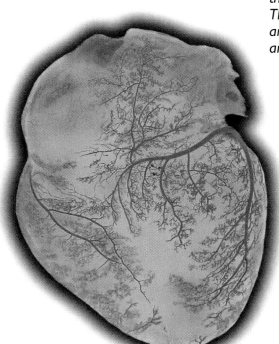

◀ *Your heart is an organ that is part of the circulatory system.*

Lesson 1 Review

1. What are the processes of life?
2. What are cells?
3. What are tissues, organs, and systems?
4. **Compare and Contrast**
   Compare and contrast living and nonliving things.

You will learn:

- how scientists classify living things.
- what the five kingdoms are.
- how scientists divide the kingdoms up.
- how ideas about classifying organisms can change.

On which shelf would you have better luck finding a book about birds? ▼

Lesson 2

How Are Living Things Classified?

WOW! Look at all the stuff in this library. How will you find what you want? Think! The books are grouped in ways that help you. Would grouping books by size or color help you?

Classifying

People usually group things by how they are alike and different. Grouping things makes them easier to find and shows relationships. The picture shows how librarians group books by the way their subject matter is related. Scientists also want a system that shows the way things are related.

You group living things whenever you call them plants or animals. You group animals when you call them birds, fish, or mammals. Scientists **classify,** or group, organisms by their similarities. They group many organisms by their body structure. Insects have six legs. Birds have two legs and are covered with feathers. However, scientists don't usually group organisms only by their appearance. Scientists also classify organisms by their cell structure, how they get nutrients and energy, and how they reproduce.

The Five Kingdoms

The largest group into which scientists classify living things is called a **kingdom.** The chart shows the five kingdoms most scientists agree on—the moneran, protist, fungus, plant, and animal kingdoms. Organisms in the same kingdom share more traits with each other than they do with any organism in any other kingdom.

You know that bacteria are tiny, one-celled organisms. Bacteria make up the moneran kingdom. They are the smallest, simplest living things. You can find them almost everywhere on earth—in the ocean, in snow at the top of mountains, on bare rocks, and inside your body. Some monerans use energy from the sun or from chemical reactions to make sugar. Others get nutrients from the bodies of other organisms. The monerans in the picture cause a disease in humans that resembles pneumonia.

Protists make up another kingdom. Most protists are one-celled organisms, but some have many cells. Some protists have a green pigment like the one in chloroplasts of plants. Like plants, they trap the sun's energy and produce sugar. Other protists, such as this paramecium, get nutrients by absorbing them from surroundings or by capturing and consuming prey.

Glossary

The Five Kingdoms

Moneran
One-celled, no separate nucleus
Example—bacteria

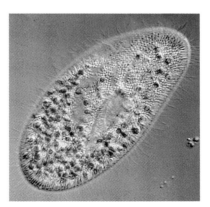

Protist
Most one-celled, have nucleus and other cell structures
Examples—algae, ameba

Fungus
Mostly many-celled, cannot move, absorb nutrients from other organisms
Examples—mushrooms, yeast, molds

Plant
Many-celled, cannot move, use energy from the sun to make sugars
Examples—trees, flowers, ferns

Animal
Many-celled, most can move, get energy by consuming other organisms
Examples—invertebrates, fish, birds, mammals

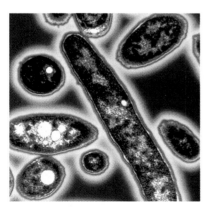

▲ *The simple cells of monerans have no separate nucleus. The material scattered through the cytoplasm does the job of the nucleus. This moneran is* Legionella pneumophia *magnified 100,000 times.*

▲ *Protist cells have a nucleus and other cell parts. Each part is surrounded by a membrane. Protist cells are like the cells of fungi, plants, and animals. This protist is* Paramecium bursaria *magnified 300 times.*

▲ These fungi send rootlike structures into the tree and absorb nutrients from it.

▲ Plants range in size from giant trees to tiny mosses that grow in moist places. Plants grow in many different climates.

Have you ever eaten a mushroom? If so, you've been in close contact with a fungus. A fungus is a member of the fungus kingdom. Fungi are mostly many-celled organisms that can't move around. The fungi in the picture get nutrients from the tree they are growing on. You've probably seen or heard of several other kinds of fungi, such as molds, mildew, and yeast. Fungi all get nutrients by absorbing them from living organisms or from organisms that are dead or decaying.

Plants are many-celled organisms. You already know that their cells have cell walls. Most plant cells have chloroplasts that contain chlorophyll, the green pigment that traps the sun's energy and makes sugar. The cells in the moss and in the green leaves of the other plants in the picture contain many chloroplasts.

Like plants and fungi, animals are many-celled organisms. Unlike plant cells, animal cells don't have a cell wall or chloroplasts. They can't trap sunlight or produce sugars. Animals get energy by consuming other organisms or their remains. The whale and the fruit fly in the pictures are both animals.

Animals range from huge whales that measure 30 meters long to insects you can hardly see. ▶

Dividing the Kingdoms into Smaller Groups

All the organisms within each kingdom are similar to each other in some ways. However, kingdoms are so large that they include very different organisms.

Scientists divide the organisms in a kingdom into smaller groups. The chart shows how one organism, the lion, is classified.

Look at the first row on the chart. All the organisms pictured in the row, including the lion, are animals. Find the animals in the second row. They all, including the lion, have backbones. Notice that the fly isn't pictured in the second row. It doesn't have a backbone.

As the groups get smaller, the animals in the group are more alike. Lions and tigers are in the same **genus,** a group of similar organisms. The animals in this group are all large cats that roar. Find the smallest group, the **species,** in the bottom row of the chart. A species has only one kind of animal in it. The lion is the only kind of animal in its species.

Glossary

Glossary

genus (jē′nəs), a group of similar species

species (spē′shēz), a group of organisms of only one kind that can interbreed in nature

▲ Tiger

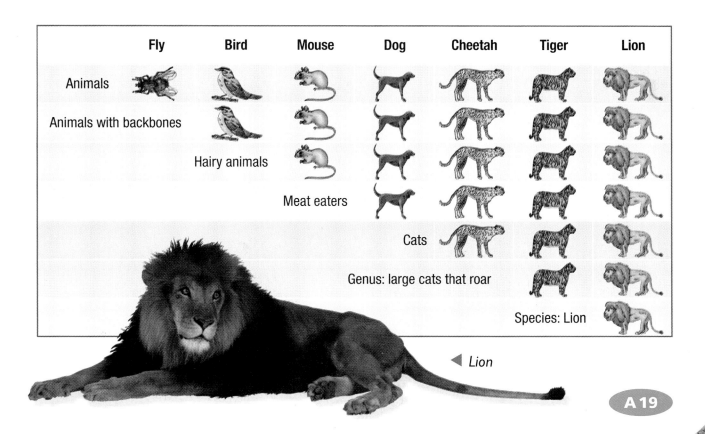

	Fly	Bird	Mouse	Dog	Cheetah	Tiger	Lion
Animals	🪰	🐦	🐭	🐕	🐆	🐅	🦁
Animals with backbones		🐦	🐭	🐕	🐆	🐅	🦁
Hairy animals			🐭	🐕	🐆	🐅	🦁
Meat eaters				🐕	🐆	🐅	🦁
Cats					🐆	🐅	🦁
Genus: large cats that roar						🐅	🦁
Species: Lion							🦁

◀ Lion

A19

Organisms in the same genus are closely related. About 250 years ago, Carolus Linnaeus, a Swedish biologist, developed a way to name organisms and show relationships. He gave each kind of organism a two-word name. One word was the name scientists use for the organism's genus. The other was the name they use for its species. Scientists still name organisms this way.

You might know some scientific names. For example, *Tyrannosaurus rex*, or *T. rex* for short, is a dinosaur that lived millions of years ago. It is in a genus scientists named *Tyrannosaurus*. One kind of dinosaur in the genus makes up the species *rex*.

The lion's scientific name is *Panthera leo*. Recall that its close relative, the tiger, is in the same genus. The tiger's species name is *tigris*. Its scientific name, *Panthera tigris,* tells you it is similar to lions and other animals in the genus *Panthera*. Which of the two animals shown is more closely related to lions and tigers?

Scientific names help avoid confusion. Sometimes people call an organism by several different names. At least four names are used for the mountain lion shown. It has only one scientific name. Scientists all over the world use that name.

People call this animal by many names, including mountain lion, Florida panther, cougar, and puma. Its scientific name is Felis concolor. ▼

Some people call this animal a leopard. Others call it a panther. Its scientific name, Panthera pardus, *tells that it is similar to lions and tigers, which are also in the genus* Panthera. ▼

Changing Ideas About Classification

Scientists classify organisms based on what they know about them. When they learn more about organisms and their structure, they also learn more about how the organisms are related to other living things. Then the scientists might change their ideas about classifying organisms.

For hundreds of years, all living things were classified as either plants or animals. Then, in the 1600s, microscopes were developed. Through the microscopes, scientists saw tiny organisms no one had seen before. When more powerful microscopes were developed, scientists learned more about the organisms.

By the 1970s most scientists agreed that the tiny organisms didn't fit with either plants or animals. They put the organisms into a new kingdom, the protists. As scientists learned more about the cells of organisms, they added kingdoms for fungi and monerans.

Today, many scientists suggest putting some of the monerans into a sixth kingdom. These bacteria have a different cell structure than other bacteria. They don't use the sun as a source of energy. They use energy from chemicals in places like volcanic vents deep in the ocean and the hot spring in the picture.

▲ *A sixth kingdom might include the bacteria that live in places like this hot spring.*

Lesson 2 Review

1. How do scientists classify living things?

2. List the five kingdoms.

3. How do scientists divide the kingdoms into smaller groups?

4. Why do scientists sometimes change their ideas about classifying organisms?

5. **Compare and Contrast**
   How do you think scientists classified protists when they divided all living things into only two kingdoms?

Observing Growth of Fungi

Process Skills

- observing
- collecting and interpreting data
- communicating
- inferring

Materials

- piece of bread
- piece of orange peel
- piece of tomato
- water
- clear plastic disposable jar with a tight-fitting lid
- masking tape
- hand lens

Getting Ready

You can learn about organisms in one of the five kingdoms by growing and observing mold on food.

Follow This Procedure

1 Make a chart like the one shown. Use your chart to record your observations.

Mold observations

Day	Bread	Orange peel	Tomato
1			
2			
3			
4			
5			
6			
7			

2 Sprinkle the pieces of food with water and put them into a clear disposable jar.

3 Put the lid on the jar tightly and wrap masking tape around the edge to seal it (Photo A).

Photo A

 Put the jar in a dark place where it won't be disturbed. **Observe** the food and **collect data** every day for seven days. Record when mold first grows on the food (Photo B). Use a hand lens to observe the mold closely. Describe the color and appearance of the mold.

⚠ *Safety Note Do not open the container or break the seal. Give the sealed container to your teacher to discard when you are done.*

Interpret Your Results

1. Compare and contrast the mold growth on the different foods. Does the same kind of mold grow on the different types of food? Does mold spread from one piece of food to the one next to it? Did any piece of food have more than one kind of mold on it?

Photo B

2. Communicate. Compare and contrast your results with the results of others in the class.

3. Like mushrooms, molds are members of the fungus kingdom. Make an **inference** based on your data and observations. Explain how you think molds get energy. Why do you think mold can grow in the dark?

Inquire Further

Could the molds grow without water? in a sunny spot? Develop a plan to answer these or other questions you may have.

Self-Assessment

- I followed instructions to **observe** mold growth on different foods.
- I **collected data** by recording my observations of mold growth.
- I **interpreted data** by comparing and contrasting mold growth on different foods.
- I **communicated** by comparing and contrasting my results with the results of other students.
- I made **inferences** about how molds get energy and why mold can grow in the dark.

You will learn:
- what invertebrates are.
- what vertebrates are.

Lesson 3

How Are Animals Classified?

Can you feel the lumpy row of bones running down your back? You should appreciate those bones. They keep your body from collapsing in a squishy heap!

Glossary

invertebrate
(in vėr′tə brit), an animal that has no backbone

▲ *A hydra's waving tentacles are covered with stinging cells that help it capture prey.*

Animals Without Backbones

The bones that run down your back make up your backbone. Fish, birds, and lions are some animals that have backbones like yours. Many animals have no backbone. Scientists call an animal without a backbone an **invertebrate.** Invertebrates are many-celled animals including sponges, jellyfish, worms, sea stars, mollusks, and arthropods.

Look at the picture of a sponge. Sponges appear more like plants than animals. They attach themselves to rocks and other objects in the water. They trap and consume tiny organisms that float in the water that passes in and out of their hollow bodies.

Like the sponges, hydras, jellyfish, and their relatives have hollow bodies. Notice the snakelike tentacles around the mouth of the hydra. The hydra and its relatives use their tentacles to capture prey.

◀ *A sponge's hollow body is made up of two layers of cells with a thick, jellylike layer between them.*

You might have met a mollusk at the dinner table. Snails, squid, and oysters are mollusks that people eat. Mollusks are animals with soft bodies. Some are supported and protected by one or two shells. Notice the snail's single shell.

The sea star in the picture lives on the ocean floor. Powerful suction cups on a sea star's underside help it pry open the shells of the clams it eats. The suction cups also anchor the sea star tightly to rocks on the sea bottom.

More than 80 percent of all animal species are arthropods. This huge group includes lobsters and crabs, spiders, centipedes and millipedes, and all the insects. Insects make up almost 70 percent of the species of arthropods. A stiff outer covering protects and supports an arthropod's body. Find the joints in the lobster's covering.

Several groups of invertebrates with narrow, tubelike bodies are called worms. Flatworms have flattened bodies. Roundworms look like tiny snakes with no heads. Worms like the earthworm in the picture are segmented worms.

▲ *The snail's coiled shell protects and supports its soft body.*

Notice the tough skin and spines on this sea star. They help protect it from enemies. ▼

▲ *This earthworm burrows into the ground. It digests the remains of dead plants and animals it finds there.*

Lobsters are like knights in armor. A stiff shell called an exoskeleton covers and protects them. Their joints let them move. ▼

▲ Fish use their fins and tails to move swiftly through the water.

▲ Do you think a lizard is slimy? Well, it's not. Its body is covered with dry scales.

Glossary

Glossary

vertebrate
(vėr′tə brit), an animal with a backbone

Frogs can breathe through their lungs, just as you do. They can also breathe through their skin. Bet you can't do that! ▼

Animals with Backbones

You know that you and lots of familiar animals all have backbones. An animal that has a backbone is called a **vertebrate.** Fishes, frogs, snakes, birds, and cats belong to the different groups of vertebrates.

The fish in the picture can get oxygen from the water. Fish use their gills to take in oxygen they need. They lay their eggs in the water and spend their whole lives there. Fish range in size from a goby about $1\frac{1}{2}$ centimeters long to a whale shark that can measure more than 12 meters.

Frogs and salamanders are amphibians. They usually lay eggs in the water and begin their lives taking in oxygen through gills like fish. Like the adult frog in the picture, most amphibians develop lungs that can take oxygen from the air. Then they can live on land.

Lizards, snakes, turtles, alligators, and crocodiles are all reptiles. They breathe with lungs all their lives. Notice that the lizard in the picture, like all reptiles, has tough scales that protect its body. Most reptiles lay eggs on land. The eggs don't dry out because they have leathery shells. A few kinds of reptiles hatch from eggs inside the mother's body.

▲ *A bird's feathers help it stay warm and help it fly.*

▲ *Notice the thick covering of hair on the bears. It helps keep their body temperature about the same all the time.*

Like reptiles, birds breathe air all their lives and lay their eggs on land. Birds' eggs have hard shells. Birds have hollow bones that make their bodies light and make it easier for them to fly.

A **mammal** is an animal that has some hair or fur on its body. The thick covering of hair on some mammals, such as the bears in the picture, helps them keep warm. Other mammals have only a little hair. Mammals have lungs and breathe air all their lives. They are the only animals that feed their young with milk produced by the mother. Dogs, bats, bears, whales, elephants, horses, cows, and monkeys are all mammals.

You can find mammals on land, in the water, and in the air. Whales and dolphins are mammals that live in the ocean. They have some hair on their bodies and they come to the surface to breathe. Did you know that bats are the only mammals that can really fly?

Glossary

mammal (mam′əl), an animal that has hair or fur and feeds its young with milk produced by the mother

Glossary

Lesson 3 Review

1. What are invertebrates?
2. What are vertebrates?
3. **Compare and Contrast**
   Compare and contrast the different groups of vertebrates.

You will learn:

- how scientists classify plants.
- what mosses are.
- what ferns are.
- what conifers are.
- what flowering plants are.

Glossary

vascular (vas´kyə lər) **plant,** a plant with long tubes inside that carry food and water to all the parts of the plant

Stringy tubes go from the base of the celery stalk all the way to the leaves. Find the tubes in this piece of celery. ▼

How Are Plants Classified?

Mmm! What's that good smell? Ahhhh, the flowers are in bloom. **Bzzz.** What's that sound? Uh-oh! The bees have found the flowers. Better not disturb them.

Classifying Plants

Scientists classify some plants as vascular plants. A **vascular plant** has cells inside it that form long tubes. The tubes carry nutrients and water through the plant. They also strengthen and support the plant. The strings in the celery stalk shown are the tubes of a vascular plant. Vascular plants are the only plants that have tubes like these.

Scientists also group plants by how they reproduce. Some plants produce seeds; others don't. Seeds such as the ones in the picture contain new, developing plants as well as stored food for the new plants. The beans, nuts, berries, and grains you eat are seeds or fruits that have seeds in them. Plants are also grouped by whether or not they produce flowers. Flowers contain the reproductive parts of flowering plants.

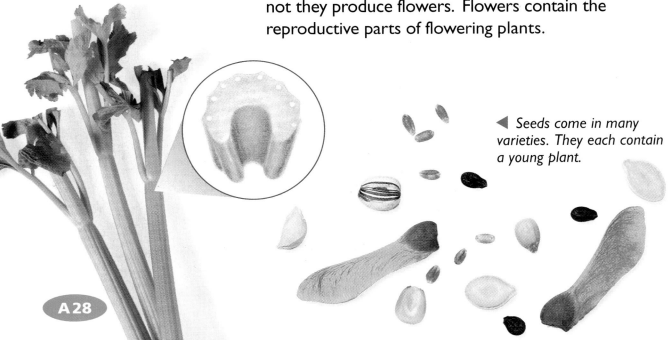

◀ *Seeds come in many varieties. They each contain a young plant.*

A28

Mosses

Mosses are not vascular plants. They don't have tubes that can carry food and water through the plant. You've probably seen a moist patch of ground with fuzzy, green moss growing on it. Most mosses live in moist places.

Notice that the mosses in the picture are small and grow near the ground. In mosses, food and water can only pass slowly from one cell to another to get to different parts of the plant. This system only works well for small plants. All the cells of a moss plant need to be near water, so moss plants can't grow very tall.

Mosses don't have roots or leaves. Some of the plant's cells grow into the ground and absorb water and nutrients. The green parts of the plants use

Moss usually grows in clumps in damp, shady places. ▼

energy from the sun to make sugar. Some mosses grow on the ground in the shade of trees and other plants. Some grow on tree trunks or decaying logs. Mosses can even grow in the soil that collects in the cracks on rocks or sidewalks.

Moss plants do not have seeds or flowers. They reproduce by forming tiny cells that can grow into new plants. Each of the tiny cells is called a spore.

Ferns

Like mosses, ferns are flowerless, seedless plants that reproduce by forming spores. The spores grow in clusters on the underside of the fern's leaves. Notice the clusters of spores on one of the fern leaves in the picture below. The wind can carry the spores far away from the parent plant. A new plant could grow from each spore that lands in a favorable place.

Unlike mosses, ferns are vascular plants. Tubes inside their stems and leaves carry food and water to all the cells of the plant. Water and nutrients move more easily through the long tubes in ferns than they do from one cell to another in mosses.

The tubes in vascular plants can carry the water and nutrients long distances through the plant. Ferns and other vascular plants can grow larger than mosses. Ferns range in size from tiny plants about 2 or 3 centimeters tall to huge plants that look like palm trees and grow more than 20 meters high.

Most ferns grow in warm, moist climates in damp, shady places. However, some ferns can grow all over the world, even in dry, cold places. Many ferns have long leaves like the ones in the picture. The green leaves of ferns, like those of other plants, use energy from sunlight to make sugar.

The long leaves of ferns are called fronds. ▼

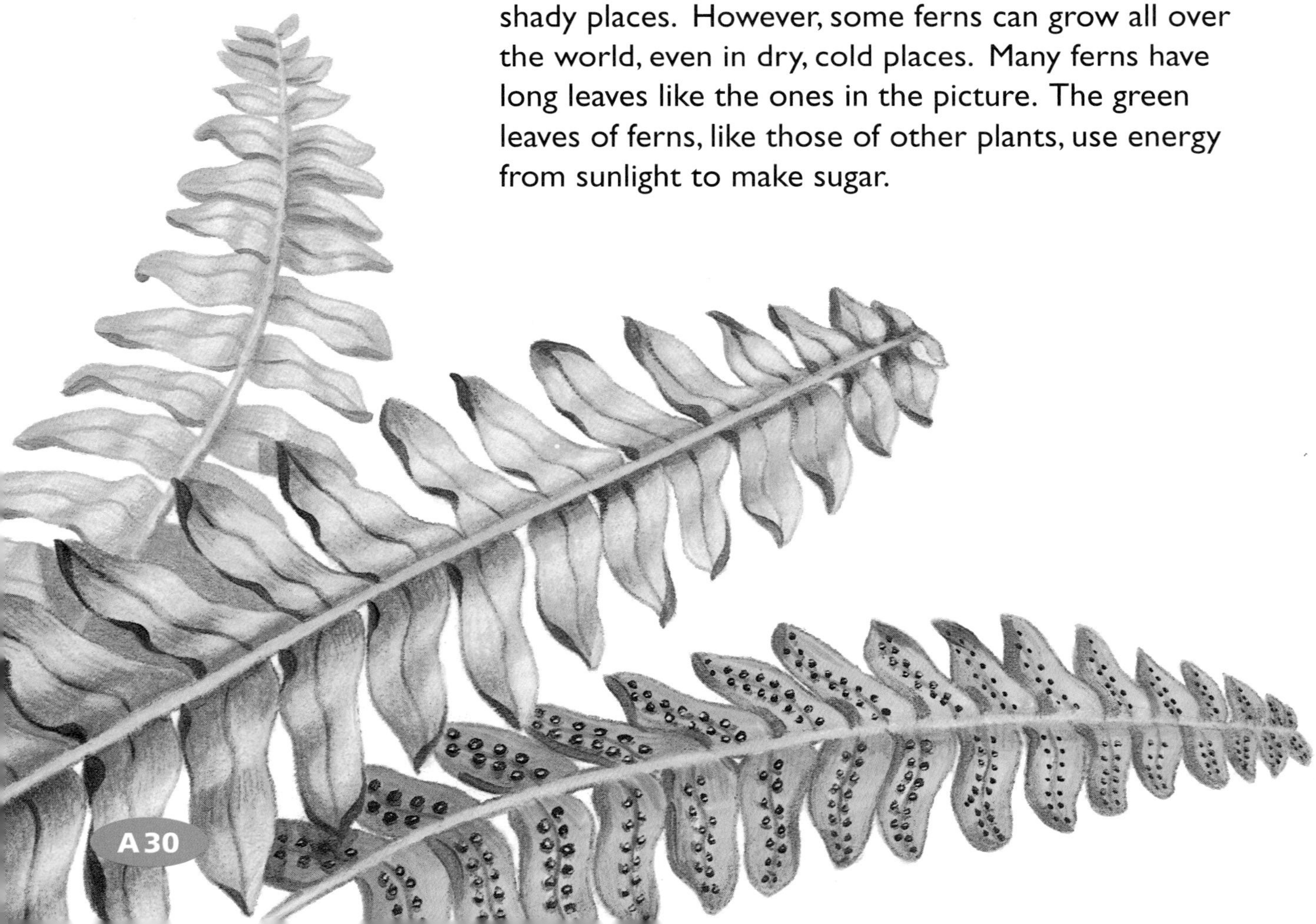

Conifers

Conifers are often called evergreens because most kinds don't lose their leaves in winter. Conifers are trees and shrubs, including pines, cedars, firs, yews, and spruces. The leaves on most conifers, like the ones on the branch in the picture, are long, narrow needles.

Conifers are vascular plants that do not have flowers. They produce seeds in cones. Conifers have two kinds of cones. The pollen cone in the picture to the right is releasing dustlike pollen into the air. The pollen will float around on the breeze.

A seed cone has a sticky covering and has egg cells inside it. Sometimes a pollen grain carried by the wind lands on a seed cone. Then a tube grows from the pollen down the cone into an **egg cell**. A **sperm cell** in the tube joins with the egg cell, and a seed develops. The seed falls out of the cone onto the ground, where it could grow into a new plant.

Glossary

egg cell, a cell that can join with a sperm cell to form a new individual

sperm cell (spėrm), a cell that can join with an egg cell to form a new individual

The cloud of pollen released when a pollen cone opens can make some people sneeze and wheeze. ▼

The green needles on conifers use energy from the sun to make sugar. ▼

A31

Flowers like the blossoms on this peach tree contain all the reproductive parts of flowering plants. ▶

Inside the seed is a developing plant and stored food that the plant can use as it begins to grow.

Flowering Plants

Most of the plants you see every day are flowering plants. Some, like grasses and oak trees, have flowers so small you might not notice them. Others have large, brightly colored blossoms.

The flowers on the peach trees in the picture are the reproductive parts of the plant. The fruits and seeds develop from the flowers. Notice in the peaches shown that the fruit you eat surrounds the seed. A developing plant is inside the seed. There are over 200,000 different species of flowering plants, more than all the other kinds of plants combined.

The fruit develops from part of the flower and grows around the seed, which can develop into a new plant.

Like conifers and ferns, flowering plants are vascular plants. Some, such as elms and oaks, grow for many years and can become huge trees. Trees and shrubs have hard, rigid, woody stems. Other flowering plants have stems that are green and flexible. Some grow for only a season. A few flowering plants are so small you can hardly see them. Duckweed, the smallest flowering plant, measures less than 5 millimeters across.

Scientists classify flowering plants into two main groups based on the number of leaflike structures inside their seeds. One group, called monocots, has one seed leaf. Monocots include grasses, lilies, orchids, corn, wheat, and rice. The other group, the dicots, has two seed leaves. Most trees are dicots. Roses, beans, tomatoes, and dandelions are dicots too. The chart shows some other differences between monocots and dicots.

Use the chart to help you find differences between the two main groups of flowering plants. ▼

	Monocots	Dicots
seed leaves		
flower parts		
leaves		
roots		

Lesson 4 Review

1. How do scientists classify plants?
2. What are mosses?
3. What are ferns?
4. What are conifers?
5. What are flowering plants?
6. **Compare and Contrast**
   List the ways different plants are grouped.

Chapter 1 Review

Chapter Main Ideas

Lesson 1
• Life processes are the activities all living things do to stay alive.
• All living things are made up of one or more cells.
• Cells working together make up tissues, organs, and organ systems.

Lesson 2
• Scientists classify living things by their similarities and to show relationships.
• Scientists classify living things into five kingdoms—moneran, protist, fungus, plant, and animal.
• Scientists divide the kingdoms into smaller groups of more similar organisms.
• Scientists sometimes change their ideas about classifying organisms because they learn more about the organisms.

Lesson 3
• Invertebrates are animals that do not have backbones.
• Vertebrates are animals that have backbones.

Lesson 4
• Scientists classify plants by certain structures and by how they reproduce.
• Mosses are plants that are not vascular and do not have seeds or flowers.
• Ferns are vascular plants that do not have seeds or flowers.
• Conifers are vascular plants that reproduce by seeds that form in cones.

• Flowering plants are vascular plants that reproduce by seeds that form in flowers.

Reviewing Science Words and Concepts

Write the letter of the word or phrase that best completes each sentence.

a. bacteria	**j.** invertebrate
b. cell	**k.** kingdom
c. cell membrane	**l.** mammal
d. cell wall	**m.** nucleus
e. chloroplast	**n.** species
f. classify	**o.** sperm cell
g. cytoplasm	**p.** vascular plant
h. egg cell	**q.** vertebrate
i. genus	**r.** virus

1. The jellylike material that fills up a cell is called ____.

2. An animal that has a backbone, breathes air, and has hair is a ____.

3. You can tell that a moss is not a ____ because it has no tubes to carry water and nutrients from cell to cell.

4. Scientists ____ organisms to show how they are related to each other.

5. Tiny, one-celled organisms in the moneran kingdom are called ____.

6. The tube that grows out of a pollen grain contains a ____.

7. An animal that has a backbone is called a ____.

8. A group that contains organisms of just one kind is called a ___.

9. The cell part that can use the sun's energy to make sugars is the ___.

10. The smallest unit of life is the ___.

11. An arthropod, which is an ___, has a stiff outer shell that supports its body.

12. In a conifer, the ___ grows inside the seed cone.

13. A ___ is a particle that can carry out some, but not all, of the life processes.

14. A group of similar species is called a ___.

15. The stiff outer layer in plant cells is called the ___.

16. The cell part that controls the cell's activities is the ___.

17. Mushrooms, molds, and mildew belong to the fungus ___.

18. A thin layer that surrounds the outside of a cell is the ___.

Explaining Science

Make a chart or write a paragraph to answer these questions.

1. How are a living thing and an automobile alike in carrying out life processes? How are they different?

2. Describe the five kingdoms and tell what some members of each kingdom are like.

3. How are the different kinds of vertebrates alike? How are they different?

4. Describe the two main groups of flowering plants.

Using Skills

1. Make a chart to **compare and contrast** mosses, ferns, conifers, and flowering plants in their structures and in the way they reproduce.

2. Recall the diagrams of the plant cell and the animal cell. List what you **observed** about the ways they are alike and the ways they are different.

3. How is the scientific way of naming organisms useful? Write a paragraph to **communicate** your ideas.

Critical Thinking

1. Nerve cells sense the things you touch. There are more nerve cells in your fingertips and on the palms of your hand than on the back of your hand. What can you **infer** about where your touch will be more sensitive?

2. **Predict** what living things you might find in a very dry place and what living things you might not find. Explain the reasons for your predictions.

3. Evaluate the usefulness of **classifying** living things into kingdoms and into smaller groups. Include what you could tell if you knew what group an organism belongs to.

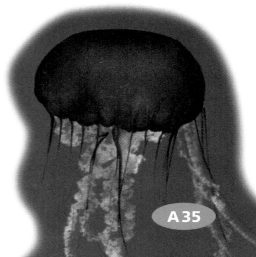

Yum, Yum!

Fruits and vegetables are better than ever! Would it surprise you to learn that an ear of corn used to be only 2.5 centimeters long?

Chapter 2
Reproduction and Change

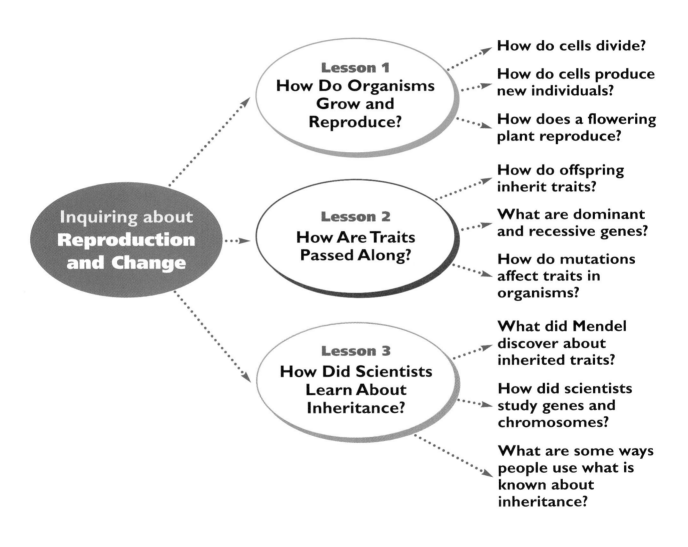

Inquiring about Reproduction and Change

Lesson 1
How Do Organisms Grow and Reproduce?

- How do cells divide?
- How do cells produce new individuals?
- How does a flowering plant reproduce?

Lesson 2
How Are Traits Passed Along?

- How do offspring inherit traits?
- What are dominant and recessive genes?
- How do mutations affect traits in organisms?

Lesson 3
How Did Scientists Learn About Inheritance?

- What did Mendel discover about inherited traits?
- How did scientists study genes and chromosomes?
- What are some ways people use what is known about inheritance?

Copy the chapter graphic organizer onto your own paper. This organizer shows you what the whole chapter is all about. As you read the lessons and do the activities, look for answers to the questions and write them on your organizer.

Exploring Cells

Process Skills

- observing
- inferring

Materials

- safety goggles
- piece of red onion
- plastic forceps
- microscope slide and coverslip
- dropper with water
- microscope
- leaf of elodea plant

Explore

1 Put on your safety goggles. Bend a small piece of onion until it breaks in two. Find the thin piece of onion skin between two layers of onion.

2 Use forceps to remove the skin and spread it out on a microscope slide.

3 Add water from the dropper to cover the skin on the slide. Place a coverslip over the onion skin.

4 Place the slide on the microscope stage. Look at the onion skin through the microscope. You should see many small cells that make up the onion skin. Look for small dark areas within a cell. Make a drawing of your **observations.**

5 Repeat steps 2–4 using a leaf from an elodea plant. Make a drawing of your observations.

Reflect

1. Compare and contrast the cells of the onion and the elodea plant.

2. Green plant cells make food for the plant. Think about the onion cells. Make an **inference.** What other things might cells do for the plant besides making food?

? Inquire Further

What do other cells look like? Develop a plan to answer this or other questions you may have.

Naming and Writing Fractions

Crisgeromie and Danikqua dig in to plant a community garden. Their hard work pays off in fresh vegetables for the school.

They planted four tomato plants in their garden. When the tomatoes grew, they saw that the tomatoes on three plants were round, but the tomatoes on the other plant were egg-shaped. They used fractions to show what part of the total number of tomato plants had round tomatoes and what part had egg-shaped tomatoes.

A fraction has a **numerator** and a **denominator**. You can use fractions to name part of a set.

Math Vocabulary

numerator
(nü′mə rā′tər), the number above the line in a fraction; the number of equal parts in a fractional amount

denominator
(di nom′ə nā′tər), the number below the line in a fraction; the number of equal parts in the whole

Did you know?
Since the 1500s, three-fourths of the food plant varieties that once grew in North and South America are now extinct because farmers do not grow them.

Example 1
What fraction of the tomato plants had round tomatoes?
Numerator   → 3 ← Number of tomato plants with round tomatoes
Denominator → 4 ← Tomato plants in all

Three-fourths, or $\frac{3}{4}$ of the tomato plants had round tomatoes

Example 2
What fraction of the tomato plants had egg-shaped tomatoes?
Numerator   → 1 ← Number of tomato plants with egg-shaped tomatoes
Denominator → 4 ← Tomato plants in all

One-fourth, or $\frac{1}{4}$ of the tomato plants had egg-shaped tomatoes

Talk About It!

1. How many fourths make up all the tomato plants?

2. Last year they planted five tomato plants. Three of the plants had round tomatoes. What fraction did not have round tomatoes?

You will learn:
- how cells divide.
- how cells produce new individuals.
- how flowering plants reproduce.

Lesson 1

How Do Organisms Grow and Reproduce?

How do living things change so much as they grow? A bird starts out in a hard-shelled egg you can hold in your hand. How does it end up as an eagle made of billions and billions of cells and covered with feathers?

Cell Division

Cells are the basic units of living things. No matter how big or how small organisms are, they are made up of cells. An ameba, an eagle, and an oak tree all start life as a single cell. As it grows, the cell divides and forms new cells. The new cells come from existing cells.

Some organisms are made up of only one cell. When the single cell that makes up a one-celled organism divides, the newly formed cells separate. Each new cell is a whole new organism.

Most of the organisms you are familiar with, such as dogs, cats, birds, and trees, are made up of many cells. When the cells of these organisms divide, they do not separate. The cells stay together and keep on dividing. As the cells divide, the organism grows and changes. A single bird or tree is made up of billions of cells.

Your body has billions of cells too. All the time you are growing, your body's cells are dividing. Notice how much the child in the picture has grown. Your cells will keep on dividing, even when you stop getting bigger and taller. Your body always needs to make new cells. The new cells replace old cells that wear away or die.

How many years did it take for you to grow as big as you are? ▼

When a cell starts to divide, it makes copies of all its parts. After the cell divides, the new cells will have parts that are identical to the ones the original cell had. The information that a cell needs to direct and control all its activities is stored inside the cell's nucleus. This information is located in a set of threadlike structures called **chromosomes.**

Look at the pictures of the dividing cell. The cell in the first picture is making copies of all its chromosomes. In the second picture, the two sets of chromosomes have lined up in the center of the cell. In the third picture, the two sets of chromosomes have separated and moved toward opposite sides of the cell. In the fourth picture, the nucleus has divided in two. One nucleus has moved to each side of the cell. The cell has divided, forming two new cells.

Each of the two new cells will have the same kinds of cell parts the original cell had. Each new cell will have its own full set of chromosomes that are just like the ones that were in the original cell before it divided.

Glossary

chromosomes (krō′mə sōmz), structures in the nucleus of a cell that control the cell's activities

These onion skin cells are magnified more than 600 times. ▼

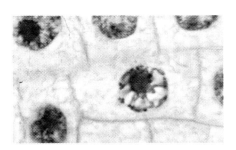

1 **Chromosomes Are Copied**
First, the cell copies its chromosomes. It makes two complete sets, one for each cell.

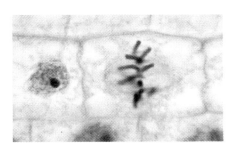

2 **Chromosomes Line Up**
The two sets of chromosomes line up in the center of the cell.

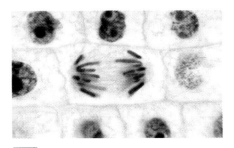

3 **Chromosomes Separate**
Then, the two sets of chromosomes separate. Each set moves toward an opposite side of the cell.

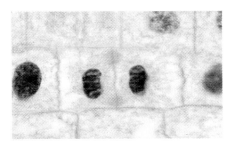

4 **Cells Divide**
Finally, the cytoplasm divides, forming two new cells.

Producing New Individuals

You know that cells produce new cells by splitting in two. In a similar way, one-celled organisms can reproduce, or make whole new individuals, by splitting in two and separating.

Look at the pictures to see how an ameba reproduces. The first picture shows the original ameba, which is the parent cell. In the second picture, the ameba is starting to divide in two. The third picture shows the two new cells, or offspring. Notice that when the parent cell divides, the two new cells separate. They are independent living things. The parent cell no longer exists. It has split apart and become two offspring cells.

The offspring cells are identical to each other. They have identical chromosomes, and the chromosomes have identical instructions. So the offspring look and behave the same way.

Organisms that reproduce by cell division often reproduce quickly. Many kinds of bacteria divide as often as once every 20 minutes. At that rate, they could produce more than 260,000 offspring in only 6 hours! Even a few disease-causing bacteria in your body might quickly produce enough offspring to make you sick.

These amebas are magnified 185 times. ▼

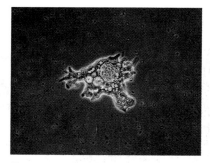

Parent Cell
In organisms that reproduce by cell division, a single individual can produce offspring all by itself. The offspring of this ameba have only one parent.

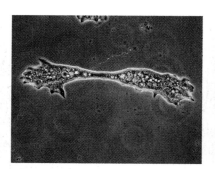

Division
The ameba is dividing. The chromosomes and other cell parts have already been copied.

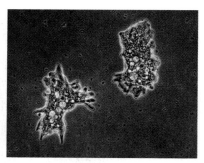

Offspring
Notice that the new cells have separated and become two new amebas. The original ameba split in two, so it no longer exists except in its offspring.

Reproduction is different in many-celled organisms than it is in one-celled organisms. When most many-celled organisms reproduce, two parents contribute to form the offspring cell.

In most many-celled organisms, a special kind of cell division takes place. Two kinds of cells, called reproductive cells, are formed. One kind of reproductive cell is an egg cell. The other is a sperm cell. These cells have only half as many chromosomes as the other cells in an organism's body.

Fertilization occurs when a sperm cell and an egg cell unite. A cell formed by fertilization is called a **fertilized egg.** It gets all the chromosomes that were in the sperm cell and all the chromosomes that were in the egg cell. As a result, a fertilized egg has the same number of chromosomes that the other cells of the parents have. It can grow and develop into a new organism.

The picture shows a colony of thousands of corals that live together under the water. They are invertebrates related to jellyfish and hydras. These corals are sending reproductive cells into the water around the colony. When a sperm cell and an egg cell from the coral meet, they unite, forming a fertilized egg. Eventually, the fertilized egg may become a new coral.

Glossary

fertilization (fėr′tl ə zā′shən), the joining of a sperm cell and an egg cell

fertilized (fėr′tl īzd) **egg,** the cell that results when an egg cell and a sperm cell unite

The coral's reproductive cells float in the water above the colony. ▼

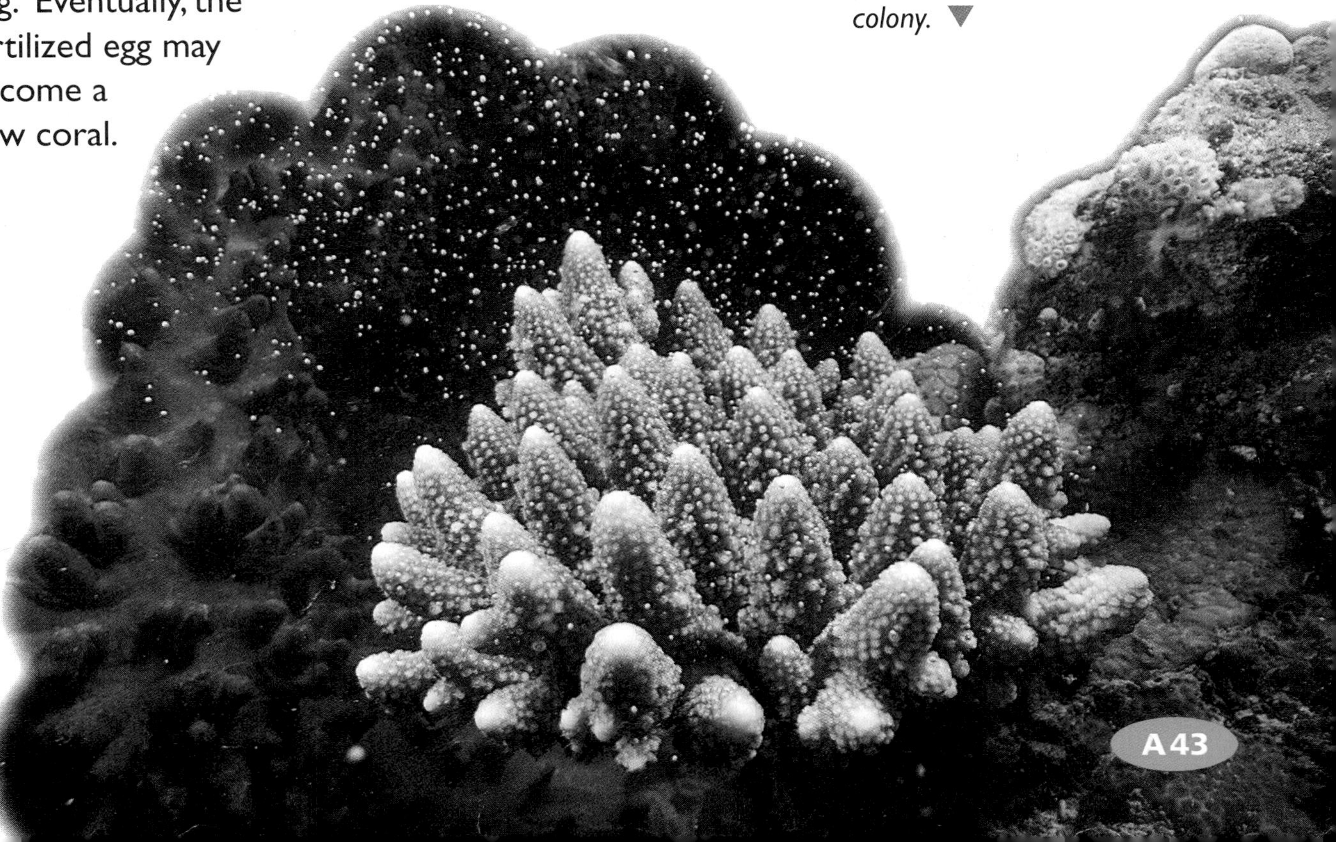

A fertilized sea urchin egg divides. (magnified 500×) ▼

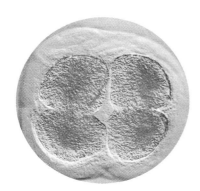

The pictures to the left show what happens to the fertilized egg of a many-celled organism as it divides. This is the fertilized egg of a sea urchin. First, the fertilized egg divides in two. The two new cells stay together. Next, each of the two new cells divides. The four cells that form stay together. Each of the cells divides in half again and again. The last picture shows sixteen cells. The new cells stay together and keep on dividing until a whole new individual has formed. When it is mature, it will look like the adult sea urchin below.

You might think that all sea urchins are exactly alike. However, they are not identical. Each sea urchin develops from a fertilized egg. It receives chromosomes from both of its parents. Half of the chromosomes came from a sperm cell from one parent. The other half came from an egg cell from the other parent.

The information in the nucleus of the fertilized egg is not exactly like the information that was in the nucleus of the cells of either parent. The sea urchin that develops from the fertilized egg will not be exactly like either of its parents. Since all of its cells have some information from each parent, it will be like each parent in some ways. How is this different from what offspring produced from only one parent are like?

◀ **Adult Sea Urchin**
Sea urchins are related to sea stars.

Look around at your classmates. You will see that they look different from each other in many ways. Perhaps you think that, unlike people, all oak trees or all peas or all plants of a particular kind look exactly alike. Look at several plants that are the same kind. At first glance, they may seem identical. However, as you look more closely, you will probably find that even individual plants of the same kind can be different. They might be like each of their parents in some ways. Some will be taller than others. Some might have a different shape or flowers of a different color. The picture shows some offspring that have traits, or characteristics, of each parent. Each of the puppies grew from a fertilized egg that got half its chromosomes from each of the two parents. The offspring have individual differences, or variations. Some variations are easy to see, such as the differences in size and color among these dogs. Other variations are harder to observe, such as whether a dog is resistant to getting a certain disease.

Notice that two of the puppies are the same color as one parent and that two of the puppies are the same color as the other parent. ▼

Glossary

pollination
(pol/ə nā/shən),
movement of pollen
from a stamen to a pistil

Reproduction in Flowering Plants

If you've seen a bee flying from one flower to another, you've watched a step in the reproduction of a flowering plant. Look at the pictures on the next page to learn more about how a flowering plant reproduces.

First find the stamens in the picture of the flower. Notice the yellow pollen grains at the top of the stamens. Inside each pollen grain is a sperm cell. Now find the pistil in the center of the flower. Egg cells grow inside the ovules that are in the ovary, which is the lower part of the pistil.

Pollination is the first step in the reproduction of a flowering plant. It takes place when pollen grains are moved from a stamen to the sticky top of the pistil. In most flowering plants, pollen from the stamen of one plant travels to the pistil of another plant of the same kind. Notice the yellow pollen grains on the bee's body. When the bee lands on a flower to find nectar, it rubs against the stamens. Pollen grains stick to hairs on the bee's body. When the bee flies to another flower, the pollen might rub off its body and stick to the top of that flower's pistil. The shape of the pollen grain helps it stick to whatever is near it.

Some flowering plants have tiny, dustlike pollen grains. Wind carries the pollen from one plant to another. Birds, bats, and many kinds of insects carry the pollen of other kinds of plants. They move the pollen when they go from one flower to another to find the sugary nectar inside the flowers.

The yellow spots are pollen grains that are stuck to hairs on the bee's body. ▼

Reproduction

Pollen Tube

A tube grows down from the pollen grain, through the pistil, and into an ovule inside the pistil. The sperm cell in the pollen grain fertilizes the egg cell inside the ovule, producing a fertilized egg cell.

= sperm cell

Pollen grains from stamen

Pistil

Stamen

Pollen grains

Pistil

Stamen

egg cells

Fruit

The ovary develops into the fruit that surrounds the seed.

A47

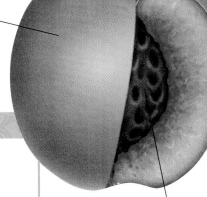

Seed

The fertilized egg cell inside the ovule will grow and become the part of a seed that can grow into a new plant. The ovule develops into the part of a seed that protects it.

Lesson 1 Review

1. How do cells divide?
2. How do cells produce new individuals?
3. How does a flowering plant reproduce?
4. **Compare and Contrast**
   Compare the number of chromosomes in an organism's body cells with the number in its reproductive cells.

Investigating the Life Cycle of a Flowering Plant

Process Skills

- observing
- collecting and interpreting data
- estimating and measuring
- predicting

Materials

- radish plant (10-15 days old)
- metric ruler
- water
- fertilizer solution
- paintbrush
- scissors

Getting Ready

You can learn about stages in the life cycle of a flowering plant by growing and pollinating a radish plant.

Follow This Procedure

1 Make a chart like the one shown. Use your chart to record your observations.

Date	Observations	Plant height	Drawing of plant

Photo A

2 **Observe** the plant and **collect data.** Record your observations of the plant in your chart. **Measure** the plant's height. Draw what your plant looks like.

3 Water your plant every other day to keep the soil moist. Add fertilizer solution once a week. Repeat your observations every other day.

④ Flowers will open in about two weeks. Now you will pollinate the plants. Swirl the brush inside an open flower to pick up pollen from the top of the stamens as shown (Photo B). Swirl the pollen-filled brush on the top of the pistil of another flower to pollinate it. Then use the pollen-filled brush to pollinate flowers of another group.

⑤ Repeat step 4 every day for three days. After three days, cut off the top of the plant above the pollinated flowers. Remove any other buds.

⑥ You should notice that the base of the flowers that were pollinated begin to swell. After five more days, remove the bases of the flowers (the fruit) and open them to remove the seeds.

Photo B

Interpret Your Results

1. Look at your chart and the drawings of your plant. Describe how the plant developed from the time you began to observe it until seeds were formed.

2. Predict what would happen if you planted your seeds. You could try planting them to test your prediction.

Inquire Further

Would the plant grow faster if you changed how much water or fertilizer you gave it? Develop a plan to answer this or other questions you may have.

Self-Assessment

- I followed directions to grow and pollinate a radish plant.
- I recorded my **observations.**
- I **measured** the height of the plant.
- I **collected** and **interpreted data** and described the plant's development.
- I **predicted** what would happen to the new seeds if I planted them.

You will learn:

- how offspring inherit traits.
- what dominant and recessive genes are.
- how mutations affect traits in organisms.

Can you curl your tongue? The ability to curl the tongue is a trait that offspring can inherit from their parents. ▼

Lesson 2

How Are Traits Passed Along?

Yuck! There goes your little brother again, showing off by curling his tongue. Your father can do it too. And your grandmother. But you can't! Why not? How come this family trait skipped you?

Inherited Traits

The ability to curl your tongue is only one of many traits that pass from parents to offspring. Dark or light hair, blue or brown eyes, and straight or curly hair are some others. Look around you. Which of these traits do your classmates have?

Perhaps you have heard someone say, "He has his father's nose." What did that mean? You know he doesn't *really* have his father's nose! Traits that pass from parents to their offspring are **inherited.** You can inherit the shape of your father's nose just as you can inherit the ability to curl your tongue, as the boy in the picture is doing.

Recall that chromosomes in the nucleus of your cells carry information that controls the activities of the cells. This information also determines what traits you have. You learned that when living things reproduce, the offspring receive chromosomes from the parents. The information your chromosomes carry determines which of their traits your parents passed to you. One of the traits it determines is whether or not your nose is shaped like your father's.

◀ *People who are closely related usually have some traits in common. Having two parents, however, means that members of a family are not exactly alike.*

Notice that the children in the picture have traits that make them look like their parents. They also have traits that are not easy to see. Some traits affect organs in the body and how they work. Some diseases are caused by traits that can pass from parents to offspring.

You know that the chromosomes in the nucleus of your cells carry information that controls what traits you have. The information controls traits that make you similar to and different from your parents. It also controls traits that make you different from other kinds of living things.

Every kind of organism has its own traits. Have you watched fireflies at night? Part of a firefly's body can glow in the dark. A firefly's traits include having six legs, hard outer wings, and antennae. Being able to give off light is another trait. The firefly's body produces a chemical that can change energy in its cells into light. Information on the chromosomes tells the cells to make the chemical. Different kinds of fireflies flash their lights in different patterns. Information on the chromosomes determines the pattern. A **gene** is the part of a chromosome that carries information that controls a trait.

▲ *Many kinds of adult fireflies produce patterns of flashing light. Even the eggs of some fireflies glow. Genes on the firefly's chromosomes control how and when light is produced.*

Glossary

recessive (ri ses´iv) **gene,** a gene whose expression is hidden by a dominant gene

dominant (dom´ə nənt) **gene,** a gene that can prevent the expression of another gene

Dominant and Recessive Genes

Every chromosome in an organism's cells is made up of a long chain of genes. Recall that offspring get half their chromosomes from each parent. So they must also get half their genes from each parent. In plants and animals, an offspring usually inherits at least two genes for a trait. One gene comes from each parent. The two genes work together to determine a trait.

Different forms of the gene for a trait may carry different information about it. Often one form of the gene hides the effect of the other form. A gene whose effect can be hidden is a **recessive gene.** A **dominant gene** is a gene that can hide the effect of a recessive gene.

Look at the two guinea pigs on the left below. One has two genes for smooth fur. Its fur is smooth. The other has two genes for rough fur. Its fur is rough. The offspring of these guinea pigs are like the two on the right. Each gets a gene for smooth fur from the parent with smooth fur and a gene for rough fur from the parent with rough fur. Each has one dominant and one recessive gene for fur texture.

Symbols for Genes

A dominant gene is represented by a capital letter. A recessive gene is represented by a lowercase letter. The letters RR stand for two genes for rough fur. The letters rr stand for two genes for smooth fur. What does Rr stand for? ▶

One guinea pig has smooth fur and one has rough fur.

These guinea pigs are offspring of the first two.

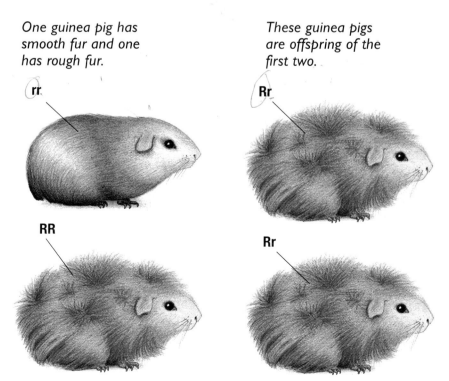

An organism with one dominant and one recessive gene for a trait is a **hybrid** for that trait. You can tell which gene for fur texture is dominant and which is recessive by observing the two guinea pigs on the right on page A 52. Remember that they each have one gene for smooth fur and one for rough fur. They are hybrids for fur texture. Notice that they both have rough fur. This tells you that the gene for rough fur is the dominant gene. The effect of the gene for smooth fur is hidden. It is the recessive gene.

What would the offspring of two guinea pigs that are hybrid for fur texture be like? They can inherit either a gene for smooth fur or a gene for rough fur from each of their parents. Look at the guinea pigs below. Find the letters that stand for the combinations of genes the offspring of two hybrids could have. Some could be hybrid like their parents. They would have one of each form of the gene. Their fur would be rough, like the fur on their parents. Some could have two genes for rough fur. They, too, would have rough fur. Some could have two genes for smooth fur. They would have smooth fur. They would not look like either of their parents. They would look like one of their grandparents!

Glossary

hybrid (hī′brid), an individual that has a dominant and a recessive gene for a trait

Glossary

These guinea pigs could be the offspring of the two hybrids.

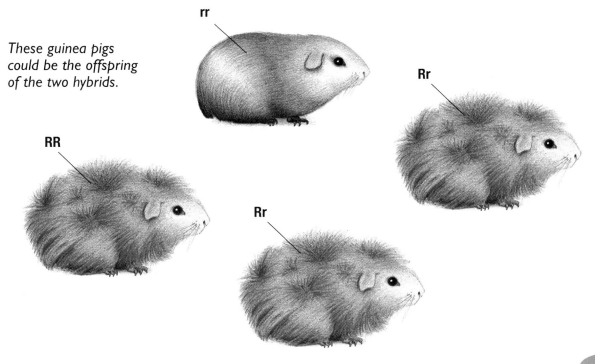

rr

Rr

RR

Rr

Diagrams can help you figure out what the offspring of different parents could be like and what genes they might have. ▼

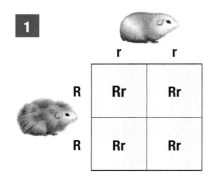

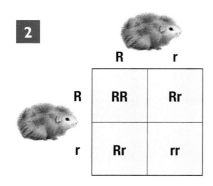

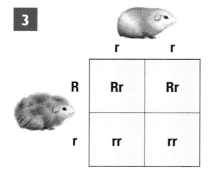

The diagrams to the left show a way you can record the traits you would observe or expect when living things reproduce. Using a diagram can make it easier for you to recognize the patterns by which gene combinations are inherited. It helps you understand what's happening.

These diagrams record what you learned about the inheritance of fur texture in guinea pigs. In the diagrams, each letter outside the square stands for a gene that one parent has. In the first diagram, one parent has two genes for smooth fur (rr). Its letters go across the top. The letters down the side of the diagram stand for the genes the other parent has. It has two genes for rough fur (RR). The letters inside the squares show what combinations of genes the offspring of these guinea pigs could have. The offspring are all hybrids (Rr). Since you know that rough fur is the dominant gene, you can predict that all of the offspring will have rough fur.

The second diagram shows how to record the possible results when two hybrid guinea pigs have offspring. The letters that stand for the genes of the hybrid guinea pigs are on the outside of the squares. Each offspring receives one gene for the trait from each parent. The letters inside the squares show the gene combinations the offspring could have. What can you infer about the fur on the offspring of two hybrids?

The third diagram records the possible offspring from a guinea pig with smooth fur and a guinea pig with rough fur that has one gene for rough and one for smooth fur. Look at the letters inside the squares to see the possible combinations of genes in the offspring. Compare the combinations with the results in the first diagram. Instead of all rough-furred offspring, about half would have rough fur and about half would have smooth fur.

Mutations

Sometimes something unexpected occurs when organisms reproduce. An offspring might have a trait unlike either parent. What's going on? Remember the guinea pig that had smooth fur like its grandparent. It's probably just a recessive gene showing up. However, it could be a **mutation.** A mutation is a change or error in the structure of a gene or chromosome. When a mutation occurs, it can produce new or different traits.

Think of the many differences you see among dogs, cats, or goldfish. Look at the eyes of the cat shown below. A mutation resulted in eyes of different colors. The cat looks unusual, but the mutation doesn't affect its vision or its survival. The mutation that produced the Cornish rex cat on the right gave the cat a short coat of soft, wavy hair. These traits are passed on to the Cornish rex cat's offspring.

The changes some mutations cause are so minor they are hardly noticeable. You can't even see some of the differences that mutations cause. Mutations can also affect things inside the body, such as how well the organs work.

Glossary

mutation
(myü tā′shən), a permanent change in the structure of a gene or chromosome

▲ A mutation gave the Cornish rex cat soft, wavy hair and large ears and eyes.

A mutation affected the genes that control eye color in this cat. Its eyes are different colors. ▼

A 55

▲ Fur Color
A mutation caused one of these squirrels to have white fur. If you were a fox, which squirrel would you be more likely to see? ▼

Short Legs
Some ranchers have bred short-legged sheep because the animals can't jump over fences and run away. In the wild, the sheep would not be able to escape from predators. ▼

Some mutations severely damage the body and can affect an organism's survival. Hemophilia, a disease in which the blood does not clot properly, is caused by a mutation. Hemophilia and other inherited diseases, such as cystic fibrosis and sickle cell anemia, can be passed on to offspring.

Many mutations can make it more difficult for an organism to survive in its environment. Most squirrels have brown or gray fur. Notice how the gray squirrel to the left blends in with the color of the tree trunk. A predator would have a hard time seeing this squirrel among the trees and dead leaves in the forest where it lives. Compare how the squirrel with white fur stands out against the tree trunk. Having white fur is a mutation. Hiding from a predator could be difficult for a white squirrel in a forest of grayish or brownish trees.

Some sheep, like the one in the middle in the picture, are born with a mutation that causes them to have unusually short legs. This would be a disadvantage for sheep living in the wild. They would have a hard time moving around to escape enemies or to find food. However, the mutation can be an advantage to sheep ranchers. Sheep with short legs can't run away by jumping over fences.

Mutations can increase the variation in a species' traits. A greater variety of traits can help a species survive changes in its environment. If an individual with a new trait survives and passes the mutation to its offspring, they too might survive the changes.

The white circles in the picture are paper disks that were soaked in an antibiotic. The cloudy areas show where bacteria are growing. The antibiotic spread out around the disks. The clear spaces show where the antibiotic prevented the bacteria from growing.

Notice that one disk has no clear space around it. A mutation made some bacteria able to survive the antibiotic on that disk. Bacteria reproduce by cell division, so every offspring cell has the same genes. All the offspring of bacteria with the mutation have the mutation. Eventually, most of the bacteria can survive the antibiotic.

If a person infected with the bacteria took this antibiotic, bacteria that don't have the mutation would die. Bacteria with the mutation would live and reproduce. When these bacteria infect someone else, taking the antibiotic won't kill them. This is good for the bacteria, but not good for the people.

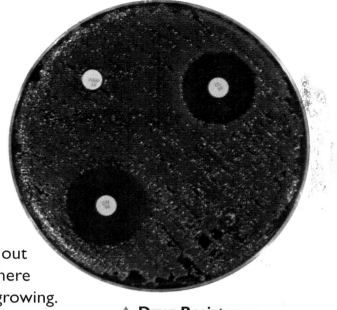

▲ **Drug Resistance**
Find the clear spaces around two circles. They show where the drug stopped the bacteria from growing. The cloudy area around one circle shows that some bacteria are resistant to the drug.

Lesson 2 Review

1. How do offspring get traits like those of their parents?

2. How do dominant and recessive genes differ?

3. How does a mutation affect a trait?

4. **Naming and Writing Fractions**
   What fraction of the offspring will probably have rough fur if both parents are hybrid?

Investigating Dominant and Recessive Traits

Process Skills

- making and using models
- observing
- inferring

Materials

- masking tape
- three plastic chips
- marker
- paper cup

Getting Ready

In this activity you can find out about the frequency of inheritance of genes and traits by making a model using chips.

Review how to use letters to represent dominant and recessive genes.

Follow This Procedure

❶ Make a chart like the one shown. Use your chart to record your observations.

Parents	Offspring		
	RR (red)	Rr (red)	rr (white)
RR x Rr			
Total			
Rr x Rr			
Total			

❷ Place small pieces of masking tape on both sides of each of the chips.

❸ With the marker, print a capital R on the tape on both sides of one chip (Photo A). This chip represents a plant with two genes for red flowers.

❹ On the other two chips, print a capital R on the tape on one side and a lowercase r on the other side. These chips represent hybrid flowers. They have one gene for red flowers and one gene for white flowers. In this activity, red flower color is dominant and white is recessive.

Photo A

Photo B

⑤ Now you will **model** how genes combine. Place the chip representing a parent with two genes for red flowers (RR) and one chip that represents a hybrid parent (Rr) in the cup. Cover the cup with your hand and shake it a few times. Spill the chips onto the desk. The letters that are face up stand for the genes one offspring of the two parents will have (Photo B).

⑥ **Observe** which letters are face up. Place a small check in the box on the chart to record which genes the offspring has.

⑦ Repeat steps 5 and 6 a total of 20 times.

⑧ Add up the number of checks in each box. Record the total for each box.

⑨ Repeat steps 5-8 using the two hybrid chips (Rr). Record your observations.

Self-Monitoring
Do I understand what the letters on each of the chips stand for?

Interpret Your Results

1. How many red-flowered offspring and how many white-flowered offspring are produced when one parent has two genes for red flowers and one is hybrid?

2. How many red-flowered offspring and how many white-flowered offspring are produced when both parents are hybrid?

3. What can you **infer** from your data about inheritance of dominant and recessive traits?

Inquire Further

How would your results be different if you tossed a chip for a hybrid (Rr) and a chip for two recessive genes (rr)? Make a plan to answer this or other questions you may have.

Self-Assessment

- I followed instructions to **make a model** of inheritance of flower color in plants.
- I made **observations** of the frequency of appearance of flower colors in a model of plant reproduction and inheritance.
- I determined how many red-flowered and white-flowered offspring are produced when one parent has two genes for red flowers and one parent is hybrid.
- I determined how many red-flowered and white-flowered offspring are produced when both parents are hybrid.
- I made **inferences** about dominant and recessive inherited traits.

You will learn:

- what Mendel learned about inheritance of traits.
- how scientists studied genes and chromosomes.
- how people use what is known about inheritance.

Lesson 3

How Did Scientists Learn About Inheritance?

How did scientists learn about traits? They grew and studied plants, insects, and molds. They used living things that reproduced quickly! They didn't want to wait 20 years or so for answers. Farmers and doctors use the information they found.

Mendel and Inheritance of Traits

History of Science   Gregor Mendel, an Austrian monk whose picture is shown on the left, studied inheritance in garden pea plants during the mid-1800s. Pea plants are small, easy to grow, and produce many offspring each year. Mendel planned and carried out experiments to study inheritance of their traits. He made careful observations and kept exact records of the results. Mendel counted and recorded exactly how many plants with each trait he found at each step of every experiment. He used mathematics to describe and analyze the results of his experiments.

In his experiments, Mendel observed many different traits. He studied one trait at a time. Mendel found that each trait he studied had two forms. Pea plants grew either tall or short. The pea seeds were either green or yellow. They were either round or wrinkled. In fact, Mendel's experiments with garden peas showed a pattern for inheritance of traits in pea plants that was like the pattern for inheritance of guinea pig fur.

▲ *Gregor Mendel was an Austrian monk who observed how traits are inherited.*

The diagrams to the right show the results of one of Mendel's experiments breeding garden peas. Compare what Mendel learned about how pea plants inherit seed color with what you learned about how guinea pigs inherit fur texture. Which color pea is dominant? Which is recessive? How do you know?

Mendel counted the offspring when he bred two pea plants that were hybrid for a trait. He found that about three of the offspring plants looked like the hybrid parents for every one that had the other form of the trait.

Mendel drew many conclusions from what he observed. He concluded that parents pass units with information about traits to their offspring. He observed that one form of a trait can hide the expression of another form of the same trait. For pea seeds, the color yellow hides the color green in plants that are hybrid for seed color. Mendel found that the way one trait, such as seed color, is inherited does not usually affect the way another trait, such as height, is inherited.

The conclusions Mendel drew about how traits are inherited still hold up today. When Mendel did his work, no one knew about chromosomes or genes or how they act in cell division and reproduction. Mendel published his work in 1866; chromosomes were not observed until 1879. Scientists did not recognize the importance of Mendel's ideas until 1900. Mendel based his conclusions on the offspring he observed when plants reproduced. Knowing about genes and chromosomes helps scientists explain what caused the results that Mendel observed.

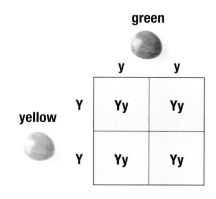

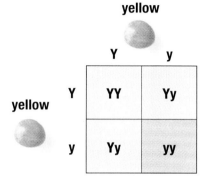

▲ *These diagrams chart the results of one of Mendel's experiments.*

Studying Genes and Chromosomes

In the early 1900s, scientists recognized that the information that controls traits is located on the chromosomes. Thomas Hunt Morgan, an American scientist, experimented with fruit flies to learn about chromosomes. He wanted to find out more about how traits are inherited.

Fruit flies are tiny insects that feed on overripe fruit. They have traits that make them easy to use in experiments. They are small, they are easy to feed, they reproduce rapidly, and they don't take up much space. They have many inherited traits that are easy to observe, such as a variety of eye colors and wing shapes. In addition, certain cells in fruit flies have giant chromosomes, about 200 times larger than the chromosomes in the other cells. When they looked at these chromosomes under a microscope, scientists could easily see what happened to them during cell division.

In 1952, scientists identified a large molecule called DNA as the material that makes up chromosomes and carries information about inheritance. Rosalind Franklin, a British scientist shown at the left, produced pictures of DNA molecules that gave clues to their structure. Her pictures suggested that the molecule was twisted, like a spring.

▲ *Rosalind Franklin produced pictures of DNA. Her pictures showed that the molecules are twisted around themselves.*

▲ *A normal fruit fly has two wings.*

▲ *This fruit fly has four wings, two on each side of its body.*

James Watson and Francis Crick, shown below, used information from pictures made by Franklin and by other scientists to design a model of DNA's structure. They built the model out of tin and wire. It showed a DNA molecule made up of two long strands twisted around each other. The DNA model at the bottom of the page shows that long strands are connected to each other by short strands, like the steps on a twisted ladder.

Genes were identified as sections of the DNA molecules. Scientists are now studying human chromosomes to produce maps that show exactly where on the chromosomes each gene is located.

◀ James Watson and Francis Crick received a Nobel Prize in 1962 for their discoveries about the structure of DNA.

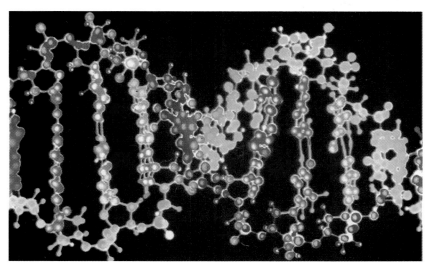

◀ This computer-generated model shows the structure of a DNA molecule. The molecule has two outer ribs connected by rungs like a ladder and is twisted around.

Glossary

selective breeding
(si lek′tiv brē′ding),
breeding plants or
animals with certain traits
to produce offspring with
those traits

▲ Ancient Incas cultivated
corn as a crop. They used
selective breeding to change
traits in corn.

Using Understanding of Inheritance

Understanding how traits are inherited is important in many ways. Farmers learned to be careful in choosing the plants and animals used for breeding. The breeding of plants or animals with desirable traits in order to produce more offspring with those traits is called **selective breeding.**

Using selective breeding results in better crops. Some of the crops resist pests and diseases. Other crops are bigger, stay fresh longer, or taste better. After many generations of using selective breeding for their crops, farmers produce offspring that are very different from the original plants or animals.

History of Science

Corn is a crop that has been greatly improved by selective breeding. The ancient Incas were one culture that cultivated corn as a crop, as shown on the left. People living in parts of Mexico about 10,000 years ago ate corn they gathered from wild plants. The corn was very different from the corn you eat today. Scientists have found remains of corncobs up to 7,000 years old. The oldest corncobs they found are only 2.5 centimeters long and had about 50 kernels.

Native Americans began growing and breeding corn in southwestern parts of North America about 7,000 years ago. They bred the corn plants with the biggest ears. Over time, offspring of these plants produced larger and larger ears. Scientists think that at some time Native Americans bred their corn with a related plant called teosinte, shown below. When teosinte was used as one parent and corn as the other, the offspring produced ears even bigger than when two corn plants were the parents.

◀ Native Americans bred corn with a cornlike grass called teosinte.

wild   farm

◄ Compare the shape of the wild turkey on the left with the farm-grown turkey. Which one has more meat?

When Europeans settled in North America, they grew corn. Like the Native Americans, they improved the corn by selective breeding. Compare the different sizes of the corn plants shown. After thousands of years of selective breeding, ears of corn today grow about 25 centimeters long, 10 times longer than the ears 7,000 years ago!

Many other farm animals and crops have been changed through selective breeding. Some have developed resistance to disease. Others grow larger or have a different shape. Look at the pictures of the two turkeys. The turkey on the right was grown on a farm. It is plumper than the wild turkey, and it has more white meat.

Compare the remains of ancient corncobs grown thousands of years ago with the giant ears of corn grown today. ▶

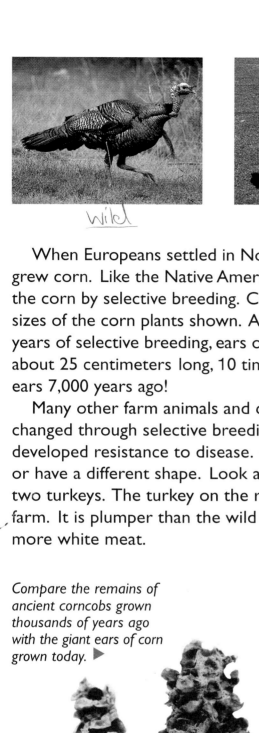

▲ The nectarine began as a mutation on a peach tree.

Breeders developed many new crops from mutations of the crops they were growing. The nectarine was a mutation on a peach tree. You can see in the picture that it is smooth-skinned, instead of fuzzy like a peach. It also has a different taste. Other mutations produced fruits without seeds. You can find seedless oranges, grapefruits, and watermelons in the produce section of grocery stores. Because they are seedless, like the watermelon at the left, they cannot reproduce normally. The picture below shows how some seedless fruit can be grown by grafting. Small branches or cuttings from trees or plants with seedless fruits are attached to the stem or trunk of a normal plant. Branches producing new generations of seedless fruits will grow on the stem or trunk of the normal plant.

◀ The seedless watermelon was a mutation that is now grown as a crop.

Find the place where the branch has been attached to the trunk. Notice how the graft is held in place. ▼

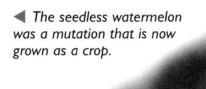

Lesson 3 Review

1. How did Gregor Mendel learn about inheritance of traits?

2. Explain how genes and chromosomes are related.

3. How does knowing about inheritance help farmers and food producers?

4. **Compare and Contrast** How are ears of corn today different from those grown thousands of years ago?

Surveying Inherited Traits

Materials

- paper
- pen or pencil
- grid paper

- formulating questions and hypotheses
- identifying and controlling variables
- experimenting (survey)
- observing
- collecting and interpreting data
- communicating

Process Skills

State the Problem

Are some forms of inherited traits more common than others?

Formulate Your Hypothesis

Which form of each of the traits shown on the next page do you think is more common among students in your class? Write your **hypothesis.**

Identify and Control the Variables

The form of each trait is the **variable** that changes among the students you survey. The number of students with each trait is another variable. Survey a sample of students, not just those who are your friends or who sit near you. Survey the same group of students for all the traits on your list. Try to survey at least 20 students.

Test Your Hypothesis

Follow these steps to conduct a **survey.**

1 Make a chart like the one on page A69. Use your chart to record your data.

2 Your chart lists the traits you will survey and the forms of each trait. Study the two forms of each trait shown in the photographs on the next page.

3 Survey your classmates. **Observe** which of the two forms of each trait each person has. **Collect** and record your **data.** In your chart, make a tally mark by the appropriate trait for each student.

Continued ➡

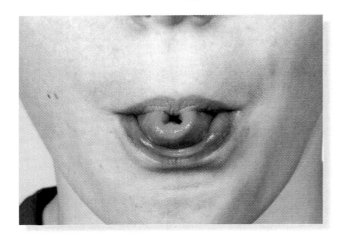

Can curl tongue

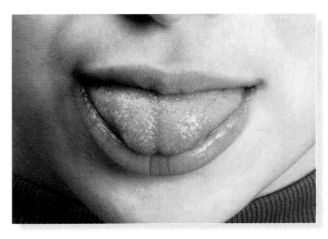

Cannot curl tongue

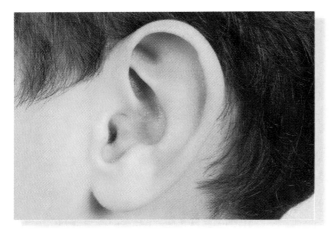

Unattached earlobes

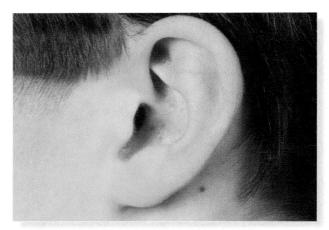

Attached earlobes

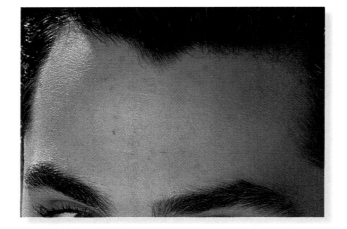

Widow's peak

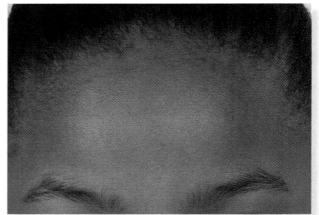

No widow's peak

Collect Your Data

	Tally of students	Total
Can curl tongue		
Cannot curl tongue		
Unattached earlobe		
Attached earlobe		
Widow's peak		
No widow's peak		

Interpret Your Data

1. Label a piece of grid paper as shown. Use the data from your chart to make a bar graph on your grid paper.

2. Study your graph. Compare and contrast the occurrence of the traits in your survey.

State Your Conclusion

How do your results compare with your hypothesis? **Communicate** your results. Which traits are more common among the students you surveyed? less common?

Inquire Further

If you surveyed a larger group of students, how would your results be affected? Develop a plan to answer this or other questions you may have.

Self-Assessment

- I made a **hypothesis** about forms of traits.
- I **identified** and **controlled variables**.
- I followed instructions to conduct a **survey** to test my hypothesis.
- I **collected** and **interpreted data** by making a chart of my **observations** and making and studying a graph.
- I **communicated** by stating my conclusion.

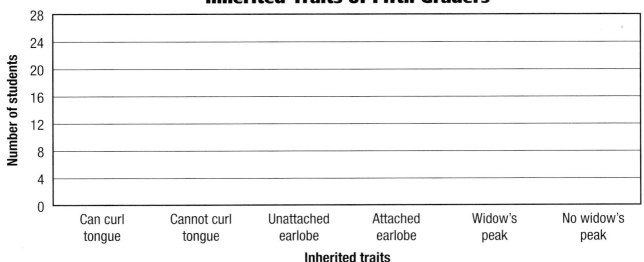

Inherited Traits of Fifth Graders

(Bar graph: vertical axis labeled "Number of students" with values 0, 4, 8, 12, 16, 20, 24, 28. Horizontal axis labeled "Inherited traits" with categories: Can curl tongue, Cannot curl tongue, Unattached earlobe, Attached earlobe, Widow's peak, No widow's peak)

Chapter 2 Review

Chapter Main Ideas

Lesson 1

• When cells divide, they split into new cells that contain copies of all the cell parts.

• New individuals are produced by cell division or by the joining of one reproductive cell from each of two parents.

• Flowering plants grow from seeds that are produced in flowers.

Lesson 2

• Information on the chromosomes in cells determines the traits that offspring inherit from their parents.

• Dominant genes hide the effect of recessive genes.

• Mutations are changes in genes or chromosomes that can affect traits in organisms.

Lesson 3

• Mendel learned about inheritance by observing and recording traits in pea plants.

• In the 1900s, scientists learned about genes and chromosomes by making observations and performing experiments.

• Knowing about inheritance helps farmers and food producers develop better crops.

Reviewing Science Words and Concepts

Write the letter of the word or phrase that best completes each sentence.

a. chromosomes

b. dominant gene

c. fertilization

d. fertilized egg

e. gene

f. hybrid

g. inherited

h. mutation

i. pollination

j. recessive gene

k. selective breeding

1. A trait that is passed from a parent to an offspring is an ___ trait.

2. A ___ has the same number of chromosomes as other cells in an organism.

3. The part of a chromosome that carries information about a trait is a ___.

4. An individual that has two different forms of a gene is a ___.

5. The effect of a ___ can be hidden.

6. In a flowering plant, ___ takes place in the ovule.

7. Genes are located on the ___ of cells.

8. A change in the structure of a gene or a chromosome is a ___.

9. Farmers use ___ to produce plants and animals with certain traits.

10. The movement of pollen from a stamen to the top of the pistil is ___.

11. The effect of a ___ is always expressed.

Explaining Science

Draw a diagram or write a paragraph to answer these questions:

1. What part does pollination play in the reproduction and life cycle of a flowering plant?

2. If two red flowers produced both red and white offspring, what could you conclude about the parents?

3. How did the large chromosomes in fruit flies help scientists understand patterns of inheritance?

Using Skills

1. Name and **write fractions** to show how many offspring are likely to have a recessive trait if the parents are hybrids.

2. How has knowledge of the way traits are inherited changed people's lives? **Communicate** your thoughts by writing a paragraph.

3. You see a picture of a cell with its chromosomes lined up in the center. **Predict** what will happen in the cell next.

Critical Thinking

1. Compare and **contrast** how offspring inherit traits in most single-celled organisms and in most many-celled organisms.

2. Design an **experiment** that will determine which of two forms of a gene is dominant for a trait.

3. Evaluate how scientists' understanding of the way traits are inherited is important to people's lives.

Go Fish!

Pretend you're a fish. You'll need tanks of air so you can breathe, a face mask to help you see, a wet suit to keep you warm, and flippers to help you swim. Even with all that gear, you're no fish!

Chapter 3
Adaptations

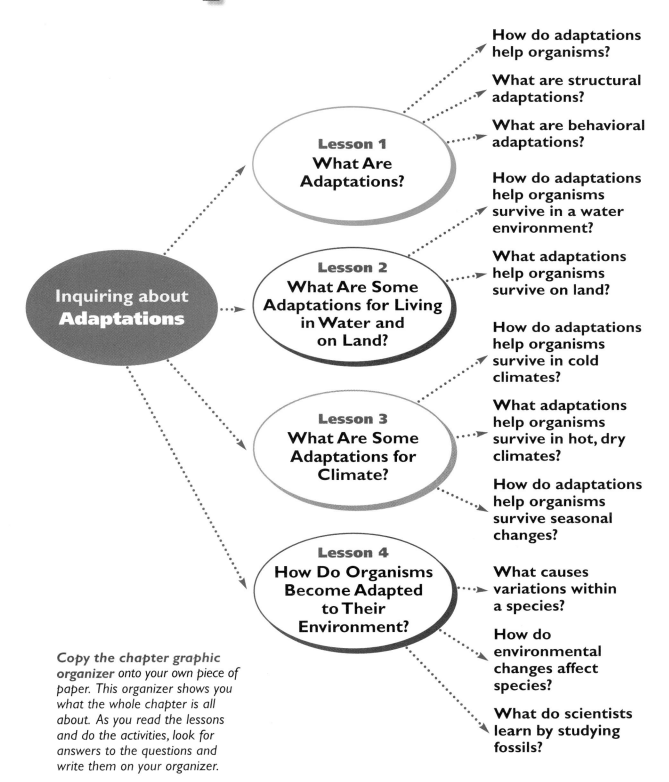

Inquiring about Adaptations

Lesson 1
What Are Adaptations?

How do adaptations help organisms?

What are structural adaptations?

What are behavioral adaptations?

Lesson 2
What Are Some Adaptations for Living in Water and on Land?

How do adaptations help organisms survive in a water environment?

What adaptations help organisms survive on land?

Lesson 3
What Are Some Adaptations for Climate?

How do adaptations help organisms survive in cold climates?

What adaptations help organisms survive in hot, dry climates?

How do adaptations help organisms survive seasonal changes?

Lesson 4
How Do Organisms Become Adapted to Their Environment?

What causes variations within a species?

How do environmental changes affect species?

What do scientists learn by studying fossils?

Copy the chapter graphic organizer onto your own piece of paper. This organizer shows you what the whole chapter is all about. As you read the lessons and do the activities, look for answers to the questions and write them on your organizer.

Exploring Protective Coloring

Process Skills

- observing
- predicting
- inferring

Materials

- pencil
- moth template
- 4 sheets of newspaper
- 4 sheets of black construction paper
- scissors

Explore

1 Trace and cut out 40 moth shapes from 2 sheets of newspaper and 40 moth shapes from construction paper.

2 Place 2 sheets of newspaper on the floor. This represents trees in the moths' habitat. Scatter moths on the newspaper.

3 Your group will work together as predators of the moths. **Observe** the moths. Which will be picked up more often, the newspaper moths or the construction paper moths? Why? Record your **prediction** and explanation.

4 Pick up the first moth you see, then turn away from the newspaper and place it in a pile. Repeat until each student has picked up 10 moths.

5 Count and record the number of each type of moth your team picked up.

Reflect

1. Was your prediction correct? Which type of moth was picked up more often?

2. Make an **inference.** Which moth would be more likely to survive in the newspaper habitat? Explain.

? Inquire Further

What would happen if the habitat was black? Develop a plan to answer this or other questions you may have.

Reading Graphs

A **bar graph** compares data and information. This bar graph gives information about the average amount of rainfall different deserts receive in a year. The numbers below the graph show the millimeters of rainfall. The names of each desert are shown along the side of the graph.

Math Vocabulary

bar graph (graf), a graph that uses vertical or horizontal bars to show data

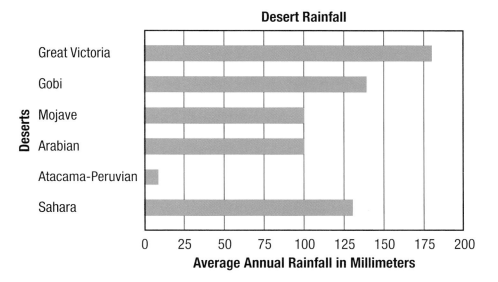

You can also use vertical bars to show data in a bar graph. The bars in a bar graph can provide information you need to analyze data and answer questions.

Talk About It!

1. Which desert gets the most rain?

2. Which desert gets the least rain?

3. How much more rain does the Great Victoria Desert get than the Atacama-Peruvian Desert?

You will learn:

- how adaptations help organisms.
- what structural adaptations are.
- what behavioral adaptations are.

The spider has special body parts that make silk. Other parts spin the silk into a web. The web helps the spider get food and protects the spider from some of its enemies. ▼

Lesson 1

What Are Adaptations?

Ever see a sparrow without feathers? A pine tree with no needles? A zebra without stripes? Of course not! Traits like feathers, needles, and stripes help organisms survive in their environments.

Adaptations That Help Organisms

You know that parents pass along inherited traits, or characteristics, to their offspring. Inherited traits can be either behaviors, such as spinning a spider web, or structures, such as thorns. Traits that help organisms meet their basic needs and survive in their surroundings are called adaptations.

Organisms have many of the same basic needs. Animals need food, water, and oxygen. Plants need sunlight, water, carbon dioxide, oxygen, and minerals. Animals and plants need to avoid being eaten. Animals need to attract a mate and reproduce. Many kinds of animals must care for and protect their young. Plants must reproduce too. Flowers must be pollinated, and seeds must send out roots and grow. Both plants and animals need protection from some things around them. How does this spider's web help it meet a basic need?

◀ *When an insect is trapped in the web, the spider wraps the insect with silk. The spider then inserts saliva into the insect. The saliva starts to digest the insect. A powerful sucking stomach and a mouth that forms a "straw" allow the spider to suck up the partly digested insect.*

The woodpecker in the picture has many adaptations that help it meet its basic needs. The bird uses its long, sturdy beak to peck holes in the bark of trees. It then uses its long, sticky tongue to remove the insects from the holes. The woodpecker eats some of the insects and feeds the rest to its young. Sharing food with its young is an adaptation too.

The woodpecker also uses its strong beak to hammer a hole in the tree for a nest. Building a nest is an adaptation. The nest protects the woodpecker and its young from the environment and helps them avoid being eaten.

The woodpecker has other adaptations as well. Strong feet and sharp claws allow it to cling to the bark of a tree. Observe how the strong tail feathers prop up the bird while it holds onto the tree.

The tree the woodpecker is on has adaptations too. The leaves have adaptations that help them collect the sun's energy. The tall trunk allows the tree to grow taller than other plants that might shade its leaves. The strong trunk makes it harder for a powerful wind to topple the tree. The tree's bark is an adaptation. Although it is no match for a woodpecker's beak, the bark does protect the tree from most birds and many insects.

This woodpecker has many adaptations that help it get food and feed its young. Its strong beak and long, sticky tongue help it get insects from the bark of trees. It clings to the tree with its sharp claws while its strong tail supports it. ▼

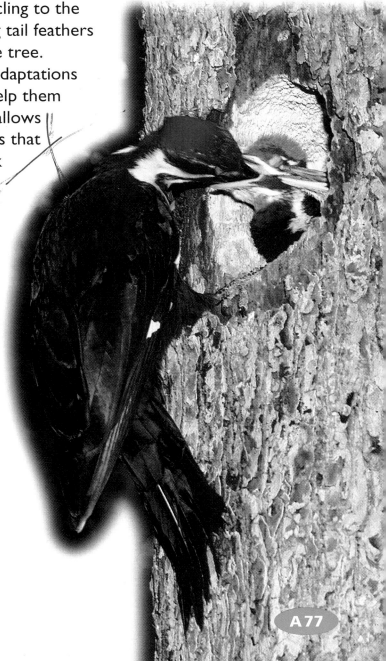

Glossary

structural adaptation
(struk′chər əl
ad′ap tā′shən), an
adaptation of an
organism's body parts or
its coloring

mimicry (mim′ik rē),
an adaptation in which
one species resembles
another

Structural Adaptations

Adaptations that affect an organism's body parts or the way it is colored are **structural adaptations.** The woodpecker's beak, tongue, tail, and feet are structural adaptations. Study the structural adaptations on these two pages.

A Protective Pouch
A special pouch helps this female kangaroo protect its young from danger. ▶

◀ **Stinky Flower**
This giant rafflesia flower smells like rotting meat. The odor attracts flies to the flower. They get pollen on their bodies, which rubs off on the next giant rafflesia flower they visit. The smell helps the flower reproduce.

Protective Coloration
Protective coloration is an adaptation in which an organism's body matches the color or pattern of the background. The flounder spends most of its life lying flat on the ocean floor. The colors of its upper side match the sand, hiding the flounder from enemies. ▶

Mimicry
Which is the venomous eastern coral snake? It has red bands next to yellow bands. The harmless scarlet king snake has red bands next to black bands. This is **mimicry,** *an adaptation in which one organism looks like another.* ▼

◀ Lightweight Seeds

The tiny seeds of the dandelion have light, feathery threads that catch the wind. The wind may blow the seeds to a place where they can put out roots and grow.

▲ Leaves Capturing Sunlight

The thin, flat shape of a leaf helps it capture lots of sunlight. Green chlorophyll inside the leaf's cells traps light energy from the sun, which the plant uses to make sugar.

▲ Sharp Thorns

Its sharp thorns protect this black raspberry plant from hungry animals. Instead of taking a thorny snack, animals look elsewhere for food.

◀ Colorful Display

This male peacock spreads colorful feathers. The bright display may attract a mate.

Warning Coloration

Many poisonous or bad-tasting organisms have bright colors and patterns that warn enemies of danger. The brightly colored poison arrow frog is poisonous. Animals that eat frogs avoid this one! ▶

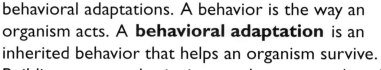

Behavioral Adaptations

Glossary

behavioral adaptation (bi hā′vyər əl ad′ap tā′shən), an inherited behavior that helps an organism survive

In addition to structural adaptations, organisms have behavioral adaptations. A behavior is the way an organism acts. A **behavioral adaptation** is an inherited behavior that helps an organism survive. Building a nest and spinning a web are examples of behavioral adaptations. These behaviors are instinctive. They are inherited, not learned.

Study the behavioral adaptations shown on these two pages and think about some of the basic needs each organism must satisfy. Basic needs include the need to find a mate, the need to care for the young, the need for protection from the environment, the need to avoid being eaten, and the need for food.

Many behaviors of organisms meet another need, the need for a place to live. The young of many animal species leave the place where they were born. Instinctive behaviors make them search for a new place to live. They must find a place large enough to meet their needs. For example, young male wolves each need large areas for hunting and other purposes.

Sometimes even with behavioral adaptations, an animal can't find a home. The kind of place the animal needs to live in may have changed. It might be used for homes, schools, farms, or businesses. A species that can't find enough places to live may become extinct. In fact, the major cause of extinction is the loss of a place to live.

Monarch Migration

By migrating each winter from the United States and Canada to Mexico, where the climate is warmer, monarch butterflies protect themselves from the harsh winter environment. ▼

◄ **Alarmed Posture**
With its back arched and its fur raised, the cat appears larger. This helps to protect it from its enemies.

"Playing Possum"

When it is frightened by an animal that might eat it, an opossum falls down. It looks dead. The other animal often loses interest, and the opossum survives. ▶

▲ The Bee Dance

A scout bee does a detailed "waggle dance" that tells other bees the location of nectar-rich flowers. This helps the bees find food for the hive.

Riding Safely on Mom

After her young are born, this mother scorpion carries them on her back, protecting them from being eaten by other animals. ▶

◀ Living Underground

This rabbit lives in an underground burrow that is cooler in summer and warmer in winter than the temperature outside. Living in a burrow protects the rabbit from its physical environment.

▲ *The weaverbird's ability to build this kind of nest is a behavioral adaptation. It is instinctive, so it does not need to be learned. The weaverbird's offspring will inherit the same ability.*

▲ *The ability to learn is a behavioral adaptation. This dog has learned to sit up on command. This behavior is not instinctive and it will not be inherited by the dog's offspring. Sitting up on command is not a behavioral adaptation.*

The behavioral adaptations you studied on the previous pages are inherited behaviors. They are called instinctive behaviors because animals are born with them. Look closely at the nest to the left. A weaverbird made it. The nest helps the bird attract a mate. Later, it protects the young. Weaverbirds know instinctively how to make a nest like this. Making the nest is a behavioral adaptation because it is an inherited ability and it meets basic needs.

The ability to learn is a behavioral adaptation that helps many animals survive. The ability to learn is inherited. However, the behaviors that an animal learns are not inherited. For example, the dog in the picture learned to sit up on command, but it won't pass that behavior on to its offspring. Sitting up on command is a learned behavior.

Lesson 1 Review

1. What are some adaptations that help organisms survive?

2. Identify a structural adaptation and explain how it helps the organism survive.

3. Identify a behavioral adaptation and explain how it helps the organism survive.

4. **Compare and Contrast**
   Compare and contrast behavioral adaptations with learned behaviors.

Lesson 2

What Are Some Adaptations for Living in Water and on Land?

Ugh! `Brrrr!` Wrinkled, puckered skin. `Cold!` Too much time in the water can make you look like a prune and feel like an ice cube. But sea otters stay warm. They have adaptations for living in water.

You will learn:
- how adaptations help organisms survive in a water environment.
- what adaptations help organisms survive on land.

Adaptations for Water

The sea otter in the picture must satisfy the same basic needs as other organisms. However, it must do some of these things in the water. It must find food but avoid being eaten by predators. It needs to attract a mate and protect its young. Finally, it must protect itself from the cold, wet environment.

Flipperlike hind feet help the sea otter move swiftly through the water as it searches for shellfish to eat. Study the picture to learn more about the sea otter's important water adaptations.

Powerful lungs let the sea otter hold its breath for 4 minutes while diving down 55 meters searching for food.

The otter's front paws can grasp and pry open shellfish.

The sea otter's flipperlike hind feet easily propel its slender body through the water. A long tail helps the sea otter steer as it swims.

Thick, waterproof fur keeps the sea otter warm and dry.

The organisms shown on these pages do not all live together, but they all face a common challenge: how to survive in a water environment. As you look at the variety of adaptations shown, think about how each one helps the organism survive.

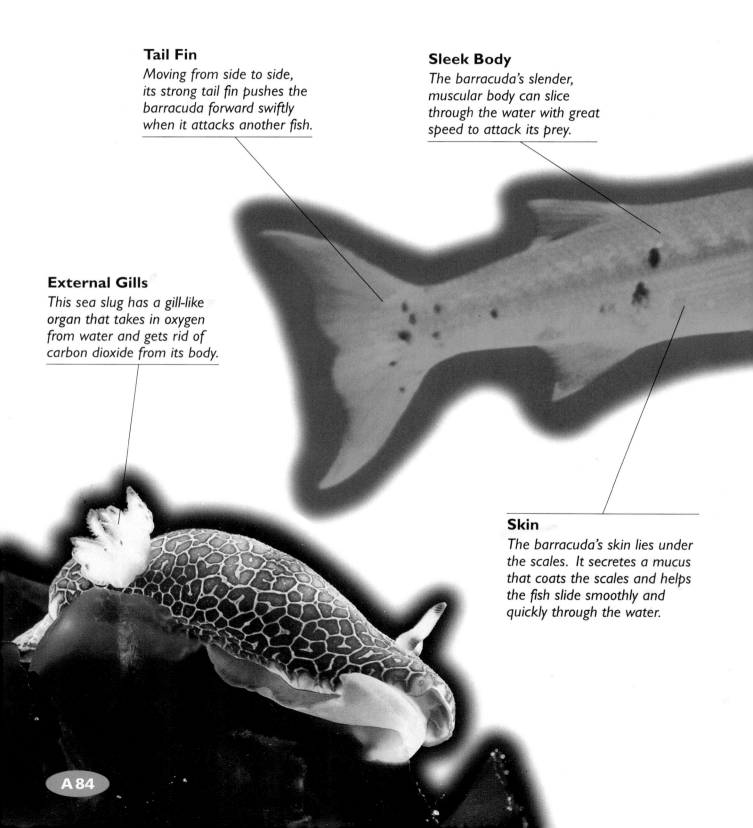

Tail Fin
Moving from side to side, its strong tail fin pushes the barracuda forward swiftly when it attacks another fish.

Sleek Body
The barracuda's slender, muscular body can slice through the water with great speed to attack its prey.

External Gills
This sea slug has a gill-like organ that takes in oxygen from water and gets rid of carbon dioxide from its body.

Skin
The barracuda's skin lies under the scales. It secretes a mucus that coats the scales and helps the fish slide smoothly and quickly through the water.

Gills

The barracuda takes in water through its mouth and forces it out through its gills. The gills absorb oxygen from the water and release carbon dioxide from the fish's blood. The water leaves the fish's body through openings in its side.

Filter Feeding

The clam gets oxygen from the water that flows over its gills. Surprisingly, it gets food too. An adaptation allows the gills to strain tiny food particles out of the water. This way of finding food is called filter feeding.

Floats and Fronds

This seaweed has small, round, gas-filled floats. This adaptation allows the plant to float near the surface of the ocean, where it gets plenty of sunlight. The seaweed lacks roots, but its leaflike fronds absorb needed minerals from the water, just as the roots of a land plant would.

▲ Jet Propulsion

An octopus takes in water and removes oxygen from it. Then it sends the water out of its body through a short funnel. When frightened, the octopus shoots the water out in a fast jet. It moves away by "jet propulsion."

Adaptations for Land

Organisms that live on land must meet the same needs as organisms that live in the water. However, they need different adaptations to meet these needs. For example, getting enough water isn't much of a problem in a watery environment. Organisms that live on land need adaptations to get and keep enough water.

Most land plants take in water from the ground through their roots. The roots help anchor the plants to the ground. Most land animals get water from food, as well as by drinking it or absorbing it through their bodies. Many plants have a waxy coating that keeps them from losing too much water. Many animals have a tough outer covering that keeps water inside. The bird eggs on the next page have a hard shell that keeps them from drying out.

You know that fish have gills that take oxygen out of the water. Land animals also need a way to get oxygen. Many land animals, such as the owl and the deer on the next page, have lungs that take in oxygen. Insects and similar animals have a system of tiny, branching tubes that take in oxygen and bring it to different parts of their bodies.

Unlike the seaweed that floats on water, land organisms need a way to support their weight. The owl, the deer, and many other land animals have a skeleton made up of bones. This adaptation supports their body, helps maintain their shape, and protects internal organs. Look at the vine and the tree it clings to on the left. They have adaptations that support their weight and help them get enough sunlight.

Animals on land must also be able to move to meet their basic needs. Many land animals walk on legs or fly with wings. Snakes slither, using S-shaped movements. Earthworms tunnel through the ground.

◀ **Clinging Vine**
The tree's strong trunk supports its branches and raises its leaves up to the sunlight. The vine clings to the tree. It receives more sunlight than it would get if it grew close to the ground.

Wings

Owls have strong wings. Their special feathers don't make the swishing sound most birds make as they fly. This adaptation helps owls hunt. They swoop down on prey unheard.

Hard-Shelled Eggs

The hard-shelled eggs of birds have tiny holes. The holes are large enough for oxygen to pass through, but they are too small for water to pass through easily. This adaptation prevents the developing bird from drying out.

Skin

The skin that covers the deer's body has many functions. It keeps the deer's body from drying out by slowing water loss.

Legs

The white-tailed deer has strong legs. Bones and muscles are adaptations that support the weight of the deer and help it run away from enemies.

Lesson 2 Review

1. Describe the adaptations each of these animals has to get oxygen from its water environment: a barracuda, a sea slug, a clam.

2. What are some ways bird eggs are adapted to a land environment?

3. **Compare and Contrast**
   Compare and contrast the adaptations that provide support for the tree and the vine shown on page A86.

Investigating Eggshells

Process Skills

- observing
- inferring

Materials

- safety goggles
- 4 cleaned eggshell halves
- scissors
- textbooks
- graduated plastic cup
- vinegar
- plastic spoon
- paper towel

Getting Ready

In this activity you will test the strength of ordinary eggshells. You will also learn about the substances in an eggshell. Remember to wash your hands after handling eggshells.

Follow This Procedure

1 Make a chart like the one shown. Use your chart to record your observations.

	Observations
Number of books to break eggshells	
Eggshells in vinegar after five minutes	
Eggshells in vinegar overnight	

2 Put on your safety goggles. Take 4 cleaned eggshell halves. With the scissors, carefully cut the edges of the shells so they are even.

3 Place the shells, open-side down, on the table. Arrange the shells so the textbooks can be placed on top of them (Photo A).

4 Carefully place the textbooks, one by one, on the eggshells (Photo B). Count the number of books the shells can support before they break. Record your **observations.**

5 Place several pieces of the broken eggshell into the graduated plastic cup. The pieces should be about the same size. Pour 120 mL of vinegar into the cup.

6 Observe the shells in the cup of vinegar for five minutes. Record your observations. Wash your hands after handling the eggshells.

7 Allow the cups to stand overnight. Use the plastic spoon to lift out the eggshells. Place the eggshells from the cup of vinegar on a paper towel. Record your observations.

Photo A

Photo B

Self-Monitoring
Have I washed my hands after handling eggshells?

Interpret Your Results

1. Do you think a chicken egg is fragile or strong? Explain.

2. Make an **inference.** How does the shell of an egg help a developing chick to survive in its habitat?

3. The shell of a chicken egg is hard because it contains a compound with calcium in it. How does vinegar affect the calcium compound?

Inquire Further

Does the size of the eggshell affect its strength? Develop a plan to answer this or other questions you may have.

Self-Assessment

- I followed instructions to test the strength of eggshells.
- I recorded my **observations** of the strength of eggshells.
- I observed eggshells in vinegar and recorded my observations.
- I explained how an eggshell is fragile or strong.
- I made an **inference** about how the shell helps the developing chick survive in its habitat.

You will learn:

- how adaptations help organisms survive in cold climates.
- what adaptations help organisms survive in hot, dry climates.
- how adaptations help organisms survive seasonal changes.

This malamute is adapted to the cold. Its thick fur keeps it warm. ▼

Lesson 3

What Are Some Adaptations for Climate?

Brrr! You are sooooo cold. You spent ten minutes putting on winter clothes, and you're still cold. For the dog, it's a nice day. What's different? The dog's adapted to the cold. You're not.

Adaptations for Cold Climates

Animals, plants, and other organisms have adaptations that help them survive in the climate where they live. Birds and mammals are animals that use the energy from food to keep their body temperature about the same all the time. Polar bears, such as the one on the next page, eat large amounts of food. The food provides energy that keeps them warm. Mammals that live in cold climates, like the dog shown, need to conserve body heat so they stay warm enough. Study the polar bear to learn some ways it is adapted to cold climates.

Even plants may have adaptations to cold climates. Some arctic plants have adaptations that allow them to carry out photosynthesis faster and at lower temperatures than plants in warmer climates can. Many plants grow close to the ground, below the cold winds. Study the arctic poppy on the next page to learn about its adaptations for cold.

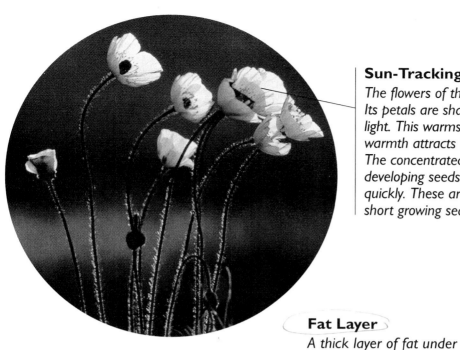

Sun-Tracking Flowers

The flowers of the arctic poppy follow the sun. Its petals are shaped so they concentrate the light. This warms the air inside the flowers. The warmth attracts insects that pollinate the flowers. The concentrated sunlight also warms the developing seeds, causing them to mature more quickly. These are important adaptations to the short growing season of a cold climate.

Warm Fur

Thick, waterproof fur insulates the polar bear from freezing temperatures and helps keep it dry while it swims in cold water. The fur's whitish color helps the polar bear blend in with the snow and ice, allowing it to stalk prey unnoticed.

Fat Layer

A thick layer of fat under its fur helps keep this polar bear warm in the winter.

Small Tail and Ears

Blood flows to the tail and ears, keeping them warm. Their small size reduces the amount of body heat the bear loses.

Hairy Paws

Hairy soles insulate the polar bear's paws from the cold and provide traction as it moves across ice.

Adaptations for Hot, Dry Climates

Organisms that live in hot, dry climates must meet all the basic life needs. However, they also face special challenges. In a place where water is very scarce, they must get water and keep it. In a place where daytime temperatures are very high, they must stay cool.

Many desert animals stay underground during the day. They come out at night when it is cooler and more moisture is present. This behavior helps their bodies retain the water they have. Desert animals need water to live, just as other animals do. However, water is rarely available to drink. The animals get most of their water from the food they eat. The kangaroo rat gets all the water it needs from food. It doesn't need to drink any water at all. The roadrunner can run quickly across the hot desert sands to find food and water.

Plants also have adaptations. The desert wild flowers have a short life cycle. They take advantage of the rare times when the desert is not dry. Mesquite grows long roots that reach far down to underground water. The barrel cactus has shallow roots that quickly absorb whatever rain falls. Examine the pictures on these two pages to discover ways plants and animals survive in the desert.

Short Life Cycle

The seeds of desert wild flowers sprout after a heavy rain. The plants grow quickly, form flowers and seeds, and die. The next time enough rain falls, these seeds sprout and the process repeats itself. ▼

▼ **Avoiding the Heat**

Kangaroo rats and many small animals dig burrows. They stay underground during the heat of the day. Kangaroo rats may even close off the entrances to their burrows to keep out the hot, dry air.

Deep Root

Mesquite plants grow very long roots that reach underground water as far as 30 meters down. ▶

Long Legs

During the day, the surface of the desert is much hotter than the air just a few inches above it. The relatively long legs of the roadrunner raise its body above the hot surface. This adaptation helps it to stay cooler. ▼

Waxy Covering

A waxy covering reduces the amount of water that escapes into the hot, dry air. ▶

Adapted Leaves: Spines

Generally, plants lose the most water through the wide, flat surfaces of their leaves. Cactus plants have needlelike spines—narrow leaves that do not let much water escape. The green stems and branches of a cactus plant carry out all the photosynthesis for the plant. ▶

◀ Water Storage

The barrel cactus bulges with stored water after a rain. It shrinks steadily as it uses up the water. The barrel shape itself is an adaptation that reduces water loss. Compared to the shape of most plants, there is less "outside" to lose water.

◀ Shallow, Widely Spreading Roots

Long, shallow roots spread in all directions from this barrel cactus. They quickly absorb water from scarce rain.

Adaptations for Seasonal Changes

In some places, the weather changes dramatically during the year. It is very hot in the summer and very cold in the winter. Most organisms in these areas have adaptations that help them survive both extremes.

As summer ends and fall begins, many organisms store nutrients. The tree below and many other plants store nutrients in their roots. As winter comes, many trees drop their leaves. A whole plant may even seem to die, as the mayapple on the left does. However, parts of the plant below the ground are alive. The plant will use the food stored there when it grows again in the spring.

▲ Dying Back

The mayapple is well adapted to winter. It stores nutrients in its roots. The top picture shows that part of the plant above the ground "dies back." The part below the ground becomes dormant until the spring. Then the plant uses its stored nutrients to send up new growth.

◀ Dropping Leaves

As days get colder and shorter, plants carry out less and less photosynthesis. The leaves stop making chlorophyll. The green chlorophyll disappears, revealing yellow, red, and orange colors. These colors were hidden by the chlorophyll. Later, the leaves fall to the ground. This adaptation helps the tree avoid water loss during the cold, dry winter. In the spring, the tree grows new leaves, using the nutrients stored in its roots.

Changing Color

As winter approaches, ermine grow heavy white fur and shed their lightweight, brown fur. This adaptation keeps them warm in winter and hides them in the snow. When warm weather returns, they grow a brown coat again. The color helps them hide among dead leaves and plants. ▶

Geese Migrating

Geese migrate to warm climates for the winter and return in the spring. ▶

Many animals store food for winter too. Bees store honey in hives. Squirrels store nuts and other food in the ground. They return during the winter and eat what they stored. Squirrels also build up a layer of fat. During the winter, this fat layer helps keep them warm and provides energy.

Some animals, such as the ermine on page A 94, grow warm winter coats. Some animals save energy by slowing their body processes until the weather warms again. Many birds and other animals avoid the cold of winter by migrating. Notice the geese flying south to warm areas to feed over the winter.

As the weather begins to warm in the spring, leaves grow on the trees. Plants sprout and flowers bloom. Some animals shed their heavy winter coats and grow lightweight ones. Migrating birds return. Caterpillars emerge from cocoons like the one to the right.

▲ **Cocoon Spun by Caterpillar**

All summer the caterpillars of the cecropia moth eat and grow. By fall they are big and fat. Each caterpillar spins a cocoon around itself. It spends the winter secure inside the cocoon, attached to the twig of a tree. In spring or early summer, adult moths emerge from the cocoons. Later the females lay eggs. Soon caterpillars hatch from the eggs, and the cycle continues.

Lesson 3 Review

1. List three adaptations that help a polar bear keep warm.

2. List three adaptations that help a barrel cactus get and keep water.

3. Describe how the ermine is adapted for seasonal changes.

4. **Compare and Contrast**
   Compare and contrast the adaptations of squirrels and geese to winter.

Investigating Insulation

Process Skills

Process Skills

- making and using models
- predicting
- observing

Materials

- safety goggles
- spoon
- shortening
- 4 plastic bags
- 4 rubber bands
- cold water in plastic pail
- clock with second hand

Getting Ready

In this activity you will make a model to observe insulating qualities of fat.

Follow This Procedure

1 Make a chart like the one shown. Use your chart to record your prediction and observations.

	Shortening	No shortening
Prediction		
Start		
30 seconds		
1 minute		

2 Put on your safety goggles. Make a **model** of fat insulation by first using the spoon to spread shortening into one of the plastic bags so it's half full.

Photo A

3 Put one hand into another plastic bag and have a partner secure it with a rubber band around your wrist. Then put your covered hand into the bag with the shortening and adjust the rubber band so both bags are secured to your wrist (Photo A).

 Safety Note *Make sure the rubber bands are not too tight.*

4 Have a partner move the shortening around in the bag so your hand is completely covered.

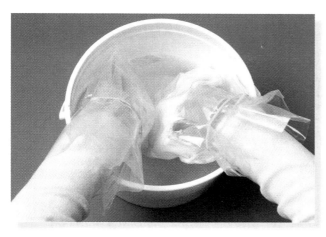

Photo B

⑤ With a partner's help, cover your other hand with two bags and secure them with a rubber band.

⑥ Which hand will be warmer in the cold water, and why? Record your **prediction** and explanation. Test your prediction by slowly placing both hands into the cold water (Photo B). Have a partner record your **observations** at the start, after 30 seconds, and after one minute.

Self-Monitoring
Have I correctly completed all of the steps? Do I have any questions?

Interpret Your Results

1. Compare your prediction with your results.

2. A good insulator keeps heat from being transferred from an object. Do you think that shortening is a good or a poor insulator? Explain.

3. Compare your model to the fatty layer an Arctic animal may have. Why is this layer of fat important?

Inquire Further

What other materials can work as heat insulators? Develop a plan to answer this or other questions you may have.

Self-Assessment

- I followed instructions to **make** and **use** a **model** of fat insulation.
- I recorded my **prediction** and **observations.**
- I compared my prediction with my results.
- I explained why I thought shortening is a good or poor insulator.
- I explained why fat is important to Arctic animals.

Lesson 4

How Do Organisms Become Adapted to Their Environment?

A chihuahua and a St. Bernard are both dogs. But they are so different. Amazingly, they belong to the same species!

Variations

Think of the many breeds of dogs. Look at the chihuahua below. It weighs less than 2 kilograms, and its height is about 13 centimeters at the shoulders. Compare it to the Irish wolfhound that is nearly 7 times as tall. The St. Bernard weighs 50 times as much as the chihuahua. Some dogs are good hunters. Others are good watch dogs. Because dogs are so varied, it's easy to forget that all domestic dogs belong to the same species.

Domestic dogs have a variety of heights and weights. What other variations do you observe? ▼

Irish wolfhound

St. Bernard

Chihuahua

Variations don't occur only in dogs. Although not nearly as dramatic, some variations exist within all species. Look at the butterflies on this page. Some are dark. Some are light. Some are larger than others, but they all belong to the same species.

New traits in a species are due to mutations. You learned about mutations in Chapter 2. Mutations are changes in a gene that may produce new traits. Some new traits may help organisms. Others may hurt them. Some have no effect. Individual butterflies that have a new, harmful trait usually don't survive. Individual butterflies with a new, helpful trait are more likely to survive and to pass the trait along to their own offspring.

Look again at the copper butterflies. How could these variations be helpful? Perhaps on a cool, sunny day, darker butterflies would warm more quickly because dark colors absorb energy from the sun better than light colors. The extra heat might make the dark butterflies more active. Perhaps they would be better able to find food and mates. Whether some variations are helpful depends on environmental conditions. On the next page, you will learn what may happen when environmental conditions change.

Copper butterflies show many variations. ▼

▲ *Air pollution changed the peppered moths' environment. Examine the light and dark peppered moths on the light tree trunk in the picture above and on the dark tree trunk in the picture below.* ▼

Environmental Change

History of Science

(H) Sometimes the environment changes. Then, over a long period of time, some species may change and become adapted to the new conditions. Other species may stay the same as before.

Scientists have studied how one species of moth living in England changed when its environment changed. In the early 1800s, tree trunks were light gray. Peppered moths had pale gray wings speckled with black. Notice in the picture at the top how the pale gray color of the moth at the left makes it hard to see when it rests on the light-colored tree. The color of its wings was an adaptation that helped the moths hide from birds that ate insects.

As factories began to pollute the air, black soot settled on trees and gradually made them darker. In 1848, a dark-colored peppered moth was found near Manchester, England. A single gene controls the color of peppered moths. A mutation, or change in the gene, might have caused the moth's dark color.

If the tree trunks had stayed light colored, birds would have quickly found and eaten dark moths. The dark moth in the top picture is easy to see against the light-colored tree. However, the environment changed. The dark moths were better adapted to survive on the dark tree trunks. Notice in the bottom picture how the light moth stands out against the dark-colored tree and the dark moth is harder to see.

Most of the trees had dark-colored bark by the late 1800s. By 1898, 99% of the peppered moths in some industrial areas of England were dark.

The peppered moths' environment changed again in the second half of the 1900s. England reduced its air pollution. As less soot settled on the trees, the bark again became light colored. The number of dark peppered moths decreased, and the number of light ones increased. Now birds find the dark moths more easily, and more light moths survive to reproduce.

You have learned how the peppered moth changed and survived when its environment changed. As the last ice age ended, the woolly mammoth and the gray fox also lived in a changing environment. Neither of them appears to have changed. However, when the climate got warmer, the woolly mammoth became extinct and the gray fox survived. Look at the pictures to see adaptations they had for living in a cold climate.

▲ Woolly Mammoth

The woolly mammoth's large size helped its body retain heat. Beneath its skin was a layer of fat up to 8 centimeters thick. It was covered by a layer of short, woolly hairs and a layer of coarse hairs up to 50 centimeters long.

The woolly mammoth and the gray fox lived in the same place at the same time. However, they did not have the same adaptations for cold. Some scientists think that the gray fox was less specialized for a cold climate and so it was able to survive when the climate got warmer. The mammoth's adaptations for cold might have kept it too warm for the new climate.

Scientists continue to study how environmental changes affect species. They look at organisms alive today and at remains of organisms that died long ago.

Gray Fox

Many scientists think the gray fox had behavioral adaptations that helped it survive the cold. It had fewer structural adaptations than the woolly mammoth. When the climate warmed, the gray fox was able to survive. Today, the gray fox is found throughout the United States. ▶

Glossary

fossil (fos′əl), any remains or trace of an organism that was once alive

mold (mōld), a fossil that is a hollow place shaped like an organism

cast (kast), a fossil formed by sediments filling up a mold

Learning from Fossils

Usually organisms die and decay without leaving a trace. Sometimes, however, an organism is preserved as a fossil. A **fossil** is any remains or trace of an organism that was once alive. Usually only the hard parts of an organism, such as bones or shells, become fossils. Occasionally other body parts become fossils. Even traces, such as a dinosaur's footprints, can form fossils.

Some fossils form when an organism dies and sinks to the bottom of a body of water. Layers of sediment cover it. The weight of the upper layers changes the lower layer into rock. When the organism decays, it leaves a **mold,** a hollow space in the rock with the imprint of its body. If soft sediment moves into the mold, it can harden to form a **cast.** The cast has the same shape as the original organism. The picture below shows a cast and a mold. Study the pictures on these two pages to learn about different types of fossils.

Scientists study fossils to learn about how the world has changed. For example, magnolias grow only in warm climates. Scientists found fossil magnolias in Greenland, far north of the United States. They concluded that at one time Greenland was much warmer than it is today. Fossils of ocean organisms high in mountain rocks indicate that the rocks were once on the ocean floor.

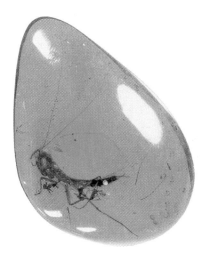

▲ **Fossils in Amber**
When it was alive, this insect became trapped in resin. The resin prevented air from reaching the insect's body. With time, the resin hardened and formed amber. This preserved the entire insect.

▲ **Molds and Casts**
Millions of years ago a trilobite, a sea animal, died and sank to the bottom of the sea. Two fossils formed—the mold at the left and the cast at the right.

▲ **Frozen Fossils**
On very rare occasions, scientists discover a frozen fossil. This baby mammoth was frozen in a glacier for more than 10,000 years.

Scientists also study fossils to learn how organisms lived. They look at the shape of an animal's bones and where muscles were attached. Sometimes they even find fossils of its food. By looking at fossils from different times, they learn how organisms changed and became adapted to a new environment.

Glossary

petrified fossil
(pet′rə fīd fos′əl),
a fossil formed when minerals slowly replace some or all of an organism, turning it to stone

▲ **Fossil Footprints**
A dinosaur made the footprints that were preserved here.

Petrified Fossils
These fossil logs are too heavy to be wood. Minerals dissolved in water soaked into the wood. When the wood dried, the minerals remained. They may have replaced some of the wood. Finally, the log was mostly minerals. A fossil preserved this way is called a **petrified fossil.** ▼

Lesson 4 Review

1. What are two variations among copper butterflies?

2. After their environment changed, what happened to the peppered moths, the woolly mammoth, and the gray fox?

3. What do scientists learn by studying fossils?

4. **Compare and Contrast**
   Compare a woolly mammoth's adaptations to cold with a gray fox's adaptations.

Chapter 3 Review

Chapter Main Ideas

Lesson 1

• Adaptations are structures or instinctive behaviors that help an organism fit its environment and help it meet its basic needs.
• Structural adaptations are adaptations of an organism's color, shape, or body parts.
• Behavioral adaptations are inherited behaviors that help an organism meet its basic needs.

Lesson 2

• Adaptations help an organism meet its basic needs in a water environment.
• Adaptations help an organism meet its basic needs on land.

Lesson 3

• Adaptations for cold climates help an organism meet its basic needs in a cold environment.
• Adaptations for hot, dry climates help an organism meet its basic needs in a hot, dry environment.
• Adaptations for seasonal changes help an organism meet its basic needs in an environment that has seasonal changes.

Lesson 4

• A species may acquire a new variation when a mutation occurs.
• When the environment changes, some species may change and others may not; some may survive and others may not.
• By studying fossils, scientists learn about life long ago and how the world has changed.

Reviewing Science Words and Concepts

Write the letter of the word or phrase that best completes each sentence.

a. behavioral adaptation
b. cast
c. fossil
d. mimicry
e. mold
f. petrified fossil
g. structural adaptation

1. When minerals replace the parts of an organism, a ____ is formed.
2. An inherited behavior that helps an organism survive is a ____ .
3. An adaptation of an organism's body or coloring is a ____ .
4. A fossil that is a hollow place shaped like an organism is a ____ .
5. An adaptation in which one organism looks like another is ____ .
6. The remains or trace of an organism that lived long ago is a ____ .
7. A fossil in rock that has the same shape as the original organism is a ____ .

Explaining Science

Write a paragraph using examples to answer these questions.

1. How can structural adaptations help organisms survive?

2. How are adaptations for living in water and on land different?

3. How does storing food for the winter help a squirrel adapt to cold weather?

4. What can happen to a species if its adaptations do not help the members of the species survive when the environment changes?

Using Skills

1. Analyze data about adaptations by **reading** a **graph.** The graph below records the observations of peppered moths made by an English scientist. He released light and dark moths in a polluted area and an unpolluted area. The bars show the percentage of light and dark moths found later still living in each area. In which area is it an advantage to be dark colored? light colored?

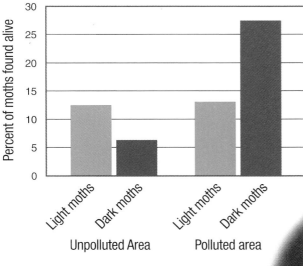

Effect of Color on the Survival of Peppered Moths

2. Suppose you saw a large animal. It was covered with thick hair and had small ears. What could you **infer** about the animal's environment based on what you know about adaptations?

3. Predict some traits you would expect to find in a plant that lives high in the mountains where the weather is cold and windy much of the year.

Critical Thinking

1. Two kinds of animals that are not related have many of the same traits. **Draw** a **conclusion** that explains why they are similar.

2. List ten adaptations and **classify** them as behavioral adaptations or structural adaptations.

3. Compare and **contrast** a polar bear's adaptations for cold to a woolly mammoth's adaptations.

What's That?

Look! Up in the sky! Is it a bird? Is it a plane? No, it's a blimp! And it's just lowered a raft into the trees. What a great way to study things that live in the tops of trees.

Chapter 4
Ecology

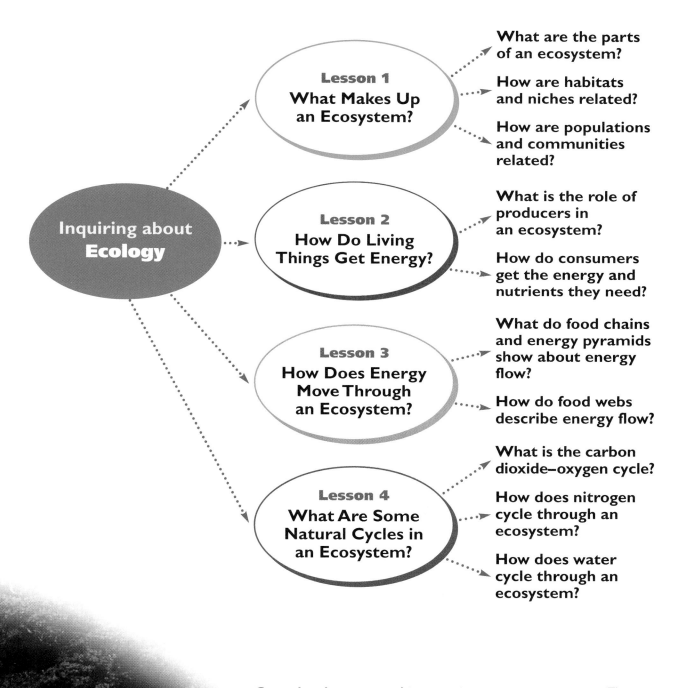

Inquiring about Ecology

Lesson 1
What Makes Up an Ecosystem?

What are the parts of an ecosystem?

How are habitats and niches related?

How are populations and communities related?

Lesson 2
How Do Living Things Get Energy?

What is the role of producers in an ecosystem?

How do consumers get the energy and nutrients they need?

Lesson 3
How Does Energy Move Through an Ecosystem?

What do food chains and energy pyramids show about energy flow?

How do food webs describe energy flow?

Lesson 4
What Are Some Natural Cycles in an Ecosystem?

What is the carbon dioxide–oxygen cycle?

How does nitrogen cycle through an ecosystem?

How does water cycle through an ecosystem?

Copy the chapter graphic organizer onto your own paper. This organizer shows you what the whole chapter is all about. As you read the lessons and do the activities, look for answers to the questions and write them on your organizer.

Exploring Parts of Soil

Process Skills

- classifying
- observing
- communicating

Materials

- garden soil or soil from a vacant lot
- spoon
- paper towel
- hand lens
- toothpick

Explore

1 Put 6 spoonfuls of the soil sample onto a paper towel.

2 Use a hand lens to observe the soil carefully. Use a spoon or toothpick to sort through the soil. **Classify** by separating the sample into three groups. Place any living organisms you see in one group. Place once-living things in the second group. Place nonliving pieces of soil in the third group.

3 **Observe** and describe at least three items in each group. (Don't worry if you didn't find any living organisms.) Ask yourself about the color, size, and shape of each item. Are there many like it, a few, or only one? Record your descriptions. **Communicate.** Write a one-sentence summary of each group.

4 Wash your hands after handling the soil sample.

Reflect

1. How did you classify items as living, once-living, or nonliving?

2. Describe the appearance of the nonliving parts of the soil.

Inquire Further

If your soil was returned to the ground, what would happen to the once-living items over time? Develop a plan to answer this or other questions you may have.

Identifying the Main Idea

As you read for science, finding the main ideas is important. Sometimes main ideas are stated directly. Look at "You will learn:" on page A 110. The three sentences there are the stated main ideas for Lesson 1, *What Makes Up an Ecosystem?* As you read the lesson, however, the main ideas might be paraphrased, or written in a slightly different way.

Example

The first stated main idea for Lesson 1 is "the basic parts of an ecosystem." In the lesson the idea has been rewritten as: "Together, the living parts and nonliving parts make up the tropical rain-forest ecosystem."

Make a chart like the one shown for the rest of Lesson 1. Write the three main ideas from "You will learn:" in the first column. As you read the lesson, decide whether each main idea is stated or paraphrased. Write the main idea sentence from each part of the lesson in the correct column.

Main Idea	Stated	Paraphrased

Talk About It!

1. Where can you find the main ideas for each lesson in your book?

2. What two ways will you find the main ideas expressed in your book?

You will learn:

- about the parts of an ecosystem.
- how habitats and niches are related.
- how populations and communities are related.

Glossary

ecosystem
(ē′kō sis′təm), all the living and nonliving parts in an area

Lesson 1

What Makes Up an Ecosystem?

Imagine you're in a tropical rain forest. **Listen** to the strange sound the howler monkey makes. **Smell** the fragrant orchid. Can you see the brightly colored frog? **Don't touch!** It's covered with poisons that keep enemies away.

Parts of an Ecosystem

You've just imagined some of the organisms that live in a tropical rain forest. Find the monkey, the orchid, and the frog in the picture on the next page. These organisms are just a few of the living parts of the rain forest. The rain forest also has nonliving parts, such as air, water, and soil. Together, the living parts and nonliving parts make up the tropical rain-forest **ecosystem.**

Three nonliving things—water, sunlight, and temperature—make a tropical rain forest what it is. In a rain forest, rain falls often, and the humidity is always high. Tropical rain forests get about the same amount of sunlight every day, all through the year. There are no short winter days. The temperature is about the same throughout the year too. It's always warm! Warm temperatures and plenty of water and sunlight explain why tropical rain forests carry out more photosynthesis per square kilometer than any other land ecosystem.

You may be surprised to learn that the soil in most tropical rain forests is very poor compared with the soil in most other forests. It has few nutrients stored in it. You know that rain forests have huge, towering trees. How can the soil be poor? Scientists have learned that almost all the nutrients in a rain forest are inside living things. When a living thing dies, specialized organisms rapidly break it down and release its nutrients. Plants nearby quickly reuse the nutrients for their own growth. Nutrients don't stay in the soil for very long.

The relationships among the living and the nonliving parts help plants in the tropical rain forest grow, even with poor soil. The plants in turn provide food and a place to live for many animals. The study of the relationships among the living and nonliving parts of an area is known as **ecology.**

Glossary

ecology (ē kol′ə jē), the study of the relationships among living and nonliving parts of an area

Many kinds of animals, plants, fungi, protists, and bacteria are found in the rain forest. They interact with each other and with nonliving factors. The nonliving factors include water, sunlight, temperature, and soil. ▼

Howler monkey

Orchid

Poison arrow frog

Glossary

habitat (hab′ə tat), the place where a species lives

niche (nich), the role of a species in an ecosystem

Habitats and Niches

Many different species live together in a tropical rain forest. Each kind of organism lives in a certain part of the rain-forest ecosystem. Look at the picture on the next page. Howler monkeys spend most of their time high in the trees. This is their **habitat**— the place where they live. Squirrel monkeys also live in rain-forest trees. They spend time not only high in the trees, but also at lower levels. Their habitat includes many different levels in the trees.

Howler monkeys spend most of their time searching for the young leaves that grow in the treetops. These leaves are the monkeys' main food. Searching for and eating new leaves is part of the howler monkey's niche. A **niche** is what an organism does—the role it plays in its ecosystem.

Compare the role of the squirrel monkey to the role of the howler monkey. Like howler monkeys, squirrel monkeys live in trees and eat leaves, but they eat other foods too. They eat fruit, insects, spiders, and other small animals. Searching for and eating these foods is part of the squirrel monkey's niche.

Now look at the other organisms in the picture. Each species has its own niche. Each niche is different. Each species uses the resources of the rain forest in a slightly different way. Find how the role of each species is different from the roles of the others. Because the organisms of the rain forest have many different niches, many different species can exist together.

Howler monkeys eat the young leaves that are found mostly in the higher parts of the trees.

Macaws fly in search of food. They use their keen eyesight to spot ripe fruit. Macaws nest in holes in rain-forest trees.

Sloths eat leaves, stems, berries, and fruits in rain-forest trees. They are usually active at night, unlike howler monkeys and squirrel monkeys.

Squirrel monkeys have a more varied diet than howler monkeys do. It includes leaves, fruits, and small animals such as insects and spiders. Squirrel monkeys are found at all levels of the rain forest.

Kinkajous eat fruit, honey, insects, and other small animals. They use their long tails to grasp branches as they move through the trees in search of food. Like sloths, kinkajous are active at night.

Ocelots spend most of their time on the ground. They eat mice, lizards, snakes, birds, sloths, monkeys, and other animals. Ocelots are active at night.

Poison arrow frogs eat insects. They live on the ground in tropical rain forests. They are also found on the trunks and lower branches and in other levels of the trees, but not at the top level.

Jaguars sometimes hunt in rain-forest trees. They spend most of their lives on the ground. Like ocelots, they eat birds, sloths, monkeys, and other land animals. Jaguars also hunt for fish in rivers and streams.

Glossary

population
(pop′yə lā′shən), all of the members of one species that live in the same area

▲ *The populations of many species of rain-forest trees are small. Although many trees look very similar, there may be no other trees of the same species within sight.*

Populations and Communities

Tropical rain forests have many species. All the members of a species that live in an area make up a **population.** The size of the population of each species is usually small compared to populations in most forests in the United States. More than 300 different species of trees might live in an area of tropical rain forest about the size of two football fields. In contrast, a similar area in many forests in the United States might have only a few species of trees, but the population of each species would be much larger.

Similarly, hundreds of species of birds may live in an area of a tropical rain forest, but the population of each species is small. A forest in the United States may have fewer species of birds, but the population of each may be ten times as large. Find the different rain-forest populations on these two pages.

▲ *All the leaf cutter ants in the area make up the population of this species.*

▲ *Howler monkeys live in groups. Their howling warns other groups of howler monkeys to stay away. The population of howler monkeys in an area includes all the groups of howler monkeys.*

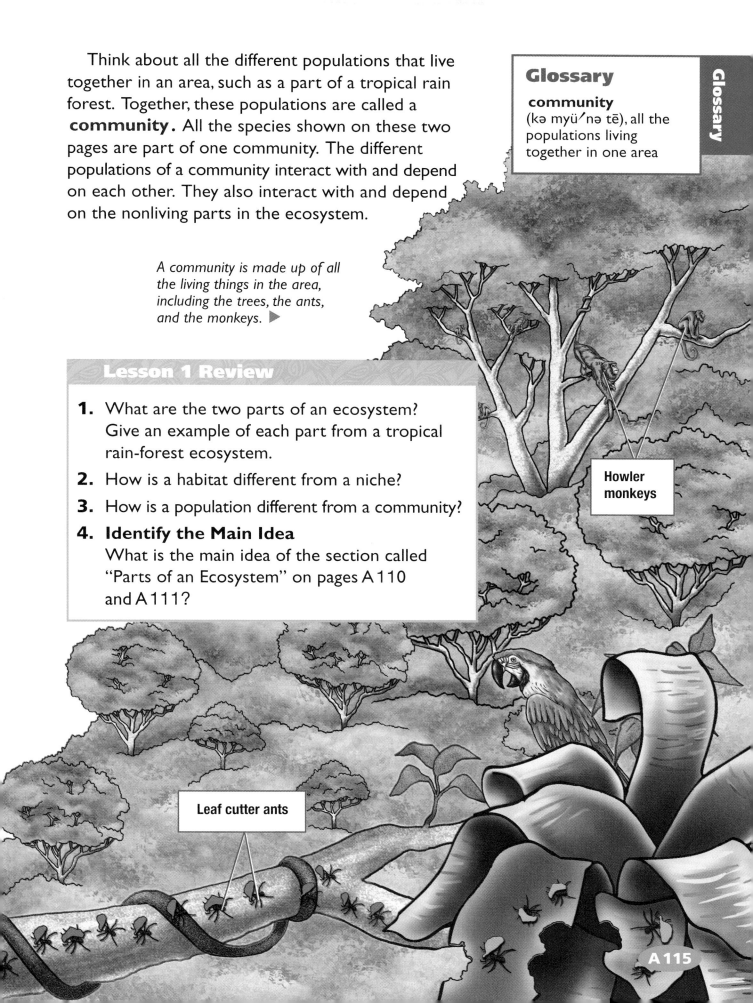

Think about all the different populations that live together in an area, such as a part of a tropical rain forest. Together, these populations are called a **community**. All the species shown on these two pages are part of one community. The different populations of a community interact with and depend on each other. They also interact with and depend on the nonliving parts in the ecosystem.

Glossary

community
(kə myü′nə tē), all the populations living together in one area

Glossary

A community is made up of all the living things in the area, including the trees, the ants, and the monkeys. ▶

Lesson 1 Review

1. What are the two parts of an ecosystem? Give an example of each part from a tropical rain-forest ecosystem.

2. How is a habitat different from a niche?

3. How is a population different from a community?

4. **Identify the Main Idea**
   What is the main idea of the section called "Parts of an Ecosystem" on pages A 110 and A 111?

Howler monkeys

Leaf cutter ants

Investigating Owl Pellets

Process Skills

- observing
- inferring

Materials

- safety goggles
- owl pellet
- paper towel
- hand lens
- plastic forceps
- round toothpick

Getting Ready

You can find out about an owl's niche by studying owl pellets.

Be sure to leave space to write and draw in your chart.

Follow This Procedure

❶ Make a chart like the one shown. Use your chart to record your observations.

	Observations
Outside of pellet	
Inside of pellet	
Teeth	
Skulls	

❷ Put on your safety goggles. Unwrap an owl pellet and place it on a paper towel. Use a hand lens to **observe** the outside of the pellet. Record your observations.

❸ Carefully use the toothpick, forceps, and your fingers to open the owl pellet (Photo A). Use a hand lens to observe the inside of the pellet. Record your observations.

Photo A

Photo B

 Safety Note *Be careful when using sharp objects such as forceps and toothpicks.*

④ Gently separate the contents of the owl pellet into groups, such as bones, fur, and feathers (Photo B). Take care not to break the tiny bones.

⑤ Separate the skulls and teeth from the other bones.

⑥ Use a hand lens to look at any teeth you found. Are they sharp, flat teeth like your front teeth; broad, flat teeth like your back teeth; or sharp, pointed teeth like those near the front of your mouth? Record your observations.

⑦ Observe any skulls you find. You may need to look at the skulls of other groups too. Compare and contrast the skulls. Record your observations.

⑧ Wash your hands thoroughly after this activity.

Self-Monitoring
Have I recorded all my observations?
    Did I wash my hands thoroughly when finished?

Interpret Your Results

1. Make an **inference.** What does the presence of fur or feathers tell you about the owl's niche in the ecosystem?

2. Make an inference. Based on your observations of skulls and bones, does the owl eat mostly one species of prey or several different species? Explain.

3. Flat teeth are good for grinding plants and seeds. Long, pointed teeth are good for grabbing, holding, and ripping flesh. Sharp flat teeth are good for cutting and tearing flesh, but sometimes can gnaw wood. Think about the types of teeth you found. Make an inference. What type or types of food are eaten by the owl's prey?

Inquire Further

How can you identify the species that the owl eats? Develop a plan to answer this or other questions you may have.

Self-Assessment

- I followed instructions to examine an owl pellet.
- I recorded my **observations** of the owl pellet and its contents.
- I made an **inference** about the owl's niche in its ecosystem.
- I made an inference about the food the owl eats.
- I made an inference about the food eaten by the owl's prey.

You will learn:
- the role of producers in an ecosystem.
- how consumers get the energy and nutrients they need.

Glossary

photosynthesis (fō′tō sin′thə sis), the process by which plants use sunlight to make sugar from water and carbon dioxide

Producers use light to make sugar and oxygen from carbon dioxide and water. ▼

Lesson 2

How Do Living Things Get Energy?

Don't look down! Imagine yourself 11 stories high in the topmost part of the rain forest. You are in bright sunlight, surrounded by a sea of green. Branches covered with leaves spread wide, capturing the sunlight. On the ground, it is dark.

Producers

Adaptations help the trees in the rain forest collect light. Their branches spread so wide and have so many leaves that they stop most of the light before it can reach the ground. The leaves use the light to change water from the ground and carbon dioxide from the air into sugar. Then they use this sugar, along with nutrients from the soil, to build other substances that form new roots, leaves, stems, and flowers. The life of the tree depends on its ability to get light.

Other plants also use sunlight to make sugar. The process that makes the sugar is called **photosynthesis.** This process is shown below. Find each of the three things plants use in photosynthesis. Notice that plants produce oxygen during photosynthesis.

Sunlight

Oxygen

Water

Sugar

Carbon Dioxide

Plants aren't the only organisms that can carry out photosynthesis. Some single-celled organisms can too. These tiny organisms carry out most of the photosynthesis on the earth, mainly in the oceans. Plants and other organisms that use light energy to make sugar from carbon dioxide and water are called **producers.**

The tall trees you see in the picture are the most noticeable producers in the tropical rain forests, but they aren't the only ones. Some producers have unusual adaptations that help them get the light and water all producers need. Certain kinds of tropical plants get sunlight by growing high in the branches of trees. Some have roots that anchor them to the tree. Others send their roots all the way down to the ground.

Glossary

Glossary

producer (prə dü′sər), an organism that uses sunlight to make sugar from water and carbon dioxide

The tall trees are the most noticeable producers in this ecosystem. ▼

Glossary

consumer
(kən sü′mər), an organism that consumes other organisms for food

▲ **Carnivore**
Jaguars eat only animals. Because they get all their energy from eating other consumers, jaguars are known as carnivores.

Consumers

You just learned how rain-forest plants get energy from the sun and use it to make the sugar they need to grow. Many organisms, such as the caterpillar below, can't do this. The caterpillar must get energy and nutrients from the food it eats. All organisms, including animals, that depend on other organisms for food are called **consumers.**

Many consumers live in the rain forest. Some consumers eat only producers. The howler monkey shown on the next page is this kind of consumer. Recall that it gets its energy mainly from eating young leaves. The howler monkey and other consumers that eat only plants are called herbivores.

Consumers that get all their energy from eating other consumers are called carnivores. Jaguars, such as the one in the picture, eat kinkajous, macaws, sloths, howler monkeys, and other animals.

Some consumers eat both plants and animals. For example, the kinkajou on the next page eats fruit as well as ants and termites. Because kinkajous are consumers that eat both plants and animals, scientists call them omnivores.

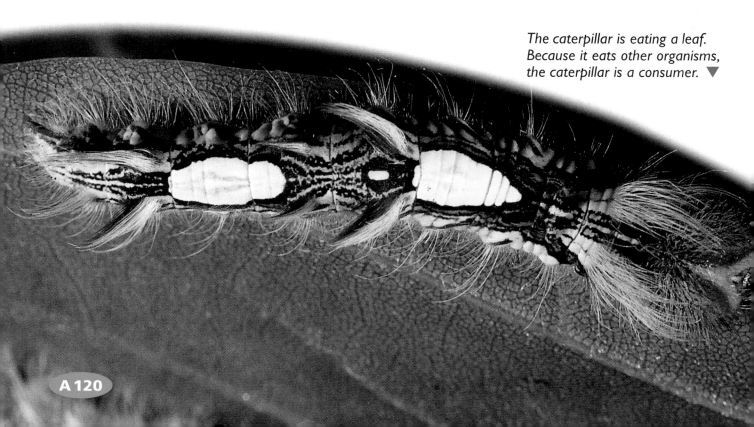

The caterpillar is eating a leaf. Because it eats other organisms, the caterpillar is a consumer. ▼

◄ Omnivore

Kinkajous eat fruit, honey, insects, and other small animals. Because kinkajous eat both plants and animals, kinkajous are known as omnivores.

Herbivore

Howler monkeys eat only plants, such as these leaves. Because they eat only plants, howler monkeys are known as herbivores. ▶

Glossary

scavenger
(skav′ən jər), an animal that feeds on the bodies of dead organisms

decomposer
(dē′kəm pō′zər), an organism that helps to break down and decay dead organisms and the wastes of living organisms

▲ **Scavenger**
Because bush dogs eat the bodies of dead animals, scientists call them scavengers.

Decomposers ▶
The bacteria in the picture on the left and the fungi on the right break down the wastes of living organisms and the bodies of dead ones. Scientists group them as decomposers. Notice that the yellow fungi completely cover the ant they are breaking down.

In addition to herbivores, carnivores, and omnivores, there are some specialized consumers. They are vital to life on earth. Without these consumers, the ground would be littered with countless dead organisms and the wastes they made while they lived.

A **scavenger** is an animal that feeds on the bodies of recently dead organisms. The bush dog shown in the picture is a scavenger. It eats dead monkeys, dead sloths, and other dead animals it finds.

A **decomposer** uses up what scavengers leave behind. Decomposers include fungi and some single-celled organisms. Given time, decomposers can decay the entire body of a large animal that scavengers missed. In addition, they break down the wastes of living organisms. Suppose all the wastes animals had ever made were still around. You'd have to be very careful where you walked! Decomposers break down dead plants too. As they consume their "food," decomposers change it into simple nutrients that plants can use. Without decomposers, soil would not contain enough nutrients for plants to grow.

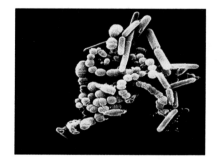
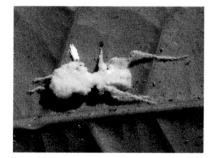

Lesson 2 Review

1. How are producers important in an ecosystem?
2. How do consumers get energy?
3. **Identify the Main Idea**
   What is the main idea of the first paragraph on page A120?

Lesson 3

How Does Energy Move Through an Ecosystem?

Look at the palm tree below. It is like a factory, making the sugar it needs, with the sun providing the energy. The energy stored in the sugar is the energy that flows through a food web.

Food Chains and Energy Pyramids

Life on the earth depends on the sun's energy. Producers, such as palm trees, change the sun's energy into energy stored in sugar. Plants use this sugar, the energy stored in it, and nutrients from the soil to grow all their parts.

All the energy that consumers get comes from plants, directly or indirectly. The macaw in the picture gets energy directly from the fruit of the palm tree. Other consumers eat plants indirectly when they eat other consumers. Because all of a plant's energy comes from the sun, all the energy consumers get comes from the sun too.

The palm tree captures energy from sunlight during photosynthesis. The tree stores some of this energy as sugar in plant parts, such as the palm fruit. Over time, the tree grew and produced the fruit you see. Energy went from the sun to the palm tree. ▼

The macaw eats the energy-rich palm fruit. Energy passes from the palm tree to the macaw. Someday, another animal may eat the macaw. Then energy will go to that animal. ▶

A 123

Glossary

energy pyramid
(en′ər jē pir′ə mid),
a diagram that compares
the amount of energy
available at each
position, or level, in
the feeding order

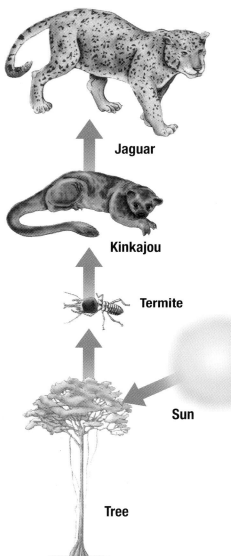

Jaguar

Kinkajou

Termite

Sun

Tree

▲ *A food chain shows a simple view of energy flow in an ecosystem. The arrows show how the energy flows.*

Food chains are diagrams scientists use to show how energy and nutrients pass from one organism to another in an ecosystem. The arrows on the food chain on the left show the path that energy and nutrients take. Notice that this food chain begins with plants that get energy from the sun. Follow the path that energy takes in the food chain from the tree to the jaguar.

Compare this food chain with the **energy pyramid** on the next page. The energy pyramid compares the amount of energy available at each position, or level, in the feeding order. The first level represents the energy trapped by the trees and all the other producers in the rain forest. This is the largest level because it is the level with the most energy. Plants get this energy directly from the sun.

Notice that the next level of the pyramid is smaller than the first. It shows the energy available to animals, such as the termites that feed on the trees. Less energy is available to these animals because the rain-forest plants use up some energy for their own needs. This energy is lost as heat.

The organisms in each level of the energy pyramid eat those in the level below them. They store some of the energy and use some energy for their life processes. This energy is lost as heat. The shape of the pyramid shows that the least amount of energy is available to the organisms in the top level.

Although both energy pyramids and food chains show the flow of energy, food chains give a simplified view. They don't show how the amount of energy changes at each position in the chain. Food chains also simplify relationships among organisms. Most organisms are part of many food chains. Besides eating termites, as shown in the food chain, kinkajous eat other foods, such as frogs, beetles, scorpions, ants, and fruit. Similarly, many consumers besides jaguars eat kinkajous.

Energy Pyramid

The energy pyramid shows the relative amount of energy available at each position, or level, in the feeding order. As you compare levels, notice that the amount of energy available decreases as you move up the pyramid. Only one species is shown at each level. In reality, there are many species at each level. ▼

A predator is an animal that hunts and eats another animal. The animal that is eaten is called the prey. A predator is always on a higher level of the energy pyramid than the prey it consumes. The energy flows from the prey to the predator.

The sun provides the energy for producers.

Organisms at each level store some energy and use some energy for life processes. Only about one-tenth of the energy flows to the next higher level. The rest is lost as heat.

Glossary

food web,
a combination of all
the food chains in
a community

Food Webs

Relationships among the species in a community are complex. A **food web** is a diagram that shows how all the different food chains in a community are linked together. It shows how energy and nutrients flow among the organisms in the different food chains in an ecosystem. A food web clearly shows how organisms are dependent on each other. The arrows show the relationships. Notice how many more arrows there are even in the simplified food web shown here than there were in the food chain. Study the simplified food web below.

Simplified Food Web

A more detailed and complete tropical rain-forest food web might show hundreds of species. Thousands of arrows would show the flow of energy and nutrients.

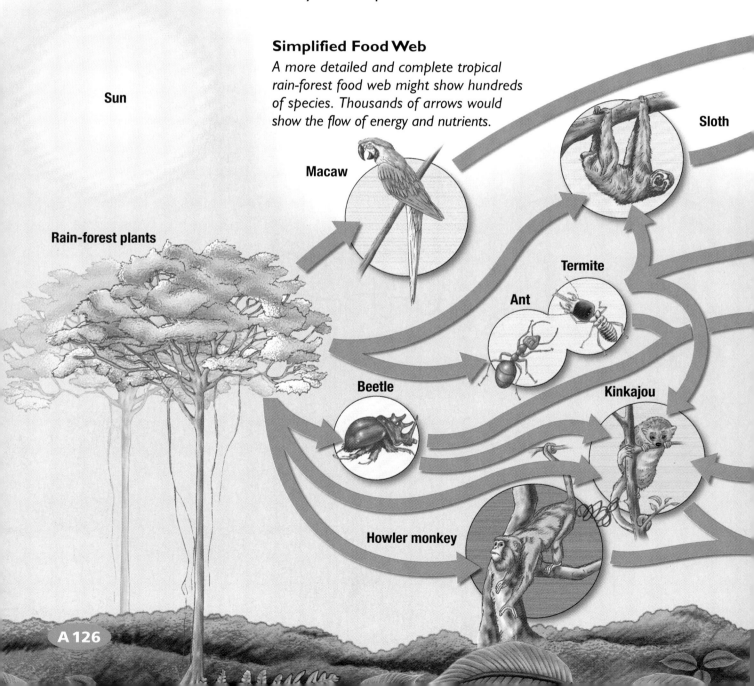

Sun

Rain-forest plants

Macaw

Sloth

Termite

Ant

Beetle

Kinkajou

Howler monkey

The food chain on page A124 showed that jaguars eat kinkajous, which eat termites, which eat plant materials. This food web shows that the kinkajou also eats frogs, beetles, scorpions, and fruit. Not all of the relationships are shown in this food web. No arrows show the role of the decomposers. Decomposers, such as bacteria and fungi, change dead organisms and wastes of living organisms into simple nutrients that plants can use. If the decomposers' role was shown, arrows would lead from every organism to the decomposers. Every plant also depends upon the nutrients decomposers release into the soil.

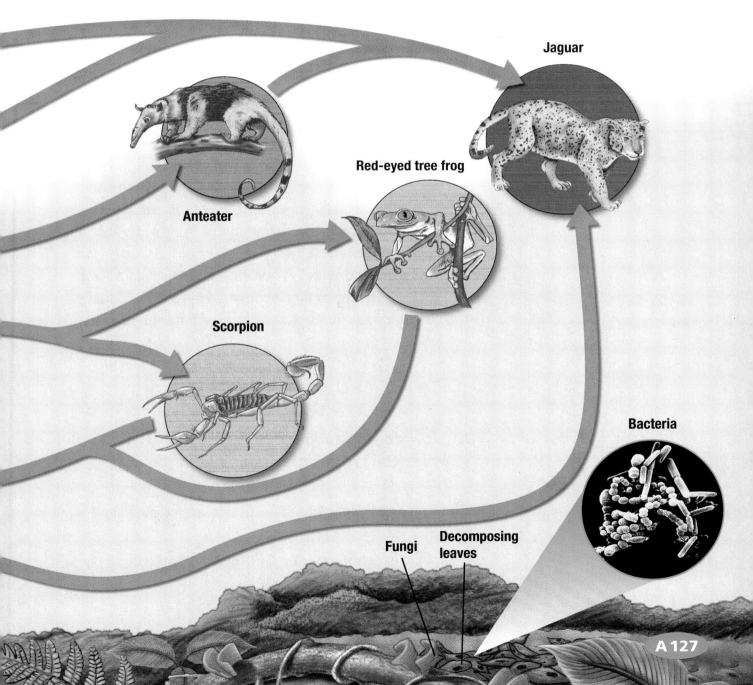

Jaguar

Anteater

Red-eyed tree frog

Scorpion

Bacteria

Fungi

Decomposing leaves

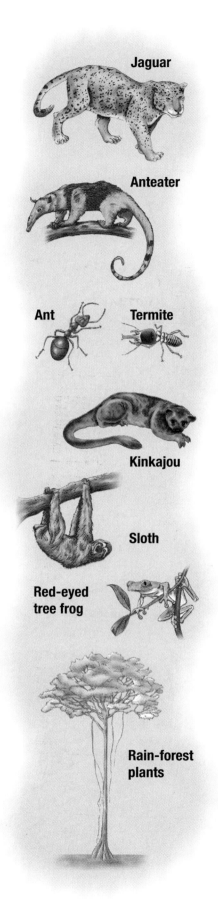

Jaguar

Anteater

Ant   Termite

Kinkajou

Sloth

Red-eyed
tree frog

Rain-forest
plants

The rain-forest food web is a part of the rain-forest ecosystem. The rain-forest ecosystem, like all ecosystems, is a complex system that has many parts, some living and some nonliving. All the parts are important. Like other systems, if one part is removed, many other parts may be affected.

Imagine what might happen if something changed the food web on pages A126 and A127 in just one way. Pretend the jaguar was removed from the food web. You might think this would be good news for its prey, such as the anteater. What would actually happen is very hard to predict. Here is one possibility.

With no jaguars to eat them, the number of anteaters might increase. However, their food supply would not increase. Anteaters would have to search harder and longer for food. There might not be enough food for all the anteaters.

With more anteaters, the number of ants and termites would decrease. This might affect the number of kinkajous, sloths, and red-eyed tree frogs, because they too eat ants and termites. Because the ants and termites help recycle nutrients in dead leaves and trees, there might be fewer nutrients for plants.

You can see how just one change could disrupt even this simplified food web. When one organism in a food web is removed, important changes may occur. Usually the changes result in an ecosystem with fewer species.

Lesson 3 Review

1. How does the amount of energy change from a lower level of an energy pyramid to the next higher level?

2. How are food webs different from food chains?

3. **Identify the Main Idea**
   What is the main idea of the third and fourth paragraphs on page A124?

What Are Some Natural Cycles in an Ecosystem?

You know what a bicycle is, but what is a carbon dioxide–oxygen cycle? No, it's not something you ride. It's a pathway that describes how carbon dioxide and oxygen move through an ecosystem.

What's the Big Idea?

You will learn:
- about the carbon dioxide–oxygen cycle.
- how nitrogen cycles through an ecosystem.
- how water cycles through an ecosystem.

Carbon Dioxide–Oxygen Cycle

The amount of material that cycles through an ecosystem stays the same. It just keeps moving through the system. The glass bubble in the picture contains producers, such as single-celled organisms, and consumers, including shrimp and snails. Producers use energy from the sun and carbon dioxide from the air inside the glass bubble. Consumers eat the producers and use energy from them to grow. They give off the carbon dioxide that producers need.

The glass bubble is like an ecosystem. Organisms sealed inside it might live for years without anything being added to the bubble. Everything they need can be used over and over again. ▶

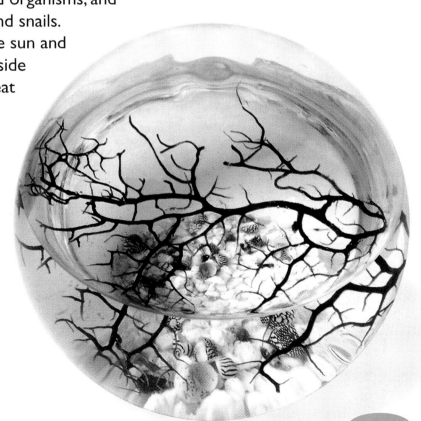

The diagram below shows how organisms use carbon dioxide and oxygen. Recall that producers in the rain forest, like other producers, carry out photosynthesis. During photosynthesis, producers use light energy to change carbon dioxide and water into sugar and oxygen. Only producers give off oxygen. Find the producers on the next page.

Notice below that the opposite of photosynthesis is respiration. Respiration is the process by which organisms use oxygen and sugar to release energy. During this process, organisms produce carbon dioxide and water. Organisms use the energy to carry out life processes. Respiration with oxygen takes place in almost all organisms, including producers. At times, all parts of plants, including roots, stems, and branches, use sugar from the leaves. Half of the sugar a plant makes may be used by the plant for respiration.

Now find the consumers in the picture on the next page. Consumers in the rain forest and in other ecosystems use the oxygen produced by plants to release energy from sugar. In this process, they produce water and carbon dioxide. Plants will use that carbon dioxide to make more sugar.

Photosynthesis
energy from sunlight + carbon dioxide + water ⟶ sugar + oxygen

Respiration
sugar + oxygen ⟶ carbon dioxide + water + energy

Carbon Dioxide–Oxygen Cycle

Key

- Carbon dioxide
- Oxygen

This tree is a producer. During photosynthesis it uses carbon dioxide and produces oxygen.

Producers don't just carry out photosynthesis. They carry out respiration, too. In the process they use oxygen and produce carbon dioxide.

The squirrel monkey and the bush dog are consumers. They use oxygen and produce carbon dioxide during respiration.

Decomposers such as this mushroom, a fungus, break down the wastes and dead bodies of organisms. The fungus can change the woody parts of the tree into sugar. Then it carries out respiration. It uses oxygen and produces carbon dioxide.

Nitrogen Cycle

Another important cycle is the nitrogen cycle. Nitrogen is a substance that is essential for life. It is a part of all proteins, the materials cells use for growth and repair. The amount of nitrogen stays the same, but it is used over and over. The nitrogen in your proteins might have once been part of a dinosaur.

Nearly 80% of the air you breathe is nitrogen gas. However, most organisms cannot use this form of nitrogen. They need nitrogen compounds. Lightning can cause nitrogen gas in the air to combine with other substances to form nitrogen compounds. Rain washes the compounds into the ground where plants can use them.

Some kinds of bacteria can also change nitrogen gas into nitrogen compounds. Some of these bacteria live in the soil. Others live in the roots of certain plants. Plants take in the nitrogen compounds from the soil through their roots. They use the nitrogen compounds to make proteins.

Animals eat the plants and use the plants' proteins to make new proteins. These animals may then be eaten by other animals. In this way, the usable nitrogen flows through the food web.

Decomposers break down the wastes organisms produce and the bodies of dead organisms. These wastes and dead bodies contain nitrogen compounds. The decomposers return the nitrogen compounds to the soil.

Nitrogen compounds can also be changed back into nitrogen gas. Some kinds of bacteria that live in the soil do this. The nitrogen gas goes into the air. Later it may be changed again into nitrogen compounds that organisms can use.

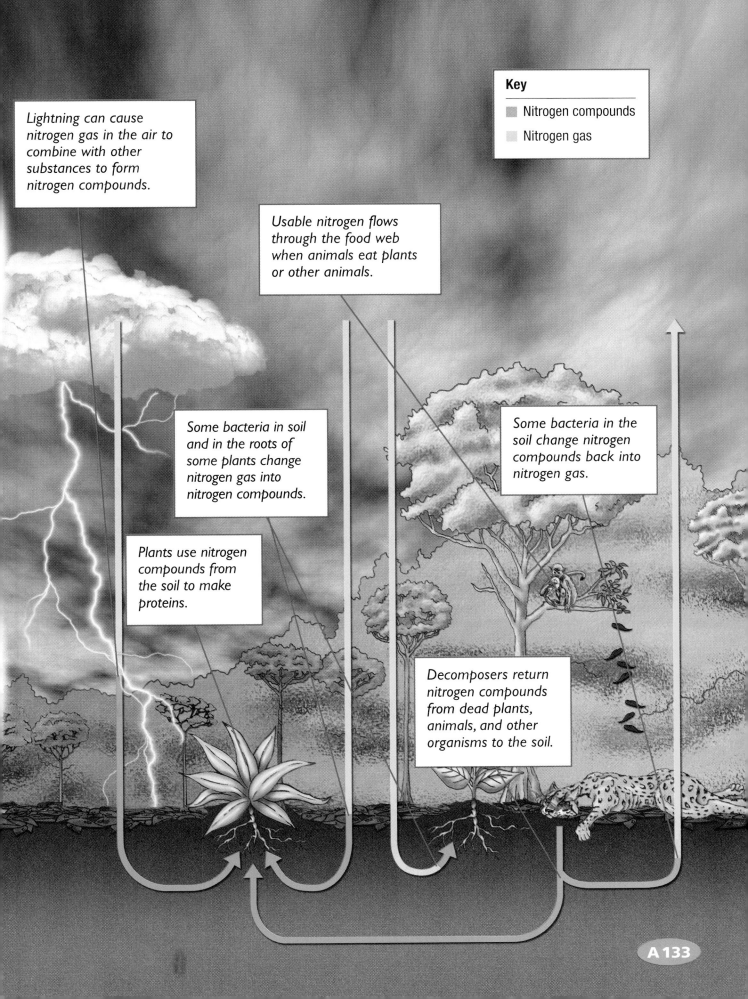

Lightning can cause nitrogen gas in the air to combine with other substances to form nitrogen compounds.

Usable nitrogen flows through the food web when animals eat plants or other animals.

Some bacteria in soil and in the roots of some plants change nitrogen gas into nitrogen compounds.

Some bacteria in the soil change nitrogen compounds back into nitrogen gas.

Plants use nitrogen compounds from the soil to make proteins.

Decomposers return nitrogen compounds from dead plants, animals, and other organisms to the soil.

Key

Nitrogen compounds

Nitrogen gas

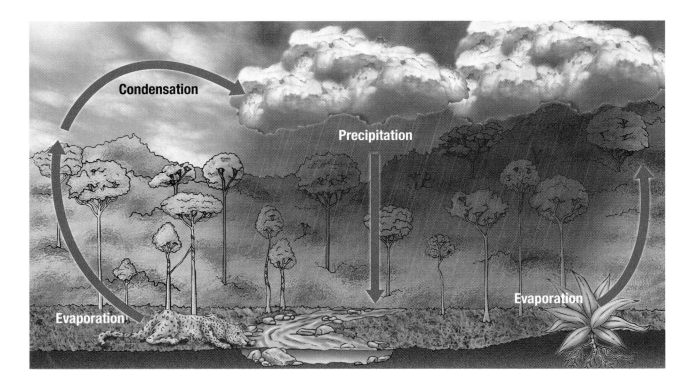

Condensation

Precipitation

Evaporation

Evaporation

▲ All organisms produce water when they use oxygen to release energy from food. Animals drink water and return it to the ecosystem through their wastes. The roots of plants take in water from the soil. Plants use some water in photosynthesis. Some evaporates from their leaves. When organisms die, the water in their bodies is recycled in the ecosystem.

Water Cycle

Water cycles through the living and nonliving parts of an ecosystem. No new water is needed. Some of the water you drink might have flowed down the Nile River when the pyramids were being built.

Notice in the picture that water on the ground evaporates, condenses into clouds, and falls to the ground as precipitation. Study the picture to learn how living things are part of the water cycle.

Lesson 4 Review

1. Explain how plants and animals use carbon dioxide and oxygen in different ways.

2. What are two ways nitrogen from the air is changed into usable nitrogen?

3. How does water cycle through the nonliving parts of the ecosystem?

4. **Identify the Main Idea**
   What is the main idea of the first paragraph on page A129?

Experimenting with Carbon Dioxide and Photosynthesis

Materials

- safety goggles
- 4 plastic cups
- marker
- masking tape
- bromothymol blue solution
- measuring cup
- 2 elodea plants
- 4 lids for plastic cups
- clock

Process Skills

- formulating questions and hypotheses
- identifying and controlling variables
- experimenting
- predicting
- observing
- collecting and interpreting data
- communicating

Process Skills

State the Problem

When a plant carries out photosynthesis it uses carbon dioxide. How does light affect the ability of a plant to use carbon dioxide?

Formulate Your Hypothesis

Will a plant exposed to light use more than, less than, or the same amount of carbon dioxide as a plant in the dark? Write your **hypothesis.**

Identify and Control the Variables

The amount of light that the plants receive is the **variable** you can change. Keep the amount of bromothymol blue solution, the length of the elodea, and the temperature the same.

Test Your Hypothesis

Follow these steps to perform an **experiment.**

1 Make a chart like the one shown on the next page. Use your chart to record your predictions and observations.

2 Put on your safety goggles.

Continued ➡

Photo A

Photo B

③ When carbon dioxide is present, bromothymol blue (BTB) solution becomes greenish yellow. You know you exhale carbon dioxide. Photo A shows BTB solution before (left) and after (right) a person exhaled into the solution through a straw.

④ Use the marker and a piece of masking tape to label the four plastic cups *A, B, C,* and *D.*

⑤ Your teacher will provide you with BTB solution that already has carbon dioxide in it. Add 100 mL of the solution to each of the 4 plastic cups. Add an elodea plant to cups A and B. Place lids on all 4 cups (Photo B). **Collect data** by recording the color of the solution in the cups.

⑥ Put cups A and C in a dark place. Put cups B and D in bright sunlight. Cups B and D serve as controls for comparison to cups A and C.

⑦ **Predict** the color of the water for each cup after 30 minutes. Record your predictions.

⑧ **Observe** all cups after 30 minutes. Record your data.

Collect Your Data

Cup	Color at start	Predic-tions	Color after 30 minutes
A			
B			
C			
D			

Interpret Your Data

1. Study the results in your chart. Which cup or cups still contained large amounts of carbon dioxide after 30 minutes?

2. Which cup or cups showed evidence that carbon dioxide had been used after 30 minutes?

State Your Conclusion

How do the results in your chart compare with your hypothesis? **Communicate** your results. Write what you conclude about how the presence or absence of light affects a plant's ability to use carbon dioxide.

 Inquire Further

What would happen if you allowed the cups to remain open for several hours or overnight? Develop a plan to answer this or other questions you may have.

Self-Assessment

- I made a **hypothesis** about how light affects the ability of a plant to use carbon dioxide.
- I **identified** and **controlled variables.**
- I followed instructions to perform an **experiment** using bromothymol blue to detect carbon dioxide in the cups.
- I **collected** and **interpreted data** by recording **predictions** and **observations** and by studying a chart.
- I **communicated** by stating my conclusion about how light affects a plant's ability to use carbon dioxide.

Chapter 4 Review

Chapter Main Ideas

Lesson 1
• An ecosystem is made up of the living and nonliving things in an area.
• An organism's habitat is the place where it lives. Its niche is its role in an ecosystem.
• A population includes all the members of a species in an area. A community is all the populations in an area.

Lesson 2
• Producers are plants and some single-celled organisms that carry out photosynthesis.
• Consumers get energy by eating producers or other consumers.

Lesson 3
• Food chains show a simplified path that energy and nutrients take in a community. Energy pyramids show how the amount of energy available decreases with each higher level in the feeding order.
• Food webs show the paths that energy and nutrients take in a community more accurately than food chains.

Lesson 4
• The carbon dioxide–oxygen cycle shows how carbon dioxide and oxygen move through an ecosystem.
• The nitrogen cycle shows how nitrogen moves through an ecosystem.
• The water cycle shows how water moves through an ecosystem.

Reviewing Science Words and Concepts

Write the letter of the word or phrase that best completes each sentence.

a. community
b. consumer
c. decomposer
d. ecology
e. ecosystem
f. energy pyramid
g. food web
h. habitat
i. niche
j. photosynthesis
k. population
l. producer
m. scavenger

1. During ___, producers use carbon dioxide, water, and sunlight to produce oxygen and sugar.

2. All the populations together in an area are called a ___.

3. An organism that depends on other organisms for food is called a ___.

4. An animal, such as a bush dog, that searches for and eats the bodies of recently dead animals is known as a ___.

5. The place where an organism lives is its ___.

6. A ___ is an organism that uses sunlight to make sugar and oxygen from carbon dioxide and water.

7. A natural system known as an ___ is made up of all the living and nonliving parts found in an area.

8. When all the food chains in a community are combined, they form a ___.

9. If an organism breaks down the wastes of living organisms, it is called a ___.

10. The study of the relationships among the living and nonliving parts of an environment is known as ___. *ecology*

11. The role of an organism in its environment is known as its ___. *niche*

12. All the members of a species in an area make up a ___. *population*

13. A diagram that compares the amount of energy available at each position in the feeding order is called an ___. *energy*

Explaining Science

Write a paragraph to answer these questions.

1. How is a niche different from a habitat?

2. Why couldn't animals survive without sunlight?

3. Why is a food web more complete than a food chain?

4. Why don't animals use up all the oxygen in the atmosphere?

Using Skills

1. Identify the **main idea** of the first paragraph on page A119.

2. Explain how scientists **classify** consumers as herbivores, carnivores, or omnivores.

3. In some places, wolves eat deer. **Formulate** a **hypothesis** about what might happen to the deer population in these areas if too many wolves were hunted.

4. Predict what would happen if the organisms in the glass sphere on page A129 received no light.

Critical Thinking

1. Usually, a smaller population is more in danger of becoming extinct than a larger one. Write a paragraph to **communicate** why this effect makes tropical rain-forest species more likely to become extinct than other species.

2. While your family was away for a month, your neighbor offered to water your houseplants. When you returned, you found well-watered plants dead in your windowless bathroom. Your neighbor moved them there so they would be easier to water. **Infer** why they died.

3. As you move up an ocean's energy pyramid, **predict** whether you would generally find more or fewer animals at each level. Explain your prediction.

Unit A Review

Reviewing Words and Concepts

Choose at least three words from the **Chapter 1** list below.
Use the words to write a paragraph about how these concepts
are related. Do the same for each of the other chapters.

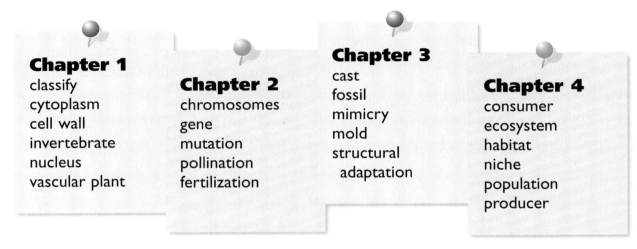

Chapter 1
classify
cytoplasm
cell wall
invertebrate
nucleus
vascular plant

Chapter 2
chromosomes
gene
mutation
pollination
fertilization

Chapter 3
cast
fossil
mimicry
mold
structural
  adaptation

Chapter 4
consumer
ecosystem
habitat
niche
population
producer

Reviewing Main Ideas

Each of the statements below is false. Change the underlined
word or words to make each statement true.

1. All living things are made up of one or more <u>species</u>.
2. Vertebrates are animals that have <u>vascular</u> <u>tubes</u>.
3. <u>Pollination</u> is the joining of a reproductive cell from each of two parents.
4. Information in <u>diagrams</u> on chromosomes determines the traits that parents pass on to their offspring.
5. The effect of a <u>hybrid</u> can be hidden by a dominant gene.
6. A <u>structural adaptation</u> is an inherited behavior that helps an organism survive.
7. Scientists can learn about how climates have changed by studying <u>moths</u>.
8. Living and nonliving things together make up the <u>niche</u>.
9. Most <u>consumers</u> make sugars by a process called photosynthesis.
10. A diagram that shows how food chains in a community are linked is called a <u>habitat</u>.

Interpreting Data

The diagram below shows a simplified food web that might exist in a meadow. Use the diagram to answer the questions below.

1. Which of the organisms shown is a producer? How do you know?

2. What might happen in the meadow if there were no owls?

3. How many different food chains are in the food web? List the organisms in each one.

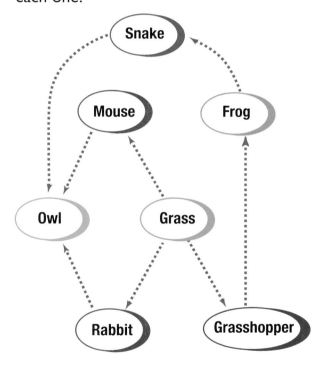

Communicating Science

1. Write a paragraph that explains ways vertebrates and invertebrates are different.

2. Draw and label a diagram that shows the part a pollen grain from one flower can play in fertilization of another flower.

3. Draw and label a diagram that shows the adaptations an organism might have to live in a water environment.

4. Draw and label a diagram showing how energy flows through an ecosystem.

Applying Science

1. Think about an animal you have seen near your home or school and write a paragraph describing how it is adapted to living in its environment.

2. Write and illustrate a travel brochure about an environment. Tell people who will go there what it will be like and what kinds of plants, animals, and nonliving things they might see.

Unit A
Performance Review

Natural History Museum

Using what you learned in this unit, complete one or more of the following activities to be included in a Natural History Museum. These exhibits will help the visitors learn more about organisms and how they live. You may work by yourself or in a group.

Ecology

Design a museum exhibit about the organisms in a rain forest. Show how they are adapted to their surroundings. Write a label for the exhibit that tells how they help one another survive.

Art

Make a chart to use in an exhibit about how scientists classify living things. Illustrate the chart with pictures that show at least one organism from each group on the chart.

History

People did not always cultivate plants for food. For thousands of years they gathered plants that grew wild. Research the history of agriculture. Prepare a time line for an exhibit on developments in agriculture from earlier times to the present.

Geography

A biome is a large geographic region that occurs in many places and has a certain kind of climate and a certain kind of community. Find out about the biomes in the United States. Draw a map showing the locations of different biomes. List some organisms that live in each biome.

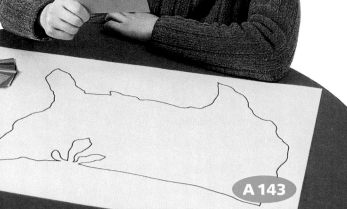

Using a List to Write Instructions

Making a List

Lists are one way that people organize their thoughts. For example, many people make grocery lists before they go to the store. The list identifies in an organized way all the things they need to buy.

Make a List of Characteristics

In Chapter 1, you learned about the characteristics scientists use to distinguish living things from nonliving things. Use this information to make a list of the characteristics of living things.

Write How-To Instructions

Look through a newspaper or magazine to find a picture of any object that interests you. Cut out the picture and mount it on a posterboard, beneath the title "Is it Living or Nonliving?" Rewrite the items on your list as questions and place the new list beside the picture. Then explain how a scientist might use these questions as a how-to guide to determine if the object shown on your poster is living or nonliving.

Remember to:

1. **Prewrite** Organize your thoughts before you write.

2. **Draft** Write your how-to instructions.

3. **Revise** Share your work and then make changes.

4. **Edit** Proofread for mistakes and fix them.

5. **Publish** Share your how-to guide with your class.

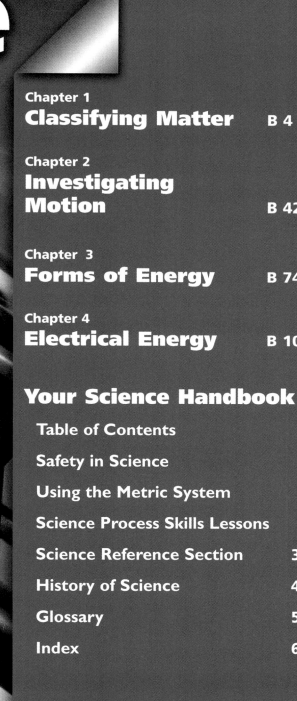

Unit B
Physical Science

Science and Technology
In Your World!

Show Off Your Glow!

Go ahead and try one! Glow sticks are fun anytime. Swing them around and make glow trails. Wear them. Use them to light your way if the power goes out. Most things that give off light also give off heat. But in glow sticks, oxygen atoms react with luminol, a chemical made by scientists. This chemical reaction gives off light but not heat. You'll learn more about atoms and chemical reactions in **Chapter 1 Classifying Matter.**

What's Rapid and Repulsive?

Zip! The latest in high-speed Maglev experimental trains reaches up to 550 kilometers per hour by riding on air! Maglev is short for *magnetic levitation*. Magnets in the track and on the train repel each other, causing the train to "float" on a "cushion" of magnetic repulsion. Rows of magnets work together to push and pull the train along at superfast speeds. You'll learn more about speed and the forces that affect motion in **Chapter 2 Investigating Motion.**

Free Falling

You step into one of the tallest, fastest thrill rides in the world—Superman: The Escape at Six Flags Magic Mountain in California. This monster reaches the height of a 36-story building. At the end you drop straight down in a free fall that resembles weightlessness. Talk about energy in motion! You'll learn more about the energy of motion and position in **Chapter 3 Forms of Energy.**

TV Unplugged!

Electricity is less of a mystery when you produce it yourself! The muscles in your legs pedaling a bicycle, can generate an electric current. How fast can you pedal? The electricity you generate could be enough to play a radio, light up a row of light bulbs, or even operate a TV. You'll learn more about ways to generate and use electricity in **Chapter 4 Electrical Energy.**

All Lit Up!

Have you ever used a glow stick? What do you think it's made of? Like everything else, it's made of matter. But what is matter made of?

Chapter 1
Classifying Matter

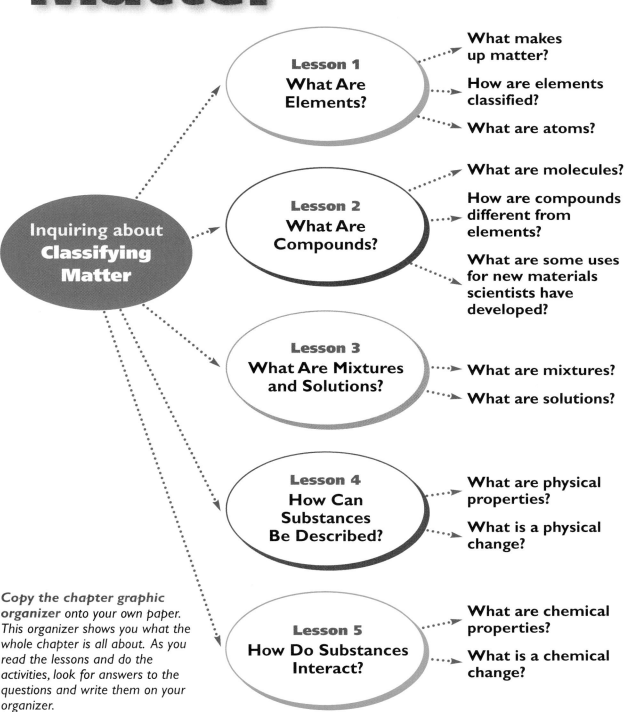

Inquiring about Classifying Matter

Lesson 1
What Are Elements?
- What makes up matter?
- How are elements classified?
- What are atoms?

Lesson 2
What Are Compounds?
- What are molecules?
- How are compounds different from elements?
- What are some uses for new materials scientists have developed?

Lesson 3
What Are Mixtures and Solutions?
- What are mixtures?
- What are solutions?

Lesson 4
How Can Substances Be Described?
- What are physical properties?
- What is a physical change?

Lesson 5
How Do Substances Interact?
- What are chemical properties?
- What is a chemical change?

Copy the chapter graphic organizer onto your own paper. This organizer shows you what the whole chapter is all about. As you read the lessons and do the activities, look for answers to the questions and write them on your organizer.

Exploring Elements

Process Skills

Process Skills

- observing
- classifying
- communicating

Materials

- aluminum foil
- penny
- paper clip
- graphite in a pencil
- hand lens
- sheet of paper

Explore

① Each of the objects is made of one or more substances called elements. Aluminum foil is made of aluminum. The penny contains zinc and copper. The paper clip is made of iron, chromium, and nickel. The graphite is a form of carbon. Place the objects on your desk. Make a list of the objects. Leave a few blank lines after each object so you have space to write about it.

② **Observe** the objects. List as many words to describe each object as you can. Use the hand lens to look closely at each object. Record your observations.

③ **Classify** the objects by dividing them into two groups on the paper. Write the properties you used to classify the objects beneath each group.

Reflect

1. Each element has its own combination of properties. Which properties did you use to classify the objects?

2. You inhale elements such as oxygen and nitrogen when you breathe. Would you classify these elements in one of your groups or would you use another group to classify them? Explain. **Communicate.** Discuss your ideas with the class.

? Inquire Further

What are some uses of the elements you observed? Develop a plan to answer this or other questions you may have.

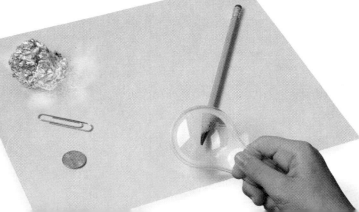

Exploring Units of Capacity

Suppose you want to bake a cake. How can you measure the volume of the ingredients? You could measure most of them in a graduated cup. Units of capacity measure volume. In the metric system you usually measure capacity using **milliliters (mL)** and **liters (L)**.

A liter is a little more than a quart.

1L = 1,000 mL

A half-gallon of milk is almost 2 liters.

A gallon of gas is a little less than 4 liters.

A milliliter of water is about 20 drops.

1 mL = 0.001 L

A small bottle of vanilla holds 60 mL.

A soda can holds 355 mL.

Example 1
350 mL = ? L
To change milliliters to liters, divide by 1,000.
350 ÷ 1,000 = 0.35
350 mL = 0.35 L

Example 2
4.5 L = ? mL
To change liters to milliliters, multiply by 1,000.
4.5 × 1,000 = 4,500
4.5 L = 4,500 mL

Math Vocabulary

milliliter (mL)
(mil′ə lē′tər), a metric unit of capacity equivalent to 0.001L

liter (L) (lē′tər), a metric unit of capacity equivalent to 1,000 mL

▲ *Dropper*

Math Tip
You can use mental math to multiply.

▲ *Soda bottle*

Talk About It!

1. Would you multiply or divide to change 2,400 mL to liters? Explain.

2. Which do you think would be more likely to be measured in milliliters: cold medicine or gasoline? Explain.

What's the Big Idea?

You will learn:

- what matter is made up of.
- how elements are classified.
- about atoms.

Glossary

element (el′ə mənt), a substance that cannot be broken down into other substances by heat, light, or electricity

Elements are the "building blocks" of matter. ▼

Lesson 1

What Are Elements?

Hey! Move over! You're taking up space. **Oops.** Moving won't change things, will it? Wherever you put yourself, your body is still a chunk of matter that takes up space.

Building Blocks of Matter

Everything that takes up space and has mass is called matter. The food you eat, the water you wash with, and the air you breathe are all matter. The things around you look different. They feel different when you touch them. They even smell different. There are so many different things, you might be surprised to learn that matter is made up of just over 100 substances.

The basic substances that make up all matter are called elements. An **element** cannot be broken down into another substance by heat, light, or electricity. You probably are already familiar with such elements as the iron in a frying pan and the aluminum in aluminum foil.

Elements are often called the "building blocks" of matter. Each element is like a letter of the alphabet. The letters on alphabet blocks can combine to make up different words, such as the word in the picture. In a similar way, elements can combine to make up different kinds of matter.

Some ancient people, including people who lived in Greece, India, and China, thought that all things in nature were made up of only a few substances. Aristotle, a Greek philosopher whose statue is shown at the right, taught that matter was made of four basic substances: earth, air, water, and fire. He thought that all other substances were made of combinations of these four substances. Ancient people used such elements as gold, iron, copper, silver, mercury, lead, carbon, and sulfur without knowing they were elements.

Early scientists recognized that some substances, including gold, copper, iron, tin, silver, sulfur, and carbon, were elements. For hundreds of years, scientists have tried to identify all the building blocks of matter—the elements.

In the 1700s and 1800s, scientists experimented with hundreds of substances as they searched for more elements. They broke down many common substances, such as salt, into their basic parts. This proved that salt and the other substances were not elements. In 1789, the French chemist Antoine-Laurent Lavoisier, whose portrait is below, published the first list of elements. By the late 1800s, more than 60 elements were identified. Today, more than 100 elements are known, including some that are made artificially.

▲ *Aristotle lived in Greece in the 300s B.C.*

◀ *Lavoisier studied how substances break down into other substances. His list of elements included substances that could not be broken down.*

You can observe that substances around you have different properties, or characteristics, by which they can be described and grouped. Different elements also have different properties. Many elements are metals. Most metals look shiny. Heat and electricity pass through them easily, and they can be hammered into thin sheets or pulled into long, thin wires. Gold, copper, silver, and iron are elements that are metals.

Some elements are nonmetals. Their properties are very different from the properties of metals. Most nonmetals are not shiny. Heat and electricity do not pass through them easily, and they cannot be hammered into sheets or pulled into a wire. Oxygen and nitrogen are nonmetal elements that are in the air. Carbon, a solid nonmetal, is black and does not look shiny. You have probably seen some of the elements that make up the objects in the picture.

Classify These Elements

Observe the properties of the objects on the tray. Each object is made up mostly of a single element. Which are metals? Which are nonmetals? How do you know? ▼

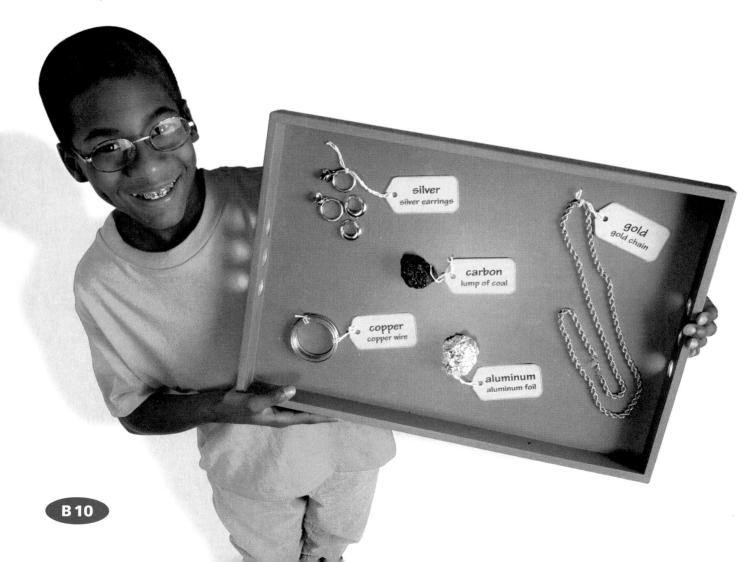

silver
silver earrings

gold
gold chain

carbon
lump of coal

copper
copper wire

aluminum
aluminum foil

The Periodic Table

History of Science

As scientists in the 1800s discovered one element after another, they wondered how the elements were related to each other and how to classify, or group, them. Scientists arranged the elements in different ways. They tried square charts and spirals.

In 1869, a Russian scientist named Dmitri Mendeleev found a way to classify all the known elements by their properties. First, he laid them out and numbered them from the least mass to the most. This put them in order from the lightest to the heaviest.

Then Mendeleev grouped the elements by other properties. He made a chart with rows and columns. He arranged the elements on the chart so that those with similar properties were near each other. He saw a pattern develop, and the properties of the elements repeated. To make elements with similar properties fall into groups, he left some empty spaces on the chart. Mendeleev predicted that new elements would be discovered and that they would have properties that made them fit into the blank spots on the table. Mendeleev was right. Elements that fit into the blanks in the table were discovered later. Today's version of Mendeleev's chart is called the **periodic table** of the elements.

The blocks below show some of the information the periodic table gives about elements. Each block has the element's name and a symbol that stands for the name. The number on the block tells the element's position on the periodic table.

Glossary

periodic (pir′ē od′ik) **table,** a chart that classifies elements by their properties

Glossary

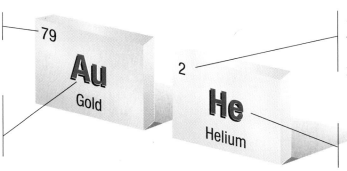

Gold is a heavy element. Its number is 79.

The symbol for gold, Au, is the first two letters of aurum, *which is the Latin word for gold.*

79

Au
Gold

2

He
Helium

Helium is a gas and is the second lightest element. It has number 2 in the periodic table.

The symbol for helium, He, is the first two letters of its name.

Sodium (Na) and potassium (K) are in the same group of elements. Look for them in the first column, on the left. ▼

The symbol for sodium (Na) comes from its Latin name natrium.

The symbol for potassium (K) is from the Latin kalium.

On the periodic table, elements are arranged so that those with similar properties appear near each other. Look at the vertical columns on the periodic table below. The elements in each column, or group, have similar properties. Find sodium (Na) and potassium (K) on the periodic table. They have similar properties. Notice in the pictures to the left that they are both shiny, silvery metals. They react in about the same way with other substances. They are in the same group.

▲ Chromium (Cr) is a mirrorlike metal sometimes used to coat metal surfaces, such as the trim on cars.

▲ Gold (Au) is a shiny, yellow metal that is often made into jewelry.

The Periodic Table of Elements
The letters in the boxes are symbols that stand for the names of the elements. ▼

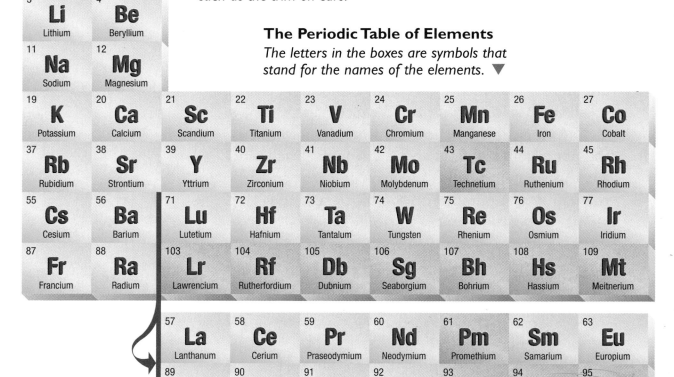

1 H Hydrogen								
3 Li Lithium	4 Be Beryllium							
11 Na Sodium	12 Mg Magnesium							
19 K Potassium	20 Ca Calcium	21 Sc Scandium	22 Ti Titanium	23 V Vanadium	24 Cr Chromium	25 Mn Manganese	26 Fe Iron	27 Co Cobalt
37 Rb Rubidium	38 Sr Strontium	39 Y Yttrium	40 Zr Zirconium	41 Nb Niobium	42 Mo Molybdenum	43 Tc Technetium	44 Ru Ruthenium	45 Rh Rhodium
55 Cs Cesium	56 Ba Barium	71 Lu Lutetium	72 Hf Hafnium	73 Ta Tantalum	74 W Tungsten	75 Re Rhenium	76 Os Osmium	77 Ir Iridium
87 Fr Francium	88 Ra Radium	103 Lr Lawrencium	104 Rf Rutherfordium	105 Db Dubnium	106 Sg Seaborgium	107 Bh Bohrium	108 Hs Hassium	109 Mt Meitnerium

57 La Lanthanum	58 Ce Cerium	59 Pr Praseodymium	60 Nd Neodymium	61 Pm Promethium	62 Sm Samarium	63 Eu Europium
89 Ac Actinium	90 Th Thorium	91 Pa Protactinium	92 U Uranium	93 Np Neptunium	94 Pu Plutonium	95 Am Americium

In the periodic table, the groups of elements are arranged in vertical columns. The color key at the bottom right will help you find out which elements are metals, which are nonmetals, and which are made artificially. Notice the pictures that show how some elements look or how they are used.

▲ Neon (Ne) belongs to a group called noble gases. They do not usually react with other substances. Neon glows when electricity passes through it.

▲ Carbon (C) occurs in different forms, such as graphite, coal, and diamond.

◀ Sulfur (S) often appears as a yellow crystal.

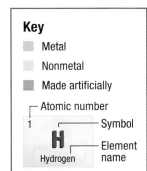

◀ Tin (Sn) is a metal used in producing containers.

							2 **He** Helium
	5 **B** Boron	6 **C** Carbon	7 **N** Nitrogen	8 **O** Oxygen	9 **F** Fluorine		10 **Ne** Neon
	13 **Al** Aluminum	14 **Si** Silicon	15 **P** Phosphorous	16 **S** Sulfur	17 **Cl** Chlorine		18 **Ar** Argon

28 **Ni** Nickel	29 **Cu** Copper	30 **Zn** Zinc	31 **Ga** Gallium	32 **Ge** Germanium	33 **As** Arsenic	34 **Se** Selenium	35 **Br** Bromine	36 **Kr** Krypton
46 **Pd** Palladium	47 **Ag** Silver	48 **Cd** Cadmium	49 **In** Indium	50 **Sn** Tin	51 **Sb** Antimony	52 **Te** Tellurium	53 **I** Iodine	54 **Xe** Xenon
78 **Pt** Platinum	79 **Au** Gold	80 **Hg** Mercury	81 **Tl** Thallium	82 **Pb** Lead	83 **Bi** Bismuth	84 **Po** Polonium	85 **At** Astatine	86 **Rn** Radon
110 **Uun** Ununnilium	111 **Uuu** Unununium	112 **Uub** Ununbium						

64 **Gd** Gadolinium	65 **Tb** Terbium	66 **Dy** Dysprosium	67 **Ho** Holmium	68 **Er** Erbium	69 **Tm** Thulium	70 **Yb** Ytterbium
96 **Cm** Curium	97 **Bk** Berkelium	98 **Cf** Californium	99 **Es** Einsteinium	100 **Fm** Fermium	101 **Md** Mendelevium	102 **No** Nobelium

Key

▢ Metal
▢ Nonmetal
▢ Made artificially

Atomic number
1
Symbol
H
Element name
Hydrogen

Glossary

Glossary

atom (at′əm), the smallest particle of an element that has the properties of the element

nucleus (nü′klē əs), the center of an atom, where protons and neutrons are located

proton (prō′ton), particle in an atom that has a positive electrical charge

neutron (nü′tron), particle in an atom that has no charge

electron (i lek′tron), particle in an atom that has a negative electrical charge

Atoms

An **atom** is a tiny particle of matter. It is the smallest particle of an element that has the properties of the element. Atoms are so small that if 4,000,000 of them were laid next to each other they would measure only about 1 millimeter across. A millimeter is about half the thickness of the lead in a regular wooden pencil.

Atoms are made up of even smaller particles. Look at the model of a helium atom. The center of the atom is the **nucleus.** Find the protons and neutrons that make up the nucleus. A **proton** has a positive electrical charge. A **neutron** has no charge. Find the electrons outside the nucleus. An **electron** has a negative charge. Electrons dart around so fast it's hard to tell where one is at any time.

All the atoms of an element have a particular number of protons. The number of protons in the atom is the atomic number of the element. It is the element's number on the periodic table. Find the number 2 on helium's block from the periodic table. It tells you that helium has two protons in its nucleus. The number of electrons in an element's atoms is the same as the number of protons. However, atoms of an element can have different numbers of neutrons. Notice that helium is so light that a helium-filled balloon rises through the air.

Helium Atom

2

He
Helium

The nucleus, or central part, of an atom contains the protons and neutrons. Most of the mass of an atom is in its nucleus.

A proton is a particle in the nucleus of an atom. It has a positive charge. A helium atom has two protons.

An electron is a part of an atom that is outside the nucleus. It has a negative charge. Helium has two electrons.

A neutron is a particle in the nucleus of an atom. It has neither a positive nor a negative charge. Most helium atoms have two neutrons.

negative

Charge

Look at the model of an aluminum atom. What is its atomic number? How many protons, electrons, and neutrons does it have?

Now look at the iron atom. What is its atomic number? How many protons, electrons, and neutrons does it have?

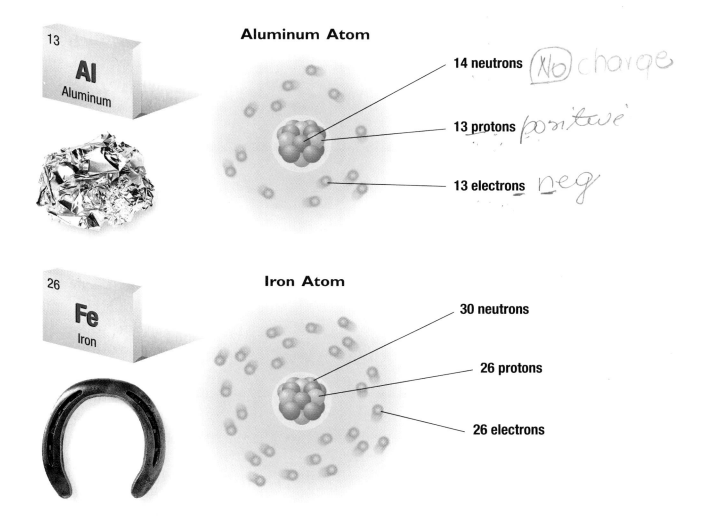

Aluminum Atom

13
Al
Aluminum

14 neutrons (No) charge

13 protons positive

13 electrons neg

Iron Atom

26
Fe
Iron

30 neutrons

26 protons

26 electrons

Lesson 1 Review

1. What makes up matter?
2. How are elements classified?
3. What are atoms?
4. **Compare and Contrast**
   Contrast the properties of metals with the properties of nonmetals.

You will learn:
- what molecules are.
- how compounds are different from elements.
- about uses of new materials scientists have developed.

Lesson 2

What Are Compounds?

Ahhh! Cool, clear water. It's good to drink, wash with, swim in, and play with. Water is wonderful, but it is not an element. Breathe deep! Air flows in and out of your body, but air is not an element either. If air and water are not elements, what are they?

Glossary

molecule (mol′ə kyül), two or more atoms joined together; the smallest unit of many substances

▲ An oxygen molecule has two oxygen atoms.

Every water molecule has two hydrogen atoms and one oxygen atom. ▼

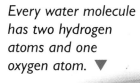

Combining Atoms into Molecules

You know that an atom is the smallest particle that makes up an element. Suppose you could take a drop of water and divide it into the smallest bit that can still be water. You wouldn't end up with an atom. You would end up with a molecule of water. A **molecule** is two or more atoms joined together. Find the model of a water molecule. Every water molecule has the same combination of three atoms—two hydrogen atoms joined to one oxygen atom. Like an atom, a water molecule is very tiny. If one of the drops of water in the picture were the size of the earth, each water molecule would be about the size of a baseball.

Unlike water, air is a mix of several different kinds of molecules. It has oxygen molecules, nitrogen molecules, and molecules of other gases. Oxygen is not usually found in nature as a single atom. An oxygen atom usually joins with at least one other oxygen atom. The two oxygen atoms together make an oxygen molecule. Find the model of an oxygen molecule.

Compounds

When atoms of two or more different elements combine, they form a **compound.** You know that when two atoms of the element hydrogen and one atom of the element oxygen combine, they form a molecule of water. You also know that atoms of oxygen join together to form molecules of oxygen in the air.

Is a water molecule a compound? Recall what you learned about water molecules. A water molecule is made up of two different kinds of atoms: hydrogen and oxygen. Therefore, it is a compound. When they are separate elements, hydrogen and oxygen are colorless gases. Joined together as a compound made up of two hydrogen atoms and one oxygen atom, they form a clear liquid.

Is an oxygen molecule a compound? An oxygen molecule like the ones in air is made up of two oxygen atoms. It has only one kind of atom: oxygen. Therefore, it is not a compound.

Carbon dioxide is another substance in the air. It is made up of more than one element. You have never seen carbon dioxide, but it is always with you. Carbon dioxide is one of the colorless gases that leaves your body when you breathe out, as the boy in the picture is doing. It is in the air around you, along with oxygen and other gases. The fizzy bubbles in soft drinks are carbon dioxide. Look at the model of carbon dioxide. What elements make up carbon dioxide? Is carbon dioxide a compound?

Every carbon dioxide molecule has an atom of carbon and two atoms of oxygen. Blow! You're sending carbon dioxide and other gases into the air. ▼

O C O

Every compound has its own properties, which are different from the properties of the elements that make up the compound. For example, sodium chloride is a compound made up of atoms of the elements sodium and chlorine. Sodium is a silvery metal that reacts violently with water, releasing a lot of heat. Chlorine is a greenish-yellow, poisonous gas. The compound they can form, sodium chloride, is the whitish crystals of table salt used to season food!

Another compound you have probably seen is rust. Rust often forms on iron objects when they are damp. Perhaps your family has an iron frying pan like the one in the picture. If an iron pan stays damp after it is washed, rust usually forms quickly. Look at the model of iron oxide. It shows one compound that forms when oxygen in the air combines with some of the iron atoms on the surface of the pan.

Like other compounds, rust has properties that are different from those of its two elements, oxygen and iron. The picture shows what rust looks like when it is magnified under a microscope. It is an orange-red, powdery substance. You know that oxygen is a colorless gas. Iron is a heavy, dark gray or black metal.

26

Fe

Iron

8

O

Oxygen

Rust

Rust is a compound made of atoms of iron and oxygen. (magnified 712×) ▶

Iron Oxide

Iron oxide is a form of rust made up of two atoms of iron and three atoms of oxygen. ▼

The pictures show some substances that contain the compound calcium carbonate. Chalk, seashells, eggshells, and pearls all have a lot of calcium carbonate. It is also the compound that makes up limestone and marble rocks. Each particle of calcium carbonate contains atoms of calcium, carbon, and oxygen. Recall that each element on the periodic table has a symbol that stands for its name. Look at the squares below to find the symbols for calcium, carbon, and oxygen.

You have learned that each particle of a compound is made up of exactly the same combination of atoms as every other particle of that compound. The picture of the atoms in a particle of calcium carbonate shows that it has one atom of calcium, one atom of carbon, and three atoms of oxygen.

Just as each element has a symbol, each compound has a formula. The formula includes the symbols for the elements in the compound. Numbers tell how many atoms of each element are in each particle. The formula for calcium carbonate is $CaCO_3$. The small number 3 after the O tells that each particle of calcium carbonate has three atoms of oxygen. If an element's symbol is not followed by a number, it means that each of the compound's particles has one atom of the element.

Limestone, seashells, and chalk are made up of forms of the compound calcium carbonate. Calcium carbonate has one calcium atom, one carbon atom, and three oxygen atoms. ▼

Limestone

Seashell

Chalk

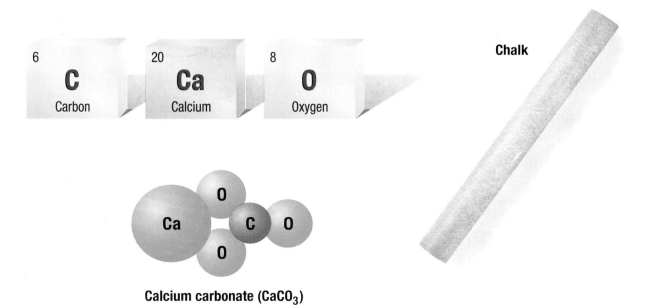

Calcium carbonate ($CaCO_3$)

New Materials

Scientists study compounds and develop new ways of combining atoms and molecules. Many of the new materials are made from polymers, or long chains of small molecules. In many materials, simple molecules of carbon and hydrogen atoms are linked together in chains that are arranged in different ways.

The way the molecules in the chains are arranged determines the properties of the resulting materials. Some polymers form long, strong fibers.

Scientists, like the one below, try to find new ways to make materials that have useful properties. Many are stronger and more durable than the materials they replace.

For sports equipment and outdoor clothing, these materials combine strength and warmth with lightness in weight. Scientists have also developed new materials for use in space exploration, medicine, and computer and communications technology. You may have seen or used some of the high-tech materials that scientists have recently developed. In fact, you may even be wearing some of them, as the child in the picture on the next page is.

"Bone Cement"

Dr. Brent Constantz developed a new material that is a mixture of calcium and phosphate. It helps the spongy ends of broken bones heal quickly. It hardens in only 12 hours, and natural bone cells eventually replace it. ▼

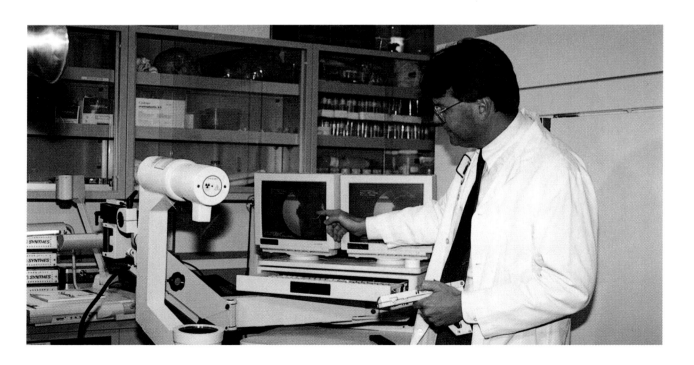

Using New Materials

Safety Helmet
Lightweight, stiff plastic foam helps this helmet protect the head.

Sunglasses
Special lenses are flexible, lightweight, and shatterproof, for use in active sports.

Weatherproof Jacket
Special fabrics protect you from rain and wind and also allow perspiration to escape. This keeps you dry and warmer.

Gel-Cushions in Shoes
Pockets of gel surrounded by plastic cushion the foot when it hits the ground.

Fleecewear Pants
Artificially made fleece is a thick, pile-type fabric that can be made from recycled plastic soda bottles. It can be four times warmer than wool.

Tennis Racket
Carbon fibers make strong, lightweight, rackets. They produce more force when the ball is hit than metal rackets do.

In-Line Skates
Durable polyurethane wheels in a single line are mounted on lightweight plastic or aluminum tracks.

Lesson 2 Review

1. What are molecules?

2. How are compounds different from elements?

3. What are some uses for new materials scientists have developed?

4. Compare and Contrast
Compare and contrast molecules and compounds.

Investigating Water

Process Skills

- observing
- inferring

Materials

- safety goggles
- measuring cup
- water
- plastic cup
- plastic spoon
- baking soda
- 2 pencils sharpened at both ends
- metric ruler
- index card
- 2 pieces of insulated wire with ends stripped
- masking tape
- 9-volt battery
- hand lens

Getting Ready

In this activity you will use electricity to split water into the elements it is made of—hydrogen and oxygen.

Follow This Procedure

1 Make a chart as shown. Use the chart to record your observations.

2 Put on your safety goggles. Pour 150 mL of water into the cup. Add a spoonful of baking soda and stir until it dissolves.

	Observations
Electric current flowing	
Electric current not flowing	

3 Use a pencil to poke holes in the index card. Poke holes about 2 cm apart. Place the card on the cup.

4 Tape one end of each wire firmly to the terminals of the battery.

5 Attach the wire ends to the pencils by wrapping the ends around the graphite point of each pencil (Photo A). The stripped wire must touch the graphite. Tape the wire firmly in place.

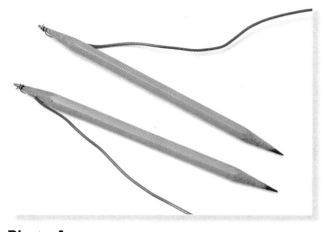

Photo A

6 Push the free ends of the pencils through the holes in the index card and into the water (Photo B). Electric current is now flowing through the wires and water.

 Safety Note This activity uses a low-voltage battery and is safe. NEVER use other electrical wires near water. That is very dangerous.

7 Use a hand lens to **observe** the pencil tips in the water. You should see small bubbles. Record differences you observe between the pencil tips.

8 Remove one pencil from the water to stop the electric current from flowing. Observe what happens at the tip of the other pencil. Record your observations. Disconnect the battery.

Self-Monitoring
Was I able to observe small bubbles on the pencil tips? If not, did I check to see that the wires were firmly connected to the battery and the pencil tips?

Photo B

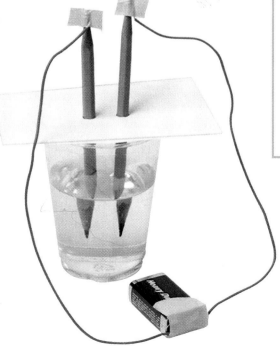

Interpret Your Results

1. Electricity flows through water, separating it into hydrogen and oxygen. What evidence do you have that this occurred in the activity?

2. There is twice as much hydrogen as oxygen in water. Make an **inference.** At which pencil point was oxygen produced? At which pencil point was hydrogen produced? Explain your answer.

Inquire Further

Would the reaction work if you didn't add baking soda to the water? Develop a plan to answer this or other questions you may have.

Self-Assessment

- I followed instructions to separate water into the elements it is made of.
- I recorded my **observations** of the pencil tips as electric current flowed through water.
- I recorded my observations of the pencil tip as the electric current was not flowing.
- I stated evidence that electric current can separate water into the elements it is made of.
- I made an **inference** about the elements produced at each pencil point.

What's the Big Idea?

You will learn:
• what mixtures are.
• what solutions are.

Glossary

mixture (miks′chər), two or more substances that are mixed together, but can be separated out because their atoms are not combined

How could you separate the parts of this mixture? ▼

Lesson 3

What Are Mixtures and Solutions?

Oranges! Avocados! Bananas! Strawberries! Blueberries! Slice them up. Toss them all together in a bowl. Guess what? You just made a mixture that tastes good and is good for you.

Mixtures

A **mixture** forms when two or more substances are mixed together but their atoms are not combined. The parts of a mixture are easily separated. The fruit salad in the picture is a mixture. All the fruit gets mixed together, but you could separate the pieces fairly easily. Pieces of avocado do not join with strawberries. They do not form a new compound that has different properties than an avocado or a strawberry. The avocado pieces remain avocado, and the strawberries are still strawberries. In a mixture, you can put the substances together in any amounts. You can add as many bananas or other pieces of fruit as you like. Your fruit salad will still be a mixture.

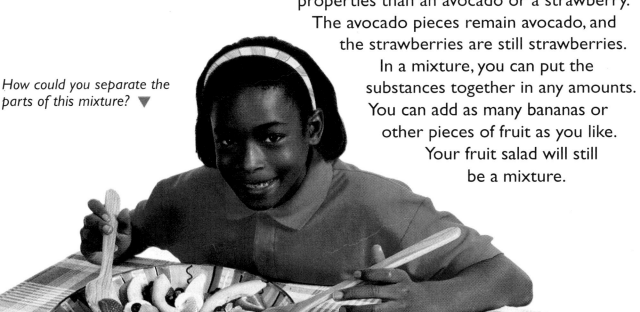

Unlike a mixture, a compound is made of different elements whose atoms are combined. The particles of a compound always have the same number and kind of atoms. Remember that water always has one oxygen atom and two hydrogen atoms. If it had another oxygen atom, it wouldn't be water. It would be hydrogen peroxide, a different compound with different properties.

Because the parts in a mixture are not combined, they are easier to separate than the parts of compounds. You could make a mixture out of sand, marbles, and water. How could you use the physical properties of the materials to separate the mixture into its parts? Perhaps you could pick out the marbles and pour the rest of the mixture through a sifting screen or coffee filter to separate out the sand and water. Or you could just let it stand until the sand sinks to the bottom and then pour off the water. Many mixtures can be separated using differences in the size of the pieces.

Find the mixture of sand and iron filings. Any amount of sand or iron filings could be added to the mixture. Notice that the iron filings are attracted to the magnet, but the sand isn't. You can see that it is fairly easy to separate the parts of this mixture by using the fact that iron is attracted to a magnet.

Pyrite, or fool's gold, contains iron and sulfur. It is not a mixture. Its atoms are joined as a compound, iron sulfide. Pyrite is a shiny, yellow mineral that looks something like gold. The iron sulfide in pyrite always has one atom of iron for every two atoms of sulfur. The elements cannot be easily separated. If extra sulfur or iron atoms are added, it becomes a different substance.

Mixtures are easy to separate. A magnet can separate iron filings from sand. ▼

Glossary

solution (sə lü′shən), a mixture in which substances break up into their most basic particles, which are too small to be seen, and spread evenly through another substance

Solutions

A **solution** is a special kind of mixture. The substances in a solution dissolve, or separate into their most basic particles. These particles are too small to be seen. In a solution, the particles of one substance are spread evenly through another substance. The substances in a solution can be solids, liquids, or gases.

Suppose you want to make something to drink, as the boy in the picture does. You squeeze some lemon juice into some water. Lemon juice is a liquid. Stir it up a little, and the juice quickly spreads through the water. You have made a solution of lemon juice and water.

Next, you add sugar. Sugar is made up of tiny white crystals. As you stir it into the liquid, it seems to disappear. The sugar crystals break up into particles. They slip among the water particles. You can no longer see them as sugar. Even though the sugar has disappeared, it is still sugar. You can taste its sweetness. The sugar molecules did not combine with the water or lemon juice molecules, or form a new compound.

◀ *Sugar crystals dissolve faster in a liquid if you stir it.*

You know that you can dissolve a solid, the sugar, and a liquid, the lemon juice, in water. Can a gas also be dissolved in a liquid? The nearest bottle of carbonated water holds the answer. Before you open the bottle, carbon dioxide gas is dissolved in, or spread evenly throughout, the liquid. When you lift the top off the bottle, thousands of bubbles of carbon dioxide gas start to rise. When the bottle is opened, some of the gas mixed into the solution separates from the liquid. The bubbles of carbon dioxide gas rise through the liquid and go into the air. Find the gas bubbles in the glass of carbonated water shown.

Go ahead and add carbonated water to your lemonade solution, if you like. Besides having made a refreshing, bubbly drink, you have also made a solution of dissolved solids, liquids, and gases.

▲ *Bubbles of carbon dioxide gas are rising through the liquid in the glass.*

Lesson 3 Review

1. What are mixtures?
2. What are solutions?
3. **Compare and Contrast**
   How are solutions different from compounds?

You will learn:
- what physical properties are.
- what a physical change is.

Glossary

physical property
(fiz′ə kəl prop′ər tē),
a way of describing an
object using traits that
can be observed or
measured without
changing the substance
into something else

What Is It Like?
*You could describe an orange
using your senses of sight, taste,
smell, and touch.* ▼

Lesson 4

How Can Substances Be Described?

Orange in color. **Round.** **Sweet** and **tangy** to taste. Shiny skin that is slightly bumpy to touch. As big as a baseball. These are ways you can describe an orange. These are also some of the physical properties of an orange.

Physical Properties

A **physical property** is a characteristic of an object that you can observe with your senses. It is a trait that can be observed or measured without changing the substance into something else. Scientists observe substances and design experiments to discover the properties of things. They want to understand substances, classify them, and find out how they are related to other substances.

Think about which of your senses you would use to observe each of the physical properties of the orange in the picture—color, shape, taste, texture, odor, and size. Scientists describe substances and objects using these physical properties and some others, including mass, hardness, elasticity, melting point, and magnetism.

Practice describing objects by their physical properties. Choose an object, such as something in your pocket, backpack, or notebook. Try listing its physical properties. Use the physical properties shown in the pictures on the next page to help you describe it.

◀ Hardness

How hard or soft is it? Is it easily scratched or broken? Will it scratch other things? A diamond is one of the hardest substances known.

◀ Texture

What is its surface like? Is it rough, smooth, soft, hard, shiny, or dull? How would you describe the texture of this stuffed animal? Soft and fuzzy!

Mass

How heavy is it? The big weight may be three times as heavy as the small one. ▶

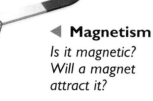

◀ Magnetism

Is it magnetic? Will a magnet attract it?

◀ Elasticity

How much will it stretch or bend before breaking? Will it bounce?

▲ Odor

What does it smell like? For example, an onion has a sharp odor. Wow! When you cut it, your eyes water.

▲ Melting Point

At what temperature will it melt or freeze? For example, water melts or freezes at 0°C.

Physical Changes

When a **physical change** takes place, the substance that changes does not become a different substance. When you grind up peanuts, you get peanut butter, as shown in the pictures. Some physical properties of the peanuts have changed. Their shape has changed. Their texture is gooey, thick, and sticky. The taste, smell, and color, however, are the same. Peanut butter is still made of peanuts.

You can fold a piece of paper to make a paper bird. The shape of the paper may change, but it is still paper. The paper bird, except for its shape, has the same properties as the sheet of paper.

Peanuts
Describe peanuts in as many ways as you can.

Physical Change
When you grind up peanuts, it changes how they look. Now they look like ground-up peanuts.

Peanut Butter
Peanut butter is made of ground-up peanuts. The peanuts have not changed into another substance.

Paper
Some of the physical properties of this paper are that it is flat, square, and orange.

Physical Change
Folding the paper changes only its shape.

Paper Bird
The physical change of shape has not changed the paper into a bird; it's still paper.

Another physical property of matter is its state—it can be a solid, a liquid, or a gas. Matter can change from one state to another if its temperature changes enough. Changing state is a physical change. When water changes state, it looks and feels different, but it's still water.

When water freezes into ice, it has changed from a liquid to a solid. A solid has a definite shape and volume. You can put it in a cup or on a desk, and it stays the same shape. It always has the same volume.

When ice melts, it changes from a solid to a liquid. A liquid takes the shape of its container, but it always has the same volume. If you pour a liquid into a different container, its shape changes to fit. If it isn't in a container, it spreads out in a puddle. That's what's happening to the snowman in the picture.

When water boils, it changes into a gas and goes into the air. A gas expands to fill up its container. Air is a mixture of gases; it fills up the room, and the earth's atmosphere. If you put air in a different container, both its volume and its shape can change.

Changing state is a physical change. As snow or ice, water is a solid. When it gets warm enough, water changes state by melting into a liquid. The snowman will soon become a puddle of water. ▼

Lesson 4 Review

1. How are the physical properties of an orange different from those of a basketball?

2. How is boiling water an example of a physical change?

3. **Identifying the Main Idea**
   Which of the following is the main idea in Lesson 4?
   a. how water changes state
   b. what physical changes are
   c. what compounds are

You will learn:

- what chemical properties are.
- what a chemical change is.

Glossary

Glossary

chemical property (kem′ə kəl prop′ər tē), describes the way a substance reacts with other substances

Physical Properties of Wood

Wood is a hard, brownish solid. ▼

Lesson 5

How Do Substances Interact?

Snap! Pop! Crackle! A log burns in the campfire, with flickering, bright orange flames. You and your family warm your hands in the heat given off as the log burns. The wood slowly turns to ashes. Quick! Add another log before the fire dies.

Chemical Properties

You know that physical properties tell you what something looks or smells or feels like. A **chemical property** is a property that describes how the atoms of a substance react with atoms of other substances.

You observe chemical properties when a substance is being changed. For example, when wood burns, it turns into something else. The log in the picture is hard, brown wood. When it burns, like the wood in the picture on the next page, wood changes into smoke, heat, and powdery gray or white ash. Afterward, it isn't wood anymore.

Wood has the chemical property of being able to burn in air. During burning, particles that make up the wood react with oxygen in the air and change into other substances, such as carbon dioxide, ash, and water vapor.

When a substance changes into something else, both its physical and chemical properties change. Think about what happened to the wood that burned and became ash and other substances.

Look at the picture of ash. Compare it to the wood. Ash has different physical properties than wood. Its color has changed from brown to gray or white. It started out hard and became soft and powdery.

The ash has new chemical properties too. You know that some of wood's chemical properties are that it can burn in air and that it can change into ash, carbon dioxide, and water vapor. Ash doesn't burn, and if it changes into other substances, they won't be the same ones that wood changed into. Like ash, carbon dioxide and water vapor have different chemical and physical properties than wood.

Chemical Properties of Wood

While everybody is enjoying the campfire, some of the atoms in the wood are combining with oxygen in the air. Feel the heat it's giving off! Don't let the ash and smoke get into your eyes. ▼

▲ **Chemical Properties of Ash**

Ash looks different than wood, and it has different chemical properties. It won't burn, and its molecules don't combine with oxygen.

Scientists study the chemical properties of things as well as their physical properties. Their properties are what make elements, compounds, and mixtures useful.

Knowing about chemical properties can help in identifying elements and compounds. You already know that the mineral pyrite is a compound made of iron and sulfur atoms. Pyrite has some of the same physical properties gold has. It is called fool's gold because prospectors, like the miner below, sometimes mistook it for gold.

Some prospectors used a simple test to identify pyrite by one of its chemical properties. They put drops of acid on the ore to find out whether it was gold or pyrite. The sulfur atoms in pyrite react with the acid to produce a gas, hydrogen sulfide. Gold does not react with the acid. If the ore was pyrite, it released a gas that smelled like rotten eggs.

This miner is prospecting for gold in the mountains of Colorado. ▼

Chemical Changes and Reactions

You know that chemical properties describe how a substance can react with other substances. For example, a chemical property of iron is that it can combine with oxygen to produce rust. A **chemical change** is a change that forms a new substance. When iron atoms actually combine with oxygen atoms and produce rust, a chemical change has occurred. A chemical change also takes place when wood burns and becomes ash and smoke.

The new substances that form when a chemical change takes place have different physical and chemical properties than the original substances did. Some chemical changes take place slowly, while others take place quickly. Combining with oxygen is a common chemical change. When a substance burns, some of its atoms combine with oxygen atoms from the air. Wood burns quickly, but it needs heat to burn. Iron combines with oxygen atoms at room temperature. Both wood and iron can combine with oxygen. However, they have different chemical properties because their atoms combine with oxygen in different ways.

The pictures show chemical changes. The properties of the new substances are different than those of the original substances.

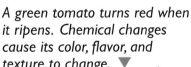

Glossary

chemical change, a change that produces new substances with new properties

Glossary

A cake bakes. The gluey batter changes into a spongy solid that tastes great. ▼

A green tomato turns red when it ripens. Chemical changes cause its color, flavor, and texture to change. ▼

Glossary

Glossary

chemical reaction
(kem′ə kəl rē ak′shən),
a process that produces
one or more substances
that are different from
the original substances

Some chemical changes, such as baking a cake, result from many steps. Each step is a chemical reaction. A **chemical reaction** is a process that produces one or more substances that are different from the original substances. Chemical reactions are always taking place in the world around you. Iron combining with oxygen to form rust is a chemical change that takes place due to a chemical reaction.

The pictures show a chemical reaction that takes place when two substances are combined. If you mix baking soda, a solid, with vinegar, a liquid, bubbles of gas rise. One of the substances formed is carbon dioxide. Notice the bubbles of carbon dioxide gas rising up through the liquid.

Human Body

When you eat food, chemical changes take place as you digest it. Digestion is a series of complex chemical changes, each consisting of many chemical reactions.

Think about what you ate for breakfast or lunch. Chemical reactions broke down the food molecules into smaller and smaller particles. Eventually, the food molecules changed into substances made up of molecules small enough to get into your bloodstream. All during digestion, chemical reactions took place. At every step, chemical reactions produced new substances from the atoms of the old substances.

A Chemical Reaction
Mixing baking soda with vinegar causes bubbles of gas to rise. ▼

Baking soda is a white powder.

A chemical reaction occurs when you add the baking soda to vinegar.

Atoms in the baking soda and vinegar react, making bubbles of carbon dioxide gas.

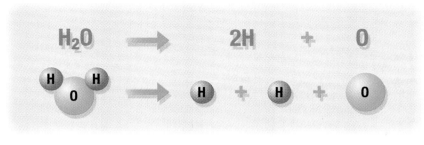

Water   Hydrogen   Hydrogen   Oxygen

◀ A water molecule is made up of two hydrogen atoms and one oxygen atom. It can be split apart into its atoms, and no atoms are lost or gained.

Recall that when baking soda and vinegar are mixed, a chemical reaction forms new compounds, including carbon dioxide. A chemical reaction can also cause compounds to be broken down into their atoms.

The diagram shows a water molecule being split apart into its atoms. When each water molecule splits apart, two hydrogen atoms and one oxygen atom are released. The number and kind of atoms in the water molecule before the chemical reaction takes place are the same as the number and kind of atoms released.

The diagram also shows how symbols and formulas are used to describe a chemical reaction. The formula for water is H_2O. The H is the symbol for hydrogen and the O is the symbol for oxygen. Remember that the small number 2 after the H shows that a molecule of water has two atoms of hydrogen. The symbols can show how the arrangement of atoms changes in the chemical reaction. The number and kind of atoms must be equal on both sides of the arrow.

Lesson 5 Review

1. Describe a chemical property of iron.

2. Describe three examples of a chemical change.

3. **Compare and Contrast**
   How is a chemical change different from a physical change?

Investigating a Chemical Change

Process Skills

- predicting
- observing
- inferring

Materials

- safety goggles
- 2 balloons
- funnel
- plastic spoon
- baking soda
- paper towels
- water
- 2 plastic bottles
- vinegar

Getting Ready

In this activity you will combine different materials and look for evidence of a chemical change.

Follow This Procedure

1 Make a chart like the one shown. Use your chart to record your predictions and observations.

2 Put on your safety goggles. Stretch two balloons by pulling gently on them. Use a funnel to put one spoonful of baking soda into each balloon (Photo A). Set the balloons aside.

	Predictions	Observations
Baking soda and water		
Baking soda and vinegar		

3 Wipe the funnel out with a paper towel. Use the funnel to add water to a bottle until it is $\frac{1}{4}$ full.

4 Stretch the opening of one of the balloons around the opening of the bottle. Be careful not to spill any baking soda into the water.

5 What will happen when baking soda is mixed with water? Record and explain your **predictions.** Lift the balloon so that the baking soda falls into the water in the bottle (Photo B). What happens to the balloon? Swirl the bottle to mix the baking soda and water. What happens to the baking soda and water? Record your **observations.**

6 Repeat steps 3 through 5 using another plastic bottle. Use vinegar in place of the water.

Photo A

Photo B

Interpret Your Results

1. Make an **inference.** When you combined baking soda and water, was there evidence of a new substance being formed? Explain.

2. Make an inference. When you combined baking soda and vinegar, was there evidence of a new substance being formed? Explain.

3. Which combination caused a chemical change to occur? Explain.

Inquire Further

What do you think would happen to the solutions if you allowed them to evaporate? Develop a plan to answer this or other questions you may have.

Chapter 1 Review

Chapter Main Ideas

Lesson 1
• Matter is made up of more than 100 basic substances called elements.
• Elements are classified by their properties and their structure.
• Atoms are the smallest structures into which an element can be divided and still be the element.

Lesson 2
• Molecules are particles made up of two or more atoms joined together.
• Elements are made up of only one kind of atom; compounds are made up of atoms of more than one element.
• Scientists have developed new materials that are useful because of their light weight and their strength or warmth.

Lesson 3
• A mixture forms when two or more substances are mixed together but their atoms are not combined.
• A solution is a mixture in which the substances are separated into their basic particles and the particles of one substance are spread evenly through the other.

Lesson 4
• Physical properties are characteristics that can be observed without changing a substance into a different substance.
• Physical change takes place when the physical properties of a substance change without changing the substance into a different substance.

Lesson 5
• A chemical property is a characteristic of a substance that describes how it reacts with other substances.
• A chemical change is a change in a substance that produces a new substance with different chemical properties.

Reviewing Science Words and Concepts

Write the letter of the word or phrase that best completes each sentence.

a. atom
b. chemical change
c. chemical property
d. chemical reaction
e. compound
f. electron
g. element
h. mixture
i. molecule
j. neutron
k. nucleus
l. periodic table
m. physical change
n. physical property
o. proton
p. solution

1. Most of the mass of an atom is in the ___.

2. A change that produces new substances with new properties is called a ___.

3. An ___ is a particle in an atom that has a negative charge.

4. In a ___, the parts are spread out evenly.

5. An ___ is made up of only one kind of atom.

6. A ____ is a particle in an atom that has a positive charge.

7. You can use your senses to observe a ____ of a substance.

8. Sand and iron filings together can make up a ____.

9. Elements are classified in the ____.

10. Melting ice is an example of a ____.

11. One step in a series of steps that take place in a chemical change is a ____.

12. The particle of an atom that has no charge is a ____.

13. The smallest particle of an element is an ____.

14. When two or more atoms that are alike or different combine, they can form a ____.

15. A substance that forms when two or more different kinds of atoms combine is a ____.

16. A ____ of a substance indicates how it reacts with other substances.

Explaining Science

Write a paragraph to answer these questions.

1. Compare the structure of the atoms of two different elements.

2. What happens when a chemical change takes place?

3. Compare the physical properties of two substances.

4. How could you separate the parts of a solution?

5. What can happen to an iron object that is left outdoors?

Using Skills

1. Use **metric units of capacity.** If you have made up a solution that measures 250 milliliters of material, how many liters do you have?

2. Explain how elements are **classified.**

3. What can you **infer** about a substance if you know it is a metal?

4. **Predict** what would happen if you boiled a solution of salt in water.

Critical Thinking

1. If you know that neon is a gas that does not easily react with other substances, what could you **infer** about other substances in the same vertical column of the periodic table?

2. How could you **classify** a particular property of a substance as a physical property or a chemical property?

3. Describe a mixture and plan an **experiment** that would show how to separate its parts.

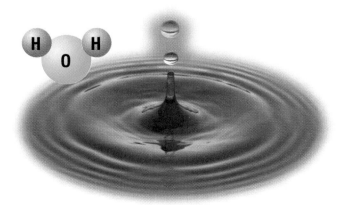

How High Can You Jump?

When you jump for the ball in volleyball, you push down against Earth and Earth pushes back just as hard. Why don't you just keep going up and up and up?

Chapter 2
Investigating Motion

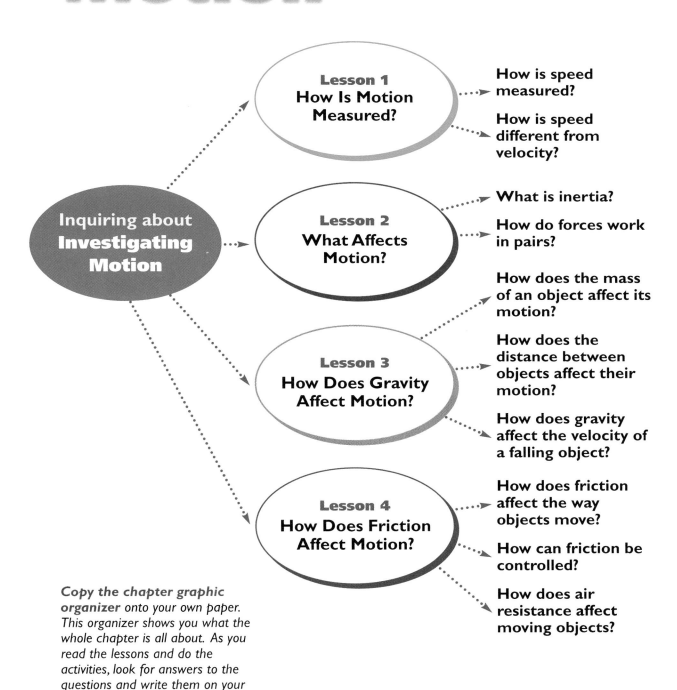

Inquiring about Investigating Motion

**Lesson 1
How Is Motion Measured?**

How is speed measured?

How is speed different from velocity?

**Lesson 2
What Affects Motion?**

What is inertia?

How do forces work in pairs?

**Lesson 3
How Does Gravity Affect Motion?**

How does the mass of an object affect its motion?

How does the distance between objects affect their motion?

How does gravity affect the velocity of a falling object?

**Lesson 4
How Does Friction Affect Motion?**

How does friction affect the way objects move?

How can friction be controlled?

How does air resistance affect moving objects?

Copy the chapter graphic organizer onto your own paper. This organizer shows you what the whole chapter is all about. As you read the lessons and do the activities, look for answers to the questions and write them on your organizer.

Exploring Motion

Process Skills

- observing
- communicating

Process Skills

Materials

- half-meter stick
- 2 desks
- masking tape
- string
- bobber
- dominoes

Explore

1 Place a half-meter stick so it is level between two desks. Tape the ends to the desks. Attach one end of the string to the bobber. Tie the other end of the string to the half-meter stick so the bobber nearly touches the floor. You have made a pendulum.

2 Swing the pendulum gently back and forth. **Observe** its motion. When is it moving the slowest? the fastest? Record your observations.

3 Hold the pendulum to one side and stand five dominoes in a line between the desks. Let the pendulum go as you try to knock down the dominoes. Record your observations.

4 Repeat step 3, but try to knock the dominoes down as the pendulum swings back to you, rather than as you let it go. Repeat once more, but swing the pendulum in a circle. Observe the order in which the dominoes fall. Think of other ways to change the motion.

Reflect

1. What did you do to control and change the pendulum's motion? How did you change the direction of the motion?

2. Communicate. Discuss your observations with the class.

Inquire Further

What would happen to the pendulum's motion if you used a shorter string to make the pendulum? Develop a plan to answer this or other questions you may have.

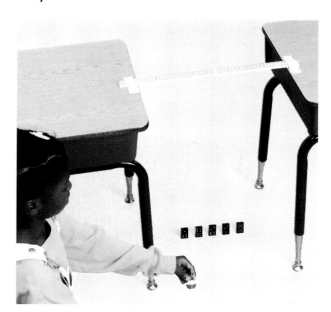

Identifying Cause and Effect

In the Explore Activity, *Exploring Motion*, you learned about cause and effect. A **cause** makes something happen. An **effect** is the outcome or result. In *Exploring Motion* you identified the cause and effect of knocking down dominoes with a pendulum. The motion of the pendulum caused the dominoes to fall. The falling of the dominoes was the effect or result of being hit by the pendulum.

Reading Vocabulary

cause (kȯz), a person, thing, or event that makes something happen

effect (ə fekt′), whatever is produced by a cause; a result

Example

As you read Lesson 1, *How Is Motion Measured?*, you will learn that to find the **speed** of something, you need to measure how far it travels **(distance)** in a certain period of time. You will learn that you can use the equation **speed = distance / time** to find the speed of any object. Speed, distance, and time are closely related. Anything that causes a change to either speed or distance or time will have an effect on the other factors. Use the equation and the chart below to answer the questions that follow.

	Speed	Distance	Time
Car	50 km/hr	100 km	2 hours
Person	4 km/hr	2 km	$\frac{1}{2}$ hour

1. If the car's speed doubles and the distance stays the same, what is the effect on time?

2. If a person walks 4 km instead of 2 km (in the same amount of time), what is the effect on speed?

Talk About It!

1. The equation above tells the speed when distance and time are known. Rewrite the equation so it tells distance when speed and time are known.

2. Identify causes that can affect your speed on a bicycle.

What's the Big Idea?

You will learn:
- how speed is measured.
- the difference between speed and velocity.

Lesson 1

How Is Motion Measured?

ZOOM! You ride along in a car. **ZZZIP!** The world seems to fly by. You pass trees and buildings that look as though they're moving fast, but they're really standing still. The needle on the speedometer points to 80 kilometers per hour.

Speed

The numbers on a car's speedometer tell how fast the car is moving at the moment. To find the **speed** of something, you need to measure how far it travels in a certain period of time. Then, you divide the distance by the time.

One way to measure an object's speed is in **kilometers per hour,** or km/hr. This tells how many kilometers something travels in an hour. Use this equation to find the speed of a car that travels 80 kilometers in an hour: distance ÷ time = speed.

$$80 \text{ km} \div 1 \text{ hour} = \frac{80 \text{ km}}{1 \text{ hour}} = \frac{80 \text{ km}}{\text{hour}} \text{ or } 80 \text{ km/hr}$$

How could you find the car's speed in kilometers per hour if the 80-kilometer trip took 2 hours?

$$80 \text{ km} \div 2 \text{ hours} = \frac{80 \text{ km}}{2 \text{ hours}} = \frac{40 \text{ km}}{\text{hour}} \text{ or } 40 \text{ km/hr}$$

Library

When you refer to the speed something travels, you often mean its average speed. It might travel faster than that speed for part of the distance and slower for another part of the distance. When the car traveled 80 kilometers in an hour, it probably moved more slowly sometimes and more quickly at other times. Perhaps it slowed down for corners and stopped for stop lights. However, it traveled 80 kilometers in an hour, no matter how fast it moved at a particular time.

The girl in the picture is riding her bicycle home from the library. She wants to know how fast she is going, but her bicycle doesn't have a speedometer. To find her average speed, she needs to know the distance she covers and the total time it takes her to ride that distance.

The distance from the library to her home is 12 kilometers. She knows that it takes her an hour to make the whole trip on her bicycle. When she goes from the library to her home, she travels a total of 12 kilometers in an hour. She can calculate that her speed is 12 km/hr.

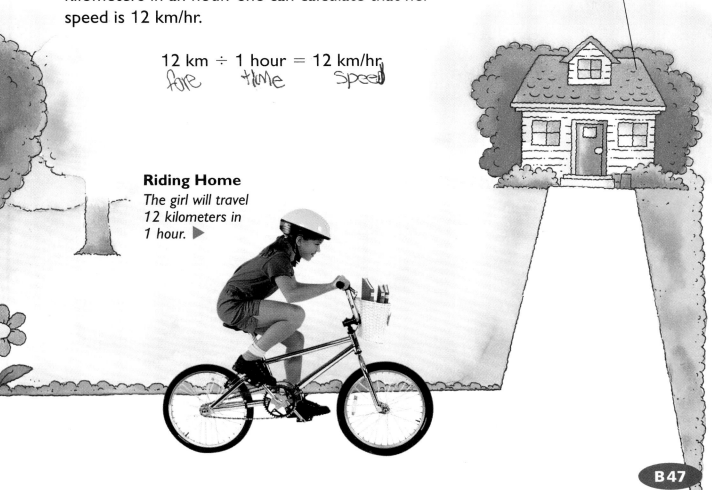

12 km ÷ 1 hour = 12 km/hr
~~fore~~ ~~time~~ ~~speed~~

Home

Riding Home
The girl will travel 12 kilometers in 1 hour. ▶

Glossary

velocity (və los′ə tē), a measure of speed in a certain direction

Velocity

You have learned that speed describes how fast you move. **Velocity** describes how fast you move and in what direction. When you change direction, you do not necessarily affect your speed, but you do change your velocity. Suppose two cars are traveling at 40 kilometers per hour. One is going east, and the other is going west. They are moving at the same speed. However, they are going at different velocities, because they are moving in different directions.

The map below shows the path the girl on the bicycle took on her way home from the library. She traveled at 12 kilometers per hour. Notice that she traveled in three directions. Her first velocity is 12 kilometers per hour south. Her next velocity is 12 kilometers per hour east. What is her third velocity? Suppose she decides not to ride north but to walk her bicycle at a speed of 2 kilometers per hour. What would be her velocity?

Library

N
W ← → E
S

Home

12 km/hr north

12 km/hr south

12 km/hr east

Lesson 1 Review

1. How can you use distance and time to measure speed?

2. How is velocity different from speed?

3. **Cause and Effect**
   Name a way to cause a change in velocity.

What Affects Motion?

WHACK! A baseball player hits a baseball squarely with a bat, sending it straight over the head of the outfielder. Even after it hits the ground, it rolls across the field until the fielder scoops it up. Why doesn't it just stop when it hits the ground?

Inertia

When a ball flies through the air, it keeps moving until a force stops it. The push of a fielder's hand is a force that can stop a ball. Force is also needed to make a ball move once it stops. Throwing or hitting the ball can provide that force.

An object either remains in motion or stays at rest until a force acts on it. The tendency of objects to stay in motion or to stay still is called **inertia.** Every object, whether it is moving or at rest, has inertia. In order to start something moving or to stop it from moving, you need to use a force to overcome its inertia.

Have you ever felt yourself jerk forward when you were riding in a vehicle that stopped suddenly? If so, you have felt inertia. That inertia is the reason you need to wear a safety belt in a moving vehicle. The safety belt helps prevent injuries. It keeps your body from continuing to move if the vehicle stops suddenly. Notice in the pictures how inertia can affect passengers in a bus. If the bus starts to move forward suddenly, inertia causes their bodies to tend to stay in the same place. The passengers' bodies seem to jerk backward. If a moving bus stops suddenly, inertia causes their bodies to keep moving forward.

What's the Big Idea?

You will learn:

- what inertia is.
- the way forces that work in pairs affect motion.

Glossary

inertia (in ėr′shə), the tendency of an object to stay at rest or to remain in motion unless an outside force causes a change

▲ *If a bus moves forward suddenly, passengers seem to jerk backward.*

▲ *If a moving bus stops suddenly, passengers keep moving forward.*

Examples of inertia are all around you. Find an object in the classroom that is at rest, such as a book on your desk. To make the book move across the desk, you would have to apply a force. Unless a force, such as a push or a pull, acts on the book, inertia keeps it still. Your muscles can provide the push or pull to overcome the book's inertia and make it move.

The pictures show how a force can overcome inertia when you ride a bicycle. When you are stopped, you must apply a force to make the bicycle start moving. You push on the pedals to provide the force needed to overcome the bicycle's inertia. The arrows in the picture on the left show where the forces act as the bicycle begins to move.

The picture on the right shows what happens if you stop pedaling while you are riding on a level road. The arrow shows that the bicycle continues to move forward for a while. To stop the bicycle, you must overcome the inertia that keeps it moving. You need to apply a force, such as putting on the brakes, to make the bicycle stop.

▲ Your legs pushing on the pedals provide enough force to overcome inertia and make the bicycle's wheels move it forward.

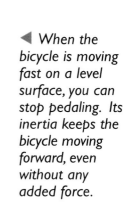

◄ When the bicycle is moving fast on a level surface, you can stop pedaling. Its inertia keeps the bicycle moving forward, even without any added force.

You know that if you stop pedaling a bicycle on a level road, inertia will keep it moving for a while. However, it will eventually stop, even if you don't put on the brakes. What makes it stop? Unless a force stops it, inertia ought to make it coast forever. Forces you can't see act on the bicycle to make it stop.

On Earth, several kinds of forces can make moving objects slow down or stop. Molecules of gas in the air push against the surface of moving objects and slow their movement. The picture shows that a rough surface, such as a carpet, can also slow moving objects. The roughness slows down a rolling marble or the wheels on a bicycle. Even a smooth-looking floor is rough enough to slow things down. You have probably experienced the effect of a rough surface on movement. You can rollerskate faster on a smooth surface than on a rough surface. A rough surface is easier to stop on.

All objects, large and small, pull on all other objects. This pull is called gravity. The pull of Earth's gravity is a force that affects how objects move. Earth's gravity is so strong its pull can overcome inertia and make things fall toward Earth. Gravity can make things slow down or stop. You will learn more about gravity in the next lesson.

Deep in space, no air exists to pull against an object. Earth is too far away for its gravity to cause much pull. For this reason, a spacecraft, once the force of a rocket has started it moving through space, can keep moving at the same speed. It doesn't meet up with forces that overcome its inertia and make it stop.

A rough surface, such as carpet, affects the inertia of a rolling marble and slows it down quickly. On a smooth surface, the marble will roll farther, but it will stop eventually. ▶

Pairs of Forces

You know that forces act on objects to make them move. The forces always work in pairs. One force pushes in one direction. Another pushes with equal strength in the opposite direction.

The pictures show the forces that can act when a frog jumps forward off a water lily leaf. As it jumps, the frog's legs push backward against the leaf. The force of this push makes the leaf move backward, away from the frog. At the same time, the leaf pushes in the opposite direction, against the frog. This force pushes the frog forward.

The force of the frog pushing against the leaf can be called the action force. The force of the leaf on the frog would be the reaction force. The two forces, working with equal strength in opposite directions, make the leaf and the frog move in opposite directions. The frog leaps forward; the leaf shoots backward.

You experience action and reaction forces every time you walk. When you step forward, you push backward on the ground with your foot. You could call this an action force.

Direction of Force

1 *Action force: The frog pushes backward against the leaf.*

2 *Reaction force: The leaf pushes forward equally against the frog.*

Direction of Movement

3 *The frog moves forward after the push.*

4 *The leaf moves backward after the push.*

You may not feel it, but Earth pushes forward against your foot with an equal reaction force. Both these forces help your body move forward. Of course, Earth doesn't shoot back when you push on it the way the leaf did when the frog pushed on it! In fact, Earth is so massive that the force of your step doesn't move it.

The same forces are at work when you use a skateboard. You push backward against the ground with your foot to start it moving. This is the action force. Earth pushes forward with a reaction force. The reaction force starts the wheels of your skateboard rolling. You and your skateboard move forward.

Lesson 2 Review

1. How does inertia affect an object's motion?

2. How do forces work in pairs when a frog jumps off a floating water lily leaf?

3. **Cause and Effect**
   When you ride a bicycle, what force can overcome inertia?

Investigating Force Used to Move Objects

Process Skills

- estimating and measuring
- inferring

Materials

- safety goggles
- 2 pieces of string
- rubber band
- small cardboard box
- masking tape
- smooth surface, such as desktop
- metric ruler
- objects of different mass
- rough surface, such as carpeted area

Getting Ready

In this activity you can use a rubber band to observe the force needed to make an object move.

Follow This Procedure

1 Make a chart like the one shown. Use your chart to record your measurements.

Object	Length of stretched rubber band	
	Smooth surface	Rough surface
Empty box		

2 Put on your safety goggles. Tie one end of a piece of string to the rubber band. Tie another string to the other end of the rubber band. Use several pieces of tape to securely connect the unattached end of one string to the box (Photo A). Place the box on a smooth surface.

Photo A

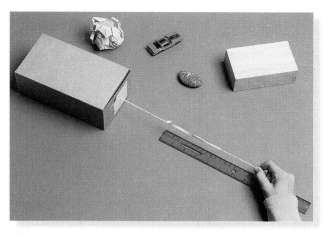

Photo B

3 Pull the unattached end of the other string. Use the metric ruler to **measure** the length of the stretched rubber band just as the object begins to move (Photo B). Record your measurement.

4 Place different objects in the box, one at a time, and repeat step 3 for each object.

5 Repeat step 4 for each object, but pull the box across a rough surface, such as a carpet.

Self-Monitoring
Have I correctly followed all the steps?

Interpret Your Results

1. Compare the amount of stretch needed to move different objects. How does the stretch change when you increase the mass of the object? Make an **inference.** How does the mass of an object affect the force needed to move the object?

2. How did your results change when you used a rough surface? Make an inference. How does the roughness of the surface affect the force needed to make objects move?

 Inquire Further

How could you reduce the force needed to move the objects? Develop a plan to answer this or other questions you may have.

Self-Assessment

- I followed instructions to **measure** the length of a rubber band when moving objects of different masses.
- I recorded my measurements when moving objects across a smooth surface and a rough surface.
- I compared the amount of stretch needed to move objects of different masses.
- I described how my results changed when moving objects across a rough surface.
- I made **inferences** about the force needed to move objects of different masses across smooth and rough surfaces.

What's the Big Idea?

You will learn:

- how an object's mass affects its motion.
- how the distance between objects affects their motion.
- the way gravity affects the velocity of falling objects.

Glossary

gravity (grav′ə tē), a force that acts to pull pairs of objects together

mass, the amount of matter in an object

What Goes Up Must Come Down

The force of a throw makes a basketball rise and move forward. Earth's gravity attracts the basketball and pulls it toward the ground. ▶

Lesson 3

How Does Gravity Affect Motion?

Ouch! A book falls off a table and lands on someone's toe. **Twang!** An arrow streaks from a bow, flies in a high arc, and then gradually falls to Earth. What makes whatever goes up, come down?

The Mass of Objects

Gravity is a force that makes any object attract, or pull toward, another object. When you throw a basketball, like the one in the picture, the force of your throw makes it rise and move forward. Then it starts to fall. Earth's gravity attracts it and pulls it down toward Earth. The ball attracts Earth, too, but Earth is so massive that the ball's pull isn't great enough to move it.

Two objects with about the same **mass,** or amount of matter, attract each other equally. Gravity has the same effect on each object. If gravity were the only force acting on the objects, they would move toward each other. They would both move the same amount because they have the same mass.

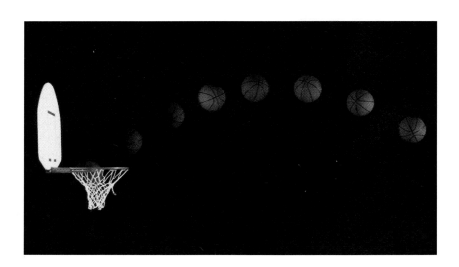

What happens to objects of different masses? They pull on each other equally, but the force moves the object with less mass more than it moves the object with more mass. Think what would happen if you pushed a massive rock and a less-massive rock equally hard. The less massive rock would move farther, because less force is needed to move it.

Why do objects fall to Earth, rather than Earth moving to them? Earth has a lot more mass than objects on it do. The force of gravity between Earth and an object can move the mass of the object. However, that force isn't strong enough to move the huge mass of Earth.

An object's mass stays the same everywhere in the universe. If you traveled to the moon, to the farthest planet, or to a distant star, your mass would stay the same. Your weight, however, would change because the pull of gravity between you and another object depends on your mass and the object's mass. **Weight** is a measure of the amount of force that gravity exerts on you.

What would happen to your weight if you went from Earth to the moon, as John W. Young, the astronaut in the picture, did? The moon has much less mass than Earth, so the force of gravity on the moon is less than the force of gravity on Earth. The moon's gravity is about one-sixth the gravity of Earth. On the moon, you would weigh about one-sixth of what you weigh on Earth. Your mass would stay the same.

Earth has enough mass to pull things toward it. If you shoot an arrow into the air, gravity keeps it from flying into space. The pull of gravity between Earth and the moon keeps the moon moving in space around Earth. Gravity keeps artificial satellites moving around Earth and keeps Earth moving around the sun.

Glossary

weight, the force gravity exerts on an object's mass

Glossary

Gravity on the Moon
The moon has a lot less mass than Earth, so the pull of its gravity is much less. Astronauts on the moon can jump much higher than they can on Earth. ▼

▲ *While they are walking to the launch pad, Earth's gravity strongly attracts the astronauts and holds them to the ground.*

The Distance Between Objects

The pull of gravity between two objects depends on more than just the masses of the objects. Gravity's effect also depends on the distance between the objects. Objects that are closer together have a greater attraction between them. The attraction is weaker when they are farther apart.

Gravity exists wherever there is mass, such as in stars and planets. The gravity of each of these objects affects other objects in space. Earth's gravity, for example, reaches millions and millions of kilometers into space. It grows weaker the farther away from Earth you get.

Recall that because the moon is less massive than Earth, an astronaut standing on the moon weighs only one-sixth as much as on Earth. The astronaut's weight would change during a trip between Earth and the moon. The effect of Earth's gravity becomes less as the distance from Earth increases. The weight of each of the astronauts in the picture was greatest at Earth's surface. The weight decreased as the spaceship moved farther away from Earth. As the spaceship moved closer to the moon, the effect of the moon's gravity increased and the effect of Earth's gravity decreased. When the lander in the picture reached the moon's surface, the weight of the astronauts on it was determined by the moon's gravity. However, the mass of the astronauts did not change during their journey.

On the moon, Earth's gravity has little effect, and an astronaut's weight is determined by the moon's gravity. ▶

Falling Objects

To understand another way gravity affects how objects move, think about what happens to your bicycle's velocity when you start at the top of a hill and coast down. As you ride down the hill, your bicycle moves faster and faster. Your velocity changes rapidly. The rate your velocity changes is your **acceleration.** As you reach the bottom, you are going fastest, but your velocity is barely changing. Your acceleration is about zero. Acceleration can be an increase or a decrease in speed or a change in direction.

The picture shows an object's velocity as it falls to Earth. Notice that the spaces between the images in the picture get larger as the object falls. The object is falling faster and faster as the distance between it and the Earth decreases. Every second it falls, its velocity is about 10 meters per second greater than it was the previous second. The force of gravity is making it accelerate. Near Earth's surface, gravity makes all objects fall at the same rate. Unless another force acts on an object, it falls to Earth at this rate.

Suppose you dropped a soccer ball and a bowling ball at the same moment from the top of a tall building. Even though their masses are different, both balls would fall at the same rate. Their acceleration would be the same. They would reach the ground at the same time.

Glossary

acceleration
(ak sel′ə rā′shən), rate of change in speed or direction of movement

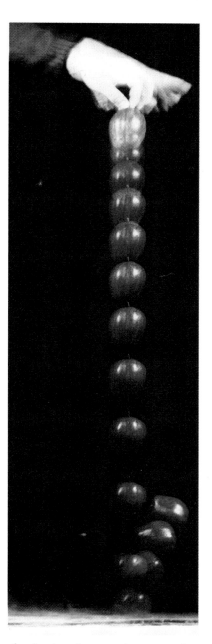

▲ *As the distance between the object and Earth decreases, the object falls faster and faster.*

Lesson 3 Review

1. How does its mass affect the way an object moves?

2. How does the distance between two objects affect the way they move?

3. How does gravity affect the velocity of falling objects?

4. **Cause and Effect**
   Why do things weigh less on the moon than they do on Earth?

Investigating Friction

Process Skills

- observing
- estimating and measuring
- classifying

Materials

- masking tape
- rectangular board
- desk or other flat surface
- eraser
- metric ruler
- stone
- coin
- button
- toy car

Getting Ready

You can see the effects of friction by experimenting with objects on a ramp.

Look at the pictures to see how to set up the ramp.

Follow This Procedure

❶ Make a chart like the one shown. Use your chart to record your observations and measurements.

Objects	Observations	Measurements
Eraser		
Stone		
Coin		
Button		
Toy car		

❷ Tape one end of the board firmly to the middle of the desk so that the end of the board will not move when the other end is lifted.

❸ Run your finger across the bottom surface of the eraser. Record your **observations** of the properties of the bottom surface. Place the eraser on the free end of the board (Photo A).

❹ Now you will raise one end of the board until the eraser moves down the ramp. Hold the ruler next to the free end of the board. Raise the end of the board one centimeter at a time (Photo B). Record your **measurement** of the height at which the eraser begins to move down the board.

❺ Repeat steps 3 and 4 for each of the objects listed in your chart.

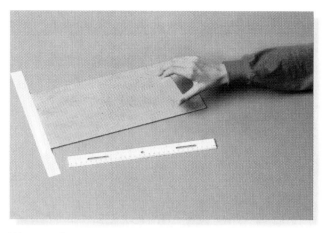

Photo A

Photo B

Self-Monitoring

Did I measure and record the ramp height for each object? Do I need to repeat any steps?

Interpret Your Results

1. Describe some properties of the objects that slide more easily. Describe some properties of the objects that slide less easily.

2. Friction keeps the objects from sliding easily down the ramp. Which object demonstrated the most friction with the board? Which demonstrated the least friction? **Classify** the objects by ranking them according to how much friction was demonstrated, from most to least.

Inquire Further

How could you reduce the friction with the board? Develop a plan to answer this or other questions you may have.

Self-Assessment

- I followed instructions to demonstrate how friction affects different objects on a wooden ramp.
- I recorded my **observations** of the properties of the objects.
- I recorded my **measurements** of the board height needed to move each object.
- I described properties of objects that affect how the objects slid down a ramp.
- I **classified** by ranking the objects according to how much friction was demonstrated.

You will learn:

- the way friction affects how objects move.
- how friction between moving objects can be controlled.
- how air resistance affects moving objects.

Glossary

friction (frik′shən), a force that resists the movement of one surface past another surface

Lesson 4

How Does Friction Affect Motion?

WHOOSH! Gravity helps you coast downhill on a bicycle. The wind whips past your ears. **WHEE!** You want to slow down, so you put on the brakes. What makes the brakes work?

What Is Friction?

You know that inertia keeps a moving object in motion unless a force stops it. However, you have probably noticed that moving objects stop eventually, even when you can't see any force stopping them.

Friction is a force that affects inertia by slowing the movement of objects. It pushes in the opposite direction to the way the object is moving. Friction takes place where two surfaces rub together. It drags on the surfaces of objects and slows them down.

Where is friction on the sled in the picture? When a sled moves, there is friction between the bottom of the sled and the surface it is sliding on. There is also friction between the ground and the shoes of the child pushing the sled. A rough surface, such as where snow is melted and dirt pokes through, would cause enough friction to stop the sled.

◀ *The sled slides over the snow. It would slide even faster on the ice.*

Knowing how a sled behaves on different surfaces can help you understand that different surfaces produce different amounts of friction. Smooth, slippery surfaces, such as a waxed floor, produce less friction. Rough, bumpy surfaces, such as a carpet, produce more friction.

Friction can work for you or against you. The picture shows a bicycle rider struggling to overcome too much friction on a rough surface. Bumps and grooves, called treads, on a bicycle tire grip the ground. They produce resistance, which helps you start your bicycle from a stopped position. It also helps you stop or slow down when necessary. If the tires and the ground were both perfectly smooth, the wheels would slip, not grip. You couldn't start—or stop.

Without friction, you couldn't pick up a piece of paper. It would slip out of your hand. Fingerprints, tiny grooves on your fingers, produce enough friction to help you pick things up.

Rub your hands together the way the child in the picture does. Feel the warmth! Warmth caused by friction builds up on your palms when you rub them together. Over time, heat and rubbing from friction can cause wear and tear on rubbed surfaces. It can eventually wear down almost any surface, even rock or steel. Friction between your foot, your sock, and your shoe can wear a hole in your sock.

▲ If you rub your hands together, you can feel the warmth that friction produces.

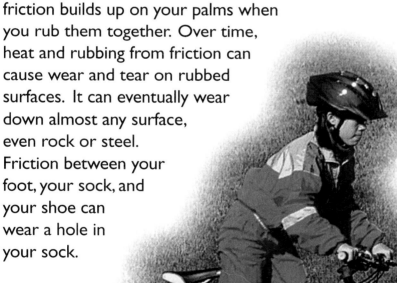

◀ On grass, the rider has to work hard to overcome friction and keep moving forward. On smooth pavement, the rider would need less force to overcome friction.

▲ *When the whole surface of the board is touching the ground, a lot of friction is produced.*

▲ *Using wheels reduces the amount of friction.*

Controlling Friction

Friction occurs when one object slides over another. Suppose you put one foot on a board, like the one in the top picture, and tried to move the board forward by pushing back with the other foot. The whole bottom of the board rests on the ground. Many tiny rough places on the wood and on the ground would produce a lot of friction between the ground and the bottom of the board. You wouldn't go very far. Friction would keep the board from sliding.

How could you reduce the friction and let the board move more easily? Suppose you put wheels on the bottom of the board, as in the second picture. Now it's a skateboard! If you stand on the board now and push with your foot, you will roll forward easily. Your push starts the wheels moving; their inertia keeps them going. The friction between the wheels and the ground is much less than the friction between the board and the ground. It doesn't slow the board's motion as much. Now you can move!

Notice how hard the girl is working to pull a heavy suitcase across a floor. Wheels on the bottom of the suitcase let her move it across the floor more easily.

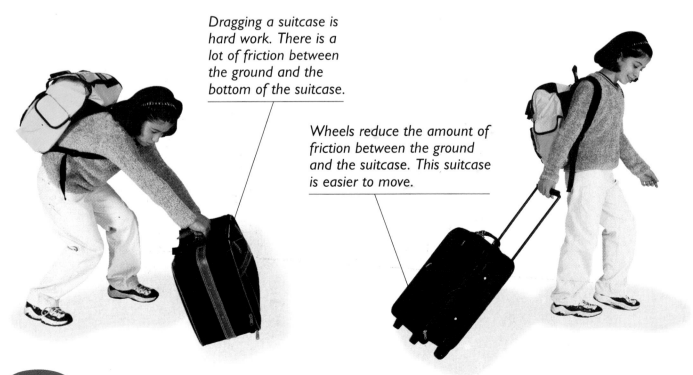

Dragging a suitcase is hard work. There is a lot of friction between the ground and the bottom of the suitcase.

Wheels reduce the amount of friction between the ground and the suitcase. This suitcase is easier to move.

Friction can also be reduced in other ways. Using slippery materials, such as oil or grease, can reduce friction. The slippery material fills in the small rough places on a surface, making it very smooth. Oil on moving parts in a machine helps the parts slip across each other easily. Oil or grease can reduce the heat and other damage that friction causes on moving parts. The top picture shows one place grease can reduce friction. Think of all the moving parts in a bicycle. The chain, gears, crank, pedals, and wheel hubs are just a few of the parts of a bicycle where oil or grease are used to reduce friction.

Sometimes you want to increase friction, not decrease it. When you are riding on a bicycle or in a car, you need good brakes. Brakes press against the wheels, increasing the friction on them. This makes the wheels move more slowly and lets you stop when you need to. If the brakes don't produce enough friction, you won't stop.

When a road is icy and slippery, sand or gravel is often spread on the ice. The sand makes the surface rougher and increases friction. The wheels of cars will not slide as easily on ice that is covered with sand. The person in the bottom picture is spreading sand on an icy sidewalk. Increasing the friction of the surface helps people walk on the ice safely, without slipping.

▲ Graphite, a form of powdered carbon, or grease helps keep a bicycle chain moving freely.

▲ Sand helps produce more friction, making icy sidewalks safer to walk on.

Glossary

Glossary

air resistance
(ri zis′təns), friction caused by gas molecules in the air hitting an object and slowing it down

Air Resistance

You already know that air is made up of molecules of gases. These gas molecules bump and rub against any objects that move through the air. This causes a kind of friction called **air resistance.** Like other kinds of friction, air resistance pushes against moving objects, slowing them down. Air resistance affects how the objects on these two pages move.

◀ **Parachute**
Air resistance helps a parachute float slowly down to Earth. Gas molecules in the air drag against the inner surface of the parachute, slowing its fall.

Air Resistance
Air resistance can slow down a bicycle. This rider is causing drag by sitting upright and by wearing loose, bulky clothing. ▼

▲ **Meteor**
A meteor is a streak of light in the sky. It is caused by a chunk of rock from space that speeds through Earth's atmosphere. Air resistance makes the solid rock so hot that it burns as it streaks to Earth.

▲ **Streamlining**
Bicycle riders can reduce drag from air resistance by wearing tight-fitting clothes and streamlined helmets, by tucking their heads down, and by keeping their arms and legs close to their bodies.

Air resistance slows an object's motion more when a large part of its surface is exposed to air. It makes a parachute drift slowly to Earth. To help objects move fast, engineers **streamline** them, or design them to reduce air resistance. Streamlined objects, like the ones below, have smooth, rounded surfaces, so air slips easily over them. They don't have parts that stick out and rub on the gas molecules in the air. Their shapes usually have less surface in the direction the object is moving. Notice that both the supersonic jet and the bullet train are pointed at the front. They have less surface at the front, where air resistance would be strongest.

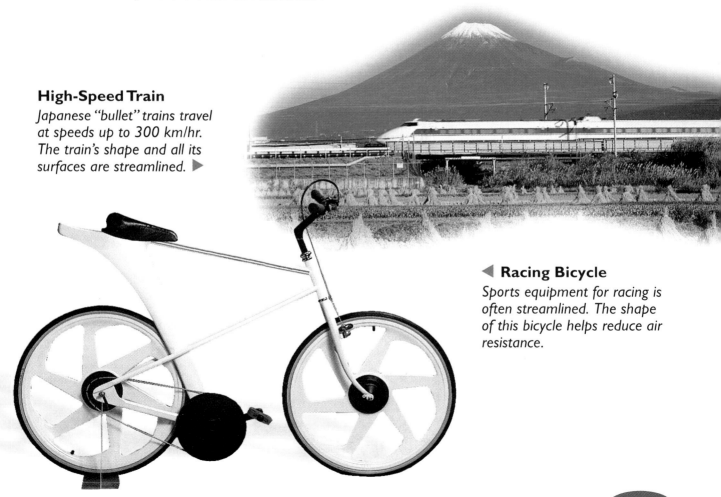

Glossary

streamline, to design smooth, rounded surfaces on an object so it slips through the air with the least possible resistance

Glossary

Supersonic Jet

The Concorde jet travels faster than the speed of sound, cruising at 16,500 meters above the earth. At this height, the air has fewer molecules, so there is less air resistance. ▶

High-Speed Train

Japanese "bullet" trains travel at speeds up to 300 km/hr. The train's shape and all its surfaces are streamlined. ▶

◀ **Racing Bicycle**

Sports equipment for racing is often streamlined. The shape of this bicycle helps reduce air resistance.

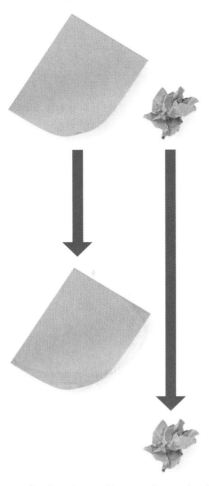

▲ *Gravity pulls equally on both papers, but the flat sheet has a larger exposed surface and more air resistance, so it falls more slowly.*

You can observe how air resistance affects the way things move. Suppose you take two identical pieces of paper and crumple one into a ball. Hold the other piece flat, parallel to the floor. Drop the two pieces of paper from the same height at the same time. You know that near Earth's surface, gravity makes all objects fall at the same rate. The two pieces of paper should fall together. Now look at the picture. The crumpled piece fell faster!

You learned that air resistance can make objects with a lot of surface, such as a parachute, fall more slowly. A flat sheet of paper has more surface exposed to the air than a crumpled sheet of paper does. More air particles push against it as it falls. This makes the flat paper fall more slowly than the crumpled paper. Air resistance is a form of friction, which is a force that can act against the force of gravity.

What do you think would happen to falling objects in a place that has no air? It certainly couldn't have any air resistance. The moon has no air, and David Scott, an astronaut who landed on the moon, made an observation. He dropped a feather and a hammer from the same height at the same time. On Earth, air resistance would slow the feather's fall. On the moon, the two objects reached the surface at the same time.

Lesson 4 Review

1. How does friction affect the way objects move?
2. Name two ways to reduce friction and two ways to increase it.
3. How does air resistance affect the way objects move?
4. **Cause and Effect**
   Name three effects that can be caused by friction.

Experimenting with Balloon Rockets

Materials

- safety goggles
- pencil
- 3 squares of index card
- metric ruler
- string
- plastic straw
- marker
- 3 balloons
- masking tape

Process Skills

- formulating questions and hypotheses
- identifying and controlling variables
- experimenting
- estimating and measuring
- collecting and interpreting data
- communicating

State the Problem

How does the size of a balloon opening affect how far a balloon rocket travels along a string?

Formulate Your Hypothesis

If you make the opening of a balloon smaller, will the distance the balloon rocket travels be reduced? Write your **hypothesis.**

Identify and Control the Variables

The opening of the balloon is the **variable** you can change. The amount of air in each balloon and the size and shape of the balloon must remain the same. You must also release the balloon at the same point each time.

Test Your Hypothesis

Follow these steps to perform an **experiment.**

1 Make a chart like the one on the next page. Use your chart to record your observations.

2 Put on your safety goggles. Use the point of the pencil to make a hole about the size of your thumb in one card. Label this card *Large*. Make a hole about the size of your little finger in the center of another card. Label this card *Medium*. Make a hole slightly smaller than the size of a pencil in the third card (Photo A). Label this card *Small*.

⚠️ **Safety Note** *Handle the sharpened point of the pencil with care.*

3 **Measure** the size of each hole in millimeters and write the measurements in your chart.

Continued ➡

B69

Photo A

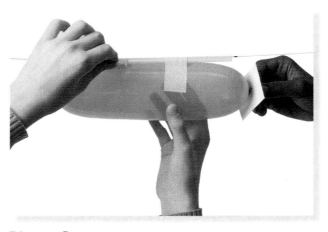

Photo C

④ Thread the string through the straw. Make a mark near one end of the string. This is where you will release the balloon rocket for each trial.

⑤ Thread the end of the balloon through the large hole. Blow up the balloon. Hold the opening tightly.

⑥ Have a partner measure and record the length of the balloon (Photo B). Tape the straw to the top of the balloon as shown (Photo C).

⑦ Have two other partners hold the ends of the string and stretch it out. Release the balloon. **Collect data** by measuring how far the balloon moved along the string. Record the data in your chart. Detach the balloon from the straw.

⑧ Repeat steps 5-7 two times, first using the card with the medium hole, then the card with the small hole. Use a new balloon each time. Measure to make sure that the balloon is blown up to the same length.

Collect Your Data

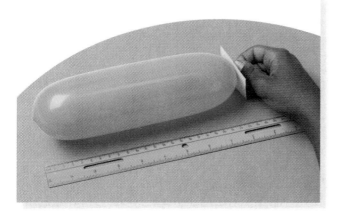

Photo B

Opening	Opening size	Distance balloon moves
Large	_____ mm	
Medium	_____ mm	
Small	_____ mm	

Interpret Your Data

Label a piece of grid paper as shown. Use the data from your chart to make a bar graph on your grid paper. Study your graph. Describe how the distance the balloon rocket traveled changed as the size of its opening decreased.

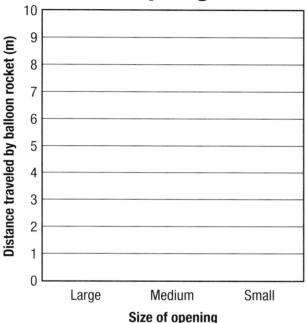

Balloon Rocket Travel and Opening Size

State Your Conclusion

How does your hypothesis compare with your results? **Communicate** your results. Explain how the size of the opening affects the distance a balloon rocket can travel.

? Inquire Further

How far would the balloon rockets travel if the string was held on an incline rather than horizontally? Develop a plan to answer this or other questions you may have.

Self-Assessment

- I made a **hypothesis** about the size of a balloon's opening and the distance it would travel.
- I **identified** and **controlled variables** and **experimented** to test my hypothesis.
- I **measured** different sizes of balloon openings and the distances the balloons traveled.
- I **collected** and **interpreted data** by making a chart and studying a graph.
- I **communicated** by stating my conclusion.

Chapter 2 Review

Chapter Main Ideas

Lesson 1

• Speed is measured by how far something travels in a certain amount of time.

• Velocity is speed in a certain direction.

Lesson 2

• Inertia is the tendency of objects at rest to stay at rest and objects that are moving to continue moving.

• Forces work in equal and opposite pairs—action and reaction.

Lesson 3

• An equal force moves an object with less mass more than it moves an object with more mass.

• Objects that are close together have a greater attraction for each other than objects that are farther apart.

• Gravity makes falling objects accelerate.

Lesson 4

• Friction slows an object's motion.

• Friction between moving surfaces can be increased or decreased.

• Air resistance is a form of friction that slows objects that are moving through the air.

Reviewing Science Words and Concepts

Write the letter of the word or phrase that best completes each sentence.

a. acceleration   g. mass

b. air resistance   h. speed

c. friction   i. streamline

d. gravity   j. velocity

e. inertia   k. weight

f. kilometers per hour

1. To find your _h_, divide the distance you travel by the time it takes.

2. Engineers _i_ objects to reduce friction with gas molecules in the air.

3. Speed in a certain direction is _j_.

4. The amount of matter that makes up an object is its _g_.

5. An object's _e_ is its tendency to continue moving or to remain at rest.

6. The force gravity exerts on an object's mass is its _k_.

7. The force that pulls objects together is called _d_.

8. The rate at which velocity is changing is _a_.

9. The force that acts to resist motion between two surfaces is _c_.

10. The friction caused by gas molecules hitting an object is _b_.

11. Speed can be measured in units of distance and time, such as _f_.

Explaining Science

Draw and label a diagram or write a paragraph to answer these questions.

1. What path might an object take that involves changing its velocity?

2. How do action and reaction forces work when you use roller skates?

3. What makes an astronaut weigh less on the moon than on Earth?

4. What changes would you suggest to make a bicycle or other vehicle more streamlined?

Using Skills

1. You are riding your bicycle to school. It becomes more and more difficult to move the bicycle forward. Make a **cause and effect** chart to suggest possible causes of your difficulty.

2. Design an **experiment** to show how the frictions of different surfaces affect the movement of an object, such as a marble rolling down a ramp.

3. How do inertia and friction affect baseball, basketball, and other sports. **Communicate** your thoughts by writing a paragraph.

Critical Thinking

1. Suggest a **hypothesis** to explain why moving heavy equipment is easier when the equipment is on a platform on wheels.

2. **Compare and contrast** speed, velocity, and acceleration.

3. **Apply** what you know about friction to suggest ways to make a familiar task at home or school easier.

Hold On!

Energy. Without it you couldn't move, see, or hear. You'd have nothing to eat. And you'd be very cold. But using energy can also be fun. It makes roller coasters work, and you're about to investigate how. Hold on!

Chapter 3
Forms of Energy

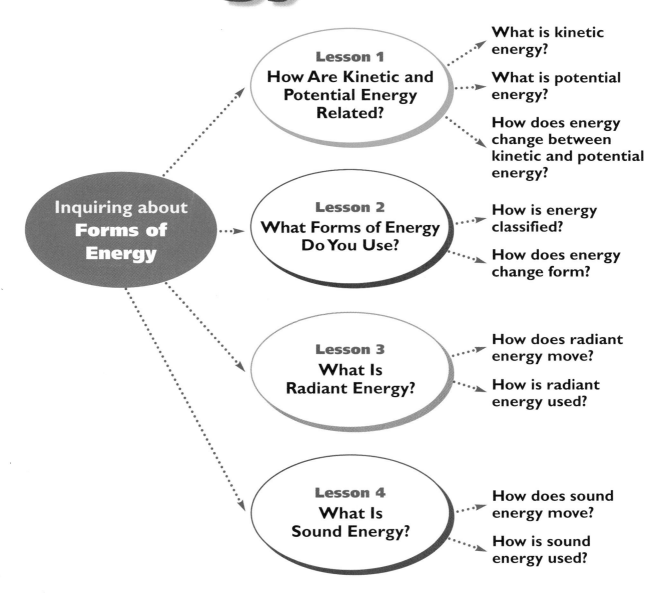

Inquiring about Forms of Energy

Lesson 1
How Are Kinetic and Potential Energy Related?

- What is kinetic energy?
- What is potential energy?
- How does energy change between kinetic and potential energy?

Lesson 2
What Forms of Energy Do You Use?

- How is energy classified?
- How does energy change form?

Lesson 3
What Is Radiant Energy?

- How does radiant energy move?
- How is radiant energy used?

Lesson 4
What Is Sound Energy?

- How does sound energy move?
- How is sound energy used?

Copy the chapter graphic organizer onto your own paper. This organizer shows you what the whole chapter is all about. As you read the lessons and do the activities, look for answers to the questions and write them on your organizer.

Modeling Roller Coaster Motion

Process Skills

- making and using models
- observing
- inferring

Materials

- masking tape
- 2 pieces of posterboard
- flat surface
- marble

Explore

1 Use masking tape to attach two pieces of posterboard together. Tape the pieces together on both sides.

2 Make a **model** of a roller coaster. Raise the center of one piece of posterboard to make a hill. Then tape the end of the posterboard to the flat surface. Hold up the other end of the posterboard.

3 Release a marble from the end of the posterboard you are holding. **Observe** how the speed of the marble changes as it travels over the posterboard. If the marble does not go all the way over the hill, hold the end of the posterboard higher and try again.

4 Make a drawing of the model. Mark on the drawing where you think the marble was moving the fastest and the slowest.

Reflect

1. What did you have to do to the posterboard to make the marble roll all the way over the hill?

2. Make an **inference.** What do you think caused the changes in the marble's speed?

? Inquire Further

Can you make the marble roll over two hills? Develop a plan to answer this or other questions you may have.

Drawing Conclusions

As you read about science and perform experiments, you will often have to **draw a conclusion,** or make a decision based on evidence you have observed. In Lesson 1, *How Are Kinetic and Potential Energy Related?*, you will explore kinetic energy, which is the energy of motion, and potential energy, which is stored energy. From observing such things as the change in speed of an object and the height from which it falls, you will be able to reach a conclusion about the relationship between kinetic and potential energy.

Reading Vocabulary

draw a conclusion (kən klü′zhən), reach a decision or opinion based on evidence and reasoning

Example

In Lesson 1, you explore the kinetic and potential energy of a roller coaster. The chart below provides information about the speed of a roller coaster. Fill in the chart to show how changes in its speed affect its kinetic and potential energy. Making a chart can help you draw a conclusion about the relationship of kinetic energy to potential energy. Use the words *least, less, greatest,* and *greater* to fill in the blanks in the chart.

	Roller Coaster at Top of Hill	Roller Coaster at Middle of Hill	Roller Coaster at Bottom of Hill
Speed	1 km/hr	70 km/hr	100 km/hr
Kinetic Energy			
Potential Energy			

▼ *Did you know that a ride on a roller coaster can teach you something about energy?*

Talk About It!

1. What is the relationship between kinetic energy and speed?

2. What is the relationship between potential energy and speed?

3. What is the relationship between kinetic energy and potential energy?

What's the Big Idea?

You will learn:
- what kinetic energy is.
- what potential energy is.
- how energy changes between kinetic and potential energy.

Lesson 1

How Are Kinetic and Potential Energy Related?

You are in the front car of a roller coaster as it reaches the top of the first hill. **ZOOM!** You rush down the track at breakneck speed. Your friend is screaming so loudly you can't even think. You're experiencing the energy of motion!

Kinetic Energy

Amusement parks use energy to make their rides exciting. Energy is the ability to do work. Here, *work* is a scientific term. You do work whenever you apply a force (a push or a pull) and move an object some distance. The more energy there is, the more work can be done.

You could use amusement park rides to investigate work. Imagine you are driving slowly in a bumper car. You bump, or apply a force to, your best friend's car and push it a short distance. You explain to your friend that you have just done some work. What would happen if you were moving faster the next time you bumped your friend's car?

Most Kinetic Energy
At the bottom of the hill, the car's speed is the greatest, but it is no longer accelerating. Its kinetic energy is greatest but is no longer increasing.

The energy you or any object has because of its motion is called **kinetic energy.** The faster an object moves, the more kinetic energy it has. When your bumper car moves faster, it can do more work to your friend's car. You can push it farther.

When you're finished with the bumper cars, you and your friend decide to ride the roller coaster. Study the roller coaster on these two pages. Where do you go the slowest? Where is your kinetic energy the least? Where do you go the fastest? Where is your kinetic energy the greatest? What is the scariest part?

Glossary

Least Kinetic Energy
At the top of the hill, the car is barely moving. Its kinetic energy is almost zero, but not for long!

Kinetic Energy Increasing
As the car goes down the hill, it moves faster and faster. Its kinetic energy is increasing.

Glossary

potential (pə ten′shəl), **energy,** stored energy or energy that an object has due to its position

Potential Energy

Scientists classify all energy as either kinetic energy or potential energy. **Potential energy** is stored energy or energy that an object has due to its position.

When you begin your roller-coaster ride, electric motors in the roller coaster move your car slowly up a long, steep hill. As it reaches a higher and higher position, your car has more and more potential energy. When you reach the top, your car has its greatest potential energy.

Find the car at the top of the hill on the next page. In this position, the car has high potential energy. It is possible for it to plunge down the track.

When the car reaches the bottom, it has used up its potential energy. Although it keeps moving along, it cannot go any faster. How much potential energy does the car have when it is halfway down the hill compared to what it had when it was at the top of the hill?

The potential energy of an object is not always due to its height. In a windup toy, energy is stored in the tightly wound spring. Even atoms—in the way they're connected to each other—can store energy. That's how a radio's batteries store the energy you use to make it play. Energy is stored in this same way in the food you need to live.

Least Potential Energy
At the bottom of the hill, the car is at the lowest point. It has used up all its potential energy. Although its speed is greatest, it has no potential to go any faster.

Most Potential Energy

At the top of the hill, the car is at its greatest height, and because of its position the car's potential energy is the greatest.

Potential Energy Decreasing

As the car goes down lower and lower, it uses up its potential energy. Halfway down, the car has used up half the potential energy it had at the top.

Changing Between Kinetic and Potential Energy

You've learned about potential energy and kinetic energy by studying a roller coaster. You can also use a roller coaster to learn how potential energy changes to kinetic energy. Start at the top of the hill on the next page and follow the roller coaster downhill to find how the energy changes. Then look at the small drawing below to find what happens next. The total amount of energy does not increase or decrease—it just changes between kinetic and potential energy.

Next time you ride a roller coaster such as the one in the picture, think about how your ride is made possible by changes between kinetic and potential energy.

▲ *Riding a roller coaster is a fun way to study science.*

Kinetic Energy Changing to Potential Energy

When the car begins to zoom back up the next hill, the process reverses. The higher the car goes, the more potential energy it has and the slower it moves. Its potential energy increases as its kinetic energy decreases—but just wait for the next drop!

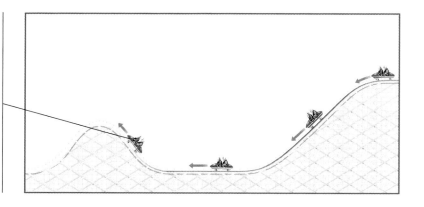

Least Potential Energy and Most Kinetic Energy

At the bottom of the hill, all the car's potential energy has been changed to kinetic energy. The car is at its lowest point, but it is going its fastest.

Potential Energy Changing to Kinetic Energy

As you move down the hill, you begin to go faster. Potential energy changes to kinetic energy. As the car goes down the track, more and more potential energy changes to kinetic energy. The car goes faster and faster as it drops lower and lower. Halfway down, half of the potential energy has changed to kinetic energy.

Most Potential Energy and Least Kinetic Energy

At the top of the hill, the car is at its greatest height. Because of this position, it has the most potential energy. Because the car is almost stopped, it has the least kinetic energy.

Lesson 1 Review

1. Give an example of an object with kinetic energy.

2. Give an example of an object with potential energy.

3. Give an example of how potential energy can change to kinetic energy.

4. **Draw Conclusions**
   While riding on a roller coaster with your eyes closed, you feel your speed increasing. Are you going uphill or downhill? Is your potential energy increasing or decreasing?

Investigating Potential Energy

Process Skills

- estimating and measuring
- predicting
- inferring
- observing
- collecting and interpreting data

Materials

- paper cup
- scissors
- blank sheet of paper
- 2 metric rulers
- 4 identical textbooks
- marble

Getting Ready

In this activity you will see how potential energy can change to kinetic energy and how kinetic energy can do work.

Review how energy and work are related. Review how potential energy and kinetic energy are related.

Follow This Procedure

1 Make a chart like the one shown. Use your chart to record your measurements and predictions.

2 Cut a rectangle 4 cm wide and 5 cm tall from the top of the paper cup (Photo A).

3 Place the cup upside-down on the paper near the edge. The rectangle opening should face the edge. Make a mark on the paper along the outside of the cup on the side opposite the opening (Photo B).

4 Place one end of your ruler into the opening as far as it will go. Place a textbook about 1 cm under the other edge of the ruler to form a ramp.

5 **Measure** the height of the ramp by measuring the height of the textbook. Record your measurement.

Number of textbooks used	Height of ramp	Predicted distance cup will move	Measured distance cup moved
1		X	
2		X	
3			
4			

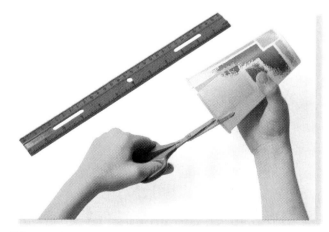

Photo A

Photo B

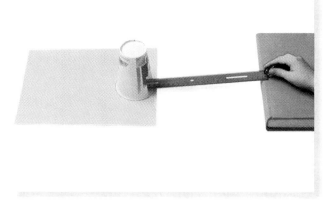

Photo C

⑥ Hold a marble at the top of the groove in the ruler (Photo C). Release the marble from the top of the ruler. **Observe** what happens to the cup.

⑦ Make a mark on the paper around the outside edge of the cup. Remove the cup and measure the distance from the new mark to the mark you made before. **Collect data** by recording your measurement. Return the cup and ruler to their original positions.

⑧ Place another textbook on top of the first textbook. Repeat steps 5–7.

⑨ **Predict** how far the marble will move the cup if you use three, then four textbooks. Repeat steps 5–7 using three, then four textbooks.

Interpret Your Results

1. How close were your predictions to your results? What is the relationship between the height of the ramp and the distance the marble moved the cup?

2. Make **inferences.** How did raising the height of the ramp affect the potential and kinetic energy of the marble? How did raising the ramp affect the amount of work the marble did?

Inquire Further

What effect would the mass of the marble have on the distance the cup moves? Develop a plan to answer this or other questions you may have.

Self-Assessment

- I followed instructions to **observe** and **measure** the distance a marble can move a cup.
- I **collected** and **interpreted data.**
- I made **predictions** based on the data.
- I stated the relationship between the height of the ramp and the distance the marble moved the cup.
- I made **inferences** about the potential and kinetic energy of the marble and the amount of work done by the marble.

You will learn:
- how energy is classified.
- how energy changes form.

Glossary

sound energy, energy of vibrations carried by air, water, or other matter

radiant (rā′dē ənt) **energy,** energy that travels as waves and can move through empty space

Lesson 2

What Forms of Energy Do You Use?

On your mark. Because of a form of energy, you can see the other runners. Get set. Because of a form of energy, you can hear. **GO!!** As you run, your muscles use a form of energy to make your body move.

Classifying Forms of Energy

You learned about potential and kinetic energy. Both can exist in many different forms. Turning on a light, running, and listening to music all use some form of energy. Study the photos on these two pages and read the captions. Think of ways you have used each of these seven forms of energy.

Sound energy is the energy of vibrations carried by air, water, or other matter. When you listen to a rock band or shout to a friend, you're using sound energy. ▼

◀ **Radiant energy** *is energy that travels as waves and can move through empty space. Scientists classify energy, such as light, X rays, and infrared rays, as radiant energy. Energy from the sun travels to the earth as radiant energy. A restaurant may use a heat lamp to shine infrared rays on your food to keep it warm until it is served.*

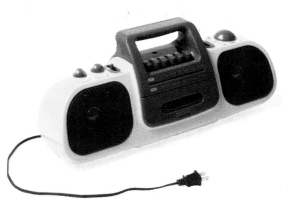

◀ **Electrical energy** is energy carried by electricity. When you play a tape, electrical energy is used to make sound.

Mechanical energy is energy an object has due to its motion, position, or condition. A person running, a bicycle stopped on top of a tall hill, and a wound spring in a windup toy all have mechanical energy. ▶

Glossary

electrical (i lək′trə kəl) **energy,** energy carried by electricity

mechanical (mə kan′ə kəl) **energy,** energy an object has due to its motion, position, or condition

nuclear (nü′klē ər) **energy,** energy produced when an atom splits apart or when two atoms join to form one atom

chemical (kem′ə kəl), **energy,** energy stored in the way atoms are connected to each other

thermal (thėr′məl), **energy,** energy of the movement of atoms and molecules

▲ **Nuclear energy** is energy produced when an atom splits apart or when two atoms join to form one atom. Nationwide, nuclear energy supplies about 14% of the electrical energy people use.

▲ **Chemical energy** is energy stored in the connections among atoms. When your body chemically changes your food, it releases the chemical energy stored in it. Your muscles use this energy when you run. In fact, your body uses this energy for all life functions.

Thermal energy is the energy of the movement of atoms and molecules. The more rapidly they move, the greater their thermal energy. When the thermal energy of this ice sculpture gets too great, the ice melts. ▶

How Energy Changes Form

Energy can change form. When you use energy, you often change its form. For example, your solar-powered calculator can change radiant energy from the sun into electrical energy. Find some examples of how energy changes form in the pictures on these two pages.

▲ Radiant energy changes to chemical energy. Long ago, ancient plants changed radiant energy from the sun into chemical energy. Over time, pressure and heat changed the remains of these plants into coal.

▲ Radiant energy changes to electrical energy. Your calculator may change radiant energy into the electrical energy it uses for its power.

▲ Radiant energy changes to thermal energy. You may have seen a house with panels like the ones on this house. The panels change the radiant energy from the sun into thermal energy to heat the home.

▲ Radiant energy changes to chemical energy. Plants change radiant energy from the sun into chemical energy.

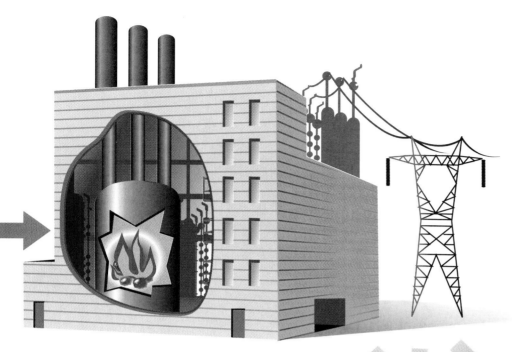

◀ Chemical energy changes to thermal energy, then to mechanical energy, and finally to electrical energy. Power plants change the chemical energy from coal into thermal energy. Then they change the thermal energy into mechanical energy to turn a generator. Finally, the generator changes the mechanical energy into electrical energy.

▲ Electrical energy changes to mechanical energy. When you use a fan you change electrical energy into mechanical energy.

▲ Electrical energy changes to radiant energy. When you turn on a light, electrical energy changes into radiant energy.

▲ Electrical energy changes to sound energy. When you play a tape, electrical energy changes into sound energy.

In the examples you've studied, energy changed from one form to another. No energy was lost. Based on careful observation and many experiments, scientists in the 1800s developed a theory about energy. It stated that energy can change forms but that it can't be created or destroyed. For example, when you use your brakes to stop your speeding bicycle, the mechanical energy of your moving bicycle isn't lost. It changes into thermal energy. Feel your brakes. They're warm!

Earlier, scientists had developed a similar theory about mass. It said that matter can't be created or destroyed. Chemical changes may occur, but the total amount of matter can't change.

By the mid-1900s, scientists had discovered that energy and matter can be changed into each other under extraordinary conditions. Nuclear energy results from matter changing into energy. Based on this new evidence, scientists revised the two theories into one new theory. The new theory says that, taken together, the total amount of matter and energy does not change.

Lesson 2 Review

1. List seven forms of energy.

2. What are three forms of energy into which radiant energy can change?

3. **Draw Conclusions**
   Will a solar powered calculator work in a dark room?

Lesson 3

What Is Radiant Energy?

Watch a colorful sunset. Tune in to a radio station. Look at an **X** ray of your teeth. What do they have in common? Without radiant energy, they wouldn't be possible.

How Radiant Energy Moves

Radiant energy from the sun includes infrared (heat) rays that warm you, ultraviolet rays that cause you to sunburn, and visible light that lets you see. All types of radiant energy travel in waves. Unlike water waves you see at the beach or sound waves that carry sound to your ears, radiant energy waves can travel where there is no matter. The sun's radiant energy travels through space to reach the earth.

The various types of radiant energy are different because their wavelengths are different. **Wavelength** is the distance from one point on a wave to the same point on the next wave. Find the wavelength in the picture below. Each type of radiant energy has a different wavelength.

Glossary

wavelength
(wāv′lengkth′), the distance from a point on one wave to the same point on the next wave

Glossary

Wavelength

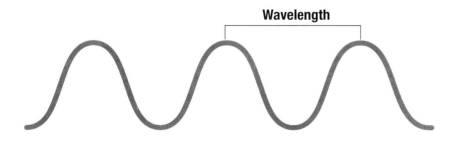

◀ **Measuring Wavelength**
Radiant energy travels in waves. Scientists use special instruments to measure wavelength. Human eyes can't see what these waves look like, not even those for visible light.

Uses of Radiant Energy

Types of Radiant Energy

The pictures on these two pages show seven types of radiant energy. Notice again that different types have different wavelengths. The shortest wavelengths are on the left. The longest are on the right. The different types have a variety of uses. Read how each type of radiant energy is used, beginning with gamma rays which have the shortest wavelengths.

Short wavelength

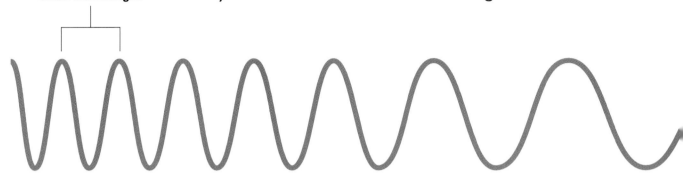

Gamma rays

X rays

Ultraviolet rays

Visible light

▲ Treating some foods with gamma rays helps preserve them by killing the organisms that cause the food to spoil. Doctors also use gamma rays to treat some cancers.

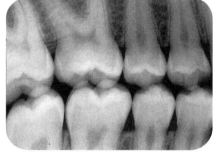

▲ X-ray images show breaks in bones or cavities in teeth. They help doctors and dentists care for you.

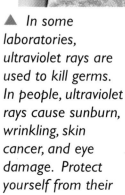

▲ In some laboratories, ultraviolet rays are used to kill germs. In people, ultraviolet rays cause sunburn, wrinkling, skin cancer, and eye damage. Protect yourself from their effects.

▲ Visible light is the only radiant energy you can see.

Long wavelength

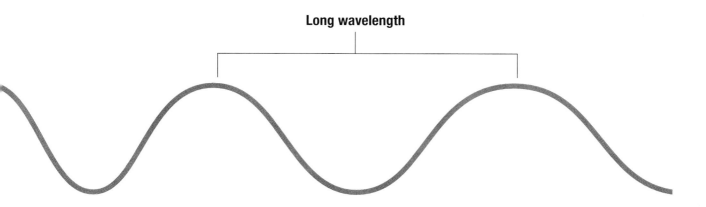

Infrared rays

Microwaves   **Shorter radio waves**   **Longer radio waves**

Shorter radio waves carry television signals.

Longer radio waves carry radio signals. ▼

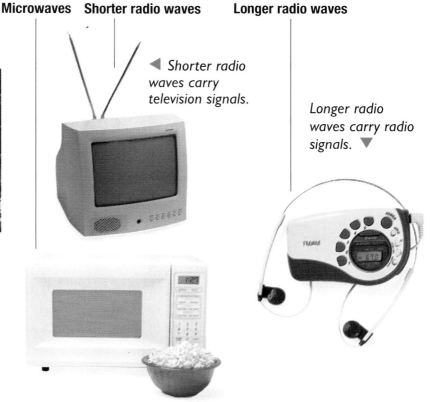

▲ *All objects give off infrared rays—the warmer the object, the more rays it gives off. Special "heat" photographs use infrared rays rather than visible light. People use these photographs to find out where buildings lose heat.*

▲ *You may pop popcorn in a microwave oven, which uses microwaves. Police catch speeders with radar, which also uses microwaves. Telephone companies use microwaves to carry portions of some phone calls.*

▲ *All the colors of visible light mix together to make white light. When white light passes through a prism, the colors separate.*

Your eyes are sensitive to a very small part of all radiant energy, the portion called visible light. Even though it makes up just a small part of all radiant energy, visible light still has a range of wavelengths. You see these different wavelengths as different colors.

Colors play a key role in how you see the world. All mixed together, the different colors make white light. You can use a prism like the one above to separate the colors. As white light travels through the prism, it bends. Because different wavelengths bend different amounts, the white light spreads out into a band of colors.

When visible light hits an object, it may behave in one of three ways. If the object is transparent, the light passes through almost unchanged, as through a window. You can see clearly what is behind it. In contrast, if the object is opaque, no light at all can pass through it. You can see nothing behind it. If the object is translucent, some light can pass through but you can't see details clearly. Look at the plastic wrap, aluminum foil, and wax paper on the next page. Which is translucent? transparent? opaque?

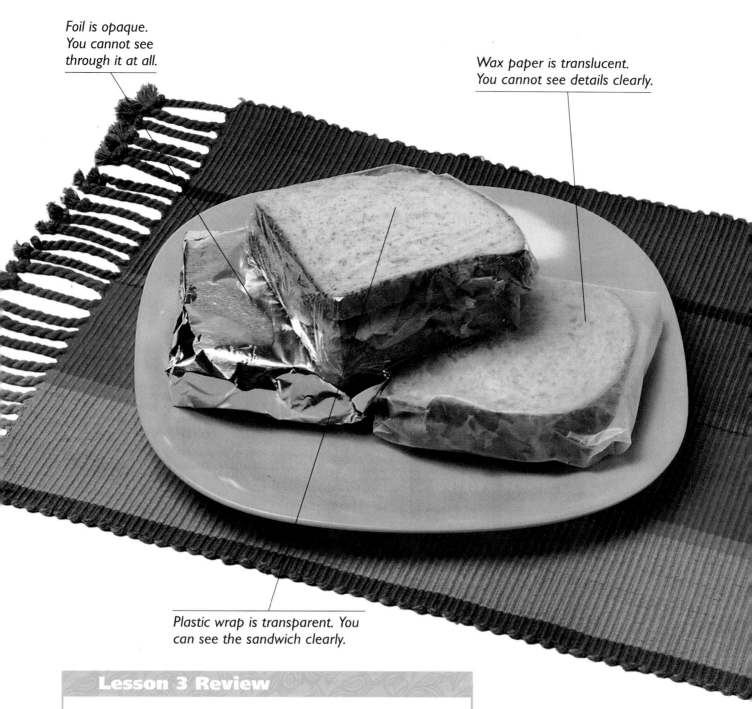

Foil is opaque. You cannot see through it at all.

Wax paper is translucent. You cannot see details clearly.

Plastic wrap is transparent. You can see the sandwich clearly.

Lesson 3 Review

1. How are all types of radiant energy the same? In what way are they different?

2. What are seven types of radiant energy?

3. Draw Conclusions
You can clearly read traffic signs through the tinted windows of a car. Are the windows transparent, translucent, or opaque?

Investigating Radiant Energy

Process Skills

Process Skills

- predicting
- observing

Materials

- plastic pail
- water
- scissors
- construction paper
- wax paper
- clear plastic wrap
- transparent tape
- light-sensitive paper
- clock with second hand

Getting Ready

In this activity you can see how radiant energy from the sun can cause a change in light-sensitive paper.

Be sure to do the first part of the activity in a darkened room.

Follow This Procedure

1 Make a chart like the one shown. Use your chart to record your predictions and observations.

Appearance of paper	Predictions	Observations
Beneath construction paper		
Beneath wax paper		
Beneath plastic wrap		

2 Fill the plastic pail about $\frac{1}{3}$ full with water. Cut out different shapes, such as a star, heart, or diamond, from the construction paper, the wax paper, and the plastic wrap (Photo A).

3 In a darkened room, use transparent tape to attach the shapes to the blue side of the light-sensitive paper (Photo B).

4 Sunlight can cause a change in light-sensitive paper. What do you think will happen to the part of the paper covered with construction paper? with wax paper? with plastic wrap? Record your **predictions.** Write an explanation.

5 Take your paper outside and allow the sun to shine directly on the paper and cut out shapes for about 1 minute.

Photo A

Photo B

⑥ Return to the darkened room and remove the cut out shapes from the light-sensitive paper. Soak the paper in the pail of water for about 1 minute. Remove the paper and allow it to dry.

⑦ Compare and contrast the three shapes on the paper. Write your **observations** on your chart. Attach a sample of each of the three shapes to your chart.

Interpret Your Results

1. Which material blocked the most sunlight? Which material blocked the least sunlight? Explain why there was a difference.

2. On pages B88–B89, you learned how energy changes forms such as from electrical energy to mechanical energy. Light is a form of radiant energy. What evidence of an energy change did you observe in this activity?

❓ Inquire Further

What other materials can be changed by radiant light energy? Develop a plan to answer this or other questions you may have.

Self-Assessment

- I followed instructions to test how radiant energy affects light-sensitive paper.
- I recorded my **predictions** and **observations**.
- I compared and contrasted the shapes produced on the light-sensitive paper.
- I stated which materials blocked the most and the least sunlight.
- I stated the evidence of an energy change I observed.

You will learn:
- how sound energy moves.
- how sound energy is used.

Glossary

vibration
(vī brā′ shən), rapid back and forth motion of air or other matter

Lesson 4

What Is Sound Energy?

You lucked out! You got the part of the bell ringer in the school play. No lines to study! When the king appears, just ring the bell that makes the deep sound. But is that the large bell or the small bell?

How Sound Energy Moves

When you shout, ring a bell, or play music through a speaker, you change some form of energy into sound energy. Sometimes you can even feel sound coming from a speaker. What you feel are **vibrations**, rapid back and forth movements of the air. These vibrations can also travel through water, wood, and other matter. Sound energy is the energy of these vibrations.

Unlike radiant energy, which can travel through empty space, sound can travel only through matter. This is because there must be something to vibrate. If you and a friend were astronauts on a space walk, you would see each other, but you couldn't hear each other. Outside your spacesuit, there is no matter to vibrate. Fortunately, you could talk using your spacesuit's radio. It uses radiant energy, which doesn't need matter to travel.

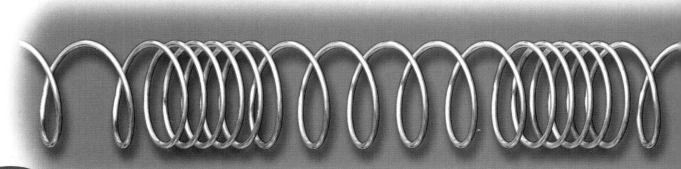

Like radiant energy, sound energy travels in waves. To understand how sound waves travel, imagine using a wire spring like the one shown below. First, stretch it between yourself and a friend on a long table. Then give it a quick push toward your friend, but hold on to the spring. As you push out, you press together part of the spring. The pressed-together area moves toward your friend. Press again and again. Notice below how the pressed-together area moves.

Similarly, vibrations from a speaker make sound waves in the air by pressing on the air again and again. Each vibration creates one wave. One wavelength is the distance from one pressed-together area to the next.

The number of waves passing a point in one second is called the **frequency.** Low-frequency sound waves have long wavelengths. You hear them as deep sounds. High-frequency sound waves have short wavelengths. You hear them as high sounds. Which of the bells shown on this page will make a high-frequency sound? Which will make a low-frequency sound?

Glossary

frequency
(frē′kwən se), the number of waves passing a point in one second

Compared to the small bell, the large bell vibrates more slowly. Because it makes fewer sound waves in one second, it has a lower frequency and a deeper sound. ▼

A quick push on the spring presses an area together. This pressed-together area moves along the spring. ▼

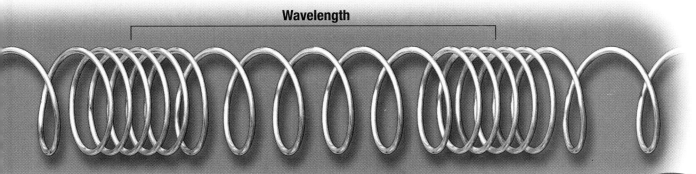

Wavelength

Uses of Sound Energy

Like radiant energy, sound energy has many uses. You use it for communication when you talk. You use it for safety when sirens warn you of danger. You use it for fun when you listen to music. Sound energy is even used in medicine. Doctors may check their patients' health with special pictures made using sound waves.

Some animals use sounds too low for people to hear. Other animals use ultrasounds, sounds too high for people to hear. Study the pictures on these two pages to learn some ways sound is used.

Range of Sound

Short wavelength
High frequency

Little Brown Bat
When they fly, many bats make very high-frequency sounds—much higher than even dogs can hear. By listening for echoes, bats avoid running into things in the dark and find mosquitoes to eat. ▶

Bat

Ultrasound machine

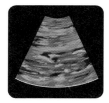

◀ Ultrasound Image
People use the highest frequency sound for making ultrasound images. These images show soft body parts such as the liver better than X rays can.

Dog Whistle
People use special high-frequency dog whistles that people can barely hear but that dogs hear easily. Compare dog hearing to human hearing. ▶

Dog Whistle

There is a wide range of sounds. The sounds with the shortest wavelengths and the highest frequencies are on the left. The sounds with the longest wavelengths and the lowest frequencies are on the right. ▼

Long wavelength
Low frequency

Human Hearing

◀ **People**
People have a certain range of hearing. All music has frequencies within this range.

◀ **Domestic Dog**
Dogs have a wider range of hearing than people. They can hear both lower-frequency and higher-frequency sounds.

Dog Hearing

African Elephant
African elephants make many sounds. Some of the sounds they make have a frequency that is too low for people to hear. These deep sounds travel well and allow elephants to communicate over long distances. The red line shows just these very low sounds. ▶

Elephant

Piano
Pianos make sounds with a large range of frequencies, but this is only a part of the range of sounds people can hear. ▼

Piano

It is important to use sound energy safely. You know that too much sound energy will damage your hearing. When using headphones, you should make sure the volume is not too high. Even a volume setting you find comfortable may let too much sound energy reach your ears.

Another way to guard against hearing loss is to wear hearing protection. Rock musicians, construction workers, and other people exposed to loud noise suffer hearing loss if they don't use hearing protection. People who use equipment that makes a great deal of noise, such as a lawnmower, should use hearing protection to stop some of the sound energy from reaching their ears and causing damage.

▲ *When the man mows his lawn he wears hearing protection. Hearing damage is usually gradual. You may not notice it until long after exposure to loud sounds. Using hearing protection helps guard your hearing, both now and for the future.*

Lesson 4 Review

1. Why must sound travel through matter?

2. List two examples of how animals use sounds that people can't hear.

3. **Draw Conclusions**
   Examine the chart on pages B100–B101. Can a dog hear the high-frequency sounds an ultrasound machine makes?

Experimenting with Sunscreens

Materials

- metric ruler
- clear tape
- clear plastic sheet
- marker
- 3 medicine cups with sunscreen lotion of different SPF values
- 3 cotton swabs
- light-sensitive paper
- clock with second hand
- plastic pail
- water
- scissors

Process Skills

- formulating questions and hypotheses
- identifying and controlling variables
- experimenting
- collecting and interpreting data
- classifying
- communicating

Process Skills

State the Problem

Are there differences in the effectiveness of sunscreens?

Formulate Your Hypothesis

Do sunscreens with higher SPF values block sunlight better than sunscreens with lower SPF values? Write your **hypothesis.**

Identify and Control the Variables

The SPF value of sunscreen is the **variable** you can change. You will have 3 samples of sunscreen with different SPF values and a control in which no sunscreen is used. Use the same amount of sunscreen for each test sample. The length of time the paper is in sunlight must be the same for all tests.

Test Your Hypothesis

Follow these steps to perform an **experiment.**

1 Make a chart like the one shown on B105. Use your chart to collect and record your data.

2 Measure four 6 cm strips of tape. Stick them on a sheet of clear plastic. Use a marker to number the strips beneath each sample (Photo A). Record the SPF value for each sample in your chart.

3 Dip a cotton swab into sample 1. Be sure the cotton is completely covered. Gently wipe the sunscreen onto the tape labeled *1* (Photo B).

Continued ➡

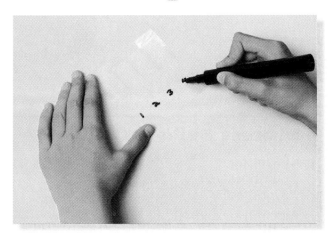

Photo A

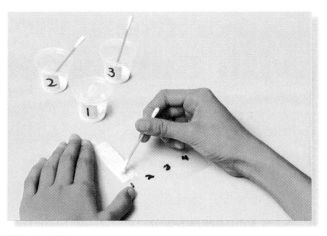

Photo B

④ Repeat step 3 using sample 2, then repeat for sample 3. Use a new cotton swab for each sample. Do not put sunscreen on the fourth piece of tape. This is your control.

⑤ Obtain a strip of light-sensitive paper from your teacher. The room should be darkened when you do this. Use the marker to make an X in the lower left corner. The X will help you identify the samples when the plastic is removed. Place the plastic sheet on top of the paper (Photo C).

⑥ Expose the paper to direct sunlight for 30 seconds. Do not overexpose the paper. Quickly soak the paper in water for one minute. Let the paper dry.

⑦ Make sure your paper is facing the right direction, and the X is in the lower left corner. Cut the four sections of the paper apart. Tape a sample of each one onto your chart next to the corresponding sample number and SPF value. This is your **collected data.**

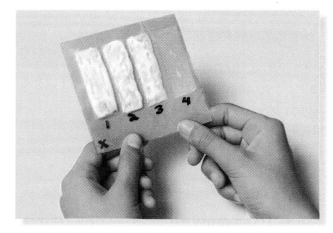

Photo C

Collect Your Data

Sample	SPF value	Sample of exposed paper	Rank (1 for most effective, to 3 for least effective)
1			
2			
3			
4	no SPF value		no sunscreen

Interpret Your Data

Dark areas on the exposed paper show where light waves went through the sunscreen. Light areas are where the sun was blocked. **Classify** the samples by ranking them in order from most to least effective in blocking sunlight. Describe the differences between the sunscreen paper samples and the control paper sample.

State Your Conclusion

How do your results compare with your hypothesis? **Communicate** your results. Were there great differences, little differences, or no differences among the sunscreen samples? Report your conclusion to the class, and compare your conclusion with those of other groups.

 Inquire Further

Does tanning lotion without sunscreen block sunlight? Develop a plan to answer this or other questions you may have.

Self-Assessment

- I made a **hypothesis** about the effectiveness of sunscreens with different SPF values.
- I **identified** and **controlled variables.**
- I followed instructions to perform an **experiment.**
- I **collected** and **interpreted** my **data** by **classifying** paper samples and ranking them from lightest to darkest.
- I **communicated** by reporting my conclusion to the class.

Chapter 3 Review

Chapter Main Ideas

Lesson 1

- Kinetic energy is the energy of motion.
- Potential energy is stored energy or energy that an object has due to its position.
- Potential energy can change to kinetic energy and kinetic energy can change to potential energy.

Lesson 2

- Energy is classified into different forms. Seven forms of energy are sound energy, electrical energy, mechanical energy, chemical energy, nuclear energy, radiant energy, and thermal energy.
- Energy can change from one form to another, but under ordinary conditions no energy is lost or created.

Lesson 3

- Radiant energy travels in waves. These waves can travel where there is no matter.
- Radiant energy is used to diagnose disease, to cook food, to send radio and TV signals, and for other purposes.

Lesson 4

- Sound energy travels in waves that move only through matter.
- Living things use sound energy for communication and navigation. People also use sound for entertainment and to diagnose disease.

Reviewing Science Words and Concepts

Write the letter of the word or phrase that best completes each sentence.

a. chemical energy
b. electrical energy
c. frequency
d. kinetic energy
e. mechanical energy
f. nuclear energy
g. potential energy
h. radiant energy
i. sound energy
j. thermal energy
k. vibration
l. wavelength

1. The energy an object has because it is moving is called ____.
2. A person at the top of a tall water slide has a great amount of ____.
3. The energy produced when atoms split or join is ____.
4. A rapid back and forth motion of air or other matter is called a ____.
5. The energy of vibrations carried by air, water, or other substances is ____.
6. The energy released by chemical changes is ____.
7. The distance from a point on a wave to the same point on the next wave is called a ____.
8. The energy carried by electricity is ____.

9. The energy that travels as waves and can move through empty space is ___.

10. The number of waves passing a point in a given amount of time is the ___.

11. As an object gets warmer, its ___ increases as the atoms and molecules it is made of move faster.

12. The energy an object has because of its position, motion, or condition is called ___.

Explaining Science

Draw and label a diagram or write a paragraph to answer these questions.

1. How can the potential energy of a bicycle stopped at the top of a tall hill be changed into kinetic energy?

2. Describe the way energy changes form when an electric light is turned on.

3. How does radiant energy travel?

4. How does sound energy travel?

Using Skills

1. You are at a baseball game. You see a batter hit the ball. An instant later you hear the crack of the bat against the ball. **Draw** a **conclusion** about which travels faster: sound waves or radiant energy waves.

2. **Classify** each as kinetic or potential energy: **a.** a rolling soccer ball, **b.** a bicycle stopped at the top of a hill, **c.** the wound spring in a wind up toy, **d.** a bicycle coasting on level road.

3. Suppose you collected the data shown below about a rollercoaster car at positions A, B, and C. **Interpret** the **data** to find where the car has the greatest potential energy, least potential energy, greatest kinetic energy, and least kinetic energy.

Position	Height (meters)	Speed (kilometers per hour)
A	50	1
B	40	50
C	10	100

Critical Thinking

1. **Classify** each of the following as a form of chemical, electrical, mechanical, nuclear, radiant, sound, or thermal energy: **a.** singing bird, **b.** a light, **c.** a flying baseball, **d.** a melting snowman, **e.** a bubbling chemical reaction, **f.** an electric clock, **g.** the splitting of atoms in a power plant.

2. Your older cousin is joining a band as a drummer. Based on what you know about sound energy, **evaluate** the health risk your cousin may face. What would you suggest if your cousin asked you to help **make** a **decision** about the best way to handle the risk?

3. Your friend from Sweden gets an outside job at a summer camp. What would you suggest to help **solve** the **problems** that can be caused by ultraviolet rays?

Crank Harder!

Electrical energy—you can make it just by turning a crank. Make all you need—as long as you don't need much! It gets tiring just lighting a single bulb. There must be a better way!

Chapter 4
Electrical Energy

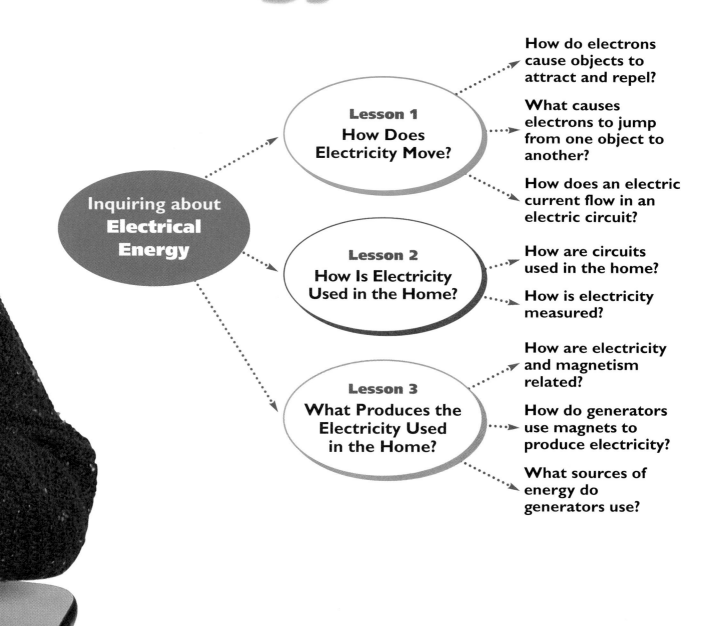

Inquiring about **Electrical Energy**

Lesson 1
How Does Electricity Move?

How do electrons cause objects to attract and repel?

What causes electrons to jump from one object to another?

How does an electric current flow in an electric circuit?

Lesson 2
How Is Electricity Used in the Home?

How are circuits used in the home?

How is electricity measured?

Lesson 3
What Produces the Electricity Used in the Home?

How are electricity and magnetism related?

How do generators use magnets to produce electricity?

What sources of energy do generators use?

Copy the chapter graphic organizer onto your own paper. This organizer shows you what the whole chapter is all about. As you read the lessons and do the activities, look for answers to the questions and write them in your organizer.

Exploring Electric Charges

Process Skills

- observing
- inferring

Materials

- 2 pieces of clear tape
- pencil
- plastic metric ruler
- plastic wrap
- clock with a second hand
- rubber comb
- wool cloth

Explore

1 Fold over a tip of each piece of tape. Write + on the smooth side of one piece and − on the smooth side of the other piece.

2 Stick the + tape onto the smooth side of the − tape. Pull the two tape strips apart quickly. They now have an electric charge. Stick them about 2 cm apart on the pencil with the folded ends hanging down.

3 Rub the plastic ruler with plastic wrap for about 30 seconds to give it an electric charge. Bring the ruler near (but don't touch) the tape strips. Record your **observations.**

4 Test these objects in the same way: comb rubbed with plastic wrap, ruler rubbed with wool, comb rubbed with wool.

Reflect

1. Which of the objects attracted the + tape? Which repelled the tape? Which of the objects attracted the − tape? Which repelled the tape?

2. Make an **inference.** Describe how charged objects act when brought near other charged objects.

? Inquire Further

Do objects without an electric charge attract the charged tape pieces? Develop a plan to answer this or other questions you may have.

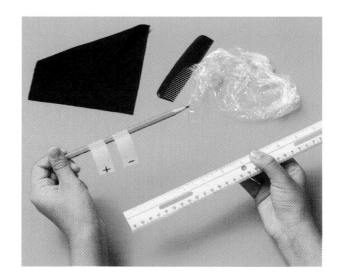

Choosing Scales for Bar Graphs

Lights. Without them, you'd be stumbling around in the dark as soon as the sun went down.

You use light bulbs all around your home. Luckily, you can buy different light bulbs for different needs — bright bulbs for the kitchen, softer bulbs for the bedroom.

The two bar graphs below show the same data, but they use different scales.

Which graph has a scale that makes it easier to give a closer estimate of each bulb's brightness?

> **Math Tip**
> The scale tells you what units are used on the axes of a graph.

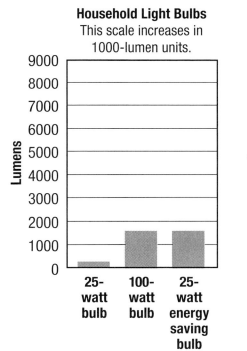

Household Light Bulbs
This scale increases in 1000-lumen units.

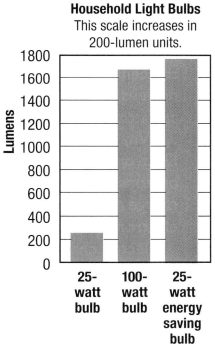

Household Light Bulbs
This scale increases in 200-lumen units.

Talk About It!

What should you look for in choosing the best scale?

You will learn:

- how electrons cause objects to attract and repel.
- what causes electrons to jump from one object to another.
- how an electric current flows in an electric circuit.

Foam peanuts stick to this wool sweater for the same reason that clothes sometimes have "static cling." ▼

Lesson 1

How Does Electricity Move?

Your cousin sends you a hand-knit wool sweater that took months to make. You eagerly pull it out of the box and hold it up! It's great! But why are those foam peanuts sticking to it?

Attracting and Repelling

You know that both the sweater and the foam peanuts in the picture are made of atoms. Protons and neutrons are packed together in the nucleus at the center of each atom. Electrons move around the nucleus. The electrons stay in the atom because they are attracted to the protons.

Why do electrons and protons attract each other? Electrons have a negative electric charge (−) and protons have a positive electric charge (+). A negative charge and a positive charge attract each other, so electrons (−) and protons (+) attract each other.

Electric charges can also repel each other. A negative charge repels a negative charge. A positive charge repels a positive charge.

Usually, an atom has the same number of protons and electrons. Positive charges balance negative charges, so the atom has no charge overall. However, two of the atoms at the top of the next page have a charge. You can see that they became charged when they gained or lost an electron.

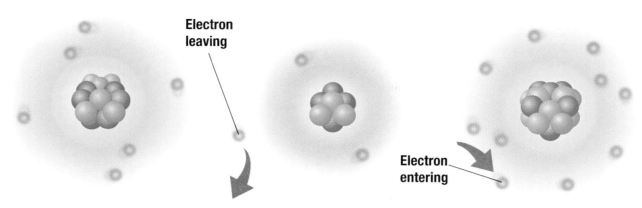

▲ The number of negative charges equals the number of positive charges. This atom is not charged.

▲ This atom has lost one of its electrons. The atom has a positive charge.

▲ This atom gained an extra electron from another atom. With one extra electron, this atom has a negative charge.

The atoms in some objects gain or lose an electron when the objects are rubbed against each other. Protons are in the nucleus of the atom, so rubbing doesn't affect them. However, the outer part of an atom has electrons, which can be rubbed off. If an uncharged object rubs against another uncharged object, some electrons may rub off one and move onto the other. Rubbing causes both objects to become charged.

The picture on the right shows what happens when foam peanuts rub against a wool sweater. Electrons rub off the sweater and onto the foam peanuts. With these extra electrons, the foam peanuts are negatively charged. The sweater is positively charged because it lost electrons. Because opposite charges attract, the foam peanuts cling to the sweater.

Imagine if you took two foam peanuts off the sweater and pushed them together. You would discover that the peanuts repel each other. This is because both peanuts are negatively charged, and like charges repel.

Key	
◦	Electrons
○	Protons
●	Neutrons

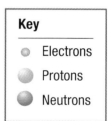

Like charges repel.

Opposite charges attract.

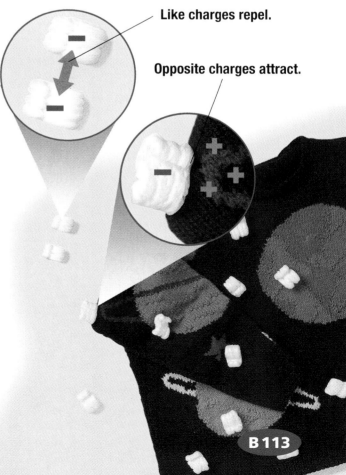

Jumping Charges

Maybe you've watched a thunderstorm through a window. You may have wondered what causes the bright flashes of lightning. Perhaps during the winter you've seen tiny flashes of light when you've pulled off a wool sweater over your head in a dark room. Are the bright lightning flashes and the tiny flashes from your sweater in some way the same? Study the pictures below to learn how the tiny flashes occur.

▲ *As you move, your wool sweater rubs against your cotton shirt. Electrons rub off the sweater's atoms and move onto the atoms of your cotton shirt. As you pull off the sweater, you rub even more electrons off the sweater onto your shirt. The sweater becomes positively charged, and your shirt, negatively charged.*

▲ *The many extra electrons on your shirt repel each other. At the same time, the extra positive charges on your sweater attract those electrons strongly. Eventually, some electrons leap from the shirt toward the sweater, making tiny sparks. You see each tiny spark as a faint flash of light.*

You may see tiny flashes when removing a sweater. ▼

Earth Science

What causes those giant sparks of moving electric charges called **lightning?** Study the pictures below to find out how lightning travels between a cloud and the ground. The steps are simplified and show only one way lightning can occur. Compare the process to the tiny flashes you saw when you removed your sweater.

The enormous sparks you see in a thunderstorm and the little sparks from your sweater are examples of one way that electric charges can move—by jumping. On the next page, you will learn how electricity can flow steadily.

On the next page, you will learn how electricity can flow steadily.

Glossary

lightning, a giant spark of electric charges moving between a cloud and the ground, between a cloud and another cloud, or within a cloud

Glossary

▲ Movements within the cloud cause the upper part of the cloud to become positively charged and the lower part to become negatively charged. This negatively charged lower part repels electrons strongly. This force is so strong it pushes away electrons on the ground. This leaves the ground underneath the cloud with extra positive charges. The ground is positively charged.

▲ The many extra electrons in the lower part of the cloud repel each other strongly. The positively charged ground attracts these electrons strongly. Eventually, electrons leap from the lower part of the cloud toward the ground, making a bright spark called lightning.

This photo shows lightning traveling between a cloud and the ground. Lightning can also travel between a cloud and another cloud or even within a cloud. ▼

Metal

The electrons move through metal wire easily. Because metals move, or conduct, electricity well, scientists classify metals as conductors.

Plastic Covering

Scientists call the special plastic that covers the wire an insulator because electricity cannot move through it.

Electric Current

You just learned how a sweater can make sparks and how lightning flashes. Imagine if the electric devices you use every day worked the same way. Your hair dryer would work for just a second. Your flashlight would flash occasionally. Fortunately, electric devices like these use an **electric current,** not jumping charges. In these devices, electricity flows steadily.

To understand how an electric current works, think of a flashlight shining a bright beam. First, the flashlight needs an energy source. A battery changes chemical energy to electrical energy. A chemical reaction in the battery makes electrons move to the negative end of a battery—that's why it's marked negative (−). At the same time, positive charges move to the positive (+) end of the battery. You can see this in the picture at the bottom.

Next, the electrons must move through the wire path. Imagine a wire from the negative part of the battery to the positive part. Electrons gathered at the negative end of the battery would repel and push some electrons out of the battery and into one end of the wire. Positive charges gathered at the positive part of the battery would attract and pull electrons. Pushed from one end and pulled from the other, electrons would move through the metal wire path. Study the picture of the wire on the left to learn why the electrons cannot leave the wire path.

A battery is a source of electrical energy. ▼

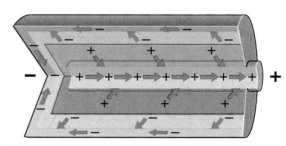

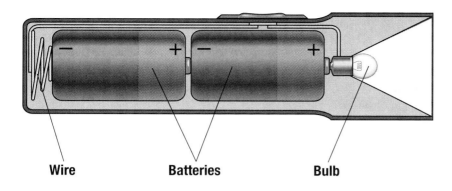

Wire   Batteries   Bulb

▲ *This cutaway view shows the basic parts of a flashlight.*

Scientists call the path that electricity takes an electric circuit. The path begins and ends at the source of electricity. Using the picture in the upper right, follow the path of electricity in a flashlight's electric circuit.

Electric currents are useful because you can use them to do things you want to do, such as shine a flashlight in a dark room. In the next lesson, you will learn more about using and controlling electricity.

Lesson 1 Review

1. What happens when two positively charged objects are brought near each other?

2. Give two examples of when electrons build up and suddenly jump from one object to another.

3. Describe the path electrons take in a simple flashlight circuit.

4. **Cause and Effect**
   When a wire leads from the negative part of a battery to the positive part, two things occur: electricity moves through the wire and a chemical reaction takes place in the battery. Which is the cause? Which is the effect?

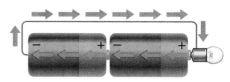

▲ **Electric Circuit of a Flashlight**

Follow the path of the electrons through the circuit. Begin and end at the left battery. As many electrons leave each part of the circuit as enter it.

1 *Electrons leave the negative end of the left battery.*

2 *Electrons move through the wire.*

3 *Electrons enter the light bulb and move through a very tiny wire inside the bulb. This wire gets so hot that it glows brightly.*

4 *Electrons leave the light bulb and move into the positive end of the right battery.*

5 *Electrons travel through the right battery, out the negative end, and into the positive end of the left battery.*

Testing Electrical Conductivity

Process Skills

- observing
- predicting
- classifying
- inferring

Materials

- safety goggles
- D-cell battery
- battery holder
- 3 insulated wires with ends stripped
- flashlight bulb and holder
- toothpick
- penny
- insulated copper wire with ends stripped
- plastic straw
- paper clip
- rubber band
- cardboard strip
- aluminum foil strip

Getting Ready

In this activity you will determine if objects are conductors or insulators of electricity.

Follow This Procedure

1 Make a chart like the one shown. Use your chart to record your predictions and observations.

2 Put on your safety goggles. Put the battery in the battery holder. Connect the wires, battery holder, and light bulb as shown (Photo A). Notice the break in the circuit.

3 Test the circuit by touching the ends of the wires together. If the bulb lights up, you have completed the circuit. Then separate the wires.

 Safety Note It is safe to touch the wires in this activity because a battery produces a small amount of electricity. NEVER touch bare wires connected to other sources of electricity.

Object	Predictions	Observations
Toothpick	X	
Penny	X	
Plastic coating on wire		
Stripped ends of wire		
Plastic straw		
Paper clip		
Rubber band		
Cardboard strip		
Aluminum foil strip		

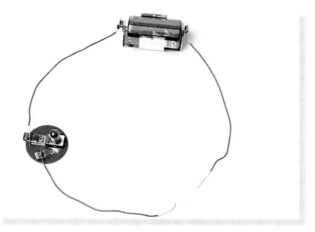

Photo A

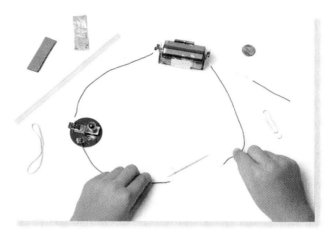

Photo B

④ Place the toothpick flat on your desk. Touch the ends of the wires to the ends of the toothpick (Photo B). Does the toothpick complete the circuit? Record your **observations.**

⑤ Repeat step 4 using a penny instead of a toothpick.

⑥ Look at the other objects. Think about the ones you tested. **Predict** which objects will complete the circuit and light the bulb. Record your predictions in your chart.

⑦ Test each object and record your observations.

Self-Monitoring
Have I correctly completed all the steps?

Interpret Your Results

1. Classify each object as a conductor or insulator. What did the objects that were conductors have in common? What did the objects that were insulators have in common?

2. Make an **inference.** Would a gold ring conduct electricity? Would a piece of wood conduct electricity? Explain.

3. Make an inference. Why do you think electrical cords in your home are covered with thick insulation?

Inquire Further

What other objects conduct electricity? Can a liquid be a conductor? Develop a plan to answer these or other questions you may have.

Self-Assessment

- I followed instructions and used the picture to build a circuit.
- I recorded my **predictions,** tested them with the circuit I built, and recorded my **observations.**
- I **classified** objects as conductors and insulators.
- I made an **inference** about objects that would or would not conduct electricity.
- I made an inference about insulation on electrical cords.

What's the Big Idea?

You will learn:

- how circuits are used in the home.
- how electricity is measured.

Lesson 2

How Is Electricity Used in the Home?

You're late! A storm has knocked out the power. Your alarm clock didn't go off, the bathroom's dark, and the toaster's not working. You'll miss electricity because you use it all over your home in important ways.

Circuits in the Home

Throughout your home, wires in the walls and ceilings form circuits. Electricity flows through these circuits to your alarm clock, toaster, refrigerator, TV, and other electric devices.

You recall that a circuit always leads back to where it started. Imagine the path you would take if you followed an entire circuit. You begin at the power plant, move through a variety of wires and equipment, and finally arrive at your home. The circuit enters your home at your circuit box and continues through a wire to your toaster. Inside your toaster, you follow the circuit through a special wire that heats up and toasts your bread. Then the circuit leaves the toaster, moves through a return wire to the circuit box, exits your home, and continues back to the power plant. Every time you use a plug-in device, you use a very long circuit!

Your home has many circuits. Find the five circuits shown on the next page. Notice that they all pass through the circuit box on their way to and from the power plant. Because of this, electricians usually say that a circuit in the home begins and ends at the circuit box.

Circuit Box

Electricity from a power plant enters your circuit box and provides electricity to each circuit. All circuits pass through your circuit box. Where in your home is your circuit box? Sometimes it is in a kitchen, a basement, a garage, or even outside.

Follow a Circuit

The picture shows some of the circuits in this home. Begin at the circuit box and follow each circuit shown. Each colored path contains a wire to bring electricity to the device and one to bring it back to the circuit box. ▼

Glossary

switch, the part of a circuit that closes the circuit and allows electricity to flow or opens the circuit and prevents the flow of electricity

▲ *When you turn the volume knob on this radio, you complete a circuit and the radio plays.*

The circuits in your home are useful because you can control them. Imagine if your TV was always on full blast and your bedroom light shone all the time.

You use a **switch,** a part of a circuit, to control the flow of electricity. You flip a switch and your radio plays. The circuit in your radio is complex, but one part is simple. One wire has a gap in it. Electricity cannot move past this gap. When you move the switch, you close the gap and your radio plays. A switch opens or closes a gap in a circuit.

In your home, you may use a dimmer switch to dim the lights. Your dimmer switch does more than a regular switch. It lets you control how much electricity moves through the circuit. This way, you can control a light's brightness.

You may control other circuits around your home with switches you don't even notice. Open your refrigerator, and the light inside comes on. Your family may use a thermostat to keep your home comfortable. Study the switches shown on this page to learn what each does.

▲ *When you turn a dimmer switch like this one, you change a lamp's brightness.*

▲ *Look around where your refrigerator door touches when it's closed, and you'll probably find a switch that looks like a lever or a button. Push it and the light will go off. When you shut the door, the door pushes the switch and turns off the light.*

▲ *Your family may use a thermostat, a switch with a built-in thermometer. The switch turns on the heat when your home gets too cold. Some families also use a thermostat to control air conditioning.*

Special switches in your home protect you and your family. If too much electricity flows through a circuit, the wires could get hot and cause a fire. To help prevent this, a circuit box has protective switches called circuit breakers. When too much electricity flows, a circuit breaker automatically flips to the off position. It leaves a gap in the circuit that stops electricity from flowing and helps prevent fires. An adult can close this gap and start electricity flowing again by flipping the circuit breaker to the on position.

Perhaps you live in an older home that uses fuses rather than circuit breakers. Fuses also make a break in a circuit. If too much electricity flows in a circuit, a special wire inside the fuse melts. This leaves a gap in the circuit. A fuse cannot be turned back on. An adult must replace it with a new fuse.

Do you have an outlet with two small buttons in your bathroom or near the sink in your kitchen? You may use one of these **GFCI outlets** (ground fault circuit interrupter outlets) every day without being aware of how it protects you. Except for those two small buttons, GFCI outlets look like regular outlets. They help prevent shocks by instantly switching off the outlet in certain situations. Hair dryers sold today have built-in GFCI plugs that work the same way.

Glossary

GFCI outlet, a special outlet with a safety switch that instantly switches off in some dangerous situations to help prevent a shock

Glossary

▲ *This circuit box holds circuit breakers. Circuit breakers switch off when too much current flows through a circuit.*

▲ *If too much current flows through the special wire in a fuse, the wire melts. This leaves a gap that stops the flow of electricity.*

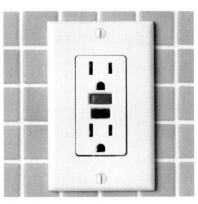

▲ *GFCI outlets help prevent shocks by instantly switching off in some dangerous situations.*

Glossary

volt (vōlt), a unit used to measure how strongly the electrons in a wire are pushed

Measuring Electricity

If it would fit, why couldn't you use a rectangular battery in your flashlight instead of the round kind? How is the electric current used by your toaster different from the current used by an electric stove? Which uses electrical energy more quickly—your toaster or a computer? To answer these questions and to really understand electricity, you need to know how it is measured.

Volts measure how strongly the electrons in a wire are pushed. The graph shows that a rectangular 9-volt battery pushes electricity through a wire 6 times harder than a round $1\frac{1}{2}$-volt battery. Compare the batteries used in the electric devices below. Using a battery with the wrong number of volts could damage an electric device.

Electric stoves and a few other devices use 220-volt electric current. Your toaster and everything else in your home that plugs in uses 110-volt electric current. For safety, 220-volt devices use special outlets and plugs that won't work with regular 110-volt ones.

The electric company makes sure the electric current it sends to your home stays at the right number of volts. This protects you and your electric equipment.

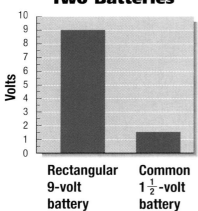

Comparison of Two Batteries

Volts

| Rectangular 9-volt battery | Common $1\frac{1}{2}$-volt battery |

▲ A 9-volt battery pushes electricity through a wire 6 times harder than a $1\frac{1}{2}$-volt battery ($6 \times 1\frac{1}{2}$ volts = 9 volts).

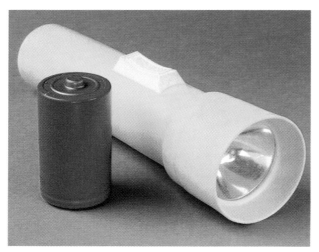

▲ Common batteries with this shape produce a $1\frac{1}{2}$-volt electric current.

▲ This rectangular battery produces a 9-volt electric current.

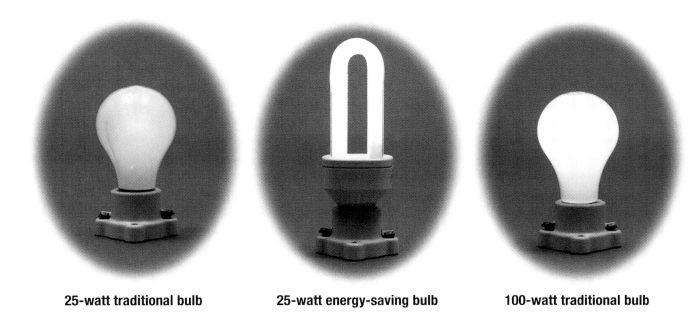

25-watt traditional bulb   **25-watt energy-saving bulb**   **100-watt traditional bulb**

The electric company also measures the electricity you use. How fast you use electrical energy is measured using a unit called a **watt.** A 1,000-watt toaster uses electrical energy ten times as fast as a 100-watt TV. The 100-watt light bulb above uses electrical energy four times as fast as the 25-watt bulbs. Notice below that the 25-watt energy-saving bulb shines as brightly as the 100-watt traditional bulb.

Because the electric company measures how fast your whole family uses electrical energy, it needs a bigger unit, the **kilowatt.** A kilowatt is 1,000 watts. This is how fast ten 100-watt light bulbs use electricity (10 × 100 watts = 1,000 watts = 1 kilowatt). In the United States, a typical home is using a little more than 1 kilowatt at any moment.

▲ Perhaps you use one of the newer, energy-saving light bulbs. They use electrical energy more slowly (fewer watts) but shine as brightly as traditional light bulbs.

Glossary

watt (wot), a unit used to measure how fast electrical energy is used

kilowatt (kil′ə wot′), 1,000 watts

▲ The 25-watt energy-saving bulb in the center shines as brightly as the 100-watt traditional bulb on the right but uses electrical energy only one-fourth as fast.

To measure the total amount of electrical energy you use, you need to take into account not just how fast you use electrical energy, but how long you use it. If left on for a long time, an energy-saving light bulb will use more energy than a traditional one left on for a short time.

Electric companies measure the amount of electrical energy you use in **kilowatt-hours.** If you measure the amount of electrical energy a 1-kilowatt heater uses in 2 hours, you will discover that it uses 2 kilowatt-hours (1 kilowatt × 2 hours = 2 kilowatt-hours). The electric company uses kilowatt-hours to figure out the electric bill for your home. In the United States, a typical home uses about 825 kilowatt-hours of electrical energy each month.

This electrical meter measures the amount of electrical energy in units called kilowatt-hours. ▼

The number of kilowatt-hours you use in your home is probably measured by an electric meter like the one shown on the previous page. You might have one like the one shown at the bottom right of this page. Most meters have five dials arranged by place value. The "ones" place is on the right and the "tens" place is to the left of it. The "hundreds" place is next, and so on. To read these meters, you look at the pointer on each dial and write down the numbers. Try this using the following example. Hint: When a pointer is between two numbers, use the lower number.

▲ On November 10 this meter showed 81,010.

▲ On December 10 this meter showed 81,819.

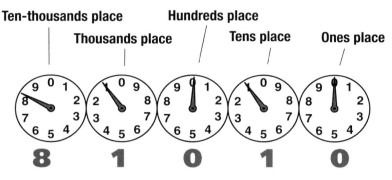

Ten-thousands place   **Hundreds place**

Thousands place   **Tens place**   **Ones place**

8   1   0   1   0

▲ This meter reads 81,010 kilowatt-hours.

To figure out how much electricity your family uses in a month, compare two readings taken one month apart and then subtract. The difference tells you how much electricity you used in one month. In the example at the top right of this page, how much electricity did the family use from November 10 to December 10? In the next lesson, you will learn how the electric company produces the electricity your family uses.

To compute how many kilowatt-hours of electricity this family used from November 10 to December 10, subtract the first reading from the second reading. ▼

December 10 reading	81,819
November 10 reading	− 81,010
Kilowatt-hours of electricity used	809

Some newer electric meters have a digital display that makes reading a meter easier. ▼

Lesson 2 Review

1. What do the electric circuits in your home do?
2. How do watts differ from kilowatts?
3. **Scales and Bar Graphs**
   How could you change the scale on the bar graph on page B124 to show a 12-volt car battery?

Making a Dimmer Switch

Process Skills

- observing
- inferring

Materials

- safety goggles
- 2 D-cell batteries
- electrical tape
- 3 insulated wires with ends stripped
- flashlight bulb and holder
- clear tape
- graphite in pencil split lengthwise

Getting Ready

In this activity you will make a simple dimmer switch.

The graphite in the pencil used in this activity is a form of carbon.

Follow This Procedure

1 Make a chart like the one shown. Use your chart to record your observations.

	Observations of bulb
As wire ends are moved apart	
As wire ends are moved closer together	

2 Put on your safety goggles. Tape two D-cell batteries together with electrical tape. The positive terminal of one battery must be against the negative terminal of the other battery.

3 Look at the incomplete circuit in Photo A. Draw the circuit and then build it. Use electrical tape to attach the ends of two wires firmly to the terminals of the batteries.

4 Notice the break in the circuit. If you connect the wire ends with a conductor the bulb will light. If you connect the wire ends with an insulator the bulb will not light. Check your circuit by touching the free ends of the wires together. The bulb should light. Separate the wires.

 Safety Note It is safe to touch the wires in this activity because a battery produces a small amount of electricity. NEVER touch bare wires connected to other sources of electricity.

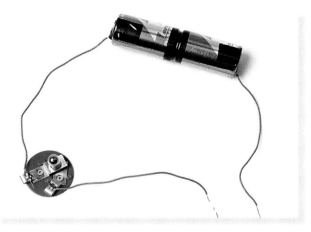

Photo A

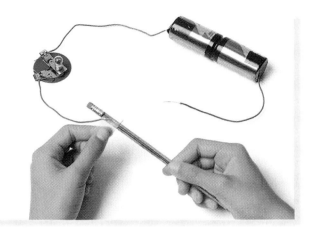

Photo B

5 Use clear tape to attach the free end of one wire to the graphite at one end of the pencil (Photo B). Add the pencil and attached wire to your drawing.

6 Touch the free end of the other wire to the graphite very close to the taped wire. **Observe** the bulb's brightness.

7 Slowly slide the free end away from the taped wire until it reaches the end of the graphite. Then slide the free end back to its starting position. Record your observations.

Interpret Your Results

1. Describe how the brightness of the bulb changed as you moved the wire ends apart and back together.

2. On your drawing, write a *B* where the wire was placed when the light was brightest. Then write a *D* where the wire was placed when the light was dimmest.

3. Make an **inference.** Is graphite a perfect conductor, a perfect insulator, or something in between? Explain.

Inquire Further

What would happen if you used a bare copper wire instead of graphite to make a dimmer switch? Develop a plan to answer this or other questions you may have.

Self-Assessment

- I followed instructions to make a dimmer switch.
- I recorded my **observations.**
- I described how the brightness of the bulb changed.
- I indicated on a drawing where the wire was placed when the bulb was brightest and dimmest.
- I made an **inference** about graphite as a conductor and insulator.

You will learn:

- how electricity and magnetism are related.
- how generators use magnets to produce electricity.
- what energy sources generators use.

Lesson 3

What Produces the Electricity Used in the Home?

Whew! Ever pedal a generator at a science museum? You work very hard to just light a bulb. After a few minutes, you're so tired you have to stop. You wonder, "How does this thing change my hard work into electrical energy?"

Magnetism Produces Electricity

History of Science

Did you know that electricity and magnetism are closely related? Scientists did not clearly understand that they are really two parts of the same thing until the 1800s. Electricity can make magnetism, and magnetism can make electricity.

Scientists learned about magnetism first. In the ancient Greek town of Magnesia, they discovered a stone with an unusual property—iron would cling to it! Later, scientists discovered the basic principles of magnetism that you know. Study them in the chart below. Compare the principles of magnetism and electricity.

Magnetism and electricity are closely related. ▼

Magnetism	Electricity
Two opposite poles attract: N attracts S.	Two opposite charges attract: + attracts −.
Like poles repel: N repels N, and S repels S.	Like charges repel: + repels +, and − repels −.
Magnetic forces can attract and repel at a distance, without touching.	Electric forces can attract and repel at a distance, without touching.
Magnetism can make electricity.	Electricity can make magnetism.

As you can see, the principles of magnetism and the principles of electricity are similar. Scientists in the 1800s thought so too. They investigated. First, they discovered that electricity could produce magnetism. When electricity flows through a wire, the wire becomes magnetic. Perhaps you have made an electromagnet like the one on the right.

Later, scientists discovered that magnetism can make electricity. If you move a magnet near a wire, the motion of the magnet causes electrons to flow in the wire. In the science museum demonstration shown below, the volunteer moves a very powerful magnet through a thick coil of wire and produces enough electricity to light the tiny bulb.

Scientists used the discovery that magnetism can produce electricity to invent a device that could make large amounts of electricity cheaply. This device changed the world. Turn the page to learn what this device is and how it works.

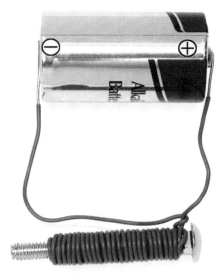

▲ An electromagnet uses electricity to make magnetism. When electricity moves in a wire, it produces magnetism. If you coil a wire around a bolt many, many times, you make this effect much stronger. You turn on the electromagnet by sending electricity through the wire.

When a magnet moves near a wire, it produces electricity. If you coil a wire many, many times, you make this effect stronger. This student pushes an extremely powerful magnet through a very thick coil of wire. This produces enough electricity to light the tiny bulb. ▼

Glossary

generator
(jen′ə rā′tər), a device that uses a magnet to change mechanical energy into electrical energy

How Generators Work

Once scientists discovered that magnetism could produce electricity, they developed electrical generators. A **generator** is a device that uses a magnet to change mechanical energy into electrical energy.

Some generators produce electricity by moving a coil of wire near a magnet. Other generators move the magnet instead, and the coil doesn't move. That's how the generators shown on these pages work. Study the generator on the next page. Find the three basic parts of the generator and discover what each does.

Moving water is the source of mechanical energy that turns the magnets in this generator. ▼

A Generator

Drive Shaft
The drive shaft is connected to the magnet inside the coil of wire. A source of energy is needed to turn the drive shaft and the magnet.

Strong Magnet
This strong magnet turns inside a large coil of wire. Most generators use electromagnets instead of regular magnets.

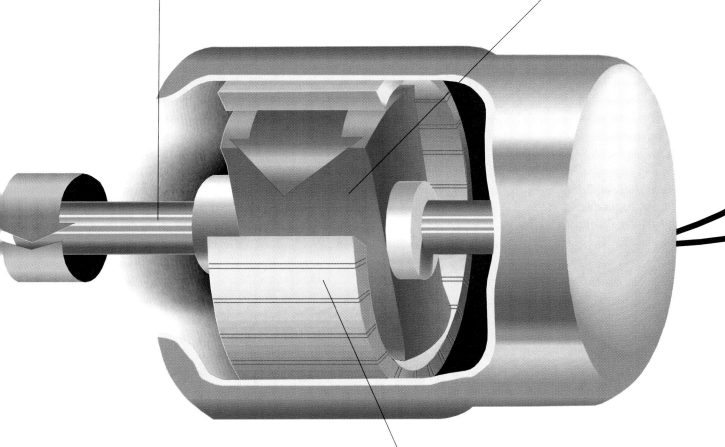

Coil of Wire
The moving magnet makes electrons flow in the coil of wire. This is an electric current. It is carried by wires to where it is needed.

Powering Generators

Different sources of energy can be used to turn a generator's drive shaft and produce electricity. Notice in each of the pictures below that the generator's drive shaft attaches to a turbine. Like a pinwheel that spins when air rushes past it, each turbine below spins as steam or water moves through it. This spins the drive shaft. The drive shaft turns a magnet inside a coil of wire in the generator. Electricity is produced.

An energy source is used to turn a turbine. The turbine turns a drive shaft. The drive shaft turns a magnet in a generator. The generator makes electricity that is delivered by power lines to homes and businesses. Trace these steps for each energy source shown below. ▼

Oil from an oil well is burned to boil water, producing steam that turns the turbine. ▼

Coal from a mine is burned to boil water, producing steam that turns the turbine. ▼

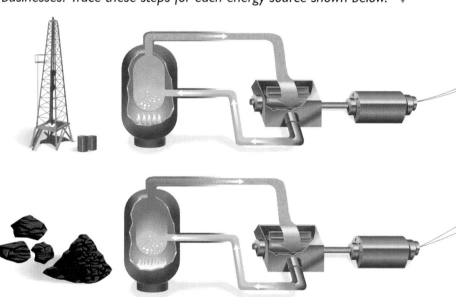

Uranium ore from a mine is used in a nuclear reactor to boil water, producing steam that turns the turbine. ▼

A river flows into a dam. The energy of moving water turns the turbine. ▼

A few power plants use tides or waves as their energy source. Modern windmills, such as those to the right, use wind energy to spin built-in generators. Altogether, generators produce almost all the electricity people use.

Some devices produce electricity without a generator. Batteries change chemical energy directly into electrical energy. Special solar panels change light energy directly into electrical energy.

▲ The blades of a modern windmill act like a turbine. Wind energy turns the turbine, which turns a drive shaft, which turns a magnet inside the built-in generator.

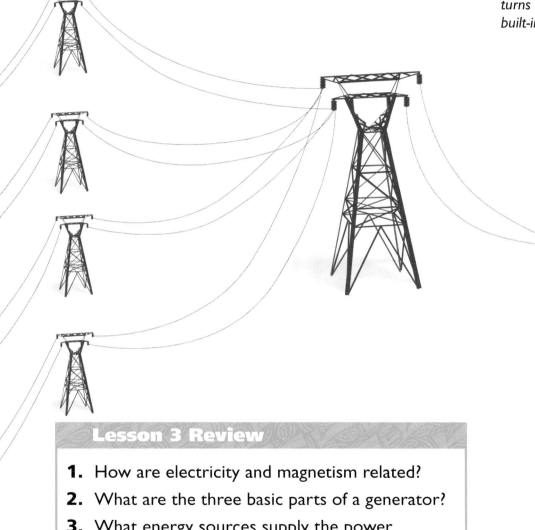

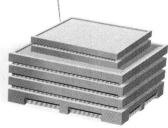

Lesson 3 Review

1. How are electricity and magnetism related?
2. What are the three basic parts of a generator?
3. What energy sources supply the power for generators?
4. **Identify the Main Idea**
   What is the main idea of the chart on page B 130?

Making a Current Detector

Process Skills

- observing
- inferring

Materials

- safety goggles
- 2 enameled wires with ends stripped
- metric ruler
- directional compass
- bathroom tissue tube
- masking tape
- bar magnet
- D-cell battery

Getting Ready

In this activity you can find out how the magnetic needle of a directional compass can be used as an electric current detector.

Keep the compass away from metal objects that may interfere with the magnetized needle.

Follow This Procedure

1 Make a chart like the one shown. Use your chart to record your observations.

	Observations of current detector
Magnet moved inside of coil	
Current detector connected to battery	

2 Put on your safety goggles. Leaving 25 cm of wire loose on both ends, wrap one of the wires around the N-S ends of the compass (Photo A). This device will be your current detector.

3 Wrap the second wire around the bathroom tissue tube. Again, leave 25 cm of wire unwrapped at both ends. Carefully remove the tube, keeping the wire coiled. Secure the coil at the top and bottom with strips of masking tape to prevent it from unraveling (Photo B).

Photo A

Photo B

④ Now try to create a current in the second coil using a magnet. Connect the ends of the second coil to the ends of the current detector.

⑤ Move the magnet back and forth within the coil (Photo C). Try to pass the magnet through the coil quickly. Be sure to put the entire length of the bar in the coil. Look closely at the compass needle. Record your **observations.**

⑥ Now compare the current you produced with current produced by a battery. Disconnect the current detector from the coil. Touch the wires from the current detector to the terminals of the battery. What happens to the compass needle? Record your observations.

Interpret Your Results

1. Why did the needle move when you moved the bar magnet back and forth in the wire coil?

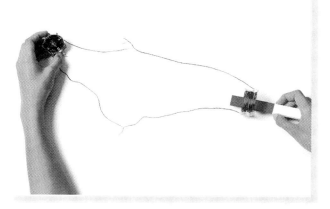

Photo C

2. Compare the results for the magnet in the coil and the battery. What can you **infer** about current produced by the moving magnet and the current produced by the battery?

 Inquire Further

What are some ways you could increase the electric current produced by the moving magnet? Develop a plan to answer this or other questions you may have.

Chapter 4 Review

Chapter Main Ideas

Lesson 1

• Electrons sometimes move from one object to another. Objects can be uncharged, positively charged, or negatively charged. Objects with opposite charges attract each other (+ attracts −). Objects with the same charge repel each other (− repels −, + repels +).

• Extra electrons on negatively charged objects repel each other. Positively charged objects attract these electrons. When these forces are great enough, some of these electrons may leap from the negatively charged object to the positively charged object.

• The same forces that attract and repel jumping charges make electricity flow in a current. Electric current flows steadily, usually in a wire.

Lesson 2

• Energy flows through a circuit controlled by a variety of switches.

• Electrical force is measured in volts. How fast electrical energy is used is measured in watts and kilowatts. The amount of electricity used is measured in kilowatt-hours.

Lesson 3

• Electricity and magnetism are closely related. Each can be used to produce the other.

• Generators produce electricity by moving a magnet near a coil of wire or by moving a coil of wire near a magnet.

• Energy sources commonly used by generators include coal, oil, nuclear fuel, and energy from falling water.

Reviewing Science Words and Concepts

a. electric current	**e.** kilowatt-hour
b. GFCI outlet	**f.** lightning
c. generator	**g.** switch
d. kilowatt	**h.** volt
	i. watt

1. A giant spark of moving electric charges is called ___.

2. A wire carries a steady flow of ___.

3. A ___ can either open a circuit or close a circuit.

4. A special outlet that instantly switches off in dangerous situations is called a ___.

5. A unit that measures how strongly the electrons in a wire are pushed is called a ___.

6. A basic unit used to measure how fast electrical energy is used is called a ___.

7. A ___ equals 1,000 watts.

8. The amount of electricity used in a home is measured in a unit called a ___.

9. A ___ uses a magnet to change mechanical energy into electrical energy.

Explaining Science

Draw and label a diagram or write a paragraph to answer these questions.

1. How can the movement of electrons from one uncharged object to another cause the objects to attract each other?

2. What is the difference between kilowatts and kilowatt-hours?

3. In what ways are magnetism and electricity similar?

Using Skills

1. In the United States, common household electric current is 110 volts. Some countries use 220-volt electric current. Everywhere, people use many of the same batteries, such as AA, C, D, and the rectangular (9-volt) batteries.

The two bar graphs show the same data. Which **bar graph** has a **scale** that is better for comparing different batteries? Which graph is better for comparing household electric current?

2. You open the refrigerator door and observe a light on. **Communicate** what

you know about circuits to explain why the light turns on and off.

3. Suppose that on March 3 your electric meter showed 22,022 kilowatt-hours. On April 3 it showed 22,919 kilowatt-hours. **Estimate** how much electricity your family used in one month.

Critical Thinking

1. Your friend decides to **experiment** with charges. She rubs a balloon on her wool shirt and places it on the wall. It sticks! Write a paragraph that explains why the balloon stuck to the wall.

2. Here are five steps in making electricity. Put them in the correct **sequence: a.** drive shaft turns a magnet in generator, **b.** power source is used to turn turbine, **c.** electricity is delivered by power lines, **d.** generator makes electricity, **e.** turbine turns drive shaft.

3. You take clothes out of the clothes dryer and notice that your socks are sticking together. You pull them apart and you see a spark! **Draw a conclusion** about why this happened. Write a paragraph to explain.

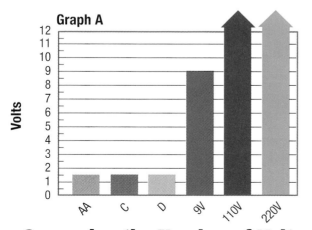

Comparing the Number of Volts

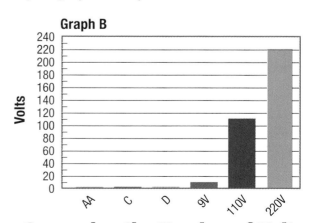

Comparing the Number of Volts

Unit B Review

Reviewing Words and Concepts

Choose at least three words from the Chapter 1 list below.
Use the words to write a paragraph about how these concepts
are related. Do the same for each of the other chapters.

Chapter 1
atom
element
mixture
molecule
periodic table
solution

Chapter 2
acceleration
friction
gravity
inertia
speed
velocity

Chapter 3
frequency
kinetic energy
mechanical
 energy
potential energy
vibration
wavelength

Chapter 4
electric current
generator
lightning
switch
volt
watt

Reviewing Main Ideas

Each of the statements below is false. Change the underlined
word or words to make each statement true.

1. The periodic table classifies compounds by the structure of their atoms.

2. Protons and neutrons make up the molecule of an atom.

3. A solution is a chemical property in which one substance is spread evenly through another.

4. Gravity is measured by how far something travels in a certain amount of time.

5. Weight is a force that resists movement of one surface past another.

6. The action force and the reaction force are a pair of masses.

7. Sound is stored energy or energy an object has due to its position.

8. Waves of radiant energy can travel where there is no vibration.

9. Electricity can flow through a circuit controlled by generators.

10. Electric current is the distance from one point on a wave to the same point on the next wave.

Interpreting Data

The following diagram shows a model of the structure of an atom of an element. Use the diagram to answer the questions below.

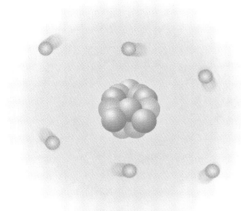

1. How many electrons are around the atom's nucleus?

2. If the atom does not have a charge, how many protons must it have?

3. What is the element's atomic number?

Communicating Science

1. Draw and label a diagram that shows one way to separate the parts of a mixture.

2. Draw and label a diagram to indicate what can happen when forces overcome inertia. You can use arrows to show the directions of the forces.

3. Draw and label a diagram that shows how kinetic energy and potential energy are related.

4. Write a paragraph explaining how electricity and magnetism are related.

Applying Science

1. Draw and label a diagram that shows how electricity travels inside a home. Identify ways the electricity is used.

2. Write a paragraph explaining a variety of ways to separate the parts of different mixtures used in the home.

Unit B
Performance Review

Science Fair

Using what you learned in this unit, complete one or more of the following activities to be included as a presentation in a Science Fair. The presentations will help the people who attend the fair learn more about matter and energy.

Cooking

Collect some recipes for healthy foods. Prepare a display or make a report explaining how preparing and cooking different foods results in physical or chemical changes in the substances used in the recipes.

Environment

Make a poster or other display for the science fair that shows ways you and your family could help the environment by using less energy.

Weather

Write a report telling what causes lightning. Illustrate your report to help others understand what happens during a thunderstorm.

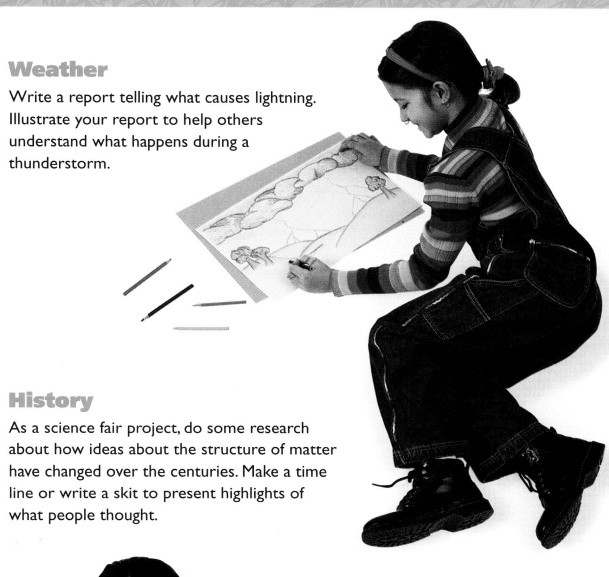

History

As a science fair project, do some research about how ideas about the structure of matter have changed over the centuries. Make a time line or write a skit to present highlights of what people thought.

Art

Design a bicycle or other means of transportation that illustrates the advantages of streamlining. You could make a drawing or build a model to communicate your ideas.

Using Reference Sources to Create a Timeline

Using Reference Sources

People use many kinds of reference sources to find information. For example, a dictionary is helpful when you want to know the meaning of a word. If you want to know more about a subject, you could use an encyclopedia or other book, or do on-line research using a computer. Dictionaries, encyclopedias, and on-line services are all types of reference sources.

Make a List

In Chapter 4, you learned about some of the ways people use electricity. Think about some of the things in your home that use electricity to work. List at least five of these things. Then use at least two different reference sources to find out when the items on your list were invented. Write these dates beside the items on your list.

Create a Time Line

A time line is a diagram that shows events and the dates they occurred. The dates on a time line are arranged in the order in which the events happened. Create a time line that shows when different kinds of items that use electricity were first invented. Use your list and the dates you researched. Be sure to put a title on your time line.

Remember to:

1. **Prewrite** Organize your thoughts.

2. **Draft** Create your time line.

3. **Revise** Share your work and then make changes.

4. **Edit** Proofread for mistakes and fix them.

5. **Publish** Share your time line with your class.

Unit C
Earth Science

Science and Technology
In Your World!

Earthquake Alert!

Thanks to the Global Positioning System, or GPS, scientists can detect the sideways movements of the earth's crust within a few millimeters. GPS uses radio signals from satellites to identify the location of things. Delivery companies use GPS to keep track of their trucks. Scientists hope to use GPS to better predict earthquakes, volcanoes, and other changes in the earth's crust. You'll learn more about movements of the earth's crust in **Chapter 1 The Changing Earth**.

Looking for What Isn't There

Up, up, and away! Scientists release a large balloon that within two hours will soar as high as 35 kilometers above the earth. Attached to it is an instrument that measures the amount of ozone high in the earth's atmosphere. This layer of ozone shields you from harmful radiation. Instruments on balloons and satellites help scientists learn about the holes that have appeared in this protective layer. You'll learn about protecting the earth's air, water, and land resources in **Chapter 2 The Earth's Resources.**

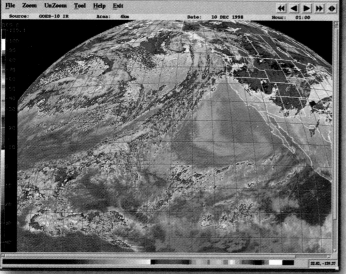

Are Clouds Really Green?

The cold air masses are easy to see in this color map. But clouds aren't really green! Computers turn satellite measurements of temperature, cloud cover, and rainfall into a grid of numbers. The numbers are assigned different colors. The resulting colorful maps show conditions in the clouds and the ocean water below. You'll read more about factors that affect climate in **Chapter 3 Climate.**

Robo-Telescopes

Don't have a telescope at home, or don't have a dark enough sky to study the stars? Not a problem! Today, any person who uses the Internet can look at fresh images made by some of the best telescopes in the world. The scientists who control the telescopes and make the images can aim, focus, and operate the telescope from far away using a computer, robotic controls, and modem connections. You'll learn more about telescopes in **Chapter 4 Astronomy.**

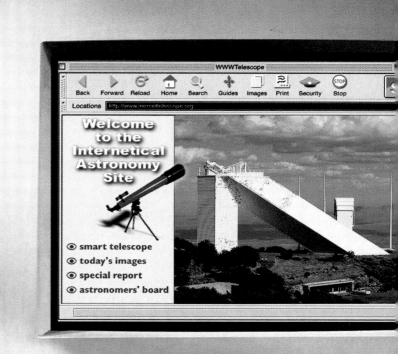

C 3

Just a Click Away!

See volcanoes erupt and continents collide. With the latest CD-ROM encyclopedias you can see the earth in action. It only takes a click!

Chapter 1
The Changing Earth

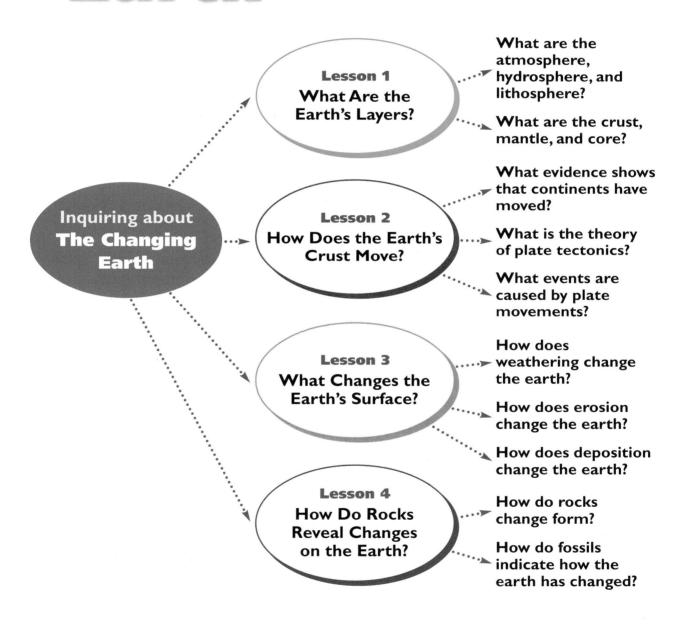

Inquiring about The Changing Earth

Lesson 1
What Are the Earth's Layers?

What are the atmosphere, hydrosphere, and lithosphere?

What are the crust, mantle, and core?

Lesson 2
How Does the Earth's Crust Move?

What evidence shows that continents have moved?

What is the theory of plate tectonics?

What events are caused by plate movements?

Lesson 3
What Changes the Earth's Surface?

How does weathering change the earth?

How does erosion change the earth?

How does deposition change the earth?

Lesson 4
How Do Rocks Reveal Changes on the Earth?

How do rocks change form?

How do fossils indicate how the earth has changed?

Copy the chapter graphic organizer onto your own paper. This organizer shows you what the whole chapter is all about. As you read the lessons and do the activities, look for answers to the questions and write them on your organizer.

Exploring a Model of the Earth's Layers

Process Skills

- making and using models
- estimating and measuring
- observing

Materials

- piece of paper
- metric ruler
- clay of different colors
- plastic knife

Explore

1 Begin **making** a **model** of the layers of the earth by drawing a circle with a diameter of 35 mm. Use the ruler to check your **measurement.** Make a dome out of one color of clay to fit on the circle. This dome represents the earth's center.

2 Use clay of a different color to add a layer 14 mm thick. Place this over the first layer. This represents a layer that surrounds the earth's center.

3 Now use clay of a different color to make a final layer. Press the clay to make the layer as thin as you can. It should be less than 1 mm thick. Place this on the second layer. This represents the earth's outer layer, including the surface of the earth.

4 Use the plastic knife to cut the model in half. You will learn more about the earth's layers in the following lesson.

Reflect

1. Compare and contrast the different layers. What **observations** can you make about the layers?

2. How do you think your model is different from the earth?

? Inquire Further

How could you change your model to show oceans and land masses of the earth? Develop a plan to answer this or other questions you may have.

Sequencing

In the activity, *Exploring a Model of the Earth's Layers*, you made a model of the different layers that make up our planet. To do so, you had to know the correct order of the earth's layers. Putting things in their correct order is called **sequencing**. Sequencing includes putting events or things in an order from first to last, top to bottom, or largest to smallest.

Reading Vocabulary

sequencing (sē′kwəns ing), putting in the correct order

Example

In Lesson 1, *What Are the Earth's Layers?*, you will learn about the three layers that make up the earth. You will learn where they are, how thick they are, and what they are made of. How would you sequence these layers based on their positions, beginning with the outer layer? As you read the lesson, fill in the chart below.

Earth's Layers
1.
2.
3.

Talk About It!

1. Is the sequence of the earth's layers the same everywhere on the planet?

2. What happens to temperature as you move from the surface of the earth towards the core?

What's the Big Idea?

You will learn:
- about the atmosphere, hydrosphere, and lithosphere.
- about the crust, mantle, and core.

Glossary

atmosphere
(at′mə sfir), the layer of gases that surrounds the earth and contains the clouds

hydrosphere
(hī′drə sfir), the water part of the earth's surface

lithosphere
(lith′ə sfir), the rigid outer shell of the earth

Lesson 1

What Are the Earth's Layers?

An apple has a peel, a tangy flesh, and a core. A boiled egg has a shell, a white, and a yolk. A peach has a thin skin, a juicy fruit, and a pit. Like these foods, the earth has different layers.

Atmosphere, Hydrosphere, Lithosphere

If you were in space looking down at the earth, you'd see clouds, oceans, and continents on a slightly flattened sphere. You'd be looking at the earth's atmosphere, hydrosphere, and lithosphere shown on the next page.

The **atmosphere** is the layer of gases that surrounds the planet. The clouds are in this layer. Thunder, lightning, wind, and rain occur here. The atmosphere contains gases that organisms need to live. It helps protect living things from being damaged by too much sunlight. Most of the atmosphere is close to the surface of the earth. As you go higher and higher, there is less and less gas and the air pressure decreases.

Beneath the atmosphere is the hydrosphere. The **hydrosphere** is the water part of the earth's surface. It includes oceans, lakes, rivers, streams, and glaciers. Water covers almost three-quarters of the earth's surface. Without this water, life could not exist.

You live on the rigid outer shell of the earth called the **lithosphere**. The lithosphere contains the rocks, soils, and minerals that plants need. Your home is attached to the lithosphere. Mines are dug into it.

Although the atmosphere, hydrosphere, and lithosphere form layers, parts of each layer can be found in the others. The atmosphere contains dust from the lithosphere and droplets of water and ice crystals from the hydrosphere. Solids and gases mix in the oceans. Even the lithosphere contains gases in the soil and water under the ground. The way the three layers interact makes it possible for you to live on the earth.

Atmosphere

The atmosphere is mostly nitrogen (about 78%) and oxygen (about 21%). Less than 0.04% is carbon dioxide. Small amounts of water vapor and some other gases make up the rest.

Hydrosphere

From space you would see that water covers most of the earth. Oceans cover about 71% of the earth's surface. Glaciers cover about 3%. Lakes and rivers cover less than 1%.

Lithosphere

When you look at the continents, you see the lithosphere, but the lithosphere extends under the oceans too. It covers the entire earth.

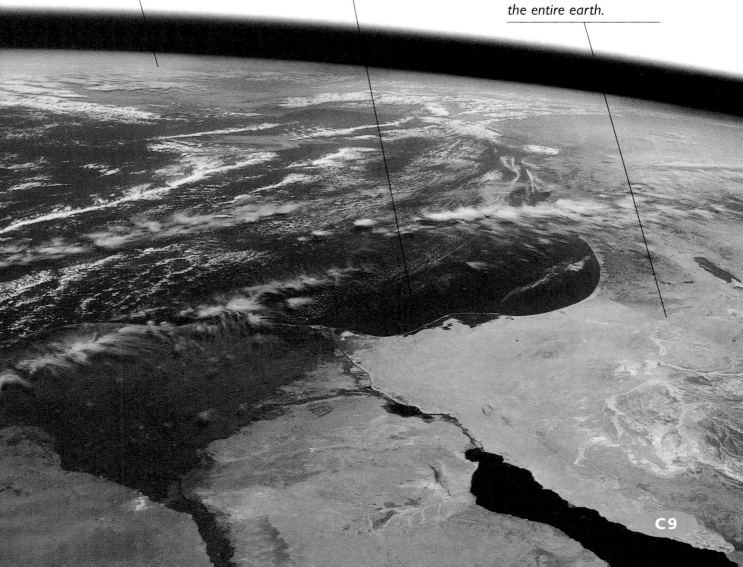

Crust, Mantle, Core

You learned a little about the lithosphere—the hard outer shell of the earth. Now pretend you have an imaginary ship that can move safely down into the earth. Get ready to explore what's beneath your school. Follow along on the diagram of the earth below.

Lithosphere

The rigid outer shell of the earth includes all the crust and the rigid top part of the mantle.

Crust

The crust is about 40 kilometers thick in many places. It is solid rock. The temperature increases from the surface to the inner edge.

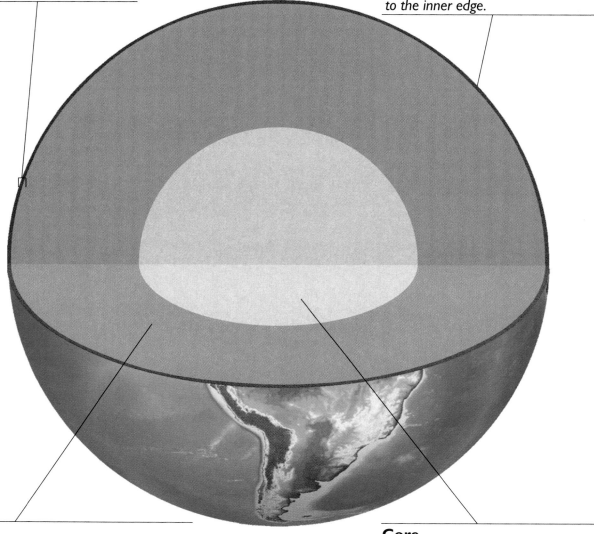

Mantle

The mantle is about 2,900 kilometers thick. Below the rigid, solid top, the mantle is partly melted rock. Below that the mantle is solid again. The temperature continues to increase with depth.

Core

The distance from the outer edge of the core to the center of the core is about 3,500 kilometers. The outer part is liquid iron and nickel. The inner part is solid iron and nickel.

As you plunge into the earth, you enter the outer layer, or **crust.** As you travel into this hard rock layer, you notice that it covers the whole earth. It is thinner under the oceans and thicker under the continents. As you dive deeper and deeper into the crust, the temperature rises.

As you continue down, you eventually enter the mantle. The **mantle**—the middle layer of the earth—is beneath the crust. Notice that the mantle is much thicker than the crust. The upper part of the mantle is rigid. This rigid part of the mantle, along with the whole crust, makes up the lithosphere. As you go deeper, the temperature continues to increase. Soon the mantle rock is not quite solid anymore. As you go even deeper, it becomes solid again.

As you continue to go deeper, you eventually enter the **core**—the center part of the earth made of iron and nickel. In the outer part of the core, the iron and nickel are melted. As you go deeper into the outer part of the core, the temperature continues to rise.

As you go still deeper, more and more of the earth is above you. The pressure becomes so great it forces the melted iron and nickel to become solid—yet the metal is white hot! Now, you are in the inner core. Finally, you arrive at the center of the earth. You can go down no further. All directions are up.

Lesson 1 Review

1. What are the three parts of the earth that are visible from space? Which is mostly liquid? mostly gas? mostly solid?

2. What are the three layers of the earth? Which is the coolest? the hottest?

3. Sequence
Place the following terms in order, beginning at the center of the earth: **a.** atmosphere, **b.** core, **c.** crust, **d.** hydrosphere, **e.** mantle.

Investigating Moving Continents

Process Skills

- observing
- making and using models
- communicating

Materials

- outline map of the continents
- colored pencils or crayons
- map of the world
- scissors
- sheet of paper
- glue

Getting Ready

In this activity you will find out how continents seem to fit together.

Be consistent with your coloring on all continents. Make sure to use the same color for all coal deposits, each fossil type, all mountains, and glacier deposit areas.

Follow This Procedure

1 Obtain an outline map of the continents, or trace the continents shown on the next page onto a piece of paper. Use colored pencils or crayons to color the features labeled on the continents. Use one color for all mountain ranges and another color for all coal deposits. Use a different color for each type of fossil and another color for glacier deposit areas.

2 Use the world map to identify the continents. Label each continent with its proper name. Use scissors to cut out the continents.

3 Arrange the continents on a sheet of paper, using the world map as a guide.

4 **Observe** the continents and the features you have colored. Now you will **model** how the continents may have once fit together. Move the continents so they fit together like a puzzle. Slide them together. Do not pick up the pieces. Use the simplest pathway to fit them together. After you have found the best fit, glue them onto the sheet of paper.

Self-Monitoring

Have I found the best fit and glued down all of the continents?

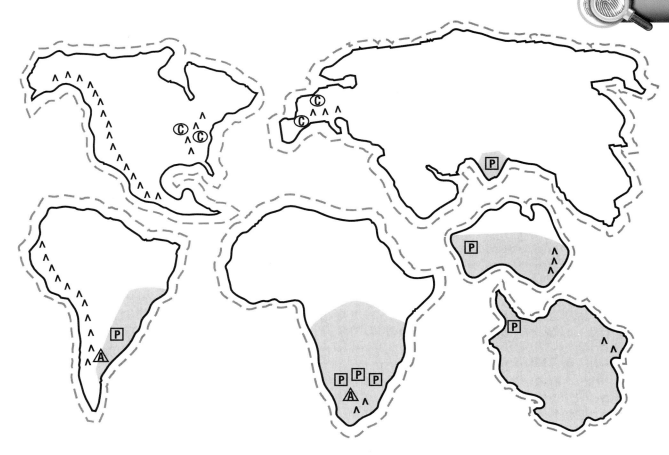

Interpret Your Results

1. How well did your continents fit together? How did you decide to fit them together this way?

2. Compare and contrast your map with the world map. **Communicate.** Discuss the differences and similarities with your group.

3. Observe the colored areas on your continents. Do you see any patterns? If so, what are they?

 Inquire Further

What other ways can the continents fit together? Develop a plan to answer this or other questions you may have.

Map key	
∧ Mountains	P Plant fossils
C Coal deposits	Glacier deposit areas
A Animal fossils	

Lesson 2

How Does the Earth's Crust Move?

It's 6 A.M. It's not time to get up. Why is someone shaking you? You turn but there's no one there. The gentle shaking stops. No damage done. You have just experienced an earthquake.

Moving Continents

History of Science

Geographers in the 1500s made the first maps that accurately showed the continents. They used information from the explorers who sailed all over the world. As the geographers studied the maps, they noticed that some continents seemed to fit together like the pieces of a jigsaw puzzle.

During the 1900s, scientists mapped the continents' edges. These edges lie beneath the oceans. When scientists included the edges, the continents fit together even better. Look at the jigsaw map on the next page. Notice how well the continents fit together.

Many scientists tried to develop hypotheses to explain the shape of the continents. One hypothesis was that continents were once connected, but they have moved apart. Scientists have found evidence that supports this hypothesis.

Life Science

Notice on the maps on the next page that fossils of *Mesosaurus* were found in only two places. The places are close to each other on the jigsaw map. Today, an ocean of salt water separates the remains of these freshwater reptiles. These remains support the hypothesis that the continents were once attached.

Evidence from Ancient Mountains

Mountain ranges on five continents fit together on the jigsaw map. Scientists discovered that the ancient rock formations of these mountains matched too.

Evidence from Coal Deposits

There are many types and grades of coal. Yet coal deposits in North America match identical deposits in Europe when the continents are connected on the jigsaw map.

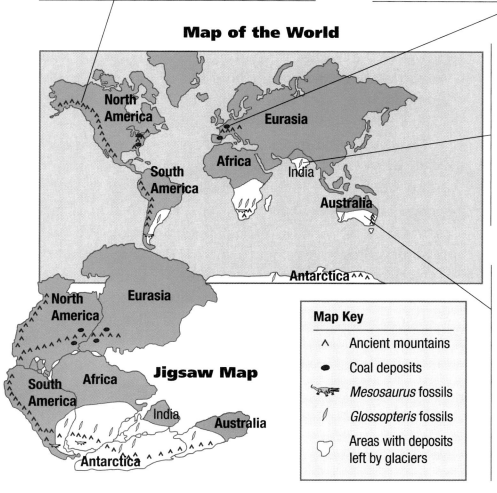

Map of the World

Jigsaw Map

Map Key

∧	Ancient mountains
●	Coal deposits
	Mesosaurus fossils
∥	*Glossopteris* fossils
	Areas with deposits left by glaciers

Evidence from Fossil Discoveries

Scientists found fossils of a warm-weather fern (Glossopteris) in Antarctica and other locations far apart from each other. When they put the continents together, the locations matched. Other fossils, such as Mesosaurus, also matched.

Evidence from Deposits Left by Glaciers

Glaciers leave behind deposits and marks that show where they were located. Scientists have found these deposits and marks in places near the warm equator. Notice on the jigsaw map that these ancient glaciers on different continents fit together.

The maps above show features on different continents such as ancient mountains and coal deposits. They too match up on the jigsaw map.

Sometimes features don't match. Oddly, this also supports the hypothesis. Features older than 150 or 200 million years match. However, younger features don't match. Scientists now think that this indicates when the continents began to separate. Features formed after continents separated would not be expected to match. Scientists have gathered many other types of evidence. The evidence supports the hypothesis that the continents were once attached and have moved apart.

Glossary

plate tectonics
(tek ton′iks), a theory stating that the earth's surface is broken into plates that move

plate, a large section of the earth's surface made of the crust and the rigid top part of the mantle

Quest. 1

How Plates Move

1 *Heat below the mantle makes even the solid part of mantle flow very slowly, as though it were a very thick liquid. The arrow shows some of the hot mantle rising toward the crust.*

2 *The hot, rising part of the mantle cools as it nears the crust. The arrow shows the cooling mantle being pushed aside by more hot, rising mantle. As the cooling mantle moves sideways, it drags along the plate floating on top of it.*

3 *The mantle continues to cool as it moves sideways. The arrow shows the cooled mantle sinking back down.*

4 *Later, the mantle may be warmed and rise again.*

Plate Tectonics

History of Science

A hypothesis that has been supported by evidence from experiments or observations becomes known as a theory. You learned that there was a great amount of evidence to support the hypothesis that the continents did move. However, the hypothesis had a major weakness. There was little evidence showing how the continents moved. Scientists have worked for nearly fifty years to find evidence that explains how the continents move.

The theory that explains how continents move is called **plate tectonics.** Scientists have learned that the surface of the earth is broken into about twenty sections, or **plates.** Each plate includes a section of the earth's crust and the rigid top part of the mantle below it. Some plates have only ocean crust on them. Most have both ocean and continental crust. Together, the plates cover the entire earth. They fit together but keep changing because they are slowly moving. The plates move at about the speed your fingernails grow. Study the illustration below to learn how the plates move.

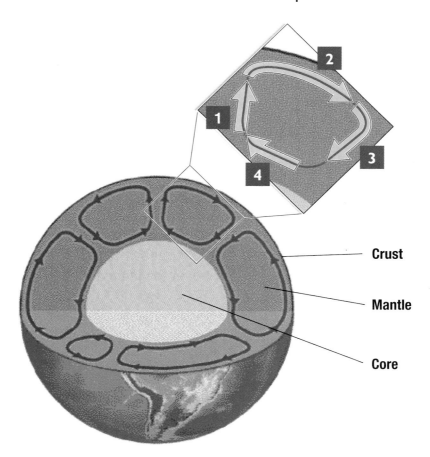

Crust

Mantle

Core

Events Caused by Plate Movements

More evidence for the theory of plate tectonics comes from observing the locations of active volcanoes, severe earthquakes, and mountains. The map below shows these locations. Scientists studied maps of these locations to learn more about plates. They also studied the directions the plates moved during earthquakes.

Scientists looked for patterns on the maps. They used the information they found to make hypotheses about where plates meet. The edges of plates—the places where plates meet—are called plate boundaries.

Look at the map below and find the patterns scientists found. The orange lines show where most scientists think the boundaries of the major plates are located. The arrows show the directions the plates are moving.

Map Key	
⊙	Earthquakes
▲	Active volcanoes
∧	Mountains
▬	Plate boundaries
➡	Plate movements

Arrows show the direction plates are moving. ▼

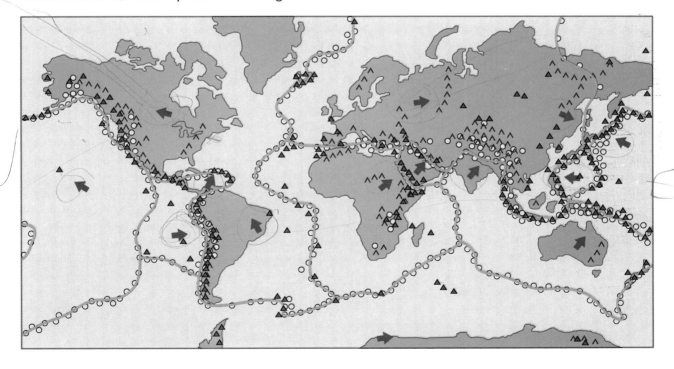

The diagram below shows the movements of four plates. At the plate boundary between Plate B and Plate C, new crust is forming. It is pushing the two plates apart. Other events occur at the other boundaries.

Notice on the left that Plate B is being pushed into Plate A. The continental crusts on the two plates are colliding. Study the drawing to learn how the mountains form at this boundary. This same process occurs as the plate that India is on collides with the plate that has Europe and Asia on it. As these plates push toward each other, rock layers rise up into huge mountains, the Himalayas. Each year the Himalaya Mountains move more than a centimeter higher.

Mountains

When the continental crusts of Plate A and Plate B collide, they wrinkle up to form a mountain range.

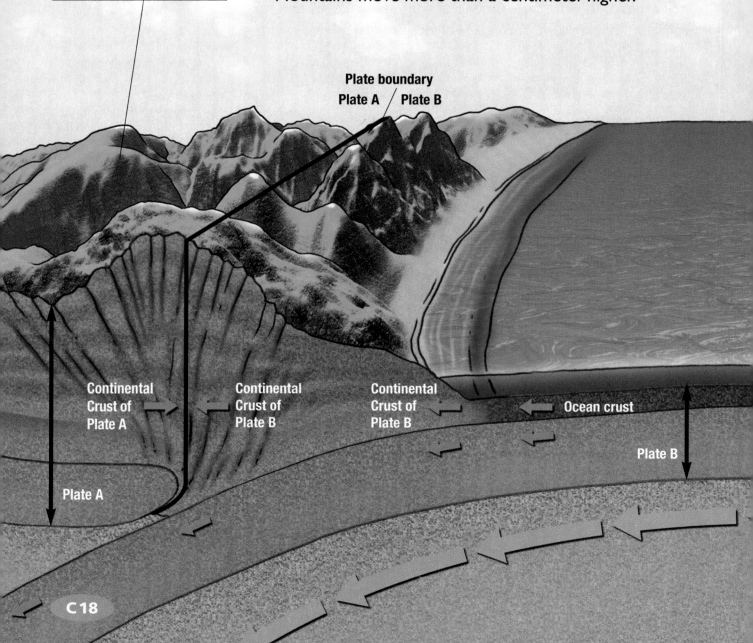

Plate boundary
Plate A / Plate B

Continental Crust of Plate A

Continental Crust of Plate B

Continental Crust of Plate B

Ocean crust

Plate A

Plate B

Mountains form elsewhere too. On the right, the diagram shows Plate C being pushed under Plate D. Slowly, gravity pulls the heavy ocean crust down under the lighter continental crust. Study the diagram to learn why volcanic mountains form when this occurs.

Mountains formed in this way include the Cascades in northern California, Oregon, Washington, and British Columbia. These volcanoes may lie quietly for many years. Their volcanic origin may not be obvious. Then, like Mount St. Helens in 1980, they may erupt again. The molten rock that forms this type of mountain is thick. It erupts violently and forms steep volcanoes.

Volcanic Mountains
Some volcanic mountains form where one plate is forced under another. New crust, formed in the center of the ocean, pushes Plate C with heavier ocean crust on it toward Plate D with lighter continental crust on it. Gravity pulls the heavier Plate C down under the lighter Plate D and down into the mantle. As the crust on Plate C moves under, friction and the earth's heat cause part of it to melt. The molten rock rises to the surface as volcanic eruptions.

The newest ocean crust is nearest the boundary between Plates B and C. The farther from the boundary, the older the ocean crust. This is more evidence for the theory of plate tectonics. ▼

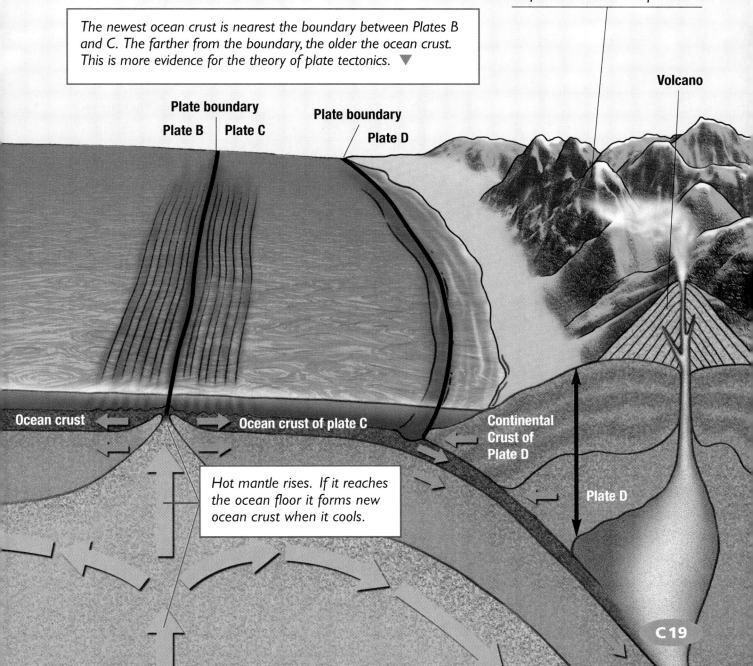

Volcano

Plate boundary

Plate B | Plate C

Plate boundary

Plate D

Ocean crust

Ocean crust of plate C

Continental Crust of Plate D

Hot mantle rises. If it reaches the ocean floor it forms new ocean crust when it cools.

Plate D

▲ Earthquakes
The part of California nearest the Pacific Ocean is on the Pacific Plate. It is moving northwest. The rest of California is on the North American Plate. It is moving southeast in relation to the Pacific Plate. When the plates suddenly move, an earthquake occurs.

The theory of plate tectonics explains how most earthquakes occur. Rocks on both sides of a plate boundary are connected at a fault. As the plates move, these rocks strain against each other. When the strain overcomes the strength of the rocks, the land moves suddenly. The sudden movement is an earthquake. The picture shows how plate tectonics explains California earthquakes.

The theory of plate tectonics has given scientists new insights into how the earth has changed. Still, scientists continue to examine theories even while they use them. Now, some scientists want to change the theory of plate tectonics based on new evidence.

The new evidence suggests that gravity pulls the cooler, heavier ocean crust down into the mantle so strongly it pulls apart the plates at the mid-ocean ridge. This pull of gravity would explain why plates move. If this new idea is true, the hot mantle rising at the mid-ocean plate boundary may not be what causes the plates to move apart. This new idea is called the gravity pull hypothesis. Scientists are discovering more evidence for this hypothesis. Over time the theory of plate tectonics, like most scientific theories, will be revised.

Lesson 2 Review

1. What evidence leads scientists to hypothesize that continents have moved?
2. What are the earth's plates?
3. What are some events caused by plate movements?
4. **Sequence**
   Place these statements in order: **a.** scientists map the location of volcanoes and earthquakes, **b.** scientists think the continents have moved, **c.** scientists develop the theory of plate tectonics.

Lesson 3

What Changes the Earth's Surface?

"Road washed out ahead." You make a detour. Later, as the car climbs a mountain road, you spot another sign. "Watch for falling rock." You don't see any rocks falling, but the road is littered with stones. What's going on?

You will learn:
- **how weathering changes the earth.**
- **how erosion changes the earth.**
- **how deposition changes the earth.**

Weathering

The surface of the earth is always changing. Even material as hard as rock can change. **Weathering** is the process that breaks down and changes rocks. Rocks can be slowly broken down by air, ice, water, chemicals, and living things.

Glossary

weathering
(weᴛн′ər ing), the process that breaks down and changes rocks

Physical Science Two types of weathering can act on rocks: physical weathering and chemical weathering. Physical weathering breaks the rocks apart, but it doesn't change what they are made of. The size and shape of a rock might change, but it is still made of the same material. For example, the rock in the picture is being broken into many pieces as water freezes into ice. A physical change takes place in the rock.

Chemical weathering changes the substance that makes up rocks. A hard material in rock, such as iron, might change into a softer material, such as iron oxide, or rust. A chemical change takes place in the rock.

Water enters tiny cracks in rocks, expands as it freezes, and enlarges the tiny cracks. Over many years, ice can split a large boulder. ▶

C21

Water can also cause a chemical change in rocks. Water often combines with chemicals such as weak acids to cause chemical weathering. Even air pollution and living things can cause chemical weathering. Study the examples of chemical weathering shown on this page. Compare them with the examples of physical weathering shown on the next page.

▲ Air pollution can weather stone. Chemicals in polluted air have caused chemical changes in the rock that forms this statue.

▲ Some organisms, such as moss and lichens, grow on rocks. Over time, weak acids released by the organisms may break down the rock on which they grow.

Often water from rain or in the ground combines with carbon dioxide from the air to form a weak acid. This acidic water soaks deep into the ground. It can settle into cracks and holes in a kind of rock called limestone. It chemically changes the rock. Slowly, the limestone dissolves, making the cracks and holes in it larger. Eventually, caves form. ▼

◀ Weathering can occur when a heavy layer of snow melts. The rock layers underneath expand when the weight is removed. The outer layers expand more than the inner layers. The layers begin to crack apart into sheets. Water and dissolved salts can enter the cracks. When the water evaporates, crystals grow. The growing crystals push apart the rock layer and enlarge the cracks. Many sheets of loose rock form. They are like the layers of an onion skin.

◀ Tiny roots may grow toward water in small cracks in rocks. As the roots slowly grow bigger, they exert enormous force, splitting the rocks.

Glossary

erosion (i rō′shən), the moving of weathered rock and soil

Erosion

You have learned how weathering breaks down rock. Loose bits of weathered rock can be moved away. The process of moving weathered rock and soil by wind, water, and ice is called **erosion.**

Flowing water is the main cause of erosion. Notice in the picture of a field how water from a heavy rain can carry away loose soil. The muddy water flows to streams and rivers after heavy rains. The fast-flowing water can erode soil and small rocks from the banks of streams and rivers. Look at the picture of the flooded Mississippi River. The river's muddy water carries away large amounts of soil and small rocks.

During heavy storms, rain falling on this field can't soak into the soil fast enough. In the picture below, identify where the water flows downhill across the field. As the water moves, it carries away small rocks, sand, and soil. The water and the soil it contains may eventually enter a stream and then a river. Over time, the flowing water could erode a measurable amount of soil. The field would be changed from rich farmland to land less usable for farming. ▼

As the brownish water of the Mississippi River flows along, it can carry soil and small rocks thousands of miles to the Gulf of Mexico. ▼

Moving water causes erosion along shorelines too. As waves crash against beaches, they can quickly carry away large amounts of sand and small rocks. The picture below and to the right shows waves eroding the land beneath a building.

Like water, wind can cause erosion. The bottom picture shows strong winds carrying away sand and soil. The loss of soil caused by wind erosion, together with that caused by water erosion, can make farmland less able to produce crops.

Powerful, fast moving waves crash against the shore. They move rocks and carry away sand. ▼

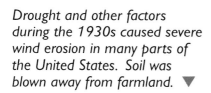

Drought and other factors during the 1930s caused severe wind erosion in many parts of the United States. Soil was blown away from farmland. ▼

Glossary

deposition
(dep′ə zish′ən), the dropping of materials moved by erosion

After flowing through many states, the Mississippi River enters the Gulf of Mexico, a part of the Atlantic Ocean. The Mississippi's flowing water spreads out and its rate of flow slows. It drops soil and other eroded materials in a "spread out" pattern. Over time, a measurable amount of materials pile up, forming new land called a delta. The soil eroded from other areas usually makes deltas good for farming. ▼

Deposition

You have learned that weathering breaks down rock and that erosion moves it away. What happens to it then? Eroded materials are dropped in new areas. The dropping of materials moved by erosion is called **deposition.** Sometimes deposition enriches the land. Over time, deposition may build new features such as deltas, beaches, and dunes.

Rivers, such as the Mississippi, carry large amounts of eroded materials as they flow, especially during floods. When a river floods, it overflows its banks and spreads out into the river valley. The water flows more slowly when it spreads out over a large area. This slower water can't carry as much eroded material. Tiny bits of rock and soil eroded from other places settle to the bottom and are left in the valley when the flooding ends. Soil deposited by flood waters in river valleys usually makes them good farmland. Study the picture below to learn what happens when a river enters an ocean.

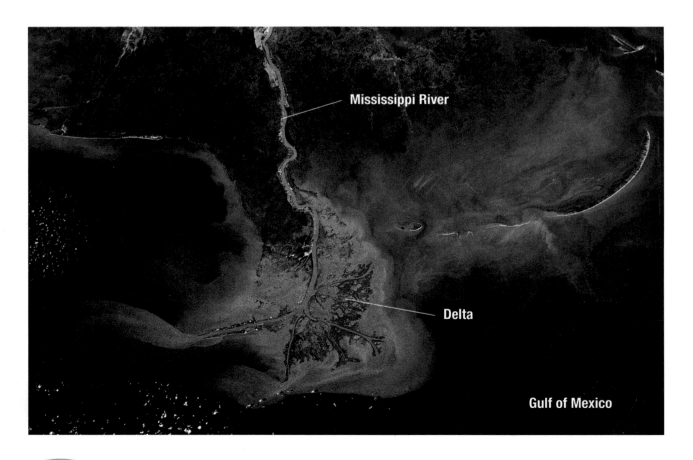

Mississippi River

Delta

Gulf of Mexico

▲ *Before deposition this seashore is mostly rocky.*

▲ *After deposition the seashore has deposits of sand.*

Waves also can make new land by deposition. They erode sand and rock. The water may carry sand toward the land until it reaches the shores of a bay where the waves move more slowly. The slower-moving water deposits the sand, forming new beaches. Compare the shore in the before-and-after pictures above.

Like water, wind can deposit sand. Sometimes it creates sand dunes near a beach as shown in the picture to the right. Wind can pick up sand from the beach and carry it along. Then a small obstacle, such as a rock or a plant, slows the wind in one place. Where the wind slows down, it can't carry as much eroded sand. As sand collects in this spot, it builds up a small mound. The mound slows the wind still more. More sand is deposited. Eventually, a large sand dune may form. Desert sand dunes form in a similar way except that the sand the winds first pick up comes from the desert, not the beach.

▲ *Dunes form as sand is slowly deposited. In time, plants may grow on the dune and cover it completely. Sometimes mature dunes appear to be ordinary hills near the beach.*

Lesson 3 Review

1. What are three things that cause weathering?

2. What are two different things that move eroded materials?

3. Describe how deposition causes deltas to form.

4. **Sequence**
   Place the processes in the order they occur:
   a. erosion, **b.** deposition, **c.** weathering.

Investigating Weathering

Process Skills

Process Skills

- observing
- making and using models

Materials

- safety goggles
- 3 sticks of chalk
- hand lens
- small stones
- 2 plastic cups
- water
- 1 plastic lid
- masking tape
- clock with second hand
- plastic spoon
- paper towel
- vinegar

Getting Ready

In this activity you will find out how physical and chemical weathering can occur. The vinegar in this activity is a solution of a weak acid dissolved in water.

Follow This Procedure

❶ Make a chart like the one shown below. Use your chart to record your observations.

	Observations
Broken chalk	
Chalk after shaking for five minutes	
Chalk after placing in vinegar	
Chalk after removing from vinegar	

❷ Put on your safety goggles. Break 3 sticks of chalk into four pieces each. Use a hand lens to **observe** several of the broken ends. Record a description of the chalk in your chart. Set four pieces of chalk aside to compare to the test samples.

❸ Make a **model** of weathering. Add small stones to a plastic cup until it is $\frac{1}{4}$ full. Then add water until the cup is $\frac{3}{4}$ full.

❹ Place 4 pieces of chalk into the plastic cup. Close the lid of the cup tightly. Tape the lid shut (Photo A). Shake the cup vigorously for five minutes. Hold on to the top of the lid while shaking the cup. Use the clock to keep time. Remove the lid.

Photo A

⑤ Use the spoon to remove the chalk and place it on the paper towel. Use the hand lens to observe the chalk for signs of weathering. Compare the chalk pieces with the 4 pieces you set aside earlier. Record your observations.

⑥ Make another model of weathering. Add vinegar to a second cup until it is $\frac{3}{4}$ full. Add the remaining 4 pieces of chalk to the cup (Photo B). Observe the chalk in the vinegar for five minutes. Record your observations.

⑦ Repeat step 5.

Self-Monitoring
Have I recorded all of my observations?

Interpret Your Results

1. Which cup or cups represented physical weathering? Which cup or cups represented chemical weathering? Explain.

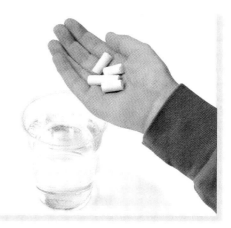

Photo B

2. Was weathering more evident in one cup than the other? Compare and contrast the chalk in the cups.

Inquire Further

How could you change the activity to investigate the combined effects of physical and chemical weathering? Develop a plan to answer this or other questions you may have.

Self-Assessment

- I followed instructions to **make a model** of weathering.
- I recorded my **observations** of the weathering of chalk by water and stones.
- I recorded my observations of the weathering of chalk by acid in vinegar.
- I identified the weathering of the chalk as physical or chemical weathering.
- I compared and contrasted the chalk in the different cups.

You will learn:

- **how rocks change form.**
- **how fossils indicate how the earth has changed.**

Glossary

rock cycle, the ways that rocks change from one form to another

Igneous rocks are rocks formed from melted mantle that comes from deep inside the earth. When it cools, the melted material hardens into igneous rock. ▼

How Do Rocks Reveal Changes on the Earth?

Pick up any rock. Although it's very old, with the right knowledge you can learn how it was formed and how it has changed. Scientists study rocks from all over the world to learn how the earth has changed.

How Rocks Change Form

You learned how rocks can be weathered and eroded. Rocks can be changed in other ways too. Rocks can be heated, compressed, cemented, twisted, and even melted. Almost all the rocks on the earth have been changed in many ways. The changes rocks go through make up the **rock cycle.** Look at the pictures on these two pages to learn about some of the ways rocks can change.

▲ Sandstone can be changed still further. As the earth's plates move, sandstone may be heated and put under enormous pressure. With time, sandstone that is made mostly of quartz sand may become quartzite. Rock formed when igneous or sedimentary rock is changed by heat or pressure is called **metamorphic rock.**

▲ Sometimes a layer of sand in a lake, river, or ocean is buried under layers of sediments—solid particles that are moved from one place to another. The weight of layers of sediments may press sand grains together. Certain chemicals can cement the sand grains together. New rock called sandstone forms. Rock formed when sediments such as sand are pressed or cemented together is known as **sedimentary rock.**

▲ Weathering eventually breaks up the igneous rocks. Tiny pieces of rock called sand are formed.

You learned how rocks can change from igneous rock to sedimentary rock and from sedimentary rock to metamorphic rock. Metamorphic rock can change too. Intense heat and pressure deep within the earth can make metamorphic rock melt. When it cools, it forms new igneous rock.

Glossary

igneous (ig′nē əs) **rock,** rock formed from melted rock that comes from deep within the earth

sedimentary (sed′ə men′tər ē) **rock,** rock formed when sediments are pressed or cemented together

metamorphic (met′ə môr′fik) **rock,** rock formed when igneous or sedimentary rock is changed by heat or pressure

▲ Organisms can be part of the rock cycle. Many animals, such as shellfish and tiny microscopic organisms, use chemicals from the ocean to make shells and skeletons.

▲ When the shellfish and tiny microscopic organisms die, they fall to the ocean floor. Over time, their shells and skeletons may collect on the ocean floor and form a sedimentary rock called limestone.

▲ Under great heat and pressure and over a long time, the limestone may change to marble, a metamorphic rock.

Glossary

mineral (min′ə rəl),
a natural, nonliving solid
with a definite chemical
structure

Mohs Hardness Scale

This scale measures the
hardness of minerals.
A harder mineral will
scratch a softer mineral.

Talc	1	softer
Gypsum	2	
Calcite	3	
Fluorite	4	
Apatite	5	
Orthoclase	6	
Quartz	7	
Topaz	8	
Corundum	9	harder
Diamond	10	

▲ Graphite used as "pencil lead"
and diamond are both made
entirely of carbon, an element.
Deep in the earth, under different
pressures and temperatures, their
atoms arranged themselves in
different patterns. Graphite is
opaque, black, and among the
softest minerals. Tiny pieces slide
off of it so easily it is used as pencil
lead. Diamond is a clear gemstone
and the hardest mineral.

As rocks change, the minerals that make up the rocks may change too. A **mineral** is a natural, nonliving solid with a definite chemical structure. The heat and pressure deep inside the earth may change the arrangements of the atoms in minerals.

This change in the arrangement of atoms occurs when the mineral quartz found in sandstone (a sedimentary rock) changes into quartzite (a metamorphic rock). The atoms in sandstone are arranged in a pattern that forms small crystals. Pressure and heat inside the earth rearrange the atoms into larger crystals. This pattern makes quartzite stronger than sandstone.

A similar effect occurs when the atoms in chalk, a type of limestone, rearrange as the limestone changes into marble. Think about the strength of a piece of blackboard chalk compared to the strength of a piece of marble. Look below to find what "pencil lead" could form if its atoms were rearranged.

The earth's forces affect how minerals form, which in turn affects their properties. These properties include color, crystal pattern, breakage pattern, luster (shininess), magnetism, and hardness. The scale used to determine a mineral's hardness is shown to the left. A harder mineral will scratch a softer one. Your fingernail has a hardness of about 2 on the Mohs Hardness Scale. You can scratch talc, the mineral used to make talcum powder, because talc is not as hard as your fingernail. Notice that diamonds are very hard. They can scratch almost anything. Scientists use hardness and other properties to identify minerals.

Quartz is one
of the hardest
minerals and is
abundant on
the surface of
the earth. ▼

Fossils That Indicate Changes

Imagine if each day you brought papers home from school and stacked them in your room. On the first day you put down the first papers. Each day you would add to the top. The oldest papers are on the bottom. The newest papers are on the top.

The drawings on the right show how something similar occurs in nature. Rocks at the earth's surface weather, and rivers often carry the eroded materials to the ocean. These eroded materials, called sediments, are deposited on the ocean bottom. Just as is the case with a pile of old papers, the oldest layers are on the bottom, and the newest layers are on the top.

Rivers may carry dead organisms as well as sediment to the ocean. Most dead organisms from both the river and the ocean are eaten. However, a few may sink to the bottom.

Occasionally, sediments quickly cover the dead organisms. The sediments may protect them from being eaten. Many decay completely, but a few may remain. Over time, many more layers of sediments may be deposited. The bottom layers form sedimentary rock. A few of the dead organisms trapped in the rock might have formed fossils. A fossil is any remains or trace of an organism. Eventually the top layers of rock may erode away. The layers of rock containing the fossils may be exposed.

Scientists study layers of rocks to learn about the earth and how it has changed. They know that if the layers are undisturbed, the oldest rocks are on the bottom and the youngest rocks are on top. They know how old each layer is in relation to the other layers.

A river carries sediments into a shallow sea and deposits them on the bottom. Layers build up.

Dead animals sink to the bottom. If sediments are quickly deposited on top, the animals may not be eaten. Layer after layer of sediments are deposited on top.

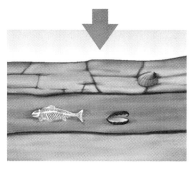

Over time, the lower layers form sedimentary rock. The remains of the dead animals form fossils.

Much later, erosion may wear away part of the rock and expose the rock layers and the fossils they contain.

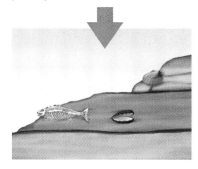

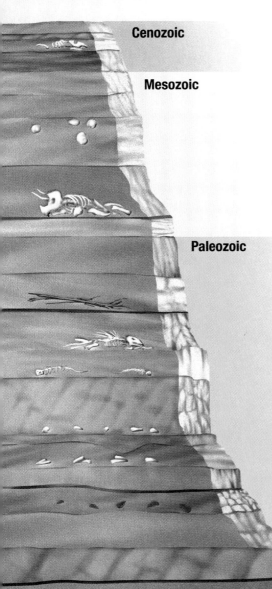

Cenozoic

Mesozoic

Paleozoic

Precambrian

▲ *The oldest fossils in the rock formation are on the bottom. The youngest ones are on the top. The Cenozoic Era is the most recent. The Precambrian is the oldest.*

Scientists learn about the history of the earth from fossils. When a layer of shells is found in rocks high in a mountain, scientists conclude that oceans once covered the area and that the land was once much lower. Trunks of fossilized trees found in places now covered by water indicate that the area was once dry land.

Fossils also provide clues about whether the climate of an area was warm or cool. For example, warm-weather plants found in snow-covered Antarctica are evidence that the continent was once in a warmer location. Similarily, fossils of warm-weather magnolias found in Greenland show that the climate there was once warmer.

Fossils help scientists figure out if the climate of an area was once dry or wet. Coal deposits often contain the fossil remains of ferns and other plants that grow in wet, swampy areas. Scientists think coal was formed from these plants. Although an area with coal deposits may be too dry for similar plants to grow today, scientists conclude that at one time the area probably was wet and swampy. Studying fossils in rock layers like the ones in the picture help scientists learn about the history of the earth.

Lesson 4 Review

1. How are igneous, sedimentary, and metamorphic rocks formed?

2. What would the fossil of a tropical plant indicate about the ancient climate where it was found?

3. Sequence
If you looked at several layers of sedimentary rock, where would you expect to find the oldest rocks?

Experimenting with Crystal Formation

Materials

- safety goggles
- 3 pencils
- masking tape
- 3 plastic cups
- 3 pieces of thread
- 3 identical buttons
- alum solution
- 3 medicine cups
- room temperature water
- ice water
- warm water
- metric ruler
- plastic wrap

Process Skills

- formulating questions and hypotheses
- identifying and controlling variables
- experimenting
- observing
- estimating and measuring
- collecting and interpreting data
- communicating

State the Problem

How does the rate of cooling affect crystal size?

Formulate Your Hypothesis

Crystals can form when molten rock from deep within the earth cools. You will use a model to experiment. This model uses alum crystals formed from a solution. When cooling is faster will the size of alum crystals be larger, be smaller, or will there be no effect? Write your **hypothesis.**

Identify and Control the Variables

The rate at which the alum solution cools is the **variable** you can change. You will cool the alum solution quickly in ice water and slowly in warm water. Then compare your results to a control—crystals formed at room temperature. Keep the concentration of the solution and the amount of solution the same for each trial.

Test Your Hypothesis

Follow these steps to perform an **experiment.**

1 Make a chart like the one on page C37. Use your chart to collect your data.

Continued ➡

Photo A

2 Put on your safety goggles. Use masking tape and a pencil to label the three plastic cups A, B, and C.

3 Tie one end of a thread to a button. Tie the other end to the middle of a pencil. Repeat, using the remaining thread, buttons, and pencils.

4 Place a pencil across the top of a cup. The attached button should be about 1 cm from the bottom of the cup. To shorten the thread, roll the extra thread around the pencil and secure it with masking tape. Remove the pencil and button. Repeat with the remaining pencils and buttons.

5 Pour the same amount of alum solution into each medicine cup. Carefully place a medicine cup in the center of each labeled cup (Photo A).

6 Carefully pour room temperature water into cup A so the water surrounds the medicine cup. Repeat this step using ice water in cup B and warm water in cup C.

7 Place a pencil across each of the cups so the attached button hangs down into the alum solution (Photo B).

8 Place the three cups where they will not be bumped or knocked over. Be careful moving the cups so they do not spill. Cover the cups with plastic wrap.

9 **Observe** the cups at the times shown in the chart. Carefully remove the crystals and use a metric ruler to **measure** the crystal sizes after four hours. **Collect data** by recording your observations and measurements.

Photo B

Collect Your Data

Cup	\multicolumn{6}{c}{Observations and measurements of crystals}					
	15 minutes	30 minutes	1 hour	2 hours	4 hours	Measurement
A						
B						
C						

Interpret Your Data

1. Study the results in the chart. In which cup did crystals form the fastest? the slowest?

2. In which cup did the smallest crystals form? In which cup did the largest crystals form?

3. Describe how the rate of cooling affects crystal size.

State Your Conclusion

How did your results compare with your hypothesis? **Communicate** your results. Write a summary of how the rate of cooling affects crystal size.

Inquire Further

What will happen if you keep the buttons in the solution until the solution evaporates? Develop a plan to answer this or other questions you may have.

Self-Assessment

- I made a **hypothesis** about the effect the rate of cooling has on the size of crystals that form.
- I **identified** and **controlled variables.**
- I followed instructions to perform an **experiment** to **observe** crystal formation.
- I **collected** and **interpreted data** by recording observations, and by **measuring** and recording the size of the crystals.
- I **communicated** by stating my conclusion about the effect of the rate of cooling on crystal size.

Chapter 1 Review

Chapter Main Ideas

Lesson 1

• The atmosphere is the layer of gases above the earth. The hydrosphere is the water part of the earth. The lithosphere is the hard outer shell of the earth, including the crust and the outer, rigid part of the mantle.

• The earth is made of three layers: a thin, rigid outer crust; a hotter, mostly solid mantle; and a melted outer core with a white-hot, solid inner core.

Lesson 2

• Scientists hypothesized that continents had moved based on the jigsaw fit of the continents, on fossil evidence, and on the locations of coal deposits, ancient mountains, and deposits left by glaciers.

• The theory of plate tectonics states that the earth's surface is composed of plates that slowly move due to forces deep within the earth.

• The movement of plates explains the location of many earthquakes, volcanoes, and mountain ranges.

Lesson 3

• During the process of weathering, rocks are broken down by air, ice, water, chemicals, and living things.

• During the process of erosion, weathered rocks and soil are moved by water, wind, and ice.

• During the process of deposition, eroded materials are deposited in locations such as river valleys, deltas, and beaches.

Lesson 4

• The rock cycle describes the processes by which igneous, sedimentary, and metamorphic rocks can be changed from one type to another.

• By studying fossils scientists learn about how the earth has changed.

Reviewing Science Words and Concepts

Write the letter of the word or phrase that best completes each sentence.

a. atmosphere
b. core
c. crust
d. deposition
e. erosion
f. hydrosphere
g. igneous rock
h. lithosphere
i. mantle
j. metamorphic rock
k. mineral
l. plate
m. plate tectonics
n. rock cycle
o. sedimentary rock
p. weathering

1. The layer of the earth that includes the crust and the rigid top part of the mantle is known as the ___.

2. When sedimentary rock is changed by heat or pressure, it forms ___.

3. The ___ is the layer of gases that surrounds the earth.

4. The ___ describes how rocks can change from one form to another.

5. Soil can be lost from a farm field through a process called ___.

6. The process that directly causes deltas to form is ___.

7. The ___ is the center layer of the earth.

8. When layers of sediments are pressed together, ___ forms.

9. The layer of the earth above the core is called the ___.

10. The water part of the earth's surface is called the ___.

11. Most earthquakes occur when a ___ moves.

12. The theory known as ___ explains how continents move.

13. The process that breaks down and changes rocks is ___.

14. When melted rock cools, it forms ___.

15. The ___ is the layer of the earth on top of the mantle.

16. The hardness of a ___ is measured by the Mohs Hardness Scale.

Explaining Science

Draw and label a diagram or write a paragraph to answer these questions.

1. Where are the atmosphere, crust, core, hydrosphere, lithosphere, and mantle located?

2. How does the flow of the mantle cause plates to move?

3. How does erosion by water cause loss of soil from farms?

4. Why do scientists expect to find the older layers of sedimentary rock below younger layers?

Using Skills

1. The rock cycle is a model of how rocks can change. Use it to put these steps in the correct **sequence: a.** sand grains are pressed together into sedimentary rock, **b.** sandstone forms, **c.** sand forms by weathering of igneous rock, **d.** melted mantle hardens into igneous rock.

2. **Classify** these as atmosphere, hydrosphere, or lithosphere: **a.** a rock, **b.** oxygen, **c.** a glacier, **d.** a puddle, **e.** smoke, **f.** a diamond.

3. How do the two maps on page C 15 **communicate** that evidence indicates continents have moved?

Critical Thinking

1. **Predict** whether the theory of plate tectonics will be revised or remain unchanged. Explain your prediction.

2. **Compare** and **contrast** the processes of weathering and erosion.

3. You received samples of calcite, quartz, fluorite, and gypsum with mixed-up labels. You learned how the Mohs Hardness Scale is used to **classify** minerals. Explain how you could use it to identify these minerals.

4. **Classify** the following as igneous, sedimentary, or metamorphic: sandstone, chalk, marble.

Get in Gear!

These kids recycle bikes. They collect unwanted bikes and teach other kids how to repair them. Reusing bikes saves resources and helps prevent pollution.

Chapter 2
The Earth's Resources

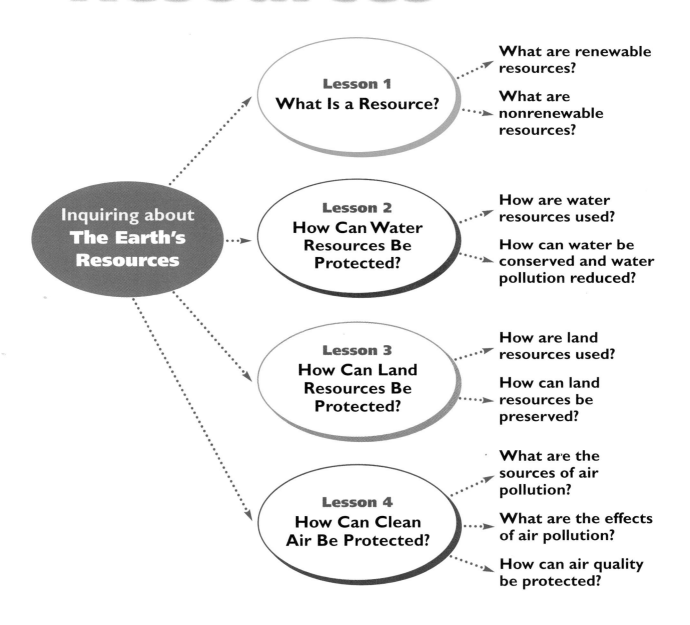

Inquiring about The Earth's Resources

Lesson 1
What Is a Resource?

What are renewable resources?

What are nonrenewable resources?

Lesson 2
How Can Water Resources Be Protected?

How are water resources used?

How can water be conserved and water pollution reduced?

Lesson 3
How Can Land Resources Be Protected?

How are land resources used?

How can land resources be preserved?

Lesson 4
How Can Clean Air Be Protected?

What are the sources of air pollution?

What are the effects of air pollution?

How can air quality be protected?

Copy the chapter graphic organizer onto your own paper. This organizer shows you what the whole chapter is all about. As you read the lessons and do the activities, look for answers to the questions and write them on your organizer.

Exploring the Earth's Resources

Process Skills

- observing
- communicating

Materials

- cup of water
- cup of soil
- piece of newspaper
- leaf from a tree
- aluminum foil
- plastic bottle
- card labeled *sunlight*
- card labeled *oil*
- card labeled *wind*
- card labeled *fish*
- plastic bag of air
- piece of paper

Explore

1 Each of the objects represents a resource, a material that people use. **Observe** each object and think about what it is made of or where it comes from.

2 Make a list of the objects on a piece of paper. Leave room to write beside each object. Beside each object, write at least one way that people use the resource.

3 Next, ask yourself which of these materials could be completely used up? Which would be replenished within a human lifetime or less? Which could never be used up?

Reflect

1. Communicate. Discuss how you decided if a resource could be used up or not. How did you decide if a resource could be replenished?

2. Compare and contrast how different groups made their decisions. You may check your answers as you read the next lesson.

? Inquire Further

Look around your classroom or home. Which resources could be used up? Which could be replenished? Which could never be used up? Develop a plan to answer these or other questions you may have.

Identifying Supporting Facts and Details

In the Explore Activity, *Exploring the Earth's Resources,* you studied different types of resources from the earth. The main idea of the activity is that some resources can be replaced and others cannot be replaced. The main idea is the most important point. Facts and details, such as the kinds and amounts of each resource, provide more specific information about the main idea.

Example

The two parts of Lesson 1 each have a main idea. Each is restated in the first column in the table below. Facts and details in the lesson provide more specific information. As you read the lesson, write in the second column the facts and details that support each main idea.

Main Idea	Supporting Facts and Details
A resource that can be replaced within a reasonably short period of time is called a renewable resource.	
A nonrenewable resource is a resource that cannot be replaced once it is used up.	

Talk About It!

1. What would happen if fish were caught at a faster rate than they could reproduce?

2. Is gold a renewable or nonrenewable resource? Why do you think so?

▼ *It takes millions of years to make a lump of coal — but only a few seconds to use it up.*

You will learn:

- what renewable resources are.
- what nonrenewable resources are.

Glossary

renewable resource
(ri nü′ə bəl rē′sôrs),
a resource that can
be replaced within a
reasonably short time

*When people limit the size and
number of fish they catch, the
remaining fish can grow,
reproduce, and replace the
ones that are caught.* ▼

Lesson 1

What Is a Resource?

Take a deep breath! Feel the air fill your lungs. Your body needs the oxygen in the air. It's a resource. A resource is something that people use. When you breathe in air, ride on a bus, or write an essay, you use resources.

Renewable Resources

You use many of the earth's resources. The oxygen your body uses, the fuel that powers your school bus, and the trees used to make the paper you write on are all resources.

Some resources can be replaced eventually. The paper you write on might be made from trees grown on a tree farm like the one on the next page. When the trees are cut down, other trees are planted. The young trees grow larger. After a time, they replace the old trees and renew trees as a resource.

A resource that can be replaced within a reasonably short period is called a **renewable resource**. If used wisely, renewable resources can last indefinitely. Like trees, fish are a renewable resource. If people like the woman in the picture catch no more than a reasonable number of fish, those that remain can reproduce and replace the ones that are caught.

Inexhaustible resources are renewable resources that cannot be used up. The sun shines no matter how much sunlight people use. The house on the next page is heated by capturing the energy from the sun.

Wind is another inexhaustible resource. Sailboats use wind energy. Wind turbines like the ones in the picture change wind energy into electrical energy.

◄ Tree farms work like other farms. A crop is planted and then harvested. Instead of producing wheat to make bread, a tree farm produces wood. The wood may be used to make paper such as that in the large rolls in the picture.

◄ Wind turbines change wind energy into electrical energy. Although wind turbines can produce electricity only when the wind blows, the wind is never "used up."

Energy from the sun heats the solar collectors on this house. In turn, this energy warms the house. ▼

Glossary

nonrenewable resource (non′ri nü′ə bəl rē′sôrs), a resource that cannot be replaced after it is used

fossil fuel (fos′əl fyü′əl), a fuel that formed over many years from the remains of living organisms

Nonrenewable Resources

A **nonrenewable resource** is a resource that cannot be replaced after it is used. Minerals and many fuels are nonrenewable resources.

The fuels used to heat most homes in the United States are nonrenewable resources. Many of these fuels, such as gas, oil, and coal, are fossil fuels. **Fossil fuels** formed over many years from the remains of plants and other organisms. Fossil fuels are being used much faster than they form. They can be used up because only a limited amount exists. The pictures below show some ways people use fossil fuels.

Oil pumped from this Texas oil well is used to make plastics, gasoline, and other products. ▶

Natural gas from this well heats homes and is used as fuel for stoves. ▶

Coal from this mine is used as fuel for power plants that supply electricity to homes, schools, and factories. ▶

Minerals from the earth, including the one used to make aluminum, are also nonrenewable resources. You may drink from aluminum cans or wrap food in aluminum foil. Aluminum comes from bauxite, a mineral that miners take from the ground. The picture below shows bauxite being mined. Only a certain amount of bauxite exists on earth. Because there is a limited amount of bauxite, there is a limit to how much aluminum can be produced.

◄ Bauxite is mined from the ground and processed into aluminum.

Aluminum is used to make many products, including aluminum foil. ▼

Lesson 1 Review

1. Describe renewable resources. Give two examples.

2. Describe nonrenewable resources. Give two examples.

3. Compare and Contrast Compare and contrast renewable and nonrenewable resources.

What's the Big Idea?

You will learn:

- how water resources are used.

- how water can be conserved and water pollution reduced.

Glossary

groundwater, water from rain or snow that sinks into the earth and is stored there

Lesson 2

How Can Water Resources Be Protected?

Water. You're hot, sweaty, and thirsty from running. You take a drink of cool water. Then you jump into a pool for a swim. Splash! Water. You can't live without it!

Water Resources

Water covers almost 75% of the earth's surface. Study the picture to see where the earth's water is located. Notice that there is plenty of water but people can't use most of it. More than 97% of the earth's water is salt water in the oceans. Less than 3% of the water is the fresh water people need.

Most of the fresh water can't be used either. It's ice, frozen in glaciers. Less than 1% of the earth's water is **groundwater**—water from rain or snow that sinks into the earth and is stored there. All the lakes, rivers, and streams on earth contain less than 0.2% of the water on the earth. A tiny part of the water is in the atmosphere, as water vapor or as droplets or ice crystals in the clouds.

Where your water comes from depends on where you live. Some regions have plenty of groundwater. Some use water from lakes and rivers. Some places must get water from far away. Study the next page to learn where some people get their water.

Location of water on the earth ▼

Groundwater, lakes, rivers, streams, and atmosphere

Glaciers

Oceans

C48

▲ Water from Nearby Rivers

Water from the Mississippi River is used by families in nearby communities.

Water from Groundwater

Wells like the one being drilled here supply the needs of many families. ▼

▲ Water from Lakes

Water from deep in Lake Michigan is used by many families in Illinois.

◄ Water from Distant Rivers

Water collects in a reservoir behind the Hoover Dam on the Colorado River and then is moved hundreds of kilometers to families in Southern California.

▲ Although paper is dry, a surprising amount of water is used in making it.

▲ Farmers irrigate their fields to make sure their crops get enough water.

People use water mainly for industrial, agricultural, and household purposes. Industries use water to make many kinds of products. Water is used to clean materials, to cool equipment, and in the processes that make products. The factory to the left uses water in several stages of the paper-making process. Some industries need so much water that their factories must be located near large supplies of water.

Farmers use water when they grow the food you eat. In some areas rain provides all the water that is needed. Other areas don't get much rain. Farming in these areas is possible only with irrigation. Without irrigation, the field in the picture might not get enough water to be good farmland.

You are probably most familiar with the household uses of water. Think of the ways you have already used water today. You used water when you washed and when you brushed your teeth. Maybe you prepared orange juice as the boy in the picture is doing. You might have used water to clean the dishes after breakfast.

Life Science

All living things use water. Cells need water for most life processes, such as getting energy from food. The cells of all living things contain water. Water makes life possible.

◀ Making orange juice is one of many ways you may use water.

Conserving Water and Reducing Water Pollution

Water may become polluted when it is used. When you brush your teeth, water carries away the used toothpaste and bacteria you brushed off your teeth. When you wash your hands, the dirt that was on them goes down the drain. Water carries away many wastes in your home. Look at the picture of a home to find some ways water can be used and might become polluted.

One way to reduce water pollution is to conserve, or to use less, water. A water-saving shower head like the one in the picture uses less water than an ordinary one.

Farmers can also conserve water. Some farmers use drip irrigation, a method that brings water to individual plants, not an entire field. Other farmers have switched to crops that need less water.

Industries and businesses conserve water too. Some manufacturers use water under very high pressure to wash parts. This method requires much less water. Some modern car washes recycle the water they use.

▲ *Many people have replaced their older shower heads with newer, water-saving ones.*

Water is used in many ways around the home. ▼

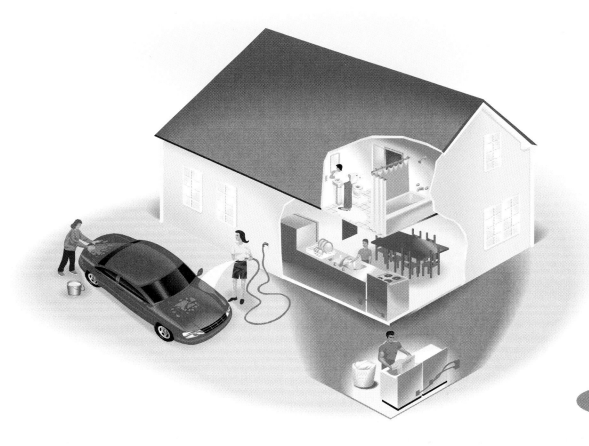

▲ *Wastewater treatment facilities clean water before it enters lakes, rivers, or oceans.*

Water used by families or factories must be cleaned before it enters rivers, lakes, or oceans. It might contain wastes from people's homes or harmful chemicals from manufacturing plants. Wastewater treatment facilities, such as the one in the picture to the left, treat water to make it safe and clean. Look at the picture below to learn the steps involved in treating wastewater.

Wastewater Treatment Process

Wastewater moves through screens that catch large solids. At each step in the process, solids that do not break down are collected and taken away.

Smaller solids settle out in a settling tank. Bacteria decompose these solids and change them into a harmless material.

Air is bubbled through wastewater. Helpful bacteria use the oxygen from the air to grow and to break down wastes.

Very small solids settle out in a settling tank.

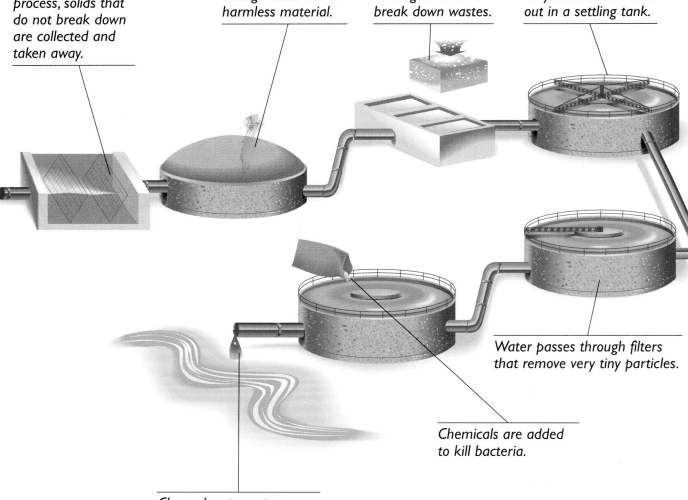

Water passes through filters that remove very tiny particles.

Chemicals are added to kill bacteria.

Cleaned water enters a river, lake, or ocean.

Water that runs off of farm fields does not flow into a wastewater treatment facility. It may go into groundwater or into streams, rivers, and lakes. It can carry chemicals used to kill weeds and insects. To reduce water pollution, many farmers use other methods to help control weeds and insects. They use fewer chemicals and use them more selectively.

Fertilizers from fields also may run off into streams, rivers, and lakes. There, the fertilizers can cause tiny organisms to grow rapidly. When these tiny organisms die, decomposers break them down. The decomposers use large amounts of the oxygen in the water in the process of breaking down the tiny organisms. Little oxygen is left for fish. Many fish may die. More and more, farmers carefully consider the amount of fertilizer they need. They may apply less each time they fertilize, and they may fertilize fewer times. However, some fertilizers may still run off.

In parts of Florida, the water that runs off of fields contains high levels of some fertilizers. To keep this polluted water from reaching the Everglades, some Florida farmers direct the polluted water into specially constructed marshes. During the weeks the water is in one of these marshes, cattails, sawgrass, and other native plants use the fertilizers to grow. When the water leaves the marsh, it has much less fertilizer. The cleaner water then continues flowing downstream, deep into the Everglades.

▲ The large marsh shown in this photo was constructed to help reduce pollution flowing into the Everglades.

Lesson 2 Review

1. What are the three main purposes for which water is used?

2. Tell one way you can conserve water, one way farmers can conserve water, and one way industry can conserve water.

3. **Identify Supporting Facts and Details** In the last paragraph on page C51, what facts and details support the main idea?

Investigating Water Pollution

Process Skills

- making and using models
- observing
- inferring

Materials

- newspapers
- clear plastic container
- scoop or cup
- sand
- water
- spray bottle
- dropper tube, no top
- metric ruler
- dropper
- red food coloring
- clock

Getting Ready

In this activity you can find out one way water can become polluted by making a model of underground water.

Follow This Procedure

❶ Make a chart like the one shown. Use your chart to record your observations.

	Observations
Level of lake water and water under hill	
Model before spraying	
Model after 15 minutes	
Model after 30 minutes	
Model after 1 hour	
Model after 2 hours	

❷ Cover your desk or table with several layers of newspaper. To **make a model,** use a scoop or cup to fill the plastic container about half full of sand. Dampen the sand with water.

❸ Form a sand hill in one corner leading to a low area in the opposite corner. The low area represents a lake (Photo A).

Photo A

Photo B

4 Pour water into the lake until the water level is about half as high as the hill. **Observe** the sand hill from the side of the model. What do you notice about the lake level and water under the sand hill? Record your observation.

5 Place the dropper tube with the top removed into the hill. Place the tip about 1 cm below the surface. The tube should touch the side of the container so the tip is visible (Photo B). This tube represents a place pollution may enter underground water. This could represent a chemical storage tank or a landfill that does not have special leakproof layers.

6 Add a dropper of red food coloring to the tube. The food coloring represents a source of pollution. Record your observations.

 Safety Note *Be careful spraying water. If the floor becomes wet, wipe it up immediately.*

7 Gently spray the hill with water for three to five minutes. This represents rain falling and soaking into the ground.

8 Observe the flow of pollution below the sand's surface over time. Record what you observe at the times shown in the chart.

Self-Monitoring
Have I written all my descriptions?

Interpret Your Results

1. Describe how pollution on land can pollute underground and surface water over time.

2. Infer what might happen over time if water could flow down through a landfill into the ground below.

3. Compare and contrast your model to a real lake and its surrounding land.

 Inquire Further

How difficult is it to clean the pollution from your model? Develop a plan to answer this or other questions you may have.

Self-Assessment

- I followed instructions to **make** and **use** a **model** of underground water pollution.
- I recorded my **observations** about water pollution.
- I described how pollution on land can pollute underground and surface water.
- I **inferred** how landfills could contribute to water pollution.
- I compared and contrasted my model to a real lake and its surrounding land.

You will learn:
- how land resources are used.
- how land resources can be preserved.

Lesson 3

How Can Land Resources Be Protected?

You and a friend are biking through a park. Pleasant trees, green grass. Very nice. The next day you return. Same trees, same grass, but trash everywhere. **Yuk!** Not so nice. What do you do?

Land Resources

If you've ever sat in a car on a long trip, it might seem as if the land goes on forever. However, land resources are limited. Land resources include the land itself, soil, and rocks and minerals.

Housing is one use of land resources. Before your home was built, the land it is on may have been a forest, a prairie, or a farm. The picture below shows new housing being built on fertile farmland. As the population grows, more land is needed for housing.

Sometimes houses are built on land that had once been used as farmland. ▼

The rich soil that makes good farmland is a valuable and limited resource. New soil forms very slowly. Soil is a mixture that forms when rock weathers into tiny pieces. Nutrients are added as dead plants, animals, and other organisms decay. Water, air, and minerals complete the mixture.

Farmers use the soil to produce the food people eat, such as fruits and vegetables, meat and poultry, milk, and grains. The grain growing in the field pictured to the right is wheat that may be used for bread or cereal. Farmers also produce cotton and wool. Your cotton shirt comes from the cotton plants farmers grow. Your wool sweater comes from the sheep they raise. All of the items shown on this page depend on fertile soil.

Like farmland, forests can be used to produce products for people. The wood that people use to build houses and schools comes from forests. Some wood is processed to make paper. People also use forests for hiking and observing nature.

▲ *The rich soil of this farmland is used to grow wheat that will be used in products such as bread.*

Dairy cattle living on farmland supply the milk you drink. Apple trees from an orchard provide a healthy snack. Trees grown in a forest are used to make notebook paper. Cotton from cotton farms and wool from sheep ranches are used to make clothes. ▶

People also use minerals from the land. The minerals removed from mines are an important land resource. For example, coal is used as a fuel for heating and generating electricity.

Some minerals removed from mines are processed and used in thousands of products, such as jewelry, silverware, bicycles, and aluminum foil. You learned earlier that aluminum comes from bauxite, a type of mineral. The pictures on these two pages show how bauxite is removed from the ground and processed into aluminum.

Production of Aluminum from Bauxite

1 *Bauxite is mined from open pits. Then it is taken to a processing plant.*

3 *At a refinery, the bauxite is treated with heat, pressure, and strong chemicals. A white powder is produced. It is a compound of aluminum and oxygen.*

2 *Bauxite is crushed, washed to remove dirt, and dried at processing plants. Then it is taken to a refinery.*

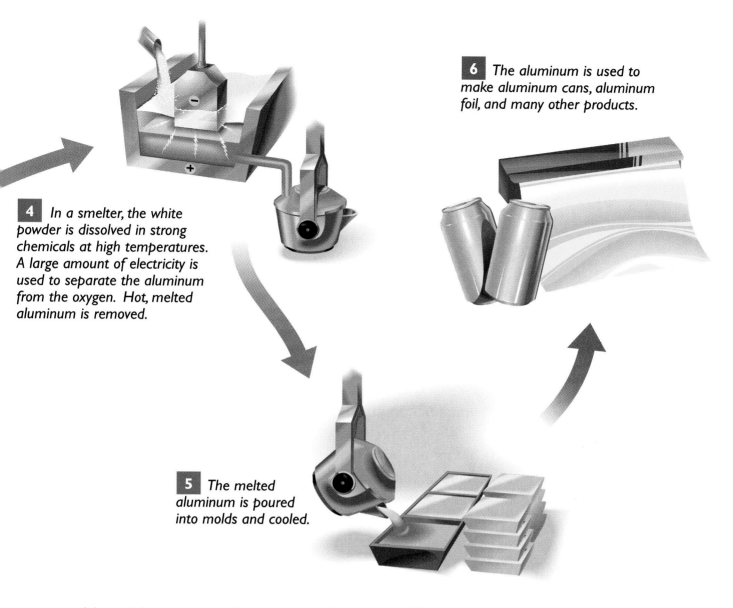

6 *The aluminum is used to make aluminum cans, aluminum foil, and many other products.*

4 *In a smelter, the white powder is dissolved in strong chemicals at high temperatures. A large amount of electricity is used to separate the aluminum from the oxygen. Hot, melted aluminum is removed.*

5 *The melted aluminum is poured into molds and cooled.*

Materials produced from mines, forests, and farms are used by factories to make most of the things you use every day. These items include bicycles, radios, tables and chairs, light bulbs, sinks and faucets, refrigerators and stoves, and pens and pencils.

Of course, industry also uses land as sites for factories. Factories are often built near the raw materials that will be used. Factories that produce frozen vegetables are frequently built near the fields where the vegetables are grown. Factories that produce aluminum use a great deal of electricity. Many have located in areas where electricity is less expensive.

Preserving Land Resources

Farms, mines, and factories produce most of the things you use every day. In producing them, land resources might be damaged or used up. Soil can be lost to erosion. Shortages of certain minerals can occur. You can't solve all these problems, but there are ways you can help.

You can help protect land resources by recycling. You learned how bauxite was mined and processed to make aluminum. Mining bauxite changes the land. Processing the bauxite produces wastes and uses large amounts of electricity. Fuels such as coal or nuclear fuel may be used to produce the electricity. Getting these fuels involves more mining.

Recycling aluminum cans and aluminum foil means that less bauxite must be mined. Compare the steps in recycling aluminum shown on these two pages with the steps needed to produce it from bauxite on pages C58–C59. No land must be mined for bauxite when an aluminum product is produced from recycled aluminum. Making a new aluminum can from an old one also helps protect land resources in two other ways. It produces far less pollution and uses far less electricity. Recycling glass and paper also helps protect land resources.

Aluminum Recycling Process

1 *Aluminum products such as recycled cans and foil are collected. They are crushed into bales and moved to a melting furnace.*

2 *In the furnace, the aluminum is melted. This process uses less electricity than is needed to make melted aluminum from bauxite.*

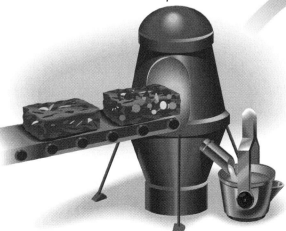

Another way to protect land resources is to reuse items. After you drink the water from a plastic water bottle from the store, you can refill it and use it over and over. Rechargeable batteries can be used again and again. A lunch box can be used for years. A paper lunch bag is usually used only once. A cloth towel can be used, washed, and reused. A paper towel is thrown away.

People can also protect land resources by reducing the amount of things they buy. They can buy only what they need and pick products that will last. In addition, they can choose products with less packaging.

By recycling, reusing, and reducing how much you use, you can help protect the resources of the land. You help reduce pollution and save nonrenewable resources for the future.

4 *The aluminum is used to make aluminum cans, aluminum foil, and many other products.*

3 *The melted aluminum is poured into molds and cooled.*

Lesson 3 Review

1. What are three ways land resources are used?

2. List three ways you can protect land resources.

3. **Identify Supporting Facts and Details**
   In the first paragraph on page C59, what facts and details support the main idea?

You will learn:
- what the sources of air pollution are.
- what the effects of air pollution are.
- how air quality can be protected.

Glossary

air pollution (pə lü′shən), the addition of any unwanted substance into the air

pollutant (pə lüt′nt), an unwanted substance added to the air, water, or land

Lesson 4

How Can Clean Air Be Protected?

Cough, cough. **Whew!** The smog is really bad today. You probably won't go outdoors for gym. There isn't much wind to blow the smog away. Where does the smog come from?

Sources of Air Pollution

The addition of any unwanted substance into the air is called **air pollution**. The unwanted substance is called a **pollutant**. You can see some kinds of air pollution. You can't see other kinds. Some pollutants make it harder to breathe. Others may cause the earth to get warmer.

People cause a great deal of the air pollution. However, air pollution comes from natural causes too. For example, the fire shown below started when lightning struck a tree in the forest. Smoke and ash from the fire can pollute the air for many kilometers. The volcanic eruption shown on the next page shot dust, ash, and gases into the air. Even wind can pollute the air by picking up large amounts of dust from the ground and blowing it through the air.

◀ *This forest fire, which was started by lightning, is a natural cause of air pollution.*

C62

◄ *Volcanoes are a natural source of air pollution. When Mount St. Helens erupted, tons of dust, ash, and gases shot into the air. These pollutants made breathing difficult for some people.*

Glossary

carbon monoxide (kär′bən mo nok′sīd), a colorless, odorless, poisonous gas made up of carbon and oxygen

ozone (ō′zōn), a molecule of oxygen that contains three atoms of oxygen

The natural sources of air pollution are not new. The difference between how clean the air is today compared with a few hundred years ago is the air pollution caused by people. Notice the smog in the picture to the right. It is caused mostly by the vehicles that people drive. Other sources of air pollution caused by people include power plants, wood-burning stoves, trash burners, and factories, such as the one in the picture. Whenever something is burned, pollutants are released into the air.

Many pollutants are gases. Carbon dioxide is the main gas produced when fuel burns. Carbon monoxide also may be produced. **Carbon monoxide** is a colorless, odorless, and poisonous gas. A reaction between sunlight and some pollutants in the atmosphere can cause the gas ozone to form. **Ozone** is a molecule with three atoms of oxygen instead of just the two atoms that an oxygen molecule usually has. Ozone in the lower atmosphere is a pollutant that may make it hard for some people to breathe.

Burning fuel is not the only way people cause pollution. When people drive on gravel and dirt roads or farmers plow their fields, dust enters the air. When people use some paints, cleaning products, hair sprays, and glues, some chemicals can evaporate and pollute the air. Industries can release similar pollutants when they produce the fuel and other products people use.

▲ *About half the air pollution in the United States is caused by the vehicles people drive.*

▲ *This factory releases air pollutants from its smokestack. The smoke looks dark because it contains tiny, solid particles that block the light.*

Effects of Air Pollution

You breathe several times a minute. Clean air is important because breathing polluted air can cause health problems. If you breathe a small amount of carbon monoxide, it becomes hard for your body to get enough oxygen. Even tiny amounts can cause headaches and dizziness. Some pollutants can irritate your eyes and the membranes around them. Ozone can irritate the lungs.

High levels of pollutants can cause coughing, make breathing difficult, and cause asthma to worsen. Dust and particles from burning fuel can be trapped in the lungs. Over time, lung damage may occur. Some areas declare air pollution alerts on particularly bad days. When this occurs, some schools may cancel outdoor activities and post notices like the one below.

Clean air is especially important to young people. Their lungs are less developed. They breathe more rapidly, are more active physically, and spend more time outdoors. When air pollution levels are high, some schools cancel outdoor activities. ▶

Air pollution can hurt animals, plants, and other organisms. For example, air pollution can cause acid rain. Some pollutants in the air react with water vapor to form acids. **Acid rain** is rain containing these acids. Rain or snow that is polluted by these acids can injure or kill organisms. Acid rain has made some lakes nearly lifeless. Notice the dead trees in the picture of the forest. They were damaged by acid rain. Some scientists think that acid rain and ozone damage farm crops.

Air pollution harms nonliving things too. Air pollution damaged the statue in the picture. It also damages buildings, monuments, and other structures, especially those made of marble and limestone. Air pollution can even damage rubber and plastic materials.

Air pollution may also cause other changes. Most scientists think that increasing amounts of carbon dioxide and certain other gases may now be causing the atmosphere to get warmer. This could cause the climate to change. Scientists also think certain pollutants are destroying the ozone that exists high in the atmosphere. You learned that ozone is a pollutant when it is close to the ground. However, high in the atmosphere, ozone protects the earth from the sun's harmful ultraviolet rays. With less protective ozone, skin cancer may become more common.

Glossary

acid (as′id) **rain**, rain containing acids formed when air pollutants react with water vapor

▲ *Acid rain killed some trees in this forest and slowed the growth of others.*

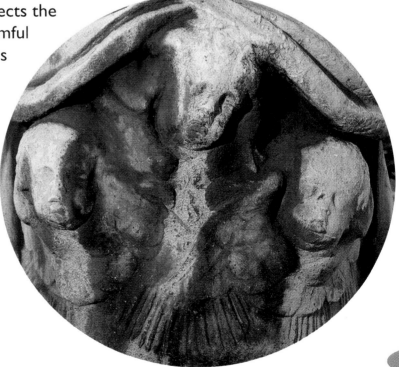

Air pollution damaged this statue. ▶

Protecting Air Quality

How can you help keep air clean? Because motor vehicles cause so much of the air pollution, anything you do to reduce their use helps. The children below are walking, riding their bikes, or taking the school bus to school. Because they do, the number of cars needed to drive children to school is reduced.

Another way to prevent air pollution is to conserve energy. That's because producing and using energy often involves polluting the air. For example, when you conserve electricity, you reduce the amount of electricity that power plants must produce. This in turn reduces the amount of air pollution the power plants make.

Walking, riding a bike, or taking the bus reduces the number of cars used to drive kids to school and helps to protect clean air. ▼

Reducing, reusing, and recycling products also saves energy and helps protect clean air. You can help by taking better care of what you have and throwing away less. If you reduce the number of new things you buy and reuse old ones, factories need to manufacture less, and so produce less pollution.

Recycling, along with reducing and reusing, also reduces the amount of trash that must be burned or hauled to landfills. The burning of trash, the trucks that haul trash to landfills, and even the landfills themselves all cause air pollution.

To reduce air pollution, many people keep their cars well-tuned. Well-tuned cars use gas more efficiently and produce fewer pollutants. As older cars wear out, many people replace them with more modern, fuel-efficient ones that pollute less. Modern cars produce 95% less pollution than cars built 30 years ago.

Many industries are working to reduce air pollution. Some find ways to reduce the amount of energy they use. Others reduce air pollution by changing how they make things. Compare the two pictures to the right to learn another way industry reduces air pollution. By thinking carefully and choosing wisely, industry and individuals can protect the air living things need.

Some factories use scrubbers that remove some pollutants before they reach the air. The top picture shows a factory without scrubbers. The bottom picture shows the same factory with scrubbers. ▼

▲ *Factory without scrubbers*

▲ *Factory with scrubbers*

Lesson 4 Review

1. List three natural sources of air pollution. List three sources of air pollution people cause.

2. What are some problems polluted air can cause?

3. What are some ways you can help keep air clean?

4. **Identify Supporting Facts and Details** In the second paragraph on page C65, what facts and details support the main idea?

Investigating Air Pollution

Process Skills

- observing
- communicating
- inferring

Materials

- safety goggles
- pencil
- 4 index cards
- 4 pieces of string
- petroleum jelly
- paper towel
- hand lens

Getting Ready

In this activity you can make your own pollution detector to check pollution levels in different locations.

Follow This Procedure

1 Make a chart like the one shown. Use your chart to record your observations.

Card number	Location	Observations
1		
2		
3		
4		

2 Put on your safety goggles. Use a pencil to punch one hole in the top center of each of the index cards. Tie a piece of string through each hole (Photo A).

Photo A

3 Label the cards *1, 2, 3,* and *4.* On the back of each card record the names of the classmates in your group.

4 Use your finger to spread a thin layer of petroleum jelly on each card (Photo B). Use the paper towel to clean off any extra jelly on your fingers or desk.

 Safety Note *The petroleum jelly is not a food. Do not taste, and avoid contact with clothing.*

Photo B

5 Pick a different location to tie each card (Photo C). Record the location of each card on your chart.

6 After one day, **observe** each card with the hand lens. Record the amount of particles you see and describe their appearance.

Self-Monitoring
Have I recorded everything I observed?

Interpret Your Results

1. Compare and contrast your four cards. Describe the similarities and differences. Which location had the most particles? Which location had the fewest?

2. Communicate. Compare and contrast your cards with those of other groups. Did cards in similar locations show similar results?

Photo C

3. Make an **inference.** Explain why there may be differences in the amount of pollution you observed in different locations.

Inquire Further

What are some other ways to detect air pollution? Develop a plan to answer this or other questions you may have.

Self-Assessment

- I followed instructions to make an air pollution detector.
- I **observed** the particles on each card and recorded my observations.
- I compared and contrasted the cards.
- I **communicated** by comparing and contrasting my cards with those of other groups.
- I made an **inference** about pollution differences in different locations.

Chapter 2 Review

Chapter Main Ideas

Lesson 1
• Renewable resources can be replaced within a reasonably short period of time.
• Nonrenewable resources cannot be replaced once they are used up.

Lesson 2
• Although there is a great deal of water on the earth, only a small part is usable by people. Water is used for industrial, agricultural, and household purposes. People get water from wells, lakes, and rivers.
• Water users can reduce the amount of water they use and reduce the amount of water pollution. Wastewater can be cleaned before it is released into rivers, lakes, or oceans.

Lesson 3
• Land resources are used for housing, farming, mining, and industry. Farms, mines, and industry produce products people use.
• By recycling, reusing, and reducing how much they use, people can protect land resources.

Lesson 4
• Some air pollution is caused by natural events. Some is caused by people.
• Polluted air can cause health problems; can harm living things, including crops and forests; and can damage nonliving things.
• Clean air can be protected by conserving energy, by using motor vehicles less, and by reducing, reusing, and recycling.

Reviewing Science Words and Concepts

Write the letter of the word or phrase that best completes each sentence.

a. acid rain
b. air pollution
c. carbon monoxide
d. fossil fuel
e. groundwater
f. nonrenewable resource
g. ozone
h. pollutant
i. renewable resource

1. People who obtain their water from wells are using ___.
2. Trees grown on tree farms are an example of a ___.
3. A resource that cannot be replaced after it is used up is called a ___.
4. In the United States, about half of the ___ comes from the cars people drive.
5. Because the smoke from a forest fire is an unwanted substance that is added to the air, it is called a ___.
6. A fuel formed over many years from the remains of living organisms is called a ___.
7. A molecule of oxygen with three atoms of oxygen is called ___.
8. Rain containing acids formed from air pollutants is called ___.
9. A colorless, odorless pollutant called ___ is poisonous to breathe.

Explaining Science

Write a paragraph to answer these questions.

1. Why is coal classified as a nonrenewable resource?

2. How can water polluted with fertilizer harm a lake?

3. Why is rich soil valuable?

4. Why is air pollution worse than it was 500 years ago?

Using Skills

1. In the first paragraph on page C52, what are the **supporting facts and details?**

2. **Predict** the effect an increase in population may have on the amount of water pollution. Explain why.

3. Make a chart to **communicate** the steps in aluminum recycling.

4. Describe what you might **observe** on a day when the air is polluted.

Critical Thinking

1. **Classify** the source of each as a renewable resource or a nonrenewable resource: **a.** a sheet of paper made from wood grown on a tree farm, **b.** a gold ring made from gold taken from a mine, **c.** a piece of bread made from wheat grown on a farm, **d.** electricity from a power plant that burns coal as fuel, **e.** electricity from a wind turbine, **f.** heat from a solar collector, **g.** heat from a gas furnace.

2. Examine the two pictures of the factory on page C67. **Infer** which picture is newer. Explain your interference.

3. Mining usually means removing a nonrenewable resource such as coal from the ground. In some places where groundwater has collected over thousands of years, the groundwater is being used far faster than it is collecting in the ground. **Infer** why this use of groundwater is sometimes called mining water.

How Cold Is It?

Perhaps you used a thermometer to find out the temperature outdoors today. Do you know what scientists use to take the ocean's temperature?

Chapter 3
Climate

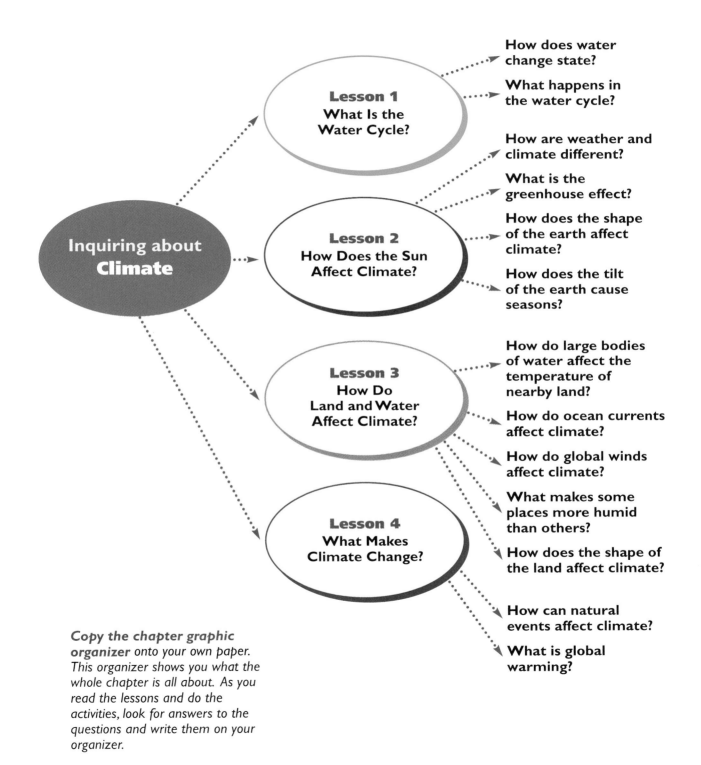

Inquiring about Climate

Lesson 1
What Is the
Water Cycle?

- How does water change state?
- What happens in the water cycle?

Lesson 2
How Does the Sun
Affect Climate?

- How are weather and climate different?
- What is the greenhouse effect?
- How does the shape of the earth affect climate?
- How does the tilt of the earth cause seasons?

Lesson 3
How Do
Land and Water
Affect Climate?

- How do large bodies of water affect the temperature of nearby land?
- How do ocean currents affect climate?
- How do global winds affect climate?
- What makes some places more humid than others?
- How does the shape of the land affect climate?

Lesson 4
What Makes
Climate Change?

- How can natural events affect climate?
- What is global warming?

Copy the chapter graphic organizer onto your own paper. This organizer shows you what the whole chapter is all about. As you read the lessons and do the activities, look for answers to the questions and write them on your organizer.

Exploring How Sunlight Moves Water

Process Skills

- observing
- communicating

Materials

- pail
- water
- large stone
- shallow plastic cup
- plastic wrap
- tape
- small stone

Explore

1 Add water to the pail until it is about $\frac{1}{3}$ full.

2 Put a large stone in a shallow cup. Place the cup in the center of the pail. The top of the cup must be lower than the top of the pail, but above the level of the water.

3 Cover the pail with plastic wrap. Seal the plastic wrap to the sides of the pail with tape.

4 Gently place a small stone in the center of the plastic wrap. It should be directly above the cup.

5 Put the pail in a warm, sunny place. Let the pail stay in the warm place for one or two days. **Observe** what happens inside the pail a few times each day. Record your observations.

Reflect

1. Communicate. Draw some pictures of what you think happened in the pail. Draw a before and after picture.

2. What role did the sunlight play in the pail setup?

? Inquire Further

How could you make more water move into the cup in the same amount of time? Develop a plan to answer this or other questions you may have.

Exploring Temperature

Maya used a thermometer to test the temperature in different parts of the classroom. She wanted to find out if it was warmer or cooler near the windows. She read the temperature in degrees **Celsius** (°C) at four places in the room every day for four days.

Math Vocabulary

Celsius (sel′sē əs), (°C), temperature scale in which water boils at 100°C and freezes at 0°C

Example 1

Find the difference between 21°C, the temperature near the classroom door, and 19°C, the temperature near the windows.

Maya read each temperature, then she subtracted to find each difference.

Difference: 21°C − 19°C = 2°C

The temperature near the windows was lower, or cooler, than the temperature near the door.

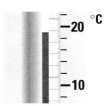

▲ *Temperature near door*

▲ *Temperature near windows*

Example 2

You can find a change in temperatures by finding the difference between high and low temperatures. If you measured a high temperature of 3°C and a low temperature of −10°C, what was the change in temperature? Hint: use the thermometer like a number line.

There was a 13°C change in temperature.

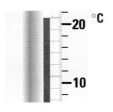

▲ *The difference between a high and a low temperature is the temperature change*

Talk About It!

If the temperature outdoors during the day reached a high of 23°C, but it dropped to 15°C at night, how would you find the change in temperature?

Math Tip
Negative numbers are numbers that are less than zero.

C75

You will learn:
- how water changes state.
- what happens in the water cycle.

Glossary

water vapor (vā′pər), water in the form of an invisible gas

humidity (hyü mid′ə tē), the amount of water vapor in the air

Lesson 1

What Is the Water Cycle?

Drip. Drip. Drip. You step outside the front door and drops of water land on your nose. Where is it coming from? It's sunny outside, but it's way below freezing! **Plink. Plunk.** How can the icicles over the door be melting?

Water Changes State

Physical Science

The pictures on these two pages show water in its three states—solid, liquid, and gas. Icicles are water as a solid. Raindrops are the liquid form of water. Water as a gas is all around you in the air.

You can see the solid icicles and the liquid raindrops in the pictures on the next page, but where is water when it's a gas? Study the picture of the teapot at the left. Do you see a gas coming from the spout? No, what you see isn't really a gas! It's a cloudy bunch of tiny droplets of liquid water. Find the place between the tip of the teapot's spout and the bottom of the cloud of water droplets. You can't see anything there. It's invisible! When water is a gas it's called **water vapor.** There's hot water vapor in the space between the cloud of droplets and the spout.

There's always some water vapor in the air. Sometimes you can feel it, even though you can't see it. Air with a lot of water vapor in it feels damp. **Humidity** is a measure of the amount of water vapor in the air.

Water droplets

Water vapor

 Icicles are solid water.

▲ Raindrops are liquid water.

You probably know that water has different properties in its different states. A solid has a definite shape and volume. As long as it stays a solid, an ice cube keeps its shape. A liquid has a definite volume, but it takes the shape of its container. If you pour a liquid into a pitcher, it will be shaped like the pitcher. If you pour it onto a table, it will spread out and form a puddle. A gas has no definite shape and no definite volume. It expands to fill its container, whether the container is a balloon or a whole room.

The diagrams show how particles of matter are arranged in each state. They are packed tightly together in a solid. They don't move around much. A solid keeps its shape and volume. In a liquid, particles are farther apart. They slide past each other, letting the liquid flow. A liquid keeps its volume, but it changes its shape to fit its container. In a gas, particles move around freely. They can be close together or far apart. They spread out to fill a big space or pack together to fill a small one.

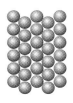

◄ **Solid**
Particles are packed together tightly. They do not move around much.

◄ **Liquid**
Particles are arranged more loosely. They can slide past each other.

◄ **Gas**
Particles are farther apart than they are in the solid or liquid state. They move around freely.

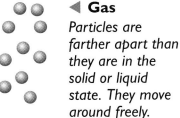

Physical
Science

Glossary

evaporate
(i vap′ə rāt′), to change from a liquid to a gas

condense (kən dens′), to change from a gas to a liquid

▲ *The sun's rays melt the solid water in icicles.*

Energy must be gained or lost for matter to change from one state to another. The energy affects how particles of matter are held together and how they move. Particles move more slowly at lower temperatures and more quickly at higher temperatures. When energy is added, particles in a solid may start to move. If they move quickly enough, the solid changes into a liquid.

What was happening inside the teapot on page C76? The water was boiling. It was changing state from a liquid to a gas. The hot plate added energy to the water in the teapot. The particles of liquid water moved faster and faster. The temperature of the water increased. Raising its temperature made the liquid water **evaporate,** or change to a gas. As the gas rose out of the teapot's spout into the air, it started to cool. It lost energy. The particles moved more slowly. Cooling made the gas **condense.** It changed into the tiny droplets of liquid water you can see.

The pictures show some ways matter around you changes state. Energy from sunlight makes solid icicles melt, or change to drops of liquid water. When the temperature drops at night, water vapor in the air condenses. Liquid dewdrops form on leaves and flowers. Later, energy from the sun makes the dew evaporate. The liquid dewdrops change back to water vapor, a gas in the air.

Dewdrops form when the air is cool. When the sun warms the air, the liquid dew evaporates and disappears into the air. ▶

7:00 AM   10:00 AM

You know that you can find water around you in all three states—as a gas, as a liquid, and as a solid. Water freezes at 0°C. Ice will melt and change to liquid water at temperatures above 0°C. Water boils at 100°C. At that temperature, water particles move so fast that the liquid evaporates and becomes a gas. Boiling is rapid evaporation.

Have you watched a puddle evaporate from the sidewalk after a rainstorm? The water slowly disappears. It changes to invisible water vapor. What's going on? The puddle isn't boiling, and the temperature isn't anywhere near 100°C. Liquids can evaporate at temperatures lower than their boiling point. Some of the particles in the liquid move faster than others. The fastest-moving particles can escape the liquid and become a gas. That's what happens when a puddle evaporates after the rain stops.

Look at the picture of the window on the right. Tiny droplets of water condensed on it. When the temperature drops, particles of water vapor in the air lose energy. They change to water droplets on the window and on other surfaces. The window below is covered with frost, a feathery pattern of ice crystals. Frost forms when the temperature is very low. Water vapor in the air changes directly into solid ice crystals on a window or other surface, without changing into liquid droplets. The crystals can make complex patterns, like the ones shown.

▲ When the temperature drops, water vapor can condense on a window. The water droplets form a thin film of liquid water.

If it's really cold, ice crystals instead of water droplets may form on the window. The feathery crystals are frost. ▼

The Water Cycle

The diagram shows the steps in the water cycle. Water evaporates from everywhere on the surface of the earth, especially from the oceans. It rises into the atmosphere and begins to cool. High in the atmosphere, water condenses and falls to the earth. The liquid water moves over the earth's surface, through the ground, and through bodies of water until it reaches the oceans. The cycle continues as more water evaporates and rises into the atmosphere. The sun provides the energy needed for water to change its state when it evaporates. Look at the diagram and follow what happens in the water cycle as you read the next page.

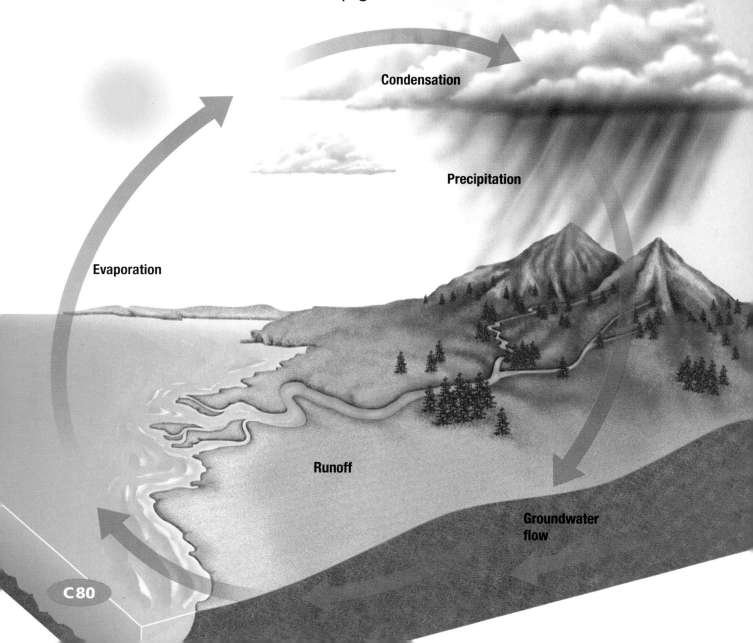

Condensation

Precipitation

Evaporation

Runoff

Groundwater flow

Find *condensation* in the diagram. Winds above the earth carry water vapor and clouds. In the atmosphere, the water vapor cools and condenses. It forms droplets of liquid water so tiny they can float in the air. Millions of these droplets together form a cloud.

When the temperature high in the atmosphere is cold enough, the droplets freeze into ice crystals. More water vapor condenses on the crystals and freezes, making them bigger. Crystals bump into each other, join, and grow still larger. When they are too big and heavy to stay in the air, they fall to the earth.

Water that falls to the earth from a cloud is **precipitation.** If the air near the earth is cold enough, the water falls to the earth as snow, sleet, or hail. If the air near the ground is warm, the water falls to the earth as rain.

Most precipitation falls onto the oceans. The rest falls on the surface of the land. Some of the precipitation that falls onto the land evaporates. Some is **runoff,** or water that falls onto land and drains away into streams and rivers. The streams and rivers flow to the ocean. The rest of the precipitation sinks into the earth. It becomes part of the groundwater, water that moves through tiny openings in rocks and soil beneath the earth's surface. Some groundwater eventually flows into streams and rivers.

Find *evaporation* in the diagram. Every day the sun heats millions of kilograms of water on the earth's surface and makes it evaporate. Close to 85% of the water vapor in the atmosphere comes from the oceans.

Glossary

precipitation
(pri sip′ə tā′shən), any form of water that falls to the earth from a cloud

runoff, water that falls onto land and drains off the surface

Glossary

▲ Hail starts as a frozen raindrop. Layers of ice form on it. When it gets heavy, it falls to earth.

▲ Snowflakes are tiny, six-sided crystals of ice. They form from water vapor in clouds at temperatures at or lower than 0°C.

Lesson 1 Review

1. How does water change state?
2. Explain the stages of the water cycle.
3. **Compare and Contrast**
   Contrast the properties of water in its three states.

Investigating Sunlight and the Earth's Tilt

Process Skills

- making and using models
- observing
- inferring

Materials

- plastic-foam ball with pencil (model of the earth)
- marker
- flashlight

Getting Ready

In this activity you will model how sunlight reaches different parts of the earth as the earth moves through its orbit.

Review what you know about how the earth moves around the sun.

Follow This Procedure

❶ Make a chart like the one shown. Use your chart to record your observations.

Tilt of the earth	Part of the earth receiving more direct sunlight
One-quarter orbit (neither pole tilted toward sun)	
One-half orbit (South Pole tilted toward sun)	
Three-quarters orbit (neither pole tilted toward sun)	
Start/end of orbit (North Pole tilted toward sun)	

❷ Observe the **model** of the earth. The eraser end of the pencil is the earth's axis at the North Pole. The other end of the pencil is the axis at the South Pole.

❸ Use the marker to draw a line around the ball halfway between the two poles (Photo A). The line represents the equator.

Photo A

Photo B

④ Hold the ball so the North Pole tilts toward the front of the room. Have your partner hold a flashlight near the ball and shine it at the center of the ball (Photo B). The flashlight represents the sun.

⑤ Move the ball through a quarter of its orbit by moving a quarter of a circle to your right, walking around your partner. Keep the eraser end of the pencil pointed to the front of the room.

⑥ Have your partner turn so the flashlight always shines on the ball at its center. **Observe** which pole is tilted toward the light and which part of the earth gets more direct sunlight. Record your observations.

⑦ Repeat steps 5 and 6 as you move the earth a quarter of the way around the sun three more times.

Self-Monitoring
Have I correctly completed all the steps?

Interpret Your Results

1. Look at your chart. Explain how the earth's tilt affects how directly light reaches different parts of the earth.

2. Explain the difference in the seasons between the Northern and Southern Hemispheres.

3. Each quarter circle you moved the ball around the flashlight is like a season. Make an **inference.** Which position of the earth would be winter in the Northern Hemisphere? Explain.

 Inquire Further

How does the length of daylight time at the earth's poles change as the earth orbits the sun? Develop a plan to answer this or other questions you may have.

What's the **Big Idea?**

You will learn:

- the difference between weather and climate.
- about the greenhouse effect.
- how the shape of the earth affects climate.
- how the tilt of the earth causes seasons.

Glossary

climate (klī′mit), the average weather conditions in an area over many years

▲ *Places near the poles are cold all year.*

Lesson 2

How Does the Sun Affect Climate?

Brrrrrrr! The weather report predicts a colder-than-usual winter for the area you live in. But you have to know what the winter is usually like to understand that, don't you? And why is it colder in winter than in summer, anyway?

How Weather and Climate Are Different

Weather is the temperature, precipitation, winds, humidity, clouds, and other conditions in a place at a particular time. In many places, the weather changes almost every day. It can even change during a day. Rain might start and stop. The temperature might be colder at night than in the daytime. In some places, weather tends to stay about the same most of the time.

Climate refers to the weather conditions in a place at different times and seasons over many years. It describes the pattern of weather for the whole year. The climate can be very different in different places. The main features of the climate are the amount of precipitation and the temperature at different times of the year. Some places are warm and humid most of the year. Others have hot, humid summers and cold, dry winters. Still other places are always cold, even in summer.

To find out about the climate of a place, scientists study records of what its weather was like every day for many years. The climate of a place usually stays about the same for hundreds of years.

The Greenhouse Effect

The sun's energy travels through space and reaches the earth's atmosphere. Notice in the diagram below that some energy bounces back into space. The rest of the energy reaches the earth's surface, which reflects some of it and absorbs the remainder.

Most of the energy the earth absorbs is changed into **infrared radiation,** a form of energy that travels in long waves. The infrared radiation is given off into the atmosphere. Some of the gases in the atmosphere absorb the infrared energy. Gases that absorb infrared energy, mainly water vapor and carbon dioxide, are called **greenhouse gases.** They let sunlight pass through the atmosphere to reach the earth. They trap the infrared radiation that is reflected from the earth's warmed surface. The greenhouse gases absorb the energy and keep the earth warm. The process is called the **greenhouse effect.**

Without the greenhouse effect, heat leaving the earth would pass through the atmosphere and go off into space. The average temperature of the earth's surface is about 15°C. Without the greenhouse effect, it would be about 33°C colder.

Glossary

infrared radiation (in′frə red′ rā′dē ā′shən), energy with a wavelength longer than the wavelength of light

greenhouse gases, carbon dioxide, water vapor, and other gases in the atmosphere that absorb infrared radiation from the earth's surface

greenhouse effect, the process by which gases in the atmosphere absorb heat and keep the earth warm

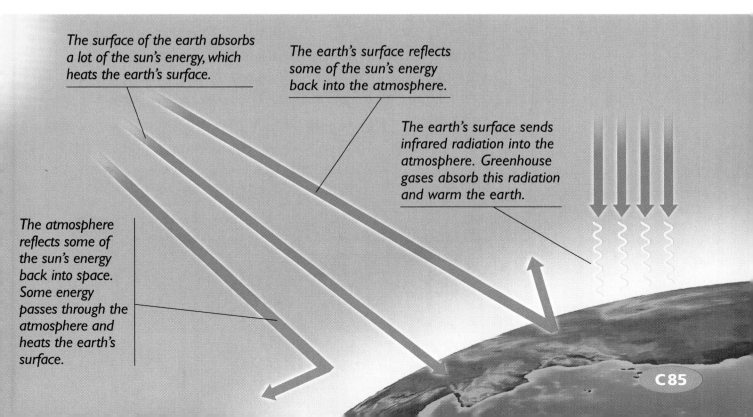

The surface of the earth absorbs a lot of the sun's energy, which heats the earth's surface.

The earth's surface reflects some of the sun's energy back into the atmosphere.

The earth's surface sends infrared radiation into the atmosphere. Greenhouse gases absorb this radiation and warm the earth.

The atmosphere reflects some of the sun's energy back into space. Some energy passes through the atmosphere and heats the earth's surface.

The Shape of the Earth

Polar climate

Sunlight spread over large area

Temperate climate

Tropical climate

Sunlight spread over small area

Equator

Tropical climate

Temperate climate

Polar climate

Because the earth is shaped almost like a ball, the sun heats the earth unevenly. Different places get different amounts of energy from the sun. The uneven heating causes different climates around the world.

Notice on the globe that at the equator, sunlight is concentrated on a small area. The earth gets more direct energy from the sun at the equator, where the rays are more concentrated. Places near the equator, where the sunlight is most direct, have a hot, tropical climate.

Now observe how the earth curves near the area of polar climate. The diagram shows that near the poles, the same amount of sunlight is spread over a larger area than near the equator. Places near the poles, where sunlight is most spread out, have a cold climate.

Find the regions on the globe between the areas of tropical climate and the areas of polar climate. The sun's rays are more intense in this area of temperate climate than they are at the poles. The rays are less intense than they are near the equator. The areas of temperate climate generally have milder weather with less extreme temperatures. The map below shows how temperatures vary in different places.

This computer-generated map was made from pictures taken by satellites in space. The different colors identify temperatures in different parts of the world. ▶

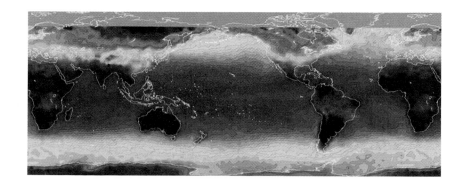

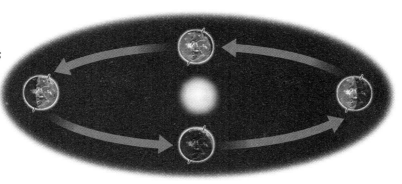

June

The North Pole is tilted toward the sun. Summer begins in the Northern Hemisphere. The South Pole is tilted away from the sun. It is winter in the Southern Hemisphere.

December

The North Pole is tilted away from the sun. Winter begins in the Northern Hemisphere. What is the season in the Southern Hemisphere?

The Tilt of the Earth

The diagram shows that as the earth follows its path around the sun, it is tilted in space. Notice that it always tilts the same way as it moves around the sun. Different parts of the earth's surface are tilted toward the sun at different points in its path.

The way the earth tilts causes the different seasons. The tilt affects how much sunlight each place on the earth gets at different times of the year. It also affects the angle of the sunlight. A place gets the most direct sunlight when it is tilted toward the sun. The days are longer, and temperatures are warmer. When a place is tilted away from the sun, the sunlight is less direct. The days are shorter, and temperatures are colder.

Lesson 2 Review

1. How does climate differ from weather?
2. What is the greenhouse effect?
3. How does the shape of the earth affect climate?
4. What causes the seasons?
5. **Predicting**
   How would life on the earth be different if the greenhouse effect did not exist?

Investigating How a Greenhouse Works

Process Skills

- making and using models
- estimating and measuring
- identifying and controlling variables

Materials

- soil
- 2 clear plastic containers
- clay
- 2 thermometers
- plastic wrap
- masking tape
- clock or watch

Getting Ready

In this activity you will make a model to find out how a greenhouse works.

Follow This Procedure

1 Make a chart like the one shown. Use your chart to record your measurements.

	Container without plastic wrap	Container with plastic wrap
At start		
After 10 minutes		
After 20 minutes		
After 30 minutes		

2 To **make** a **model** of a greenhouse, put a thin layer of soil in each plastic container. Use the same amount of soil in each container and spread it evenly.

3 Place a ball of clay in the center of each container. Prop a thermometer on each ball of clay. Be sure to place the bulb end of the thermometer above the soil to measure the temperature of the air.

4 Cover one of the containers tightly with plastic wrap. Tape the plastic wrap to the container. Do not cover the other container.

5 **Measure** temperatures by reading the thermometers in the containers. Record your starting measurements in your chart.

6 Place the containers in a place that receives direct sunlight.

7 Read the thermometers every ten minutes for half an hour. Record your measurements in your chart.

Self-Monitoring
Have I followed all the directions in the activity?

Interpret Your Results

1. How did the air temperatures of the two containers compare before they were placed in sunlight? How did they compare after they were exposed to light for half an hour?

2. You were **identifying** and **controlling variables** when you used the same amount of soil in each container and exposed them to sunlight for the same amount of time. Explain why this is important.

3. Based on your measurements, which container do you think was like a greenhouse?

4. Explain how your model is similar to the greenhouse effect on the earth and how it is different.

Inquire Further

Would the results be different if you used water in the container instead of soil? Develop a plan to answer this or other questions you may have.

Self-Assessment

- I followed instructions to **make** a **model** of a greenhouse.
- I recorded my **measurements** of the temperatures of each container every ten minutes.
- I compared the air temperatures in the containers before and after they were exposed to sunlight.
- I **identified** and **controlled variables** in the activity and discussed why that is important.
- I compared my model to the greenhouse effect on the earth.

What's the Big Idea?

You will learn:

- how bodies of water affect temperature.
- the ways ocean currents affect climate.
- how global winds affect climate.
- what affects humidity.
- how the shape of the land affects climate.

San Francisco is near the ocean. Its winters are usually mild. Most of the time you need only a lightweight jacket. ▼

Lesson 3

How Do Land and Water Affect Climate?

Crash!! Crash!! Crash!! That noise you're hearing is made by waves. As you know, you can sometimes hear water. Did you know you might also feel it in the air?

Differences in Temperature

The temperature of a large body of water, such as a lake or ocean, doesn't change much during the day. Even when the air temperature rises in daytime and falls at night, the water temperature stays about the same. Water warms and cools more slowly than land. Land absorbs energy from the sun and warms quickly in the daytime. It loses energy and cools quickly at night.

The climate of a place close to an ocean or large lake will probably be affected by the constant temperature of the water. Hawaii, an island surrounded by ocean water, has about the same temperature day and night. Many places near an ocean or lake have less temperature variations through the year than places farther inland.

Places that are not near the water are more likely to have big changes in temperature from day to night and throughout the year. For example, in San Francisco, average temperatures are 8.8°C in January and 16°C in July. Temperatures in St. Louis are −0.5°C in January and 27°C in July. The Pacific Ocean moderates the climate in San Francisco. The boy in the picture only needs a lightweight jacket most of the year. St. Louis has a greater temperature range.

◄ You can make inferences about the climate of a place if you know its location on a map.

Find San Francisco and St. Louis on the map above. Notice that they are at about the same distance from the equator. They are also about the same height above sea level. San Francisco is on the coast of the Pacific Ocean. St. Louis is inland, far from any large body of water. The girl in the picture needs a warm jacket during the winter.

Winds can influence how much a nearby body of water affects the temperature of the land. In the United States, winds generally blow from west to east. As they move east, they carry weather conditions from the places they passed over.

The climate of places near the Pacific Ocean is usually affected by the ocean to the west. Along the Atlantic Ocean, the water is to the east. Because of the wind direction, the climates of many cities along the Atlantic are more affected by the temperatures of the land, which is west of them, than they are by the temperatures of the ocean to the east. New York City is on the Atlantic Ocean, so you might think its temperature range would be like San Francisco's. Actually, New York has a range almost as great as St. Louis has. Winds from the west bring weather to New York City from the land that is west of it. New York has cold winters and hot summers, just like an inland city.

St. Louis is far inland. Temperatures are cold in winter. You need a warm jacket. ▼

C91

Ocean Currents

Currents are like rivers of water that move through the ocean. Surface currents flow through the upper parts of the ocean. Their movement is caused by the earth's rotation and by winds that always blow across the globe in the same directions.

Surface currents can carry water that is warmer or colder than the ocean water around them. The map below shows where major surface currents of the world's oceans flow. Reddish arrows show the paths of warm currents. Blue arrows show the paths of cold currents. The temperature of the water in the currents can affect the climate of land they pass near.

The map shows where warm and cold surface currents flow in the world's oceans. ▼

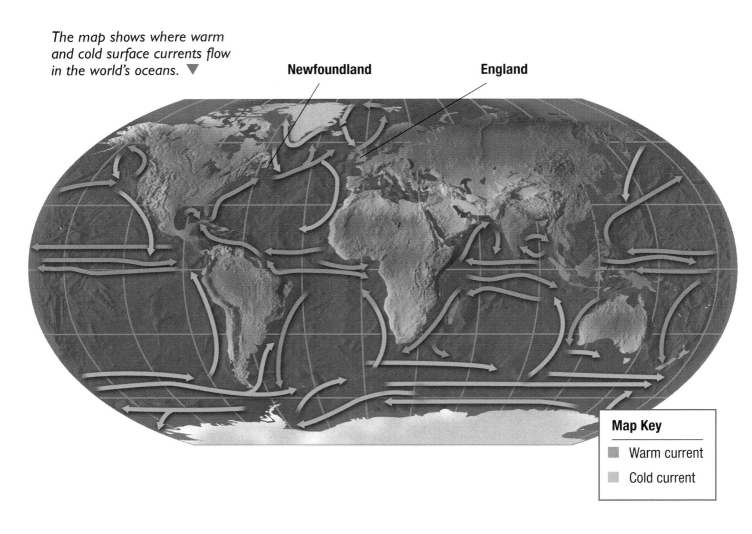

Newfoundland   **England**

Map Key

■ Warm current

■ Cold current

The Gulf Stream is a surface current that carries warm water from the Gulf of Mexico. It moves north along the eastern coast of the United States. It travels as fast as 10 kilometers per hour. Then it turns east and moves more slowly toward Europe. The different colors on the map below show the temperatures of the surface water of the Gulf Stream and of the nearby land at the left.

Locate England on the map on page C 92. Notice that part of the Gulf Stream flows close to the coast of England. Warm water in the current warms the air near the land. Then find Newfoundland. Notice the cold current that flows from the north and passes near Newfoundland. Cold water in the current affects Newfoundland's climate. England and Newfoundland are about the same distance from the equator. However, because of the different temperatures of the surface currents, the climate of England is warmer than the climate of Newfoundland.

◀ *This view of the Gulf Stream was taken from a satellite.*

Wind Patterns

Look at the map below showing the pattern of the most common winds that blow across the earth. Notice that in some places, the winds usually blow from west to east. In other places, the winds usually blow from east to west. The earth's rotation makes the path of the global winds curve.

Global winds occur because the temperature of the air is different in different places. The air above the equator is warmer than the air over the poles. When air is warmed, the particles in it spread out. The warm air from the equator rises. Particles in cooling air move closer together. Cold air from the poles slips beneath the rising warmer air. The movement of the cooler air creates wind.

Winds carry heat energy and water vapor with them when they move. Recall that winds blow west to east across the United States, carrying weather conditions with them. To learn about tomorrow's weather, look at today's weather map to see conditions in a place west of you.

Global Wind Patterns

The arrows show the directions of global winds that blow across the earth. ▼

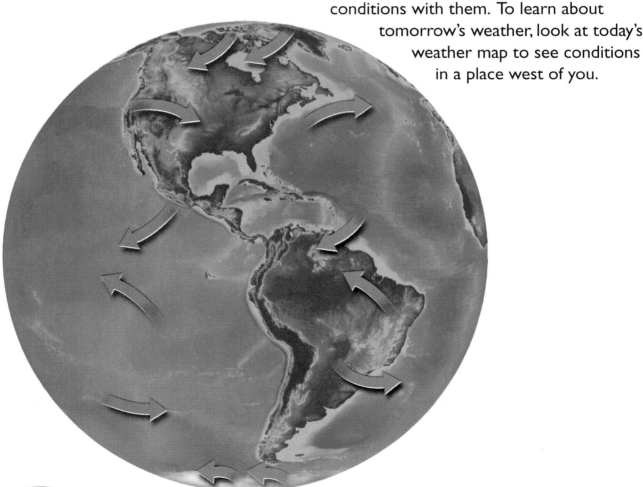

Differences in Humidity

Many places near an ocean or a large lake have a humid climate during all or part of the year. Large amounts of water are always evaporating from oceans and lakes. When it evaporates from a body of water, water vapor goes into the air above the water and above the nearby land. It makes the air more humid.

Places that are not near large bodies of water can also have humid climates. Winds can move air that carries water vapor to places far from the oceans. Wind currents carry moisture from the Gulf of Mexico into the Midwest. The water vapor they bring provides most of the moisture for that area.

The roots of trees and other plants take up water from the ground. Plants add humidity to the air when they send out water vapor through their leaves. A single tree can give off 7,000 liters of water each year. Cactus plants grow mostly in dry places. Their needlelike leaves do not give off much water. Which picture shows a place that probably has high humidity?

▲ Many trees and other plants give off water vapor and can increase the humidity in the air around them.

▲ A desert has few trees or large bodies of water. The air is almost always very dry.

The Shape of the Land

The shape of the land can affect the climate in an area. The climate at the top of a mountain can be very different from the climate at the bottom. The difference is caused by changes in elevation. Air that is closer to low, flat land is usually warmer than air at higher elevations. Higher places usually have colder climates.

Look at the diagram below. Denver and St. Louis are about the same distance from the equator. Both cities are inland from the ocean, and they aren't near large lakes. However, they are at very different elevations. Denver is 1,610 meters above sea level. St. Louis is 163 meters above sea level. Which city do you think has a cooler average temperature?

The shape of the land can also affect the amount of precipitation. You know that air above the ocean is full of water vapor. Winds can move the humid air above the ocean and carry it over the land. The diagram on the next page shows what can happen when humid winds from the ocean meet tall mountains near the coast. The wind is carrying warm, humid air picked up over the Pacific Ocean. It is moving eastward toward the Cascade Range near the northwestern coast of North America. As it moves east, the wind rises upward when it meets the mountains. As it rises up the side of the mountains, the air gets cooler. Water vapor in the moist air condenses, and clouds form. As the air continues to rise and to get cooler, water falls from the clouds as rain or snow.

Land at higher elevations usually has cooler temperatures. The average temperature for the year in Denver is 10.1°C. In St. Louis, it is 13.3°C. ▼

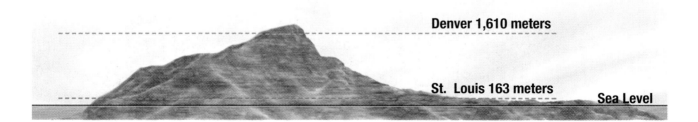

Denver 1,610 meters

St. Louis 163 meters

Sea Level

Humid wind

Precipitation

Dry wind

Pacific Ocean

Desert

Notice in the diagram above that most of the precipitation falls west of the mountains. The pictures to the right show how this can affect the land. Rain or snow keeps the western slopes of the mountains wet. The winds are dry by the time they reach the eastern side of the mountains, and the land is dry and desertlike.

▲ The western side of the Cascade Range is humid.

Lesson 3 Review

1. How do large bodies of water affect the temperature of nearby land?

2. How can ocean currents affect climate?

3. How do global winds affect climate?

4. Why are some places more humid than others?

5. How does the shape of the land affect climate?

6. **Sequencing**
   Put the items in the order they would occur:
   a. air cools at higher elevations;
   b. air picks up moisture over the ocean;
   c. rain or snow falls;
   d. air is dry as it moves eastward.

▲ Mount Rainier is the highest peak in the Cascade Range.

▲ The land east of the Cascade Range is dry.

You will learn:

- how natural events affect climate.
- what global warming is.

Lesson 4

What Makes Climate Change?

KABOOM!!!! You probably know that volcanoes often erupt with a lot of noise, ash, and lava. What a mess! Some eruptions throw out so much ash and dust that they make day look like night. Some eruptions can even affect weather.

Natural Events

Some natural events can change climate and weather. The pictures on these two pages show how some volcanic eruptions affect weather. The eruptions release sulfur dioxide gas along with dust and ash. Sulfuric acid droplets form when the gas mixes with oxygen and water in the atmosphere. Strong winds high above the earth carry the tiny droplets long distances. They keep some of the sun's energy from reaching the earth's surface.

In April 1815, a volcano called Tambora erupted in Indonesia. Droplets of sulfuric acid spread through the atmosphere, along with more than 1.5 million tons of debris and dust. In the next year, called "the year without a summer," temperatures in North America and Europe were unusually cold. The cold caused crop failures and famine.

In 1883, Krakatoa, a volcano in Indonesia, erupted, releasing dust and gases. It caused three years of brilliant sunsets in the Northern Hemisphere. It may have contributed to the worldwide low temperatures of the next five years.

Erupting volcanoes shoot clouds of matter into the atmosphere. The matter usually includes gases, dust, and ash. Most ash quickly falls to the earth's surface. ▼

Volcanoes

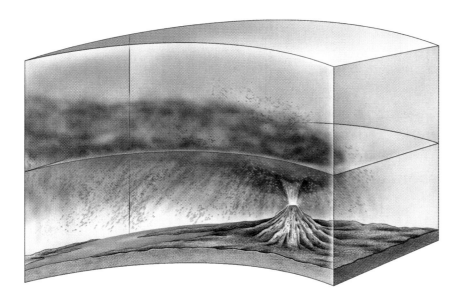

◀ Gas and acid droplets from volcanic eruptions can rise above the first layer of the atmosphere, the troposphere, into the second layer, the stratosphere. There, winds can carry the droplets all over the world. The layer of droplets above the earth can reflect some of the sun's energy back into space. This keeps the energy from warming the earth.

In 1991, Mt. Pinatubo in the Philippines erupted, producing a huge cloud of sulfur dioxide gas. It sent 20,000,000 tons of gas into the stratosphere. An instrument on a NASA satellite measured the sulfur dioxide gas released. This picture was recorded the day after the June 16, 1991 eruption. The colors show the concentration of sulfur dioxide in the atmosphere. ▶

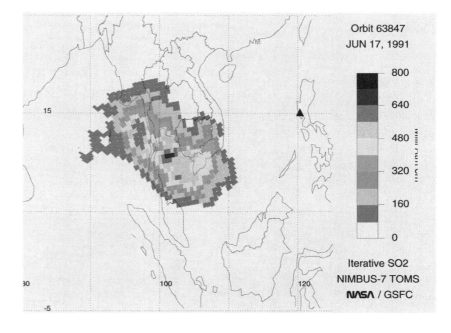

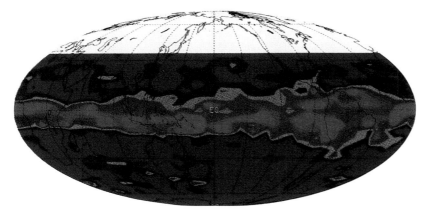

◀ The cloud of gas from the eruption of Mt. Pinatubo, shown here in red and green, spread around the world in about 22 days. It may have been the cause of low temperatures that lasted several years.

Another natural event that can change weather is called an El Niño. Every two to seven years, the temperature of the water in the Pacific Ocean near the equator increases. Winds in that area usually blow from east to west. When an El Niño starts, the winds weaken. Warm water in the area can drift eastward.

Look at the satellite pictures of ocean temperatures during the 1997 El Niño. White areas near the center show warm water flowing toward South America. Air above the water warms. It rises, then it starts to cool. Storm clouds can form.

An El Niño affects different parts of the earth in different ways. In 1997, warm ocean water brought warm, wet weather and severe storms and floods to the western coast of South America. Brazil, on the east coast away from the warm water, had a drought. Southeast Asia had a severe drought.

The pictures on the next page show some of the damage caused by storms resulting from the El Niño. The southern and western United States had severe winter storms. Heavy rains in California and tornadoes in Florida also caused destruction. Other parts of the United States, such as parts of the Midwest, had an unusually mild winter.

These maps were made with data from an orbiting satellite. Yellow, red, and white areas are waters that are warmer than usual. The blue and purple areas are waters that are colder than usual. ▼

April 1997
Notice that the white area in this picture is very small.

July 1997
The white area shows an increase in the amount of unusually warm water in the Pacific.

October 1997
The white area is a huge mass of warm water flowing toward South America. It contains 30 times more water than all the Great Lakes put together.

◀ Tornadoes and other wind storms caused severe damage in Florida and in many other parts of the world.

▲ Unusually heavy snows fell in some parts of the United States.

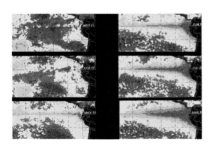

▲ These maps, drawn from satellite information, show temperatures of ocean water in 1997. Reds indicate water that is warmer than usual. Blues indicate water that is cooler than usual. In some places, water temperatures rose 5°C.

▲ Wet weather and storms in California resulted in mudslides.

Glossary

global (glō′bəl)
warming, an increase in the earth's temperature

Global Warming

You learned that the greenhouse effect keeps the earth warm. If greenhouse gases in the atmosphere didn't absorb the energy and send it back to the earth, the earth would be a frozen ball of ice.

Some activities people do, such as driving cars and burning wood or other fuel, send carbon dioxide and other greenhouse gases into the atmosphere as wastes. Trees and other plants use carbon dioxide from the atmosphere when they make sugars. When forests are cleared for lumber or farming, less of the carbon dioxide gets used. Carbon dioxide in the atmosphere has increased about 28% since the mid-1700s, when the Industrial Revolution began.

Many scientists think that the greenhouse effect increases when there are more greenhouse gases in the atmosphere. A rise in the earth's temperature, called **global warming,** could result. The diagram shows how global warming might occur. As a result, the earth's temperature could rise 1°C in the next 100 years. Maybe that doesn't sound like much. However, water expands when it gets warmer, and ice in glaciers melts. The level of the ocean could rise. Land near coastlines could flood. The climate might change, bringing violent storms and severe floods and droughts.

Sun warms the earth.

Greenhouse gases in the atmosphere keep some heat from escaping into space. When there are more greenhouse gases, more heat stays near the earth. The temperature rises.

Many scientists think the effect of global warming could be reduced if the amount of greenhouse gases added to the atmosphere were reduced. Using energy for heating, electricity, and transportation adds greenhouse gases to the atmosphere. Avoiding the cutting and burning of forests would also help reduce the amount of carbon dioxide. The chart shows ways you and your family could help reduce adding greenhouse gases to the atmosphere.

Use less energy for heating and cooling

- Be sure furnace and air conditioner are in good repair and are working efficiently.
- Clean or change air filters on furnace and air conditioner regularly.
- Plug leaks around doors and windows.
- Insulate walls and ceilings.

Use less hot water

- Wash clothes in warm or cold water, not hot water.
- Take shorter showers and use water-saving shower heads.
- Set temperature of the water heater no higher than 49°C.
- Run only full dishwasher and washing machine loads.

Transportation

- Walk, ride a bicycle, car pool, or use mass transit instead of driving.

Recycle and Reuse

- Recycle paper, plastic, and metal objects.
- Choose reusable rather than disposable items.
- Start and use a recycling program at school.

Lesson 4 Review

1. What natural events affect climate?

2. What is global warming?

3. Compare and Contrast
Explain how global warming differs from the greenhouse effect.

Chapter 3 Review

Chapter Main Ideas

Lesson 1

• Water exists in three states—solid, liquid, and gas—and can change from one state to another when temperatures change.

• In the water cycle, water evaporates from the earth and its oceans, rises into the atmosphere, condenses, falls to the earth as precipitation, runs over the surface or sinks into the ground, and eventually makes its way back to the oceans, completing the cycle.

Lesson 2

• Weather refers to conditions of temperature, humidity, winds, precipitation, and clouds every day; climate refers to weather conditions over many years.

• The greenhouse effect is the process by which certain gases in the atmosphere absorb heat and keep the earth warm.

• The shape of the earth affects the amount of energy from the sun a particular place gets.

• The tilt of the earth causes the seasons by affecting how much sunlight a place gets at different times of the year.

Lesson 3

• The temperature of a nearby body of water can affect the temperature of the land.

• The temperature of ocean currents can affect the climate of land near their path.

• The temperature and humidity of global winds affect the climate of the land.

• Bodies of water and wind currents can affect the humidity of different places.

• The way the land is shaped can affect temperature, humidity, and the amount of precipitation.

Lesson 4

• Natural events, such as volcanic eruptions and changes in ocean temperature, can affect climate.

• Addition of excess greenhouse gases to the atmosphere can increase the greenhouse effect, causing global warming.

Reviewing Science Words and Concepts

Write the letter of the word or phrase that best completes each sentence.

a. climate
b. condense
c. evaporate
d. global warming
e. greenhouse effect
f. greenhouse gases
g. humidity
h. infrared radiation
i. precipitation
j. runoff
k. water vapor

1. A form of energy that travels in long waves and heats the earth is ____.

2. Water that drains off the land into rivers and streams is called ____.

3. When there is a lot of water vapor in the air, the ____ is high.

4. When the temperature falls, water vapor can ____ into liquid water.

5. Increasing the amount of carbon dioxide in the atmosphere might cause ___.

6. Gases in the atmosphere that absorb heat are called ___.

7. Rain and snow are forms of ___.

8. Weather conditions over many years make up the ___ of a location.

9. Water in the form of a gas is ___.

10. Water in the ocean can ___ and go into the atmosphere.

11. The earth would be much colder if it were not for the ___.

Explaining Science

Draw and label a diagram or write a paragraph to answer these questions.

1. How does water change as it moves in the water cycle through the ocean, the atmosphere, and the land?

2. How do greenhouse gases affect the way energy from the sun warms the earth?

3. What can happen when a warm, moist wind blows over a mountain range?

4. How can a volcano's eruption affect climate?

Using Skills

1. The average temperature of the earth is 15°C. The thermometer on the right shows what the average temperature would be without the greenhouse effect. What difference does the greenhouse effect make in **temperature?**

2. Suppose you read about a city that has almost the same temperature day and night and throughout the whole year. What could you **infer** about its possible location?

3. How could you **measure** the temperature for one month in the place where you live and **estimate** the average temperature?

Critical Thinking

1. Your friend wants to help develop a recycling program at your school. **Make a decision** about supporting the program. List the advantages and disadvantages of a recycling program.

2. **Sequence** the following events.
 a. Small amounts of warm water drift eastward.

b. Winds blowing to the west get weaker.

c. Wet weather occurs in western South America.

 d. Large amounts of warm water reach South America.

3. Suppose the earth was not tilted as it revolves around the sun. **Predict** the effect this would have on climate.

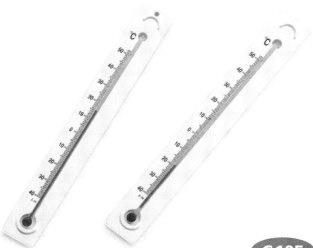

What's Up?

You look up at the night sky. A streak of light zips across the darkness. How could you find out more about objects in space? You could use a telescope to help you see.

Chapter 4
Astronomy

Lesson 1
What Makes Up the Solar System?

How have models of the solar system changed?

What are planets like?

What objects besides planets are in the solar system?

How do objects in the solar system affect Earth?

Inquiring about Astronomy

Lesson 2
What Is Known About Stars?

How does the sun compare with other stars?

How do scientists measure distances in space?

What are the properties of stars?

What are constellations and galaxies?

Lesson 3
How Do Scientists Study Planets and Stars?

How do scientists use spectroscopes to analyze light?

How do telescopes work?

How are images from telescopes recorded?

Why do scientists use telescopes in space?

Copy the chapter graphic organizer onto your own paper. This organizer shows you what the whole chapter is all about. As you read the lessons and do the activities, look for answers to the questions and write them on your organizer.

Making a Model of the Solar System

Process Skills

- making and using models
- estimating and measuring

Materials

- posterboard
- metric ruler
- scissors
- markers or crayons

Explore

1 Use the data in the table to help you **make models** of the planets. Find the diameter of each planet. Then find the size to make each planet model.

2 Make a model of each planet from the posterboard. **Measure** each planet with a metric ruler to make sure it has the correct diameter. Cut out the planets and color them. Record the color you use for each planet.

3 Arrange the models in the order shown on the chart. Mercury is closest to the sun. Remember, this model helps you compare sizes, not distance. The distances are very great.

Reflect

Hold the Earth model next to the Venus model, then next to the Jupiter model. Describe how Earth compares in size to Venus and Jupiter.

Inquire Further

How many Earth models could be lined up along the diameter of the Jupiter model? Develop a plan to answer this or other questions you may have.

Planet	Diameter	Diameter of model
Mercury	4,900 km	5 mm
Venus	12,100 km	12 mm
Earth	12,800 km	13 mm
Mars	6,800 km	7 mm
Jupiter	143,000 km	143 mm
Saturn	120,500 km	121 mm
Uranus	51,100 km	51 mm
Neptune	49,500 km	50 mm
Pluto	2,300 km	2 mm

(1 mm = approximately 1,000 km)

Exploring Place Value Through Millions

How great a distance do you think you can see? A kilometer? Two kilometers? You can see the sun, can't you? Would you be surprised to know that the sun is 149,597,900 kilometers from Earth?

A place value chart shows the value of each **digit** in this number. Each group of three digits—millions, thousands, and ones—is a **period**.

Math Vocabulary

digit (dij′it), symbol used to write numbers: 0, 1, 2, 3, 4, 5, 6, 7, 8, 9

period (pir′ē əd), a three-digit group of numbers, separated from other groups by a comma

Millions Period			Thousands Period			Ones Period		
hundreds	tens	ones	hundreds	tens	ones	hundreds	tens	ones
1	4	9 ,	5	9	7 ,	9	0	0

This number can be written in several ways:

Standard Form
149,597,900

Expanded Form
100,000,000 + 40,000,000 + 9,000,000 + 500,000 + 90,000 + 7,000 + 900

Word Form
one hundred forty nine million, five hundred ninety seven thousand, nine hundred

Write each number in the two other ways.

1. 3,406,237

2. 60,000,000 + 100,000 + 8,000 + 10 + 5

3. four hundred sixty million, two hundred six thousand, six hundred two

Math Tip

The place value chart helps you read greater numbers. You say "149," then at the comma you name the period, "million."

Talk About It!

What pattern can you find in the place names in each period?

You will learn:

- **how models of the solar system have changed.**
- **what planets are like.**
- **about other objects in the solar system.**
- **how objects in the solar system affect Earth.**

Glossary

elliptical (i lip′tə kəl), oval-shaped, like a flattened circle

model (mod′l), a representation of how something looks or works

What Makes Up the Solar System?

The sun sets, the sky grows dark, and the moon rises. One or two very bright points of light shine among the stars. **WOW!** Maybe they're planets, like Earth. Earth goes around the sun, and the moon goes around Earth.

Solar System Models

As people long ago watched the night sky over many months, certain bright objects seemed to move from one group of stars to another. Because they seemed to wander through the stars, people called these objects *wanderers.* Today we call them *planets,* from the Greek word meaning "to wander." Earth is one of nine planets that travel in **elliptical,** or oval, paths around the sun. The sun is a star at the center of this group of planets. Earth and some of the other planets have moons that revolve, or move around them. The sun, the planets and their moons, and other objects that revolve around the sun make up the solar system.

History of Science As people observed the sun, moon, planets, and stars, they made models to represent how they thought these objects were related to one another. A **model** shows how something looks or works. Early solar system models showed Earth as the center of everything that exists. It was thought to be the center of the whole universe. Look at the models on the next page to see how ideas about the solar system have changed over time.

▲ Ptolemy's Model

Ptolemy, who lived in Greece in the A.D. 100s, believed that the sun and other objects in the sky revolved around Earth. Find Earth in his model.

▲ Copernicus's Model

In 1543, almost 1,400 years after Ptolemy, the Polish astronomer Copernicus published a new model. He suggested that the sun was at the center of the solar system, with planets revolving in circles around it. Locate the sun and the planets in Copernicus's model.

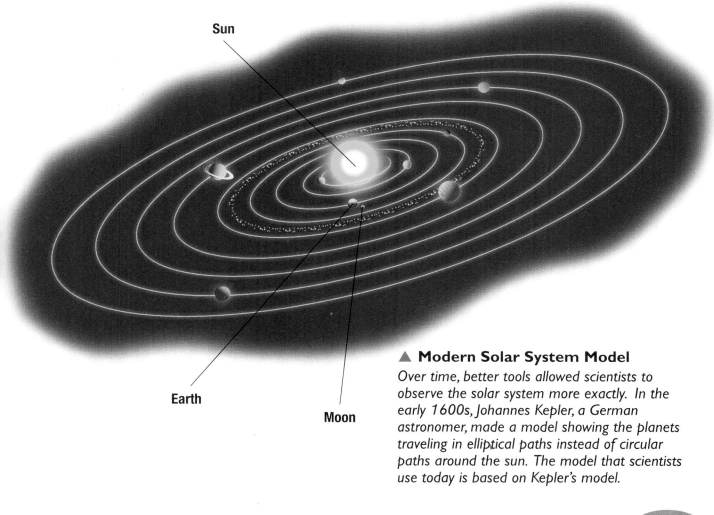

Sun

Earth

Moon

▲ Modern Solar System Model

Over time, better tools allowed scientists to observe the solar system more exactly. In the early 1600s, Johannes Kepler, a German astronomer, made a model showing the planets traveling in elliptical paths instead of circular paths around the sun. The model that scientists use today is based on Kepler's model.

The Planets

On Earth, long distances can be measured in kilometers or miles. But in our solar system, the distances between objects are too large to use these units of measure conveniently. Astronomers measure distances in the solar system in astronomical units, or AUs. One AU is the average distance from the sun to Earth, about 150,000,000 kilometers. The chart on these two pages tells about planets, including their distances from the sun in AUs.

	Mercury	Venus	Earth	Mars
Average Distance from Sun	0.39 AU 57,900,000 km	0.72 AU 108,200,000 km	1 AU 150,000,000 km	1.5 AU 227,900,000 km
Moons	None	None	1	2
Discovery	Known in ancient times; mapped by Mariner spacecraft, 1974–1975	Known in ancient times; mapped by Pioneer and Magellan spacecraft, 1979–1990	Known in ancient times	Known in ancient times; mapped by Viking spacecraft, 1976; landing by Mars Pathfinder, 1997
Special Features	Moonlike surface; second-smallest planet	Brightest object in evening or morning sky (other than the moon); surface covered with clouds of sulfuric acid	Only planet known to have living things; has lands, seas, and an oxygen-rich atmosphere	Reddish-brown "deserts" and dark blue-gray or greenish "seas" with no water

What keeps the planets in their paths, or orbits, as they revolve around the sun? In the late 1600s, Sir Isaac Newton reasoned that the same force that pulls an apple to Earth when it falls from a tree could hold the planets in their orbits. He called this force *gravity*.

The planets are much closer to Earth than any star except the sun. Because they are so close, they often look brighter than stars. However, planets do not glow from their own heat, the way the sun and other stars do. Planets shine the way the moon does, by reflecting light from the sun.

Jupiter	Saturn	Uranus	Neptune	Pluto
5.2 AU 778,300,000 km	9.5 AU 1,427,000,000 km	19.2 AU 2,869,600,000 km	30 AU 4,496,600,000 km	39.4 AU 5,900,100,000 km
16	23	15	8	1
Known in ancient times; Galileo discovered four moons by telescope in 1610; photos by Voyager spacecraft, 1979	Known in ancient times; photos by Voyager spacecraft, 1980–1981	Discovered in 1781 by William Herschel; photos by Voyager 2, 1986	Existence predicted in 1845; discovered by telescope in 1846; photos by Voyager 2 in 1989	Discovered by Clyde W. Tombaugh in 1930
The largest planet; made of gases (a "gas giant"); covered by colored bands of thick clouds; has a stormy area, the Great Red Spot; has one thin ring	Second-largest planet; a "gas giant" with six major rings and hundreds of thousands of ringlets; has yellowish surface covered with liquid hydrogen	Made of gases; smaller than Jupiter and Saturn; has eleven narrow rings; appears blue-green	Made of gases; has a great dark spot (a spiral storm); looks blue-green; has four complete rings, several incomplete rings	Smallest planet—smaller than Earth's moon; has single moon, Charon, more than half the size of the planet

Glossary

asteroid (as/tə roid/), a rocky object that revolves around the sun

meteoroid (mē/tē ə roid/), a small piece of rock or metal that travels in space around the sun

meteor (mē/tē ər), a bright streak of light that passes through Earth's atmosphere

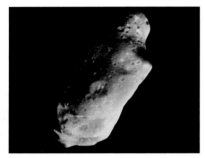

▲ **Asteroid**

At least 100,000 asteroids orbit the sun in the space between Mars and Jupiter.

▲ **Meteor**

The meteor is a glowing streak of light among the stars as it falls toward Earth.

Other Objects in the Solar System

The moon is nearer to Earth than any other object in the solar system. It revolves around Earth at a distance of about 384,500 kilometers. The moon's diameter is about a quarter of the diameter of Earth. It is almost as big as Mercury and is bigger than Pluto, the smallest planet. The moon shines by reflecting light from the sun. It seems to change shape depending on how much of the lighted side is facing Earth.

The moon and the planets are not the only objects that orbit the sun. An **asteroid** is like a small planet. The largest asteroids are about 1,000 kilometers in diameter, about the size of the moons of some planets. Others are less than a kilometer across. Asteroids like the one in the picture orbit the sun in an area called the asteroid belt, which is located between the orbits of Mars and Jupiter.

A **meteoroid** is a small piece of rock or metal that revolves around the sun. The smallest meteoroids are about the size of a grain of sand. The largest may be 100 meters in diameter, about the length of a football field. Meteoroids form when asteroids collide or comets break up.

Sometimes a meteoroid passes through Earth's atmosphere. Friction from air particles rubbing against its surface make it so hot that the rock burns. The streak of light caused by the burning rock is a **meteor.** Meteors are sometimes called "shooting stars." Find the meteor streaking across the sky among the stars in the picture.

A comet's head is a huge ball of gases and dust. The frozen center is a few kilometers in diameter. It is surrounded by a cloud of gas and dust, up to 1,000,000 kilometers in diameter.

A **comet** is a ball of ice, dust, and gases that revolves around the sun in a long, narrow path. A comet can be seen because the gas and dust particles in it reflect light from the sun. Some comets are seen from Earth only once. Then they disappear forever. Others return near Earth regularly. Find the parts of a comet in the picture below.

Glossary

comet (kom′it), a ball of ice, dust, and gases that travels through space and orbits the sun

◀ This photograph of Comet Halley has been color-enhanced by computer.

A comet's tail forms when it gets near the sun. It may be more than 100,000,000 kilometers long. The tail streams out away from the sun.

▲ Some comets pass near the sun in their long, elliptical orbits. Comet Halley reappears in Earth's part of the solar system every 76 years.

Glossary

meteorite
(mē′tē ə rīt′), a piece of a meteoroid that lands on Earth after passing through the atmosphere

▲ *All living things depend on the sun for light and warmth. The green leaves of plants change sunlight into sugar and give off the oxygen almost all organisms need.*

▲ *A 300,000-ton meteorite crashed to Earth almost 50,000 years ago. It formed Meteor Crater, which is in Arizona. The crater is 175 meters deep and 1,275 meters across.*

How Objects in the Solar System Affect Earth

Life Science

The sun is an average-sized star, located at the center of the solar system. Energy from the sun provides the heat and light that is needed for all life on Earth, including the crops in the picture. Without energy from the sun, Earth would be a frozen ball of ice. Like other stars, the sun is a glowing ball of hot gas. It seems much bigger, brighter, and hotter than other stars because it is so much closer to Earth. You will learn more about the sun in the next lesson.

The sun affects Earth without touching it. Unlike the sun, some objects from the solar system actually reach Earth's surface. Most objects from space that enter Earth's atmosphere burn up completely. However, if they are very large, like asteroids, they may not burn up completely. A piece of rock and metal that lands on Earth, such as the one shown below, is called a **meteorite.** Most meteorites came from the asteroid belt, but a few seem to be made of rock from the moon or Mars. Large meteorites can hit the ground with such force that they make craters like the one in the picture. About every million years, a very large meteorite probably hits Earth and makes a huge crater. Look at the picture below to see what a small meteorite can do.

▲ *This car was damaged when a meteorite hit it.*

▲ *Small pieces of rock or metal are all that remain of most meteorites that reach Earth. About 500 meteorites hit Earth each year.*

◀ **Tides on Earth**
The pull of gravity from the sun and moon causes the oceans on Earth to form bulges called tides. One bulge always stays on the side of Earth that is under the moon. The other bulge is on the opposite side of Earth.

The moon and sun also affect Earth by causing the rise and fall of the tides. The diagram shows that the moon's gravity pulls ocean water toward the moon. The water piles up in a bulge on the side of Earth facing the moon. The water also bulges out on the opposite side of Earth. This is caused by the way forces pull on the water as the moon and Earth move through space. Low tides are in the area between the two bulges.

When the sun and moon are lined up with Earth, their pulls combine and cause very high tides. When they pull at right angles, the tidal bulges are flatter, or lower, than usual.

Lesson 1 Review

1. Compare three models of the solar system.

2. What are the planets like?

3. List three objects besides planets that are found in the solar system.

4. List three ways the sun affects Earth.

5. **Place Value Through Millions**
   An AU is 150,000,000 kilometers . Write the number in expanded form and in words.

You will learn:

- how the sun compares with other stars.
- how scientists measure distances in space.
- about the properties of stars.
- what constellations and galaxies are.

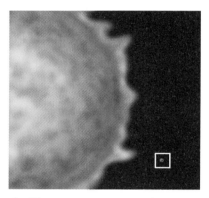

▲ *The sun measures about 1,392,000 kilometers in diameter. The picture compares the size of the sun to Earth. The sun's diameter is more than 100 times greater than Earth's.*

Lesson 2

What Is Known About Stars?

From a dark sky, stars **twinkle** above you. If you looked through a telescope, you might see that the stars are not all the same color. Some are white, some are blue, some are yellow, and some are red. What makes them look like that?

The Sun

You know that the sun is a star at the center of the solar system. Even though it looks much brighter than the other stars, the sun's brightness is just average. Some stars give off more light than the sun, others give off less. The sun looks brighter because it is so much closer to Earth than any other star is.

Like the other stars, the sun is a hot ball of glowing gases. Deep inside the sun, atoms combine in nuclear reactions. These nuclear reactions change small amounts of matter into gigantic amounts of heat and light energy. The huge amounts of energy the reactions give off are what make the sun and all the other stars so hot that they glow.

The sun is hotter than some stars and cooler than others. The sun, like some stars, is yellow. Other stars are white, blue, or red. Still others are dark and don't glow at all. In size, the sun is an average star. It is bigger than some stars and smaller than others. The picture at the left shows how much bigger than Earth the sun is. Look at the pictures on the next page to learn about the parts of the sun.

Size

The sun is a medium-sized star. The smallest stars may be 450 times smaller than the sun and have one-twentieth the sun's mass. The largest stars may be more than 1,000 times bigger than the sun and have up to 50 times more mass. ▼

▲ The sun's corona can be seen only when the center of the sun is covered. In a solar eclipse, the moon passes between the sun and Earth, blocking light from the bright center part of the sun.

Convection Zone

Currents of hot gases carry energy as they rise to the surface and then sink.

Core Temperature

Deep inside the sun the temperature is 15,000,000°C.

Corona

The corona surrounds the sun's surface. It is made of very hot, glowing gas. It has a temperature of about 2,000,000°C. The corona reaches millions of kilometers into space.

◀ Surface

The total surface of the sun is about 12,000 times greater than the surface of Earth. The sun's temperature at the surface is less than 6,000°C. Loops, flares, and arching jets of gas occur on the sun's surface.

Glossary

light year, the distance light travels in one year

Distances in Space

Scientists use kilometers as a unit to measure distances from one place to another on Earth. Using kilometers to measure distances to the stars would be very awkward. The distance to the nearest star outside the solar system, called Proxima Centauri, is about 40,678,000,000,000 kilometers! You learned that astronomical units, or AUs, are used to measure distances to the planets. AUs are based on the distance from Earth to the sun. But AUs are not big enough to be useful to measure distances to the stars. Instead, scientists use a unit based on the speed of light to measure these distances.

On Earth, light travels so fast it seems to take no time at all to get where it's going. It travels 300,000 kilometers in a second. Light travels so fast that it could circle Earth seven times in a second. In one year, light travels as far as 9,500,000,000,000 kilometers. That distance is called a **light year.** It is used as a unit to measure distances in space.

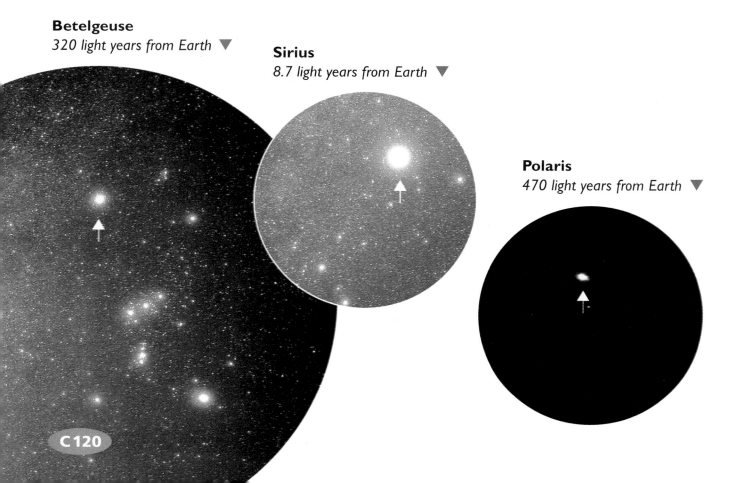

Betelgeuse
320 light years from Earth ▼

Sirius
8.7 light years from Earth ▼

Polaris
470 light years from Earth ▼

The stars are so far away from Earth that light from Proxima Centauri, the closest star, takes 4.3 years to reach Earth. Suppose you could look at that star in the sky right now. You would see light that left the star more than 4 years ago.

Some stars are much farther away. Find the star Cassiopeia A in the star group called Cassiopeia shown at the right. Light from this star travels for 11,000 years before it reaches Earth. When you see that star in the sky, you see light that left it 11,000 years ago. How many light years away from Earth is Cassiopeia A? Light from the sun, shown below, takes only 8 minutes to reach Earth.

Cassiopeia A

Light from the star named Cassiopeia A travels for 11,000 years before it reaches Earth. ▼

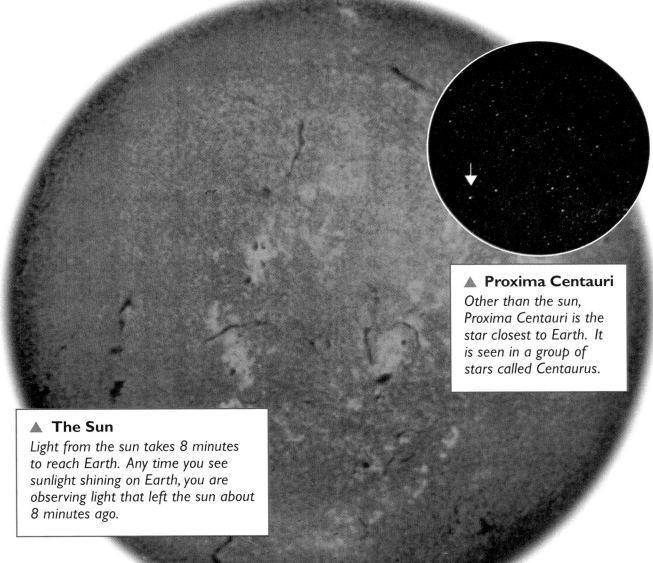

▲ **Proxima Centauri**

Other than the sun, Proxima Centauri is the star closest to Earth. It is seen in a group of stars called Centaurus.

▲ **The Sun**

Light from the sun takes 8 minutes to reach Earth. Any time you see sunlight shining on Earth, you are observing light that left the sun about 8 minutes ago.

The Properties of Stars

Astronomers group stars by their properties, such as brightness, color, and size. These properties can depend on other characteristics, such as temperature.

Some stars are so bright you can see them on almost any night, even in a lighted city. Others are so faint they can be seen only through a telescope. A star's brightness depends on how big the star is, how hot it is, and how far away from Earth it is.

The bigger and hotter the star, the more light it gives off. However, its brightness also depends on its distance from Earth. Imagine looking at a row of streetlights on a dark night. They all give off the same amount of light. However, a streetlight that is close to you looks brighter than one that is far away. In the same way, a star that is nearer Earth looks brighter than one that gives off the same amount of light but is farther away.

A star's color depends on its temperature. The pictures show how a steel bar changes color from red, to orange, to yellow, to white or blue-white when it is heated in a furnace. In a similar way, stars give off a red, orange, yellow, white, or blue-white glow, depending on their temperature. Red stars are the coolest. The sun gives off a yellow glow because it is a medium-hot star. Blue-white stars are the hottest.

▲ Color can depend on temperature. A steel bar starts out black. When it is heated, it begins to glow red.

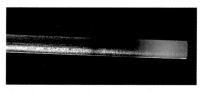

▲ As it gets hotter, it glows orange.

▲ As the metal gets still hotter, it turns yellow.

◀ At its hottest, molten steel glows with a white or even blue-white color.

Look at the picture of the group of stars on the right above. This group is known as Orion. Notice that it includes stars of several different colors. The large reddish star is Betelgeuse, one of the stars in the chart below. Some of the stars in Orion are blue and some are white.

Stars range greatly in size. The smallest stars are even smaller than Earth. Recall that the sun is an average star and that its diameter is 100 times Earth's diameter. Betelgeuse is 500 times bigger than the sun. Other large stars can be as much as 1,000 times the diameter of the sun. Some stars vary in size. One of these is Polaris, also known as the north star. Polaris is actually three stars close together that move around each other in space. The chart shows the properties of several stars, including the sun.

▲ *Find the different-colored stars in the group on the right, called Orion.*

	Sirius	Polaris	Betelgeuse	Sun
Color	Blue	Orange	Red	Yellow
Diameter	4,300,000 km	Varies in size	640,000,000 km	1,400,000 km
Temperature	More than 9,000°C	5,700°C	3,000–3,500°C	Less than 6,000°C

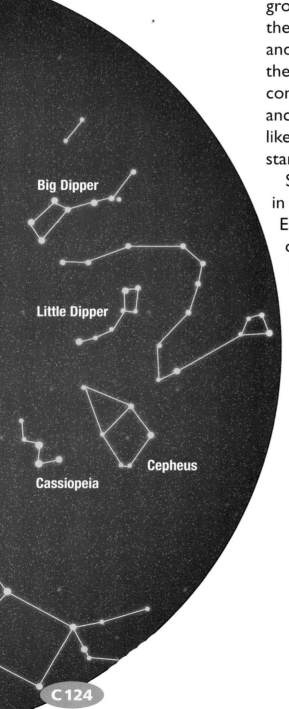

Glossary

constellation
(kon′stə lā′shən), stars that appear to be in groups when viewed from Earth

Glossary

Constellations and Galaxies

When you look at the stars, the brightest ones seem to form patterns or groups in the sky. Most people have seen groupings known as the Big Dipper, the Little Dipper, Cassiopeia, Orion, and others. Stars that seem to be in a group make up a **constellation.**

People in ancient times told stories about the constellations they saw. Different groups of people made up different stories. For example, look at the group of stars called the Big Dipper in the star map on the left. The star group looks like a dipper, with a bowl and a handle. Greeks saw these stars and others near them as a Great Bear. Ancient Romans saw the constellation as a team of oxen pulling a plow. The ancient Babylonians thought the Big Dipper looked like a wagon. Make up your own story for a group of stars you can see.

Stars in constellations are not really close together in space. They only look that way when viewed from Earth. The pictures below show how the constellation Cassiopeia looks from Earth and how it would look if you could see it from somewhere in space.

Big Dipper

Little Dipper

Cassiopeia

Cepheus

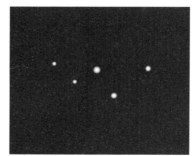

▲ **Cassiopeia Viewed from Earth**
The constellation Cassiopeia looks like a W as you look overhead and slightly north in December.

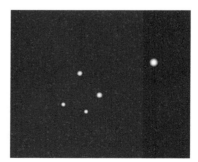

▲ **Cassiopeia Viewed from Space**
From space, the stars in Cassiopeia would seem to be in different positions, so the grouping would look different.

◄ **Milky Way**
You can see the Milky Way on a very clear, very dark night.

Glossary

galaxy (gal′ək sē), a group of billions of stars, dust, and gases in space held together by gravity

The images of these galaxies were taken by the Hubble Space Telescope. The telescope is on a human-made satellite that orbits Earth. ▼

The stars in a constellation only look like a group in space. However, huge numbers of stars really are clustered in groups, called galaxies. In a **galaxy**, gas, dust, and hundreds of billions of stars are all fairly close together in space. Some bright spots you see in the night sky are not single stars, but distant galaxies. They are so far away, they look like faint stars. The pictures to the right show how distant galaxies look when recorded by a telescope on a satellite in space.

The solar system is located near the edge of the Milky Way Galaxy. Look at the picture above of the cloudy band of millions of stars called the Milky Way. The stars in the Milky Way lie between the sun and the edge of the Milky Way Galaxy.

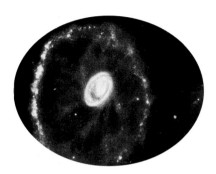

Cartwheel Galaxy

Spiral Galaxy

Lesson 2 Review

1. How does the sun compare to other stars?
2. What units do scientists use to measure distances in space?
3. What properties do scientists use to group stars?
4. Compare a galaxy and a constellation.
5. **Place Value Through Millions**
   The sun measures 1,392,000 kilometers in diameter. Write this number in expanded form and in words.

Small Spiral Galaxy

Making a Spectroscope

Process Skills

- predicting
- observing

Materials

- safety goggles
- paper towel tube
- sharpened pencil
- small sheet of cardboard
- scissors
- masking tape
- diffraction grating
- incandescent lamp
- colored pencils or crayons

Getting Ready

In this activity you will make and use a spectroscope to separate light from a bulb into the colors of the visible spectrum.

Follow This Procedure

1 Make a chart like the one shown. Use your chart to record your prediction, observations, and drawing.

Prediction	Observations	Drawing

2 Put on your safety goggles. Use one end of the paper towel tube to trace two circles on the sheet of cardboard. Cut them out with the scissors.

3 Cut one of the circles in half. Tape the halves to one end of the tube with a little space between them to make a narrow slit. Do not cover the slit with the tape, but seal all other spaces (Photo A).

Photo A

4 With a sharp pencil, punch a hole in the center of the other cardboard circle. Cover the hole with the diffraction grating. Tape the circle and diffraction grating to the other end of the cardboard tube (Photo B).

Self-Monitoring

Except for the slit and small hole, have I sealed all of the edges with tape so no light comes into the tube?

Photo B

5 A defraction grating works like a prism. **Predict** how the light will appear when you look at the light bulb through the spectroscope. Record your prediction in your chart.

6 Point the slit of the spectroscope at the light bulb. Look through the small hole and diffraction grating at the other end (Photo C). Record your **observations** and draw a picture of what you see.

⚠ *Safety Note Do not look at the sun with your spectroscope.*

Interpret Your Results

1. Look at the drawing of the color patterns you drew. Have you seen a pattern like this before? If so, where?

2. Explain how the diffraction grating in the spectroscope changes the light from the light bulb.

Inquire Further

What patterns do other sources of light produce when viewed with the spectroscope? Develop a plan to answer this or other questions you may have.

Self-Assessment

- I followed instructions to make a spectroscope.
- I **predicted** how light would appear when looking through the spectroscope.
- I **observed** light from a bulb through the spectroscope.
- I recorded my prediction and observations, and made a drawing.
- I explained how the diffraction grating in a spectroscope changes the light from a light bulb.

Photo C

You will learn:

- how scientists use spectroscopes to analyze light.
- how telescopes work.
- how images from telescopes are recorded.
- why scientists use telescopes in space.

How Do Scientists Study Planets and Stars?

You peer through binoculars at a tree far away. The tree looks **close**, and you can see it more clearly. The binoculars make it look **larger!** In a similar way, scientists use powerful telescopes to observe objects in space.

Analyzing Light

Physical Science

Astronomers study objects in space by observing the light and other forms of radiation they give off. To do this, they use special tools to record, focus, magnify, and analyze the light and other radiation. To analyze something is to separate it into its parts so it can be studied.

Notice how the prism splits white light into all the colors of the rainbow. A **spectroscope** is a tool that scientists use to analyze light. It can separate light from a glowing star into bands or patterns of light. Each element present in the star has its own pattern. The picture below shows the pattern a spectroscope makes when it analyzes glowing hydrogen. Astronomers study the patterns the spectroscope makes to find out what elements a star contains.

Glossary

spectroscope (spek′trə skōp), an instrument that separates light into a pattern of lines of different colors

A prism separates white light or sunlight into a rainbow spectrum, or pattern of colors. ▼

◀ **Spectrum of an Element's Light**
A type of spectroscope analyzes the light from a glowing element. It produces a pattern or spectrum of bands and dark lines. This is the spectrum for the element hydrogen.

Telescopes

Telescopes make distant objects look clearer and show detail. Do you know how they do it? Mirrors and lenses in telescopes bend and focus light to produce an image with more detail.

If you have used binoculars or a hand lens, you know that a lens can magnify objects. You may also know that the lens in your eye focuses light and produces an image. Some people's eyes do not form a clear image. Specially shaped lenses in eyeglasses can help the eye focus.

Refraction and reflection are two different ways to gather and focus light. Lenses work by **refraction,** or the bending of light as it passes from one material to another. Notice in the pictures below that the way light bends as it passes through a lens depends on the shape of the lens.

Mirrors work by **reflection,** or bouncing light off a surface. The pictures to the right show that the shape of a mirror changes the direction of light that bounces off it.

Glossary

refraction
(ri frak′shən), the bending of light as it passes from one material to another; a way to gather and focus light

reflection
(ri flek′shən), the bouncing of light off a surface; a way to gather and focus light

Glossary

Mirrors

The image in a mirror is formed by reflection, the bouncing of light off a shiny surface. Use your fingers to trace the direction the mirrors in the pictures make the light bounce.

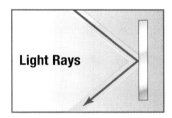

▲ *Flat mirror*

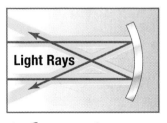

▲ *Concave mirror*

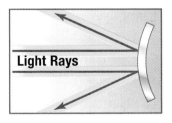

▲ *Convex mirror*

Lenses

The shape of a lens determines the angle of bending and where the light rays that pass through it focus. Trace the bending of light by the lenses in the pictures.

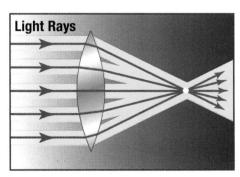

◀ *A convex lens is thicker in the middle and thinner at its edges. It brings light rays together at one point. The thicker the lens, the more it bends the light rays and the closer to the lens the focus point will be.*

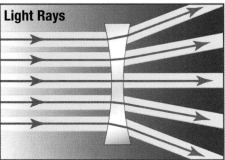

◀ *A concave lens is thinner in the middle and thicker at the edges. It makes light rays spread apart.*

Optical telescopes produce images by focusing light rays. They work by either refraction or reflection. The diagrams on these two pages are basic patterns of how refracting and reflecting telescopes work. Use your fingers to trace the path of light in each kind of telescope. Find where the light enters the telescope. Follow it to where it passes through the eyepiece and to the observer. The earliest telescopes, like Galileo's telescope in the picture below, were refracting telescopes.

Refracting Telescope

This refracting telescope works like binoculars do. A large convex lens at the end of the telescope captures light from the stars and bends it to focus an image. A convex lens in the eyepiece magnifies the image for viewing. ▼

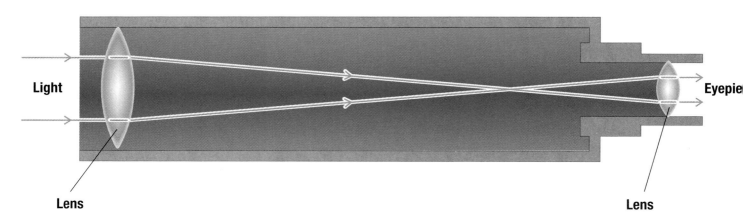

Light

Eyepie

Lens

Lens

▲ Galileo's Refracting Telescope

Galileo built many refracting telescopes. He observed things that no one had seen before, including moons of Jupiter and the craters on Earth's moon. He saw ten times as many stars as anyone had ever seen before.

The first important discovery made with a refracting telescope was that there are craters on the moon. The discovery was made in 1609 by the Italian astronomer Galileo. In 1668, Isaac Newton designed a reflecting telescope like the one shown below. It solved a problem with blurred images that Galileo had with his telescope. More complex designs used today include large reflecting telescopes that have many small, six-sided mirrors mounted close together, instead of one large mirror.

Reflecting Telescope
This reflecting telescope uses mirrors to bounce light and form a clear image. A concave mirror magnifies and focuses an image toward a flat mirror, which then reflects it toward an eyepiece. A convex lens in the eyepiece focuses the image for viewing. ▼

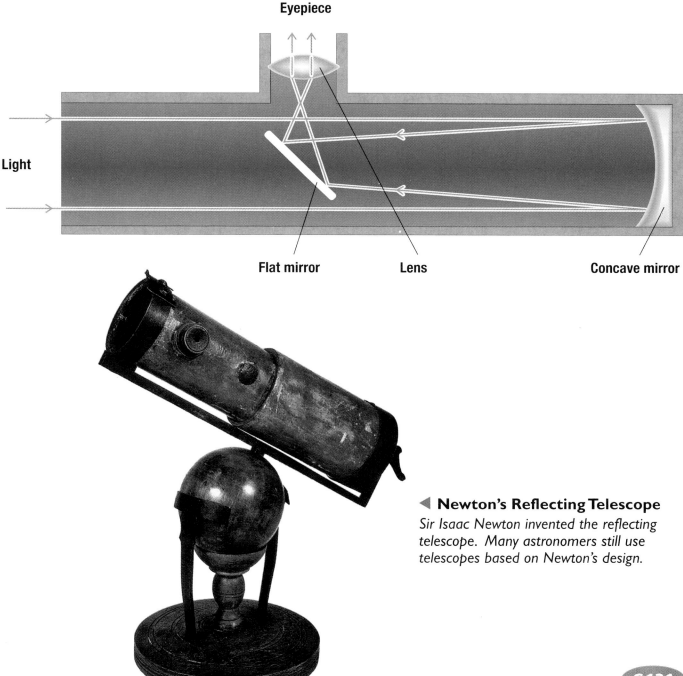

Eyepiece

Light

Flat mirror   Lens   Concave mirror

◀ **Newton's Reflecting Telescope**
Sir Isaac Newton invented the reflecting telescope. Many astronomers still use telescopes based on Newton's design.

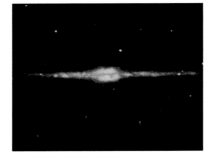

▲ Milky Way Galaxy

▲ Whirlpool Galaxy

▲ Infrared telescope

Radio Telescope

A radio telescope has a huge dish-shaped reflector that focuses radio waves onto an antenna. ▼

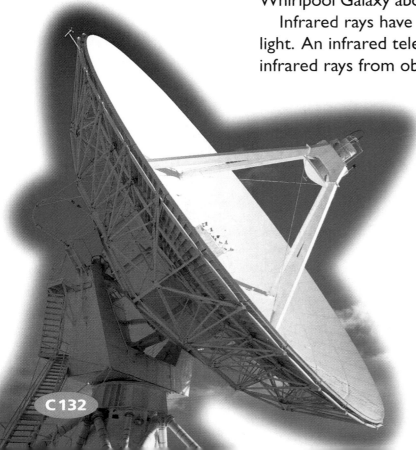

Visible light waves are only one kind of radiation that stars and other objects in space give off. Other kinds of radiation cannot be seen by the human eye. The wavelengths are shorter or longer than visible light. This means they are too short or too long for the eye to detect. Scientists use special telescopes, as well as satellites in space, to collect and make images from these invisible kinds of radiation.

A radio telescope, like the one in the picture below, collects and measures the radio waves that objects in space give off. Radio telescopes have been used to discover objects that optical telescopes cannot see, such as dust clouds in dark parts of the sky. The image of the Whirlpool Galaxy above was taken by a radio telescope.

Infrared rays have longer wavelengths than visible light. An infrared telescope like the one above collects infrared rays from objects in space. An infrared telescope is built like a reflecting telescope. However, it has an infrared detector instead of an eyepiece. The picture above of the Milky Way Galaxy was taken by an infrared telescope on a satellite in space.

Recording Images

To record images from optical telescopes, astronomers often use film or photographic plates. Film can be exposed for a long time, so it can collect enough light to make dim objects appear bright. The camera attaches to the eyepiece of the telescope and collects light on film during long, "elapsed-time" exposures. It can record objects that might be too faint for the eye to see, even through a telescope.

The pictures below were taken with a camera attached to a telescope. Compare how many stars you can see in each picture. The first picture, exposed for 12 seconds, shows only a few stars. In the second picture, exposed for 2 minutes, more stars are visible. The third picture, exposed for 8 minutes, shows hundreds of stars, as well as dust and gases. The increased exposure time has brought out a great deal of detail about the part of the sky shown.

Electronic detectors are also used with all types of telescopes to record images from space. These instruments collect light or other rays and change their radiation pattern into a pattern of electrical charges. Then the pattern can be shown as a picture on a computer screen. Different wavelengths of radiation may be shown in different colors. The colors may not be the real colors of the dust clouds and other objects in space. However, the colors help scientists understand the image. For example, places or objects that have different temperatures can be shown in different colors.

The telescope was aimed at the constellation Sagittarius. ▼

▲ *12-second exposure*

▲ *2-minute exposure*

▲ *8-minute exposure*

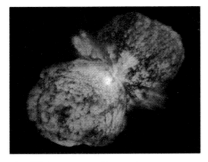

▲ This unusual star exploded 150 years ago and has divided into two sections. It is 100 times more massive than the sun.

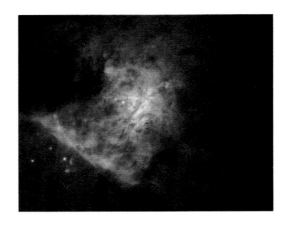

◄ This picture of the Orion Nebula, a mass of stars, gas, and dust particles in space, was put together from 45 separate images taken by the Hubble Space Telescope. The nebula is near the center of the constellation Orion.

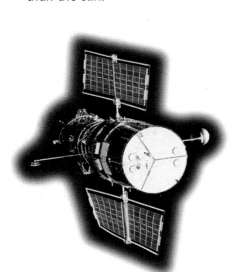

▲ The Hubble Space Telescope can detect objects 50 times fainter than telescopes on Earth can.

Telescopes in Space

Telescopes on rockets or satellites in space, such as the Hubble Space Telescope on the left, have an advantage over telescopes on Earth. They can record light and other radiation from objects in space, without the radiation having to pass through Earth's atmosphere. Telescopes on Earth often produce a blurred image as light passes through the atmosphere. The air contains many particles, including water vapor, dust, carbon dioxide, and other substances. Also, in some places the air is warm or hot; in other places it is cool or cold. All these things affect the way light moves through air. They keep a lens from focusing an image clearly. The pictures of objects in space on these two pages were taken by the Hubble Space Telescope from far outside Earth's atmosphere.

When studying infrared rays from objects in space, even heat absorbed by the telescope itself can affect the image being recorded. For this reason, infrared telescopes have to be cooled, even in the extreme cold of space. Water vapor and carbon dioxide gas in Earth's atmosphere block many infrared rays. To avoid blurred images, infrared telescopes are usually placed on very high mountains or on satellites.

◄ Two rings of glowing gas surround a place where a star exploded.

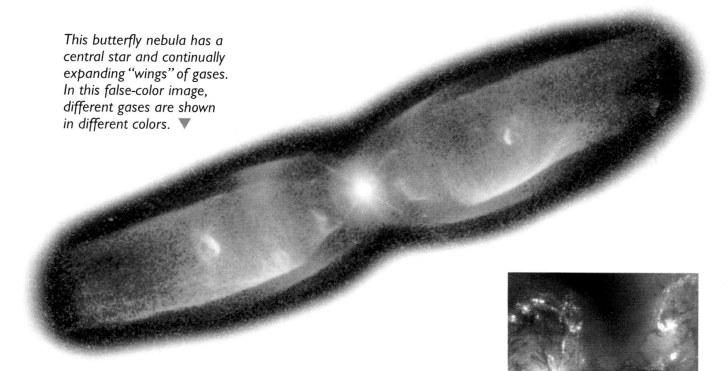

This butterfly nebula has a central star and continually expanding "wings" of gases. In this false-color image, different gases are shown in different colors. ▼

The Hubble Space Telescope was launched in 1990. It observes objects in space from above the Earth's atmosphere. It contains a 2.4-meter reflecting telescope. It also has cameras, supersensitive radiation detectors, and spectroscopes. It can collect and make images of infrared, visible, and ultraviolet rays from objects, and it can record bright images of very faint objects. It produces much clearer images than telescopes on Earth can produce.

▲ The orange-colored blobs in the picture are two colliding galaxies.

Lesson 3 Review

1. What do scientists learn from using spectroscopes to analyze light?

2. How do telescopes work?

3. How are images from a telescope recorded?

4. Why do telescopes in space produce better images than those on Earth?

5. **Compare and Contrast**
   How are refraction and reflection alike? How are they different?

▲ These three columns of dust and gas are located in the Eagle Nebula. Hot, massive stars heat the surrounding gas, making it glow. Scientists estimate that this nebula is 2,000,000 years old.

Investigating Lenses

Process Skills

Process Skills

- observing
- making operational definitions

Materials

- lens paper
- glass convex lens
- plastic hand lens

Getting Ready

In this activity you can find out how convex lenses change the way objects appear. Then you can use lenses to make a simple telescope.

Follow This Procedure

❶ Make a chart like the one shown. Use your chart to record your observations.

	Observations
Description of lens shape	
Drawing of lens	
Change caused by glass convex lens	
Change caused by smaller convex lens	
Appearance of object through telescope	

❷ Place a piece of lens paper around the glass convex lens. Carefully feel the shape of the lens. What is the shape of the lens? Record your **observations.** Then draw a side view of the lens in your chart.

 Safety Note *Use care when handling the glass lens.*

❸ Hold the glass convex lens near to your eye. Looking through the lens, hold the index finger of your other hand out at arm's length. Bring your finger toward the lens until it is in focus (Photo A). How does the lens change the way your finger looks? Record your observations.

❹ Repeat step 3 using the smaller convex lens of the hand lens. Which lens made your finger look larger? Record your observations.

Photo A

Photo B

⑤ Now you will make a simple telescope. Hold the small lens of the hand lens near your eye. Hold the glass convex lens in front of the hand lens so you can see through both of them.

⑥ Face a distant object. Move the glass lens back and forth until the distant object comes into focus (Photo B). You have just made and focused a simple refracting telescope. How does the object appear through your telescope? Record your observations.

 Safety Note Never look through lenses at direct sunlight or other very bright sources of light.

Interpret Your Results

1. Write an **operational definition** of a convex lens. Be sure to include how the lens is shaped and how objects appear when viewed through the lens.

2. Describe how to make and use a simple refracting telescope. Describe how to place the lenses and how to focus the telescope. Describe how objects appear when viewed through the telescope.

 Inquire Further

What happens if you use a concave lens as the eyepiece of a simple refracting telescope? Develop a plan to answer this or other questions you may have.

Self-Assessment

• I followed instructions to record **observations** of objects viewed through convex lenses.

• I drew a diagram of a convex lens.

• I followed instructions to make and use a simple refracting telescope.

• I wrote an **operational definition** of a convex lens.

• I described how to make and use a simple refracting telescope.

Chapter 4 Review

Chapter Main Ideas

Lesson 1
• As better tools enabled scientists to learn more about the solar system, they developed new models.
• The nine planets that move around the sun are different in size, atmosphere, distance from the sun, and number of moons.
• The sun, planets, asteroids, meteoroids, and comets are objects in the solar system.
• Objects in the solar system can affect Earth if they enter Earth's atmosphere, if their radiation or energy reaches Earth, and through the effect of gravity on the tides.

Lesson 2
• The sun is an average star in size, brightness, and temperature.
• Scientists measure distances to stars and galaxies in units called light years, the distance light can travel in a year.
• Scientists group stars by their size, brightness, and color.
• Constellations are groups of stars that appear to be near each other; galaxies are huge groups of stars that actually are fairly close to each other.

Lesson 3
• Spectroscopes identify the elements in a star by separating starlight into a pattern of lines and colors.
• Lenses and mirrors in telescopes focus light and magnify images.

• Images from a telescope can be recorded on film or by electronic detectors.
• Light and other radiation that is recorded by telescopes in space do not pass through the atmosphere, which could blur the image.

Reviewing Science Words and Concepts

Write the letter of the word or phrase that best completes each sentence.

a. asteroid
b. comet
c. constellation
d. elliptical
e. galaxy
f. light year
g. meteor
h. meteorite
i. meteoroid
j. model
k. reflection
l. refraction
m. spectroscope

1. The distance light can travel in a year is called a ____.
2. A group of stars that forms a pattern in the sky is a ____.
3. A ball of ice, dust, and gases that revolves around the sun in a long, thin orbit is a ____.
4. A piece of rock from space that passes through the atmosphere and lands on Earth is a ____.
5. A streak of light that passes through the atmosphere is a ____.

6. A ___ is an instrument that identifies substances by separating the light they give off into patterns of lines and colors.

7. A large rocky object that revolves around the sun is an ___.

8. A ___ shows how something looks or works.

9. The bouncing of light off a shiny surface is ___.

10. An orbit that is shaped like a flattened circle is ___.

11. A piece of rock or metal that revolves around the sun is a ___.

12. The bending of light as it passes from one substance to another is called ___.

13. A huge group of stars in space, along with dust and gases, makes up a ___.

Explaining Science

Draw and label a diagram or write a paragraph to answer these questions.

1. How is the orbit of a comet different from the orbit of a planet?

2. In what two ways are AUs and light years different?

3. How are radio telescopes and infrared telescopes different from optical telescopes?

Using Skills

1. The star Sirius is 4,300,000 kilometers in diameter. Show that you understand **place values through millions** by writing this number two other ways.

2. Suppose you look into the sky on a dark, clear night. List the different things you would expect to **observe.**

3. Suggest a way to **make a model** of what could happen when a meteorite lands on Earth. List the materials you would use and tell how you would use them.

Critical Thinking

1. Compare and contrast what you might see if you looked at a distant galaxy through a telescope on Earth with what you might see in an image of the galaxy sent to Earth by a camera on a satellite in space.

2. Suppose you see a large crater in Earth's surface. **Make a hypothesis** to explain how it might have formed, and tell what evidence you would look for to support your hypothesis.

3. Predict what you might see in the sky if Earth passed through the tail of a comet.

Unit C Review

Reviewing Words and Concepts

Choose at least three words from the **Chapter 1** list below.
Use the words to write a paragraph about how these concepts
are related. Do the same for each of the other chapters.

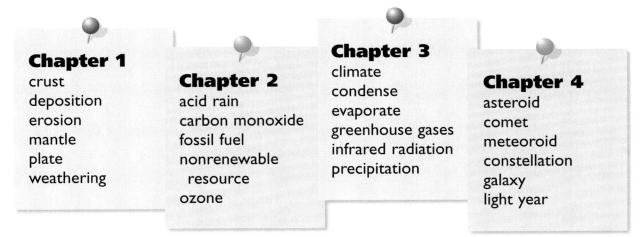

Chapter 1
crust
deposition
erosion
mantle
plate
weathering

Chapter 2
acid rain
carbon monoxide
fossil fuel
nonrenewable
  resource
ozone

Chapter 3
climate
condense
evaporate
greenhouse gases
infrared radiation
precipitation

Chapter 4
asteroid
comet
meteoroid
constellation
galaxy
light year

Reviewing Main Ideas

Each of the statements below is false. Change the underlined
word or words to make each statement true.

1. The <u>lithosphere</u> is the layer of gases that surrounds Earth.
2. The hot, central part of Earth is the <u>mantle</u>.
3. <u>Deposition</u> is the process of breaking down and changing rock.
4. A resource that can be replaced within a short time is a <u>fossil</u> <u>fuel</u>.
5. A <u>mineral</u> is an unwanted substance in the air or water.
6. In the <u>greenhouse</u> <u>effect</u>, water in its different forms moves through the land, air, and water on the earth.
7. The tilt of the earth affects how much sunlight a place gets at different times and causes the <u>ocean</u> <u>currents</u>.
8. Astronomers usually measure distances to the stars in <u>kilometers</u>.
9. A star's color indicates its <u>brightness</u>.
10. A group of stars clustered together in space is a <u>constellation</u>.

Interpreting Data

The following chart provides information about the properties of some stars. Use the chart to answer the questions below.

	Color	Diameter	Temperature
Sirius	Blue	4,300,000 km	More than 9000°C
Polaris	Orange	Varies in size	5,700°C
Betelgeuse	Red	640,000,000 km	3,000–3500°C
Sun	Yellow	1,400,000 km	Less than 6000°C

1. Of the stars shown on the chart, which is the hottest?

2. Which star is coolest?

3. Put the star colors in order from hottest to coolest.

4. Astronomers group stars by their color and size. One group of stars are called red supergiants. Which of the stars on the chart might be a red supergiant?

Communicating Science

1. Write a paragraph explaining how scientists can use layers of rock to learn about how the earth has changed.

2. Write a paragraph explaining what events can occur at plate boundaries.

3. Draw and label a diagram that shows how the greenhouse effect keeps the earth warm.

4. Draw and label a diagram that shows how light bends when it passes through a lens.

Applying Science

1. Write a paragraph suggesting ways your community could better protect water or land resources.

2. Write a paragraph describing the climate in your area. Remember that climate is weather conditions over many years.

Unit C
Performance Review

Earth and Space Day

Using what you learned in this unit, complete one or more of the following activities to be included in an Earth and Space Day celebration. These activities will help people learn more about the earth and space.

Drama

Draw a picture of a constellation. You can use a star pattern in the sky or make one up. Make up a skit that tells the story of your constellation and act out the skit.

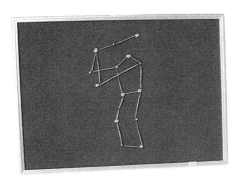

Science News

Write a news report that tells new things scientists are learning about objects in space. Sources of new information include telescopes, satellites, and spaceships.

Physics

Draw a diagram of the water cycle. Identify the steps where the water changes state. Show the arrangement of the particles of matter in each state. Use the diagram to explain how matter changes state.

Safety

Find out ways to stay safe during an earthquake. Draw a chart to report your findings. Use the chart to communicate what you learned to others.

Environment

Give a report on air pollution in your community. Tell what people could do to improve the quality of air and other resources in the environment.

Using a Graph to Write a Description

Using Graphs

Graphs can be useful ways of showing comparisons. The three most common types of graphs are the pie chart or circle graph, the bar graph, and the line graph. A pie chart or circle graph is used to show data as parts of a whole. A bar graph is used to compare similar things, such as the heights or weights of people. A line graph is usually used to show how one thing changes in response to another, such as how someone's height changes over time. What kind of information is shown in each of the graphs below?

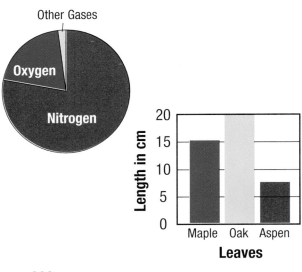

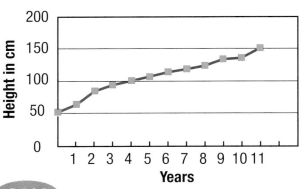

Make a Graph

In Chapter 1, you learned about the three layers that make up the Earth—the crust, the mantle, and the core. Use the information provided about the thickness of each layer to calculate the percentage of the Earth each layer makes up. Use the type of graph you think is most appropriate to display this data. Be sure to label your graph clearly and give it a title.

Write a Description

Use your graph and information from the chapter to write a three-paragraph description of the three layers of the Earth. Include information about the characteristics of each layer and tell how much of the Earth each layer makes up. Use one paragraph to describe each layer.

Remember to:

1. **Prewrite** Organize your thoughts.

2. **Draft** Write your description.

3. **Revise** Share your work and then make changes.

4. **Edit** Proofread for mistakes and fix them.

5. **Publish** Share your description with your class.

Unit D
Human Body

Science and Technology
In Your World!

No Air Out There? No Problem!

Ever wonder how astronauts breathe in space? Imagine you're a crew member on the space shuttle. Tanks supply you with a mixture of oxygen and nitrogen similar to the air on Earth. So far, so good! But each time you breathe out, carbon dioxide leaves your body. Equipment on the shuttle prevents the carbon dioxide from building up and poisoning you. A fan removes air from the crew cabin and sends it into containers called canisters. Chemicals in the canisters absorb the carbon dioxide, and the air is returned to the cabin. Replacing the used canisters is one of your daily jobs. If you leave the shuttle, you carry equipment that provides oxygen and removes carbon dioxide from your breath. You will learn more about breathing in **Chapter 1 Respiration and Excretion.**

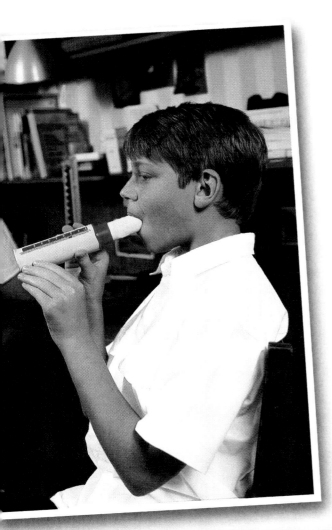

Tools Aid Medical Detectives!

You may have seen TV dramas in which doctors save lives with experimental treatments or dazzling high-tech equipment. Such things do happen. But many medical advances are less glamorous than what you see on TV. Tests to detect early signs of illness are an example. Although many such tests must be done in a hospital or laboratory, others can be done at home. For example, someone with the disease called asthma can use a tool known as a peak flowmeter to measure the amount of air breathed out. A low reading indicates that an asthma attack, in which breathing becomes difficult, is coming. The person can then take medicine to prevent or lessen the attack. You will learn more about disease treatment and prevention in **Chapter 2 Living a Healthy Life.**

Take a Deep Breath!

Your lungs have an important job. The oxygen in the air your lungs breathe in makes life possible! You can measure how much air you can breathe in. So, take a deep breath!

Chapter 1
Respiration and Excretion

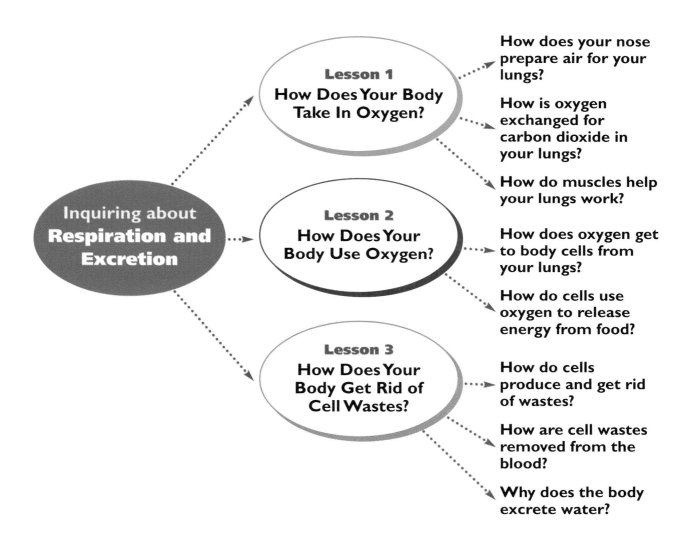

Inquiring about Respiration and Excretion

Lesson 1
How Does Your Body Take In Oxygen?

- How does your nose prepare air for your lungs?
- How is oxygen exchanged for carbon dioxide in your lungs?
- How do muscles help your lungs work?

Lesson 2
How Does Your Body Use Oxygen?

- How does oxygen get to body cells from your lungs?
- How do cells use oxygen to release energy from food?

Lesson 3
How Does Your Body Get Rid of Cell Wastes?

- How do cells produce and get rid of wastes?
- How are cell wastes removed from the blood?
- Why does the body excrete water?

Copy the chapter graphic organizer onto your own paper. This organizer shows you what the whole chapter is all about. As you read the lessons and do the activities, look for answers to the questions and write them on your organizer.

Exploring Lung Volume

Process Skills

- estimating and measuring
- inferring

Materials

- garbage bag
- masking tape
- soap solution in graduated cup
- paper towel
- 4 plastic straws
- half-meter stick

Explore

1 Tape the garbage bag to the desk. Pour about 60 mL of the soap solution onto the garbage bag and spread the solution out over the surface. Wipe your hands with a paper towel.

2 Dip a straw in the soap solution. Touch the straw to the soap on the garbage bag. Take a deep breath. Blow into the straw until you are out of breath. A bubble dome should form.

3 After the bubble bursts, **measure** and record the diameter of the soap ring left on the bag. Use the table to find your lung volume. Have each student in your group use a new straw to find his or her lung volume.

Reflect

There may be differences in lung volume among students. Make an **inference.** What might account for differences in lung volumes?

Diameter	Lung volume	Diameter	Lung volume
14 cm	0.7 L	19 cm	1.8 L
15 cm	0.9 L	20 cm	2.1 L
16 cm	1.1 L	21 cm	2.4 L
17 cm	1.3 L	22 cm	2.8 L
18 cm	1.5 L	23 cm	3.2 L

? Inquire Further

Can regular exercise help you increase your lung volume? Develop a plan to answer this or other questions you may have.

Using Graphic Sources

An ancient Chinese proverb says: "One picture is worth more than ten thousand words." Studying a picture can provide information at a glance that would take many words to describe. In science, using a picture or other **graphic source** can help you understand a complex topic like the one presented in Lesson 1, *How Does Your Body Take in Oxygen?*

Reading Vocabulary

graphic source
(graf′ik sôrs), a drawing, photograph, chart, table, or diagram that shows information visually

Example

In Lesson 1 you will learn that the air we breathe is made up of different gases. A pie chart, like the one below, is an effective way of showing this fact. In a pie chart, all the parts, or sections, add up to 100 percent. Use the pie chart below to answer the following questions:

1. Which two gases make up most of the air we breathe?

2. What percentage of air is made up by oxygen? Approximate.

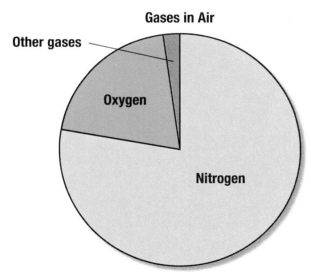

Gases in Air

Other gases

Oxygen

Nitrogen

Talk About It!

Look at the picture on page D12.

1. What function of the respiratory system does the picture explain?

2. What information does the photograph provide?

What's the Big Idea?

You will learn:

- how your nose prepares air for your lungs.
- how oxygen is exchanged for carbon dioxide in your lungs.
- how muscles help your lungs work.

Glossary

respiratory system (res′pər ə tôr′ē sis′təm), the group of organs that take oxygen from the air and remove carbon dioxide from the body

Lesson 1

How Does Your Body Take In Oxygen?

Have you ever tried to hold your breath? If so, you know what happened before very long. **WHOOSH!** Air rushed out. You couldn't help it—you just had to take another breath. Why does your body force you to breathe?

Preparing Air for Your Lungs

About one-fifth of the air that you breathe in is a gas called oxygen. Your cells must have oxygen to do their work. Without oxygen, cells will die—some within three to five minutes. That is why you can hold your breath for only a short time. Your body forces you to breathe to keep your cells alive.

When you breathe in, your **respiratory system** brings air containing oxygen into your body. The cells in your body use the oxygen. As your cells work, they make a gas called carbon dioxide. This gas leaves your body as a waste when you breathe out.

The respiratory system includes your nose, your lungs, and the tubes that connect them. Air enters the body through the nose, which has the job of getting the air ready for the lungs. Air that is very cold, dry, or dirty could harm your lungs. Your nose warms, moistens, and cleans the air that you breathe in. Study the picture on the next page to learn more.

Nose and Nostrils

Air usually enters the nostrils, which are the two openings in the nose. When you exercise, you may breathe through your mouth instead of your nose. That is because you need extra oxygen, and your mouth can take in more air in one breath than your nose can. You also may breathe through your mouth when you have a stuffy nose.

Glossary

mucus (myü′kəs), a sticky liquid produced by the linings of the nose and other body parts that open to the outside

trachea (trā′kē ə), the tube that leads from the throat toward the lungs, also called the windpipe

Tissue inside nose

Mucus

Tiny hairs

Blood vessel

▲ Lining of Nose

*This close-up of the inside of the nose shows that the tissue that lines the nose contains blood vessels. Blood in the blood vessels helps warm and moisten the air that you breathe in. The nose's lining makes a sticky liquid called **mucus**, which adds more moisture to the air. Mucus and tiny hairs inside the nose also trap dust from the air. When you blow your nose, you get rid of anything trapped in the mucus, including some germs.*

Trachea

*After the air is warmed, moistened, and cleaned by the nose, the air goes to the throat and down the **trachea,** or windpipe. The air is headed toward the lungs.*

Inside Your Lungs

When you **inhale,** or breathe in, air comes into your body. As you read on, use the picture on the next page to help visualize what happens as air moves through your respiratory system.

You know that air moves through your nose, throat, and trachea. The trachea divides into two **bronchial tubes,** each of which goes into a lung. Inside the lungs, the bronchial tubes divide into smaller and smaller tubes. The smallest tubes lead to clusters of tiny pouches called **air sacs.** Notice in the picture below that a net of tiny blood vessels surrounds each air sac.

Inhaled air, which is rich in oxygen, enters the air sacs. At this moment, the blood in the vessels around the air sacs contains a lot of carbon dioxide, which the blood has picked up from body cells. The blood contains little oxygen.

An exchange of gases quickly takes place. Oxygen passes from the air sacs into the blood vessels. The blood now has oxygen to deliver to body cells. At the same time that oxygen passes out of the air sacs, carbon dioxide passes from the blood vessels into the air sacs. The carbon dioxide leaves your body when you **exhale,** or breathe out.

Air sacs

Blood vessels

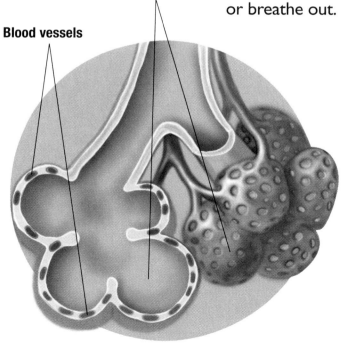

◀ **Exchange of Gases in the Air Sacs**

As the cutaway shows, air sacs are hollow. The walls of the air sacs and the walls of the surrounding blood vessels are so thin that gases can pass right through them. Oxygen passes from the air sacs into the blood vessels. Carbon dioxide passes from the blood vessels into the air sacs. The lungs have more than 300 million air sacs.

The Respiratory System

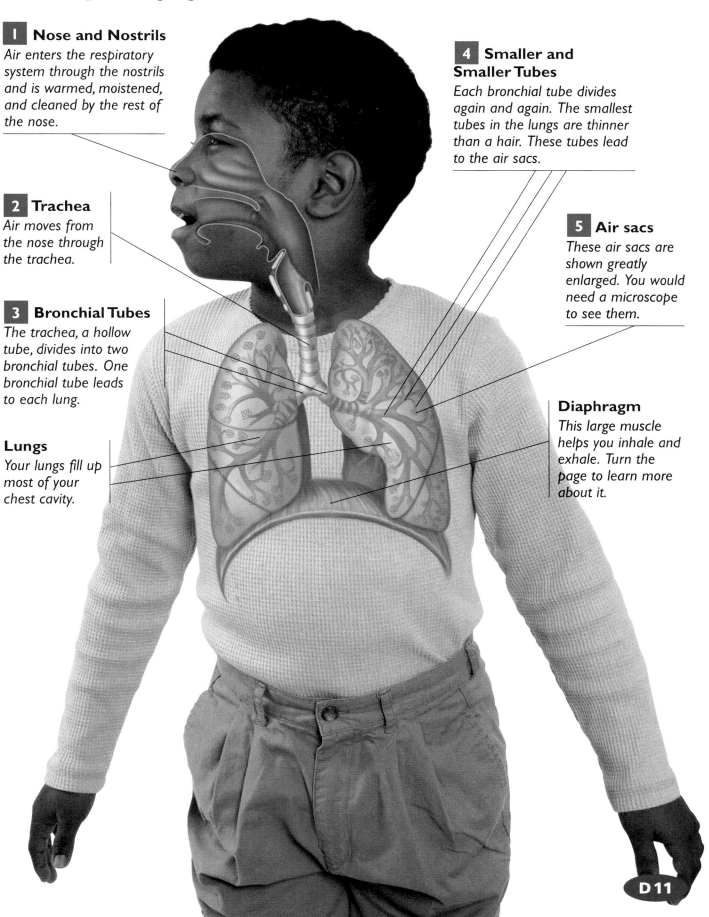

1 Nose and Nostrils
Air enters the respiratory system through the nostrils and is warmed, moistened, and cleaned by the rest of the nose.

2 Trachea
Air moves from the nose through the trachea.

3 Bronchial Tubes
The trachea, a hollow tube, divides into two bronchial tubes. One bronchial tube leads to each lung.

Lungs
Your lungs fill up most of your chest cavity.

4 Smaller and Smaller Tubes
Each bronchial tube divides again and again. The smallest tubes in the lungs are thinner than a hair. These tubes lead to the air sacs.

5 Air sacs
These air sacs are shown greatly enlarged. You would need a microscope to see them.

Diaphragm
This large muscle helps you inhale and exhale. Turn the page to learn more about it.

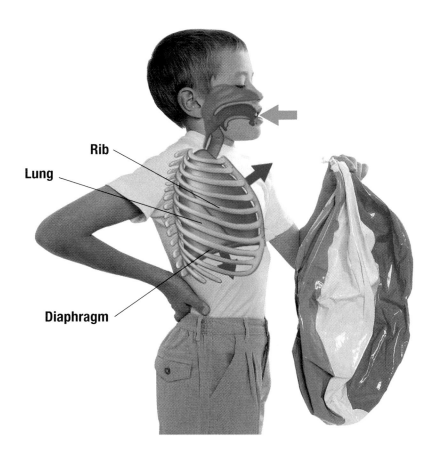

Rib

Lung

Diaphragm

◀ Inhaling

To take the most air into your lungs, you need to stand or sit up straight with your shoulders back. You can prove that by doing the opposite. Hunch forward. Try to take a deep breath. What happens? Why?

Glossary

diaphragm
(dī′ə fram), the large muscle below the lungs that helps you breathe

Muscles That Help Your Lungs Work

You know about the path that air takes into and out of your lungs. You may wonder, though, what forces the air to move. How do you inhale and exhale? The answer involves muscles.

Your soft, spongy lungs have no muscles. The muscles that allow you to breathe are outside your lungs. The **diaphragm** is a large sheet of muscle below your lungs. You can see the diaphragm on page D11. You also have muscles between your ribs. They work with your diaphragm to help you breathe.

Suppose you want to blow up the beach ball in the picture above. First, you must take a deep breath. For this to happen, your diaphragm contracts, or tightens. As it contracts, it flattens and moves down. The muscles between your ribs also contract, pulling your ribs up and out. These movements make the space inside your chest larger. Air rushes into your lungs to take up the extra space.

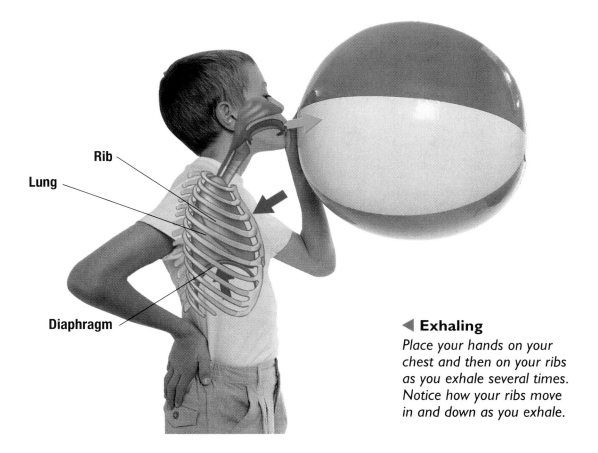

Rib

Lung

Diaphragm

◀ **Exhaling**
Place your hands on your chest and then on your ribs as you exhale several times. Notice how your ribs move in and down as you exhale.

When you are ready to exhale into the beach ball, your diaphragm relaxes. It moves up, taking its normal domelike shape. The muscles between your ribs also relax. Your ribs move down and in. With these movements, the space inside your chest becomes smaller. Air is forced out of your lungs.

Lesson 1 Review

1. What are the three ways that your nose changes the air that you breathe in?

2. Describe the exchange of gases that takes place in the air sacs of the lungs.

3. How do muscles below your lungs and between your ribs help you inhale?

4. Graphic Sources
Use the information in the picture on page D 9 to compare and contrast breathing through your nose and mouth.

Making a Breathing Model

Process Skills

- making and using models
- predicting
- observing
- inferring

Materials

- safety goggles
- small balloon
- plastic straw
- twist tie
- plastic cup with hole cut in the bottom
- modeling clay
- scissors
- large balloon

Getting Ready

You can make a model of the respiratory system to show how the diaphragm aids breathing.

You will need to study the pictures of the model carefully to complete the activity.

Follow This Procedure

1 Make a chart like the one shown. Use your chart to record your predictions and observations.

	Predictions	Observations
Balloon pulled down		
Balloon pushed up		

2 Put on your safety goggles. Begin making a **model** by attaching the open end of the small balloon to the plastic straw. Use the twist tie to hold the balloon in place.

3 Hold the plastic cup upside down. Push the open end of the straw up through the hole in the cup. Be sure the balloon does not hang below the cup's rim. Seal the hole around the straw with the clay (Photo A). The straw represents the trachea, the balloon represents a lung, and the cup represents the space inside the chest.

4 Use scissors to cut the neck off the large balloon. Discard the neck. While another student holds the cup, carefully stretch the cut balloon over the open end of the cup. The stretched balloon represents the diaphragm.

Photo A

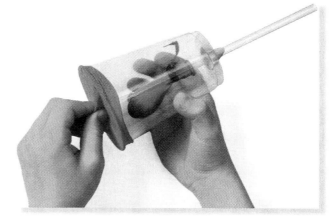

Photo B

⑤ What will happen to the small balloon if you pull down on the stretched balloon? What will happen if you push up on the stretched balloon? Record your **predictions**.

⑥ Gently pull down on the large balloon while holding the cup with your other hand (Photo B). Then gently push up on the large balloon. Record your **observations**.

Self-Monitoring
Have I correctly completed all the steps?

Interpret Your Results

1. Compare your predictions and observations. How well did your predictions match your observations?

2. Compare and contrast the workings of your model with the actual process of breathing. What similarities and differences do you note?

3. Make an **inference**. What might be the advantage of having an especially strong diaphragm?

 Inquire Further

What happens if there is an open hole in the cup? Develop a plan to answer this or other questions you may have.

Self-Assessment

- I followed instructions to **make a model** of the respiratory system.
- I recorded my **predictions** and **observations** about the workings of the model.
- I compared my predictions and observations.
- I compared and contrasted the model with the actual process of breathing.
- I made an **inference** about the advantage of having an especially strong diaphragm.

What's the Big Idea?

You will learn:

- how oxygen gets to body cells from your lungs.
- how cells use oxygen to release energy from food.

How Does Your Body Use Oxygen?

WHACK! **Your bat sends the ball flying! As you charge to first base, the workings of your body cells are the last thing on your mind. Yet every move you make depends on your cells getting and using oxygen.**

Glossary

capillary (kap′ə ler′ē), a tiny blood vessel with thin walls through which oxygen, nutrients, and wastes pass

Carrying Oxygen to Your Cells

You have learned that oxygen moves from your lungs into your blood. In the blood, the oxygen is carried by red blood cells. These cells float in plasma, which is the watery part of blood. When red blood cells are carrying oxygen, they are bright red.

Blood vessels carry oxygen-rich blood from your lungs to your heart. The heart pumps the blood into a large blood vessel called an artery. This large artery divides into smaller arteries. The smaller arteries eventually divide into **capillaries,** tiny blood vessels with very thin walls. Thousands of kilometers of capillaries carry blood throughout your body. Almost every body cell is near a capillary.

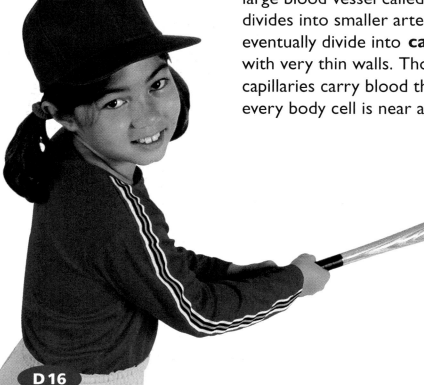

◀ *Play ball! Read a book! Draw a picture! No matter what you do, your body cells use oxygen supplied to them by your blood.*

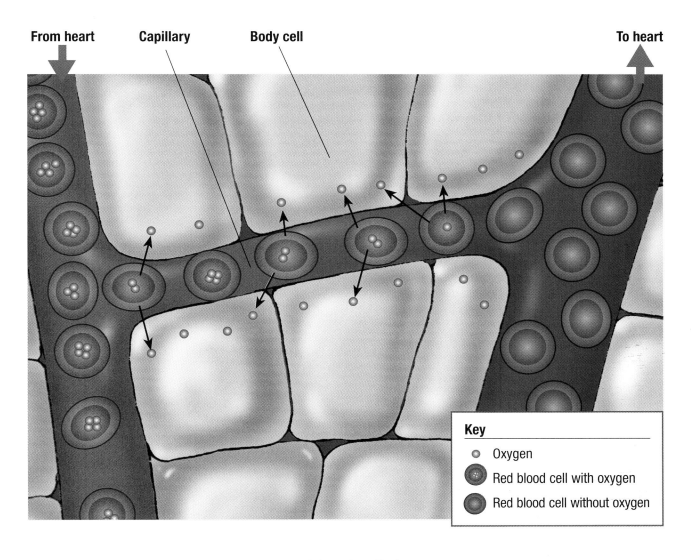

From heart   **Capillary**   **Body cell**   **To heart**

Key
- ⊙ Oxygen
- ⊕ Red blood cell with oxygen
- ⬤ Red blood cell without oxygen

Capillaries are so narrow that red blood cells have to move through them in single file. As red blood cells move through a capillary, they release their oxygen to body cells outside the capillary. The picture above shows this process.

After red blood cells give up their oxygen, they become dark, dull, and purplish. Now the blood flows from the capillaries into blood vessels called veins. Veins carry the blood to your heart, which pumps the blood to your lungs. There, the red blood cells pick up more oxygen from the air sacs. Almost all your blood goes through your lungs about once a minute.

▲ Red blood cells moving through capillaries release the oxygen they carry. The oxygen passes through the thin capillary walls and enters body cells. Having delivered its oxygen, the blood now flows back toward the heart.

▲ All of these activities use energy. Even if you sit or stand perfectly still, your body needs energy for breathing, digestion, and other essential activities. Your body cells even use energy while you sleep!

Using Oxygen to Release Energy

Almost all living things need oxygen to stay alive. You have learned how oxygen gets from the air to your lungs and into your body cells. Like other living things, you also need food. Your digestive system changes food into nourishing substances called nutrients. The nutrients pass from your digestive system into your blood. Nutrients are carried by plasma, just as red blood cells are. Nutrients get into body cells the same way oxygen does.

Many nutrients are simple kinds of sugar. Your cells use oxygen to break the sugar down into carbon dioxide and water. When your cells break sugar down, they release energy from the sugar. The equation below shows this process. Most of the energy that your body needs is made this way.

Every activity that you can think of uses energy. Which of the activities shown at the top of these two pages do you suppose uses the most energy?

Respiration

sugar + oxygen ⟶ carbon dioxide + water + energy

For activities such as running or swimming, the body's need for energy is obvious. The need may be less obvious with other activities. For example, did you know that body cells use energy to keep you warm? Cells also use energy to grow, to divide, and to repair damage. Brain cells use energy to help you think. The cells of your heart use energy to pump blood.

Sometimes you use your muscles so much that muscle cells cannot release enough energy from nutrients. Your muscles feel tired. While you rest, the muscle cells get more oxygen and nutrients from your blood. Then the cells can release more energy.

Lesson 2 Review

1. How does oxygen get from red blood cells to body cells?

2. What do body cells do with the oxygen that they receive?

3. **Sequence**
   Arrange these steps in the correct order:
   a. oxygen-rich blood arrives at capillaries;
   b. oxygen enters body cells; **c.** heart pumps oxygen-rich blood; **d.** oxygen moves through capillary walls.

What's the Big Idea?

You will learn:

- how your cells produce and get rid of wastes.
- how cell wastes are removed from your blood.
- the reasons why your body excretes water.

Glossary

excretory system
(ek′skrə tôr′ē sis′təm), the group of organs that get rid of cell wastes

Lesson 3

How Does Your Body Get Rid of Cell Wastes?

"Don't forget to take out the trash!" your friend's father calls out as the two of you get ready to go skating. **"Ugh,"** your friend grunts as she lifts the bulky bag. "How can one small family make so much trash?"

How Cells Produce and Get Rid of Wastes

Families produce wastes in the form of trash. As body cells do their work, they also produce wastes such as carbon dioxide and wastes containing nitrogen. Some cell wastes are harmless, but your body cannot use them. Your body excretes—gets rid of—cell wastes. Your **excretory system** does most of the work. Your lungs and skin also help.

Cell wastes are different from solid wastes, which are materials from food that your body cannot digest. Solid wastes are stored in your large intestine before passing out of your body.

Your body cells constantly produce cell wastes. Carbon dioxide and water are produced when body cells break down sugar to release energy. Other wastes containing nitrogen are produced when body cells break down another nutrient—protein—for use in growth and repair.

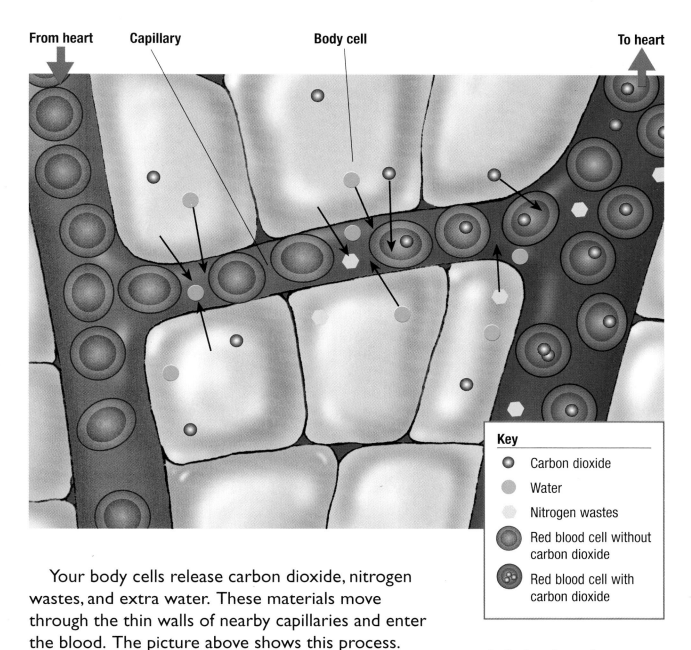

From heart   Capillary   Body cell   To heart

Key

- ● Carbon dioxide
- ● Water
- ⬡ Nitrogen wastes
- ◎ Red blood cell without carbon dioxide
- ◉ Red blood cell with carbon dioxide

Your body cells release carbon dioxide, nitrogen wastes, and extra water. These materials move through the thin walls of nearby capillaries and enter the blood. The picture above shows this process.

Some carbon dioxide attaches itself to red blood cells, but most travels in plasma. Water and nitrogen wastes also are carried by plasma. The blood carries cell wastes to body organs that get rid of the wastes. Carbon dioxide is exhaled from the lungs. Certain other wastes are eliminated in sweat from the skin. Nitrogen wastes are removed by the kidneys.

▲ Body cells produce wastes and release them into the capillaries. The blood carries cell wastes to the organs that get rid of the wastes.

Removing Wastes from the Blood

You may already know that you have two kidneys. Your **kidneys** are the main organs of your excretory system. These fist-sized organs have the job of removing nitrogen wastes, as well as some other wastes, from your blood. The picture on the next page shows the organs of the excretory system, including the kidneys.

Blood containing cell wastes enters the kidneys through arteries. Inside the kidneys, the blood flows through smaller and smaller blood vessels until it reaches capillaries. Wastes from the blood pass through the thin capillary walls into tiny tubes. These tubes remove nitrogen wastes, some salts, and extra water from the blood. These wastes form a liquid called **urine**.

The urine flows from the kidneys into tubes, one tube for each kidney. These two tubes lead to the **urinary bladder**. This muscular, baglike organ stores the urine temporarily. Meanwhile, the cleaned blood moves through the capillaries in the kidneys. These capillaries join together into veins that carry the cleaned blood away from the kidneys and back to the heart. The heart pumps the cleaned blood throughout the body.

Your kidneys clean all of your blood about forty times every day. This nonstop activity means that the kidneys make urine constantly. As the urinary bladder fills with urine, nerve cells send a message to your brain. You know that it is time to empty your bladder. The urine then leaves your body through a tube.

The Excretory System

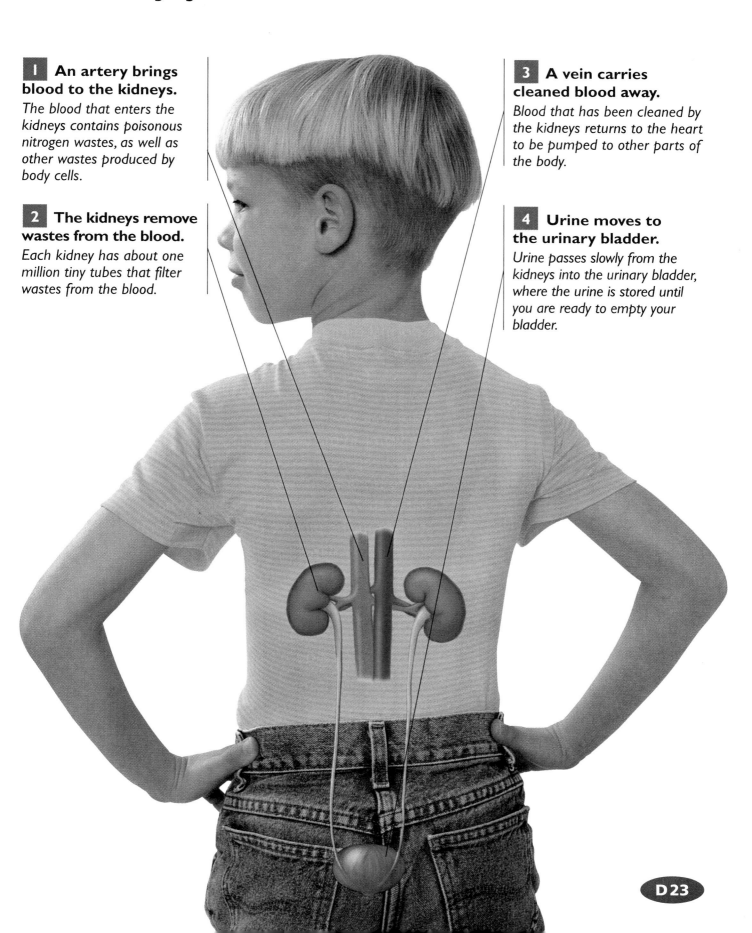

1 An artery brings blood to the kidneys.

The blood that enters the kidneys contains poisonous nitrogen wastes, as well as other wastes produced by body cells.

2 The kidneys remove wastes from the blood.

Each kidney has about one million tiny tubes that filter wastes from the blood.

3 A vein carries cleaned blood away.

Blood that has been cleaned by the kidneys returns to the heart to be pumped to other parts of the body.

4 Urine moves to the urinary bladder.

Urine passes slowly from the kidneys into the urinary bladder, where the urine is stored until you are ready to empty your bladder.

Water Excretion and Replacement

Just as they need oxygen and nutrients, your body cells need water to live and do their work. In fact, did you know that about two-thirds of your body weight is water? Much of that water is inside your cells.

Although your body needs water, it excretes some water every day. For example, when you exhale, you lose some water as well as carbon dioxide. When you "see your breath" on a cold day, you are seeing water.

One reason that your body excretes water is to prevent extra water from building up. Water excretion also helps the body get rid of certain wastes. For example, the watery part of urine carries nitrogen wastes and salts out of the body.

Water excretion also helps your body maintain a normal temperature. For example, when you are very active, your cells produce a great deal of heat. Your body gets rid of the extra heat by sweating. Glands in your skin make sweat from water, salt, and other wastes. You cool down as the water in the sweat evaporates.

To keep your excretory system and your entire body healthy, you need to replace the water that your body loses. Do what the student in the picture does: drink plenty of water every day.

Plain water is refreshing and good for you, but you also can get water from liquids such as milk, fruit juice, and sports drinks. Drink extra liquids on hot days and after exercising to replace the water lost by sweating. ▼

Lesson 3 Review

1. How do carbon dioxide and nitrogen wastes get into your blood?

2. What happens inside your kidneys?

3. Give one reason why your body excretes water.

4. **Graphic Sources**
   Use the drawing on page D23 to put these steps in order: **a.** arteries bring blood to kidneys; **b.** veins carry clean blood away from kidneys; **c.** kidneys remove wastes from blood.

Experimenting with Exercise and Carbon Dioxide

Materials

- safety goggles
- masking tape
- marker
- 3 plastic cups
- measuring cup
- 150 mL bromothymol blue solution
- 3 plastic straws
- clock with a second hand

Process Skills

- formulating questions and hypotheses
- identifying and controlling variables
- experimenting
- estimating and measuring
- collecting and interpreting data
- inferring
- communicating

State the Problem

How does the body's activity level affect the amount of carbon dioxide exhaled?

Formulate Your Hypothesis

If you increase your activity level, will the amount of carbon dioxide exhaled increase, decrease, or stay the same? Write your **hypothesis.**

Identify and Control the Variables

Your activity level is the **variable** you can change. You will perform three trials. Do Trial 1 after resting. Do Trial 2 after 2 minutes of walking. Do Trial 3 after 2 minutes of running. Use the same amount of bromothymol blue solution for each trial.

Test Your Hypothesis

Follow these steps to perform an **experiment.**

1 Make a chart like the one on the next page. Use your chart to record your data.

2 Put on your safety goggles. Use the masking tape and marker to label the 3 plastic cups *1, 2,* and *3.*

3 Use the measuring cup to **measure** and pour 50 mL of bromothymol blue (BTB) solution into each plastic cup. Bromothymol blue solution will turn greenish yellow as carbon dioxide is added to it. Put a straw in each cup. Sit and rest quietly for at least 2 minutes.

 Safety Note *Do not inhale through the straw. Do not drink the bromothymol blue solution.*

Continued ➡

4 Have a partner time how long it takes for the BTB solution to change color. Exhale through the straw into cup 1 as shown. As soon as you see the bromothymol blue solution turn greenish yellow, stop timing. **Collect data** by recording the time in your chart. Set the cup aside.

5 Walk briskly in place for two minutes. Stop. Repeat step 4, using cup 2. Try to exhale with the same force as you did in Trial 1. Also make sure you stop exhaling as soon as the color of the solution in cup 2 matches the color in cup 1.

Safety Note *Do not perform exercise if you have a medical condition that makes it unsafe for you.*

6 Run in place for two minutes. Stop. Repeat step 4, using cup 3.

Collect Your Data

Trial	Activity level	Amount of time for color change
1	After resting	
2	After walking	
3	After running	

Interpret Your Data

1. Label a piece of grid paper as shown. Use the data from your chart to make a bar graph on your grid paper.

2. Study your graph. Describe what happened to the amount of time it took for bromothymol blue to turn greenish yellow as the activity level increased. The faster the change, the more carbon dioxide was present.

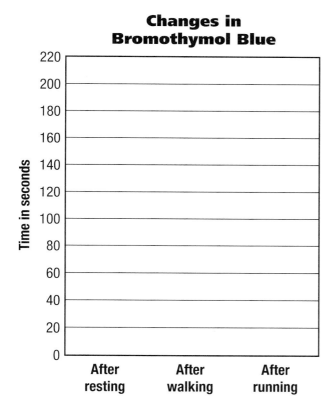

Changes in Bromothymol Blue

State Your Conclusion

How do your results compare with your hypothesis? **Communicate** your results by writing a paragraph. In your paragraph, state how exercise affects the amount of carbon dioxide exhaled.

 Inquire Further

Does the amount of carbon dioxide exhaled by people of different heights vary? Develop a plan to answer this or other questions you may have.

Self-Assessment

- I made a **hypothesis** about exercise and exhaling carbon dioxide.
- I **identified** and **controlled variables.**
- I followed instructions to perform an **experiment.**
- I **collected** and **interpreted** my **data** by recording **measurements** and making and studying a graph.
- I **communicated** by stating my conclusion.

Chapter 1 Review

Chapter Main Ideas

Lesson 1

• The nose warms, moistens, and cleans air that the body breathes in.

• In the lungs, oxygen in the air passes from the air sacs into the surrounding blood vessels, while carbon dioxide passes from the blood vessels into the air sacs.

• The diaphragm and rib muscles contract and relax to allow a person to inhale and exhale.

Lesson 2

• Red blood cells carry oxygen from the lungs through capillaries, where the oxygen is released to nearby body cells through the capillary walls.

• Body cells use oxygen to break sugar down into carbon dioxide and water, and energy is released in the process.

Lesson 3

• Carbon dioxide, nitrogen wastes, and water are produced when body cells break down nutrients. These materials are released into the blood through capillary walls.

• The kidneys filter nitrogen wastes, salts, and extra water from the blood, forming urine that eventually leaves the body.

• The body excretes water to prevent extra water from building up, to help get rid of certain wastes, and to help maintain a normal temperature.

Reviewing Science Words and Concepts

Write the letter of the word or phrase that best completes each sentence.

a. air sac
b. bronchial tube
c. capillary
d. diaphragm
e. excretory system
f. exhale
g. inhale
h. kidney
i. mucus
j. respiratory system
k. trachea
l. urinary bladder
m. urine

1. The ____ is the group of organs that get rid of cell wastes.

2. A tiny pouch in the lungs where gas exchange takes place is an ____.

3. The large muscle below the lungs that helps you breathe is called the ____.

4. A ____ is a tiny blood vessel that supplies body cells with oxygen and nutrients.

5. An organ of the excretory system that filters cell wastes from the blood is a ____.

6. When you breathe in, you ____.

7. A ____ is a tube that branches off from the trachea and goes into a lung.

8. The waste liquid formed in the kidneys is ____.

9. The ___ is the group of organs that take oxygen from the air and remove carbon dioxide from the body.

10. The lining of the nose makes ___, a sticky liquid.

11. Urine is temporarily stored in a muscular, baglike organ called the ___.

12. The tube that carries air to the bronchial tubes is the ___.

13. When you breathe out, you ___.

Explaining Science

Draw and label a diagram or write a paragraph to answer these questions.

1. How does oxygen get from the air to the blood in the lungs?

2. What happens to a red blood cell between the time it leaves a lung and the time it returns?

3. How do nitrogen wastes get from body cells to the urinary bladder?

Using Skills

1. The **graphic source** to the right shows how body cells get oxygen. Explain the process.

2. Make an **inference.** Why do you suppose that breathing through your nose is usually better for you than breathing through your mouth?

3. Suppose you put a small plastic bag over one hand. With your other hand, you hold the bag around your wrist so that no air can get inside. What do you think you will see after five minutes? Why? **Communicate** your thoughts by writing a paragraph.

Critical Thinking

1. When you exercise, you breathe faster than normal. Your heart beats faster too. Based on what you have learned in this chapter, **draw** a **conclusion** about why these things happen.

2. Robin and David get thirsty while hiking. Their water bottles are nearly empty. They have oranges, trail mix, and crackers. **Decide** which would be best to eat. Why?

3. A small child holds his breath for a short while. Make a **prediction.** Just before the child starts to breathe again, will his blood contain a buildup of carbon dioxide or a buildup of oxygen? Explain.

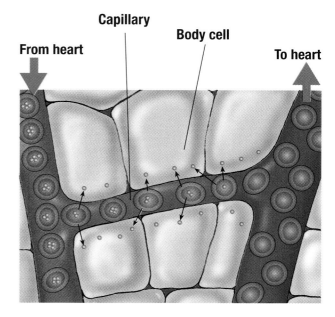

From heart Capillary Body cell To heart

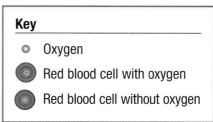

Key

◎ Oxygen

◉ Red blood cell with oxygen

● Red blood cell without oxygen

To Your Healthy Future!

What's the best way you can fight disease and stay healthy? Participate in healthy activities you enjoy. Learn about ways to stay safe. Find out how to prevent disease.

Chapter 2
Living a Healthy Life

Inquiring about Living a Healthy Life

Lesson 1
What Are Communicable Diseases?

- What are the causes of communicable diseases?
- How do communicable diseases spread?
- How does the body defend against pathogens?
- How can communicable diseases be prevented and treated?

Lesson 2
What Are Noncommunicable Diseases?

- What are some noncommunicable diseases and their causes?
- How can noncommunicable diseases be treated and controlled?

Lesson 3
What Is a Healthy Lifestyle?

- How can you prevent injuries?
- How can you get the nutrients you need?
- Why is it important to avoid tobacco, alcohol, and other drugs?
- How do rest and exercise help your body?

Copy the chapter graphic organizer onto your own paper. This organizer shows you what the whole chapter is all about. As you read the lessons and do the activities, look for answers to the questions and write them on your organizer.

Exploring How Diseases Spread

Process Skills

- making and using models
- observing
- inferring
- communicating

Materials

- marker
- 4 sheets of dark construction paper
- flour in a pail
- hand lens

Explore

1 Use the marker to number the sheets of construction paper 1–4.

2 To **model** how some diseases may be spread, have one student in your group dust his or her right hand with flour. Student 1 uses this hand to shake hands with student 2. Then student 2 shakes hands with student 3 and student 3 shakes hands with student 4.

3 Have student 1 press his or her hand on sheet 1. Each of the other students does the same with his or her numbered sheet.

4 Use the hand lens to study the four sheets. Record your **observations.**

Reflect

1. Imagine that the flour represents germs. Describe how shaking hands can spread germs from person to person.

2. Make an **inference.** Besides shaking hands, what are some ways that germs can get on your hand? **Communicate.** Discuss your ideas with the class.

Inquire Further

How can washing your hands affect the spread of germs? Develop a plan to answer this or other questions you may have.

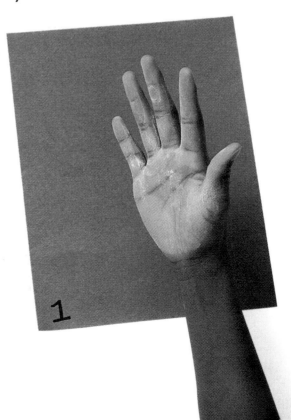

Solving Word Problems

Exercise is an important part of a healthy lifestyle. Some students answered a survey about their favorite kind of exercise. The bar graph shows the results of the survey.

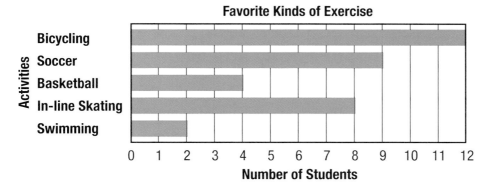

Favorite Kinds of Exercise

Activities: Bicycling, Soccer, Basketball, In-line Skating, Swimming

Number of Students: 0 1 2 3 4 5 6 7 8 9 10 11 12

How many students did not choose bicycling or soccer? Use the four-step guide below to help you solve this problem.

Understand	Read the problem carefully. Find the information you need. Find the question.	4 students chose basketball, 8 chose in-line skating, and 2 chose swimming. How many did not choose bicycling or soccer?
Plan	Think about what you need to do.	You need to combine the number who chose basketball, in-line skating, and swimming.
Solve	Use the plan. Find the solution.	$4 + 8 + 2 = 14$ 14 students did not choose bicycling or soccer.
Look Back	Decide whether the answer makes sense.	35 students in all −21 choosing bicycling or soccer 14 The answer makes sense.

Talk About It!

What can you do to understand a problem?

You will learn:
- about the causes of communicable diseases.
- how communicable diseases spread.
- how the body defends against pathogens.
- how communicable diseases can be prevented and treated.

▲ *A cold can make a person feel miserable.*

Lesson 1

What Are Communicable Diseases?

AH-CHOO! Remember the last time you had a cold? Perhaps you sneezed and coughed and blew your nose again and again! Your family and friends may have been sick too! Why?

Causes of Communicable Diseases

Life Science

The girl in the picture has a cold. The symptoms of a cold can include runny nose, sneezing, coughing, watery eyes, sore throat, headache, fever, and tiredness. A cold is an example of a communicable disease. A **communicable disease** is an illness that can spread, usually from person to person. That is why family members and friends may have colds at the same time. An agent that causes a communicable disease is called a **pathogen**. Pathogens include bacteria, viruses, protists, and fungi. Pathogens are sometimes called germs, and communicable diseases are sometimes called infectious diseases or infections.

Many pathogens are so small that they can be seen only through a microscope. An electron microscope uses a beam of electrons instead of light rays to magnify pathogens up to two million times their actual size.

Bacteria live in the air, in water, and in soil. They live in your body too. Bacteria are so tiny that millions of them could fit on the head of a pin. Most kinds of bacteria are harmless, and many are even helpful. However, some kinds of bacteria cause diseases.

Bacteria reproduce quickly, especially in dark, warm, moist places such as inside the human body. Harmful bacteria give off poisonous wastes, or toxins, that can damage cells. A large number of them can produce enough toxins to make you sick.

Bacteria cause a variety of diseases, including ear infections, sinus infections, bacterial pneumonia, whooping cough, and tuberculosis. Notice the picture of some of the bacteria that cause strep throat.

Viruses are even smaller than bacteria. Unlike bacteria, viruses cannot carry out all the processes of life. They cannot reproduce on their own. However, viruses can invade body cells. Once inside a cell, a virus takes control of the cell and reproduces rapidly. The new viruses rob the cell of energy and crowd the inside of the cell. The cell can no longer work properly. Then the viruses invade other cells. These cells begin producing and releasing new viruses, which can lead to the death of the cells.

If enough new viruses are produced, they can damage and kill so many cells that you become sick. Diseases caused by viruses include colds, measles, mumps, chicken pox, influenza (flu), and viral pneumonia. Find the picture of the virus that causes flu.

Like bacteria, most fungi are harmless, and many are helpful. However, certain fungi can cause disease. The most common diseases caused by fungi are skin infections such as athlete's foot.

Protists also can be harmless or harmful. Malaria is one disease caused by a type of protist. The dark objects in the top picture are protists that can cause malaria. The lighter colored objects shown are red blood cells.

These streptococcus bacteria cause strep throat. (magnified 14,600×) ▶

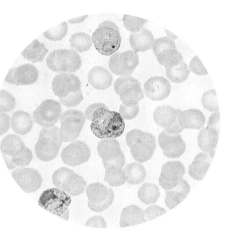

▲ Malaria is caused by a kind of protist. (magnified 1,500×)

▲ This picture of influenza viruses was taken with an electron microscope. The viruses are magnified 900,000 times.

How Communicable Diseases Spread

Many communicable diseases spread from person to person through the air. The man in the picture has a cold. When he sneezes without covering his nose and mouth, droplets containing viruses are sprayed into the air. Other people may breathe in the viruses.

Suppose the same man covered his sneeze with his hands but then failed to wash them. He shook hands with another man, who also failed to wash his hands and then touched his own mouth or nose. Cold viruses might enter the second man's mouth or nose. Similarly, some communicable diseases spread when a person's hands or mouth come in contact with an object used by a sick person. Sharing a drinking glass with someone who has a cold is one example.

Communicable diseases can spread even when no sick people are nearby. Some diseases spread when people drink water containing pathogens. Cholera, caused by a bacterium, can spread this way. Other diseases spread when people eat food containing pathogens. For example, salmonellosis is a disease caused by bacteria that can grow in foods such as poultry and eggs.

Insects and other animals carry the pathogens that cause some other communicable diseases. Such animals are called carriers. For example, a certain kind of mosquito can be a carrier of the protist that causes malaria. The mosquito spreads the pathogen to people when it bites them. The picture on the next page summarizes some of the ways that diseases spread.

The water droplets from a single sneeze can contain thousands of pathogens. ▼

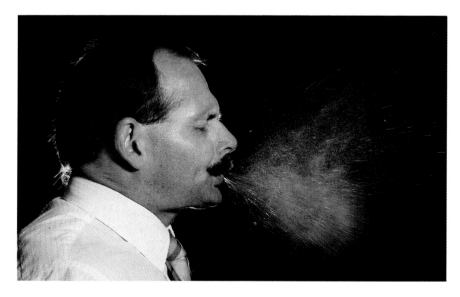

Some Ways Communicable Diseases Spread

This character is a communicable disease disaster. Luckily, she doesn't really exist!

Sneezes and Coughs

Colds, flu, measles, mumps, chicken pox, pneumonia, strep throat, tuberculosis, and whooping cough are some diseases that can spread when a sick person sends pathogens into the air by sneezing or coughing.

Contaminated Food

Food poisoning results from eating food containing harmful bacteria or their toxins. The bacteria are usually found in foods that are not kept clean or are inadequately cooked or stored. Symptoms can range from mild stomach upset to difficulty in breathing.

Contaminated Drinking Water

Cholera and typhoid fever are both caused by bacteria. They were once common in the United States but are rare here today. They occur mainly in regions of the world where drinking water is polluted as a result of poor sanitation.

Contaminated Hands and Objects

Diseases that spread by sneezes or coughs also may spread through contact with sick people's hands or with objects they have touched. The fungus that causes athlete's foot can be spread by contact with a shower floor, a towel, or a bath mat that someone infected with the fungus has touched.

Animal Bites

Malaria is spread by certain mosquito bites. Mosquito bites also spread some kinds of encephalitis, an inflammation of the brain. Some viruses that cause encephalitis can live in the blood of horses and other animals. Ticks can be carriers of the bacterium that causes Lyme disease. Animals such as dogs, cats, raccoons, and bats can carry the virus that causes rabies.

Body Defenses Against Pathogens

Knowing that pathogens are all around, you may wonder why you don't get sick more often than you do. The reason is that your body has several ways of defending itself against pathogens.

One line of defense involves keeping pathogens out. Your skin is a major part of this line of defense. Most pathogens cannot pass through unbroken skin. Pathogens can enter the body through such openings as the nose and mouth. However, the pathogens are likely to be trapped in the sticky mucus made by the lining of the nose, the mouth, and the passages leading to the lungs. The mucus can then be coughed out, sneezed out, blown out, or swallowed. If mucus is swallowed, digestive juice in the stomach kills many pathogens in the mucus.

Tears and saliva also serve as defenses. Pathogens carried by dust or by your fingers can get in your eyes. However, the tears that continuously wash your eyes contain a substance that kills some pathogens. If you eat food with pathogens in it, your saliva may kill some pathogens. Some other pathogens die when they mix with the acid and digestive juice in your stomach.

Sometimes your body's defenses cannot keep pathogens from getting into your blood or other tissues. When this happens, another line of defense goes to work. White blood cells, shown at the left, form this line of defense. Some white blood cells travel to parts of the body that have been invaded by pathogens. The white blood cells surround and destroy the pathogens. The photographs at the top of the next page show how the white blood cells destroy pathogens.

Blood contains red blood cells, which give the blood its color, and white blood cells, which fight pathogens. (magnified 3,750✕) ▼

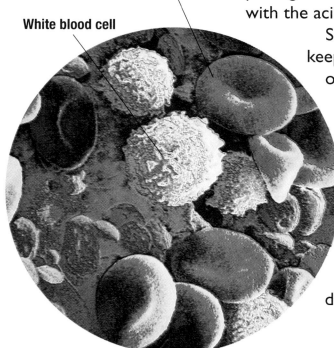

Red blood cell

White blood cell

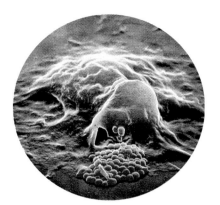

▲ A white blood cell approaches a colony of bacteria, shown in green. (magnified 3,600×)

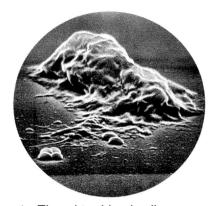

▲ The white blood cell surrounds much of the colony. (magnified 1,500×)

▲ The colony has become a harmless jellylike mass inside the white blood cell. (magnified 2,900×)

Sometimes white blood cells cannot destroy pathogens fast enough. Antibodies are still another line of defense against the pathogens. An **antibody** is a substance made by certain white blood cells. The diagram below shows how antibodies work. Each kind of antibody can fight only one kind of pathogen. If a new kind of pathogen invades, your white blood cells must make a new kind of antibody.

Antibodies can give you **immunity,** or resistance, to some diseases. Suppose you get sick with chicken pox. Some white blood cells make antibodies that attack the chicken pox virus right away, so you can get well. Other white blood cells become "memory" cells that can "remember" to make the correct antibodies. If the chicken pox virus ever enters your body again, the memory cells will make antibodies so quickly that you probably will not get sick a second time.

Glossary

antibody (an′ti bod′ē), a substance made by certain white blood cells that attaches to a pathogen and makes it harmless

immunity (i myü′nə tē), the body's resistance to a disease through the presence of antibodies

Glossary

When certain white blood cells are exposed to a pathogen, they make antibodies against that kind of pathogen. The antibodies attach themselves to the pathogens and make the pathogens harmless. Later, other white blood cells destroy the pathogens. ▼

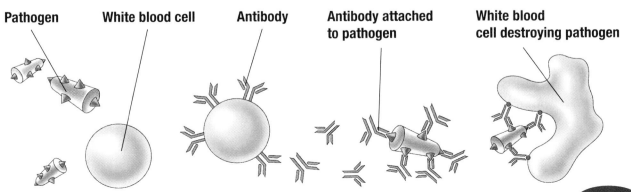

Pathogen **White blood cell** **Antibody** **Antibody attached to pathogen** **White blood cell destroying pathogen**

Prevention and Treatment

You can develop immunity to some communicable diseases without getting sick. The way to do that is to get the vaccines your doctor recommends. A vaccine is a dose of weakened or killed pathogens of one kind. The pathogens cause white blood cells to "remember" how to make antibodies if you are exposed to the same kind of pathogen in the future. In this way, the vaccine gives you immunity to the disease caused by the pathogen.

Chicken pox, mumps, measles, and whooping cough are some diseases that can be prevented by vaccines. The child in the picture below is drinking one kind of vaccine. Other vaccines are given as injections, or "shots."

Many communicable diseases have no vaccines. However, you can take other steps to help prevent them. For example, you can boost your body's ability to fight pathogens by eating a healthy diet and getting enough exercise. Washing fresh fruit and vegetables before eating them and storing and cooking food properly can help you avoid getting communicable diseases. The pictures on this page show some other ways to prevent communicable diseases.

▲ *Wash your hands with soap and water to get rid of pathogens. Be especially careful to wash after you use a tissue, after you touch an animal, after you go to the bathroom, and before you handle or eat food.*

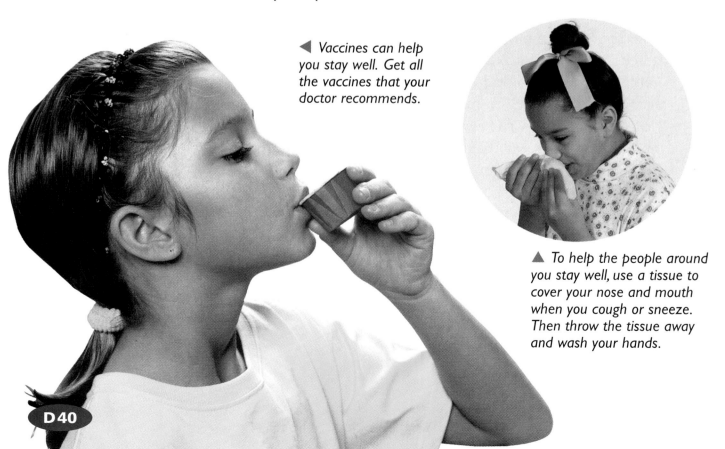

◀ *Vaccines can help you stay well. Get all the vaccines that your doctor recommends.*

▲ *To help the people around you stay well, use a tissue to cover your nose and mouth when you cough or sneeze. Then throw the tissue away and wash your hands.*

Your body's defenses and your best efforts are not always enough to prevent communicable disease. When you do get sick, you may need a medicine to help destroy pathogens.

An **antibiotic** is a medicine that kills bacteria. The top picture shows bacteria growing in a dish. The four colored disks are pieces of paper that were soaked in different antibiotics. The clear areas around three disks show that the antibiotics prevented the growth of bacteria. The disk with bacteria around it shows that some antibiotics cannot destroy some bacteria.

Your doctor might give you an antibiotic if you have a disease caused by a bacteria, such as strep throat. Antibiotics can't kill viruses, so they won't help cure diseases such as colds and flu.

Your body's defenses will eventually destroy the pathogens that cause colds and flu. You can help your body recover by getting plenty of rest and sleep and by drinking more fluids than usual, as the children in the pictures are doing.

▲ *Antibiotics can kill some kinds of bacteria, but not all kinds.*

▲ *Getting plenty of rest and sleep when you are sick can help you get better.*

▲ *Drinking lots of fluid, such as fruit juice, also can help your body recover from illness.*

Lesson 1 Review

1. Name three kinds of agents that cause communicable diseases.

2. Describe one way that a cold can spread from one person to another.

3. What are the body's three lines of defense against pathogens?

4. How do vaccines prevent communicable diseases?

5. **Sequence**
   Put the following steps in the development of immunity in order: **a.** antibodies attach to pathogens; **b.** white blood cells make antibodies; **c.** white blood cells are exposed to pathogens; **d.** white blood cells destroy pathogens.

What's the **Big Idea?**

You will learn:

- about some noncommunicable diseases and their causes.

- how noncommunicable diseases can be treated and controlled.

Glossary

allergy (al′ər jē), a harmful reaction to certain substances

noncommunicable (non′kə myü′nə kə bəl) **disease,** an illness that cannot spread and is not caused by a pathogen

Lesson 2

What Are Noncommunicable Diseases?

It's a gorgeous spring day. The sun is shining, a breeze is blowing, and colorful flowers are blooming all over. Nearby, some people are sniffling and sneezing. They seem miserable. What's going on?

Noncommunicable Diseases and Their Causes

Those people may have colds, or they may have an allergy to the pollen produced by spring's flowering plants. An **allergy** is a reaction that some people have when they are exposed to certain substances, such as those in the pictures on these two pages. Allergies are examples of **noncommunicable diseases.** Such illnesses cannot spread from person to person, and they are not caused by pathogens. There are three main causes of noncommunicable diseases: heredity, surroundings, and behavior.

◄ *Wheat*

◄ *Strawberries*

◄ *Shrimp*

▲ *Peanuts*

Heredity involves the passing of genes from parents to children. Some diseases, such as sickle-cell anemia and hemophilia, are caused by heredity. People can inherit a tendency to get certain other diseases. However, whether or not they develop the disease may depend on their surroundings, their behavior, or both.

Allergies provide a good example of how heredity, surroundings, and behavior can combine to make a noncommunicable disease develop. People inherit the tendency to develop allergies. However, people only experience allergic reactions when they are exposed to certain substances. The pictures show a few things that can trigger allergic reactions. People who are allergic to certain things may be able to avoid them and therefore avoid allergic reactions.

When allergic reactions occur, they can involve various parts of the body. For example, an itchy skin rash may develop from contact with poison ivy. Hives (red bumps on the skin), stomach upset, or swelling of the lips or tongue may result from eating certain foods. Pollen often triggers hay fever, in which the eyes may water and itch. The respiratory system also is affected. The tissue that lines the inside of the nose becomes swollen, causing a "stuffy" feeling. Other hay fever symptoms include runny nose and sneezing.

Ragweed pollen (magnified 1,000×) ▼

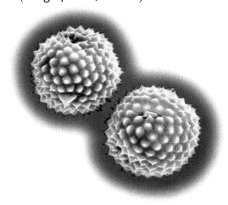

▲ *Dust mites are microscopic animals that live on dust particles. (magnified 500×)*

▲ *Poison ivy*

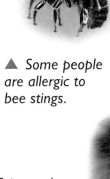

▲ *Some people are allergic to bee stings.*

Dander consists of tiny scales shed from the skin of cats and other mammals. ▶

Glossary

asthma (az′mə), an allergy that affects the respiratory system and may result in breathing difficulty and wheezing

emphysema (em′fə sē′mə), a disease of the lungs in which air sacs are damaged

Like hay fever, **asthma** is an allergy that involves the respiratory system. In asthma, the lining of the bronchial tubes and the smaller tubes in the lungs becomes swollen. Mucus builds up. As a result, breathing becomes difficult. There may be a wheezing sound as air forces its way through the narrowed tubes. Thousands of substances can trigger an asthmatic reaction, often called an asthma attack. Smoke, dust, and pollen are some common triggers.

Allergies, including asthma, are not the only diseases that can affect the respiratory system. **Emphysema** is another noncommunicable disease of the respiratory system. You know that your lungs have millions of tiny air sacs. In emphysema, the walls of some air sacs lose their elasticity and become overstretched. Air sacs next to one another may burst, forming one large space instead of many small ones. Compare the picture of normal air sacs with the picture of air sacs damaged by emphysema.

Damage to air sacs means that blood passing through the lungs cannot take in oxygen or get rid of carbon dioxide very well. The heart must work harder to get enough oxygen to body cells. A person with emphysema often feels short of breath.

Emphysema takes years to develop. Some people may inherit a tendency to develop emphysema. However, the main cause of emphysema is a certain behavior. That behavior is smoking.

Normal air sacs (magnified 100×) ▼

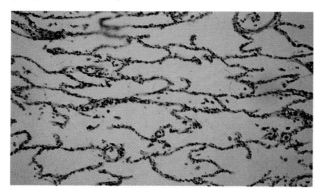

Air sacs with walls damaged by emphysema (magnified 80×) ▼

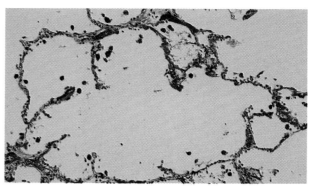

Any noncommunicable disease that affects the heart or blood vessels is called a **cardiovascular disease**. Compare the pictures to the right. **Atherosclerosis** occurs when fatty substances build up on the inside walls of arteries. As arteries become clogged, blood flow decreases. Some body cells may not get enough oxygen. If arteries leading to the heart or brain become completely blocked, a heart attack or stroke may result. People may inherit a tendency to develop atherosclerosis. However, behaviors such as smoking, eating a high-fat diet, and being inactive increase the risk.

The noncommunicable disease known as **cancer** involves body cells that develop abnormally and grow uncontrollably. The cancer cells damage normal body cells and interfere with the way the body works. You can see normal and cancerous skin cells in the pictures below.

Heredity and surroundings play a role in causing some cancers. However, a person's behavior can affect the risk of developing cancer. For example, the main cause of skin cancer is the sun's radiation, which is part of the surroundings. People who inherit light-colored skin have a greater tendency to develop skin cancer. How can you protect yourself? When you will be in the sun, apply a sunscreen with an SPF (sun protection factor) of 15 or higher. Try to wear a wide-brimmed hat, long sleeves, and long pants. Smoking causes most lung cancer. Using smokeless tobacco increases the risk of mouth cancer. A high-fat diet may contribute to cancer of the colon, which is part of the large intestine.

Glossary

Glossary

cardiovascular
(kär′dē ō vas′kyə lər)
disease, a disease of the heart or blood vessels

atherosclerosis
(ath′ər ō sklə rō′sis), a disease in which fatty substances build up on the inside walls of arteries

cancer (kan′sər), the uncontrolled growth of abnormal cells

Normal coronary artery (magnified 13✕) ▼

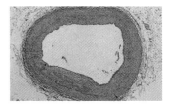

Moderate atherosclerosis (magnified 13✕) ▼

Normal skin cells (magnified 42✕) ▼

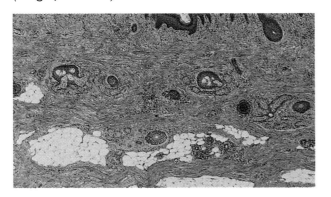

Cancerous skin cells (magnified 67✕) ▼

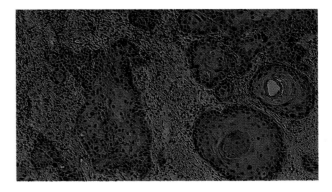

Treating and Controlling Noncommunicable Diseases

Some noncommunicable diseases can be cured. Others cannot be cured, but they can be treated and controlled. Doctors may use such methods as medicines and surgery. They also may suggest changes in a person's lifestyle to keep a noncommunicable disease under control.

An inhaler sends medicine for asthma directly to the bronchial tubes and lungs. ▼

Suppose medical tests show that a person is allergic to a particular food. The doctor will advise avoiding that food. However, a person with an allergy such as hay fever or asthma may find it impossible to avoid pollen and other triggers. In these cases, medicines may be used. Medicines for allergies range from hay-fever remedies sold at grocery stores and drugstores to allergy shots given by a doctor on a regular schedule. People with asthma may use an inhaler, as the child in the picture is doing. The inhaler dispenses medicine to prevent or relieve asthma symptoms.

Suppose a person has atherosclerosis. His or her doctor may prescribe a medicine to try to lower the level of fat in the blood. The doctor also may advise the person to practice the same kinds of behaviors that can help prevent the buildup of fatty substances in the first place. These behaviors include getting regular exercise, eating a diet low in fat, and not smoking.

If arteries that supply the heart are severely clogged with fatty substances, the doctor may perform bypass surgery to try to prevent a heart attack. In bypass surgery, a short length of vein, usually taken from the patient's leg, is attached to either side of the blocked part of an artery in the heart. Blood then flows through the attached vein, bypassing the blockage and ensuring that the heart muscle gets enough oxygen.

Traditionally, doctors have treated cancer with surgery, radiation, or powerful drugs that kill cancer cells. Today, scientists are developing and testing a wide range of treatments that they hope will be more effective against cancer cells and less harmful to healthy cells. Scientists are also working on drugs to prevent cancer.

Early diagnosis is the key to curing, controlling, or reducing the damage done by noncommunicable diseases. If you ever have any unusual or upsetting symptoms, tell an adult who is responsible for you. You may need to see your doctor. It's also a good idea to get regular health checkups, even if you're feeling well. That is what the child on this page is doing. When your doctor sees you regularly, he or she can detect changes that might indicate a health problem. Your doctor also can work with you to develop a lifestyle that can help prevent disease.

Communication is part of a successful health checkup. Take the opportunity to ask questions and explain concerns you have about your health. ▼

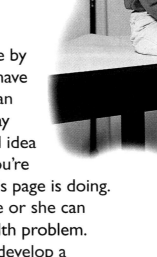

Lesson 2 Review

1. Identify some of the causes of a noncommunicable disease such as skin cancer.

2. How might a noncommunicable disease such as atherosclerosis be treated?

3. **Compare and Contrast**
   Describe how normal air sacs and air sacs of a person with emphysema are different.

You will learn:

- how you can prevent injuries.
- how you can get the nutrients you need.
- why it is important to avoid tobacco, alcohol, and other drugs.
- how rest and exercise help your body.

Lesson 3

What Is a Healthy Lifestyle?

Almost everywhere you look, you see people exercising, eating low-fat foods, and giving up unhealthy habits such as smoking. A healthy lifestyle can help prevent both communicable and noncommunicable diseases.

Preventing Injuries

You may want to begin living a healthier lifestyle too. Before you go charging off, though, you need to realize the importance of safety. For example, exercising won't do you much good if you hurt yourself doing it. The children on these two pages stay safe by following simple safety rules. Whether exercising, riding in a car, or just hanging around, you too can take steps to prevent accidents and injuries.

Always wear your safety belt when riding in a car or other vehicle. You won't be thrown from your seat if there's a crash.

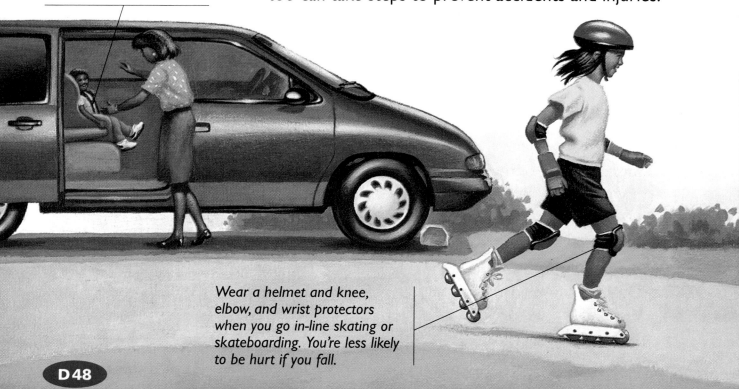

Wear a helmet and knee, elbow, and wrist protectors when you go in-line skating or skateboarding. You're less likely to be hurt if you fall.

You can have fun and still be safe. When you play an organized game or sport, follow its rules. Avoid unnecessary roughness. Wear appropriate clothing, shoes, and protective equipment. For example, wear the right kind of helmet if you play baseball, softball, football, or hockey.

In addition to obeying traffic signs and signals, use special care when crossing streets, whether on foot or on a bicycle. Cross only at corners or crosswalks and only when no traffic is coming. Look in all directions to be sure, even when the green light or walk sign is on.

Avoid falls at home or school by wiping up spills immediately. Don't leave any objects, big or small, lying around where someone could step on or trip over them.

Wherever you are and whatever you do, keep safety in mind. Don't take unnecessary risks. Always ask yourself, "What is the safe thing to do here?" Then do it.

Do warm-up and cool-down activities when exercising. You loosen your muscles and help prevent soreness or injury.

Wear a helmet for bicycling. Always obey all traffic signs and signals when bicycling or crossing streets on foot. You're less likely to get hurt by colliding with a car, a bicyclist, or a pedestrian.

Getting the Nutrients You Need

A healthy diet is an essential part of a healthy lifestyle. A healthy diet is one that gives you all the nutrients you need in the right amounts. Nutrients are substances in food that body cells use to do their work, get energy, and grow.

The six kinds of nutrients that your body needs are carbohydrates, fats, proteins, vitamins, minerals, and water. Carbohydrates and fats give you energy. Your body uses proteins mostly for growth and repair, though proteins provide energy too. Vitamins and minerals do many different jobs to keep your body working properly. For example, some vitamins help fight disease, and some minerals help build body cells. Among other jobs, water helps remove cell wastes and helps keep your body temperature steady.

No single food has every nutrient. To be healthy, you need a variety of foods. The Food Guide Pyramid, shown on the next page, can help you plan meals and snacks that provide the right amounts of each nutrient. The pyramid has a range of servings you need each day for most food groups. Eat at least the lower number of servings in each range. Eat more if you lack energy or are too thin. Start with additional servings of bread, cereal, rice, and pasta. These foods should make up the largest part of your diet. Choose healthy snacks, like the celery, raisins, and peanut butter on the left.

Watch out for foods at the top of the pyramid! You can get the small amount of fat that you need from the two groups just below the top. Fatty foods increase the risk of cardiovascular disease and some kinds of cancer. Fatty and sugary foods can cause you to gain too much weight. Sugary foods can cause tooth decay too.

Fruits, vegetables, and whole-grain breads and cereals do more than provide nutrients. They also provide a material called fiber. Fiber helps food move through the digestive system as it should. Fiber also may help prevent colon cancer.

Healthy snacks like this one can provide added nutrients. ▼

The Food Guide Pyramid

Plan meals and snacks to include foods from the groups below the top group. For example, a healthy snack might consist of an apple, whole-wheat crackers, and low-fat cheese.

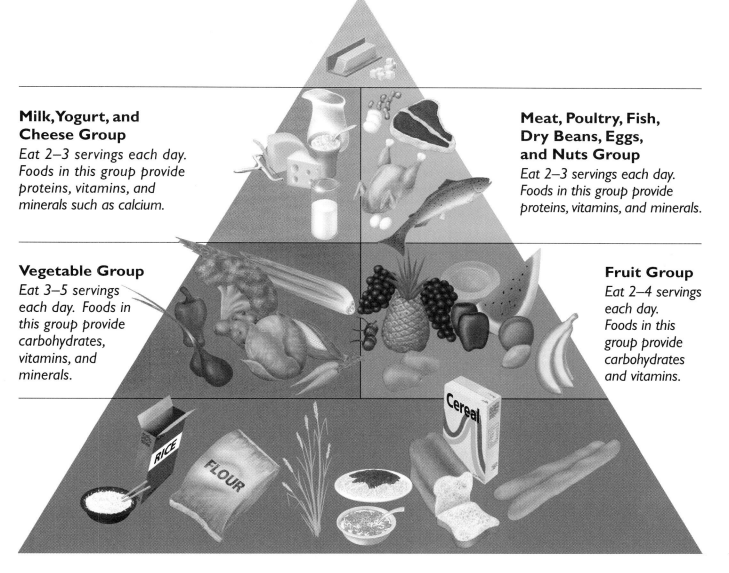

Fats, Oils, and Sweets
Eat very little of these foods.

Milk, Yogurt, and Cheese Group
Eat 2–3 servings each day. Foods in this group provide proteins, vitamins, and minerals such as calcium.

Meat, Poultry, Fish, Dry Beans, Eggs, and Nuts Group
Eat 2–3 servings each day. Foods in this group provide proteins, vitamins, and minerals.

Vegetable Group
Eat 3–5 servings each day. Foods in this group provide carbohydrates, vitamins, and minerals.

Fruit Group
Eat 2–4 servings each day. Foods in this group provide carbohydrates and vitamins.

Bread, Cereal, Rice, and Pasta Group
Eat 6–11 servings each day. Foods in this group provide carbohydrates, vitamins, and minerals.

Glossary

dependence
(di pen′dəns), the need
for a drug, which may be
a mental need, a physical
need, or both

Avoiding Tobacco, Alcohol, and Other Drugs

Drugs are chemicals that change the way the body works. Medicines are drugs used to prevent, cure, and treat illnesses. If used carefully, medicines can be helpful to health. Other drugs have no place in your healthy lifestyle.

Cigarettes and other products made from the tobacco plant contain a drug called nicotine. It makes the heart beat faster than normal. It narrows the blood vessels so that less blood flows through them. Nicotine also causes **dependence,** which is the need for a drug. People who use tobacco often find it extremely difficult to quit.

Tobacco smoke also contains carbon monoxide, a poisonous gas that replaces some oxygen in the blood. A sticky material called tar is another substance found in tobacco smoke. As you can see in the picture, tar builds up in a smoker's lungs, where it can cause cancer cells to grow. Substances in tobacco smoke also can cause emphysema and contribute to atherosclerosis.

A simple demonstration shows how tar builds up in the lungs of a smoker. The substances in tobacco can lead to lung cancer, cardiovascular disease, and other diseases that can kill a person. ▼

Alcohol, found in beer, wine, and liquor, is another drug to avoid. Alcohol slows down the work of the brain, changing the way a person thinks, feels, and acts. After several drinks, a person may have trouble remembering things or making decisions. Muscles may not work together correctly. The picture shows how vision may be blurred. Someone who drinks and then tries to drive a car or a bicycle may have an accident.

Drinking large amounts of alcohol over a long period can lead to brain damage, liver disease, and cancer of the stomach and other organs. Alcohol can also cause dependence. Alcoholism is an illness in which a person is dependent on alcohol and cannot control his or her drinking.

Drug abuse is the intentional use of drugs for reasons other than health. Some people abuse alcohol. Others abuse drugs such as marijuana, cocaine, and heroin. Those drugs are illegal. They can harm health. They can cause dependence. The only drugs you should take are medicines from a doctor, a nurse, or an adult who is responsible for you. If anyone else offers you any other drug, say "no."

Glossary

drug abuse (ə byüs′), the intentional use of drugs for reasons other than health

Glossary

This is how a street scene at night might look to someone who has been drinking alcohol. ▼

Getting Enough Rest and Exercise

Getting enough rest and exercise is another important part of a healthy lifestyle. Resting after working or playing helps tired muscles recover. Rest also can help relieve emotional fatigue, or stress. Sleep is a special kind of rest. During sleep, your heartbeat, breathing, and some other body processes slow down. This means that more energy is available to build or repair body cells. At your age, you should get nine to twelve hours of sleep each night.

Regular, vigorous exercise benefits your body in many ways. For example, exercise can help you keep a healthy body weight. Exercise helps keep arteries clear of fatty substances. Exercise makes muscles flexible. Exercise also strengthens muscles, including the heart muscle, diaphragm, and muscles between the ribs. The children on these pages are getting exercise in different ways.

A stronger heart muscle can pump more blood with each beat. A stronger diaphragm and rib muscles make it possible for the chest cavity to expand more as you inhale. This means you can take in more air with each breath. The result is that body cells get the oxygen they need with less effort by your heart and lungs.

Sports such as basketball and soccer are good for your entire body, including your heart and lungs. However, you do not have to play sports to be healthy. You also do not have to do exercises that you think are boring. Bicycling, in-line skating, jogging, swimming, and jumping rope are all good exercises. Walking, dancing, cross-country skiing, and doing chores such as sweeping floors and raking leaves also are good for you. Try to do some vigorous activity every day, or at least three times a week.

Before you exercise, warm up. Get your muscles ready for vigorous activity by doing slow, gentle stretches or by walking or jogging slowly for a few minutes. After you exercise, cool down the same way. This will loosen tight muscles and help prevent soreness.

It's a good idea to rest for a while and drink some water after you do any vigorous activity. ▼

Lesson 3 Review

1. How can you prevent injury while riding a bicycle?

2. What kinds of foods should you eat to get the nutrients your body needs?

3. Why should you say "no" to tobacco and other drugs?

4. What are three ways that regular, vigorous exercise helps your body?

5. **Cause and Effect**
   Identify some effects that can result from living a healthy lifestyle.

Measuring Heart Rates

Process Skills

- estimating and measuring
- collecting and interpreting data
- inferring
- communicating

Materials

- clock with a second hand

Getting Ready

In this activity you will find out how your heart rate is affected by exercise.

It may take some practice and patience to be able to feel your pulse.

Follow This Procedure

1 Make a chart like the one shown. Use your chart to record your data.

Activity	Heartbeats in 10 seconds	Number of heartbeats per minute
Resting heart rate		
Exercising heart rate		

2 Sit quietly with one arm palm up. Place the first two fingers of your other hand against your upturned wrist near the base of your thumb (Photo A). Press gently until you can feel your pulse.

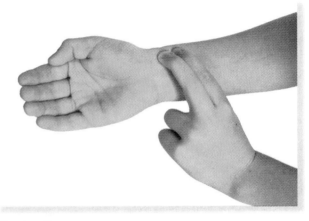

Photo A

3 Watching the clock, count the number of heartbeats in 10 seconds. **Collect data** by recording the **measurement** in your chart. Multiply the number by 6. This is your resting heart rate: the number of times your heart beats per minute when you are at rest. Record it in your chart.

 Safety Note *Be sure you have enough space to exercise without bumping into people or objects. If you have a health problem, do not do jumping jacks without your doctor's permission.*

④ Stand up and do 20 jumping jacks (Photo B). Immediately sit down and measure your exercising heart rate. Count the heartbeats in 10 seconds, and multiply that number by 6. Record both numbers in your chart.

Self-Monitoring
Have I correctly completed all the steps?

Photo B

Interpret Your Results

1. Describe how your heart rate changed after exercise.

2. Make an **inference.** Why do you think your heart rate changed in this way?

3. There may be differences among students' resting heart rates and exercising heart rates. **Communicate.** Discuss possible reasons for the variations in resting heart rates and exercising heart rates.

Inquire Further

If you continue doing jumping jacks, how will your heart rate change? Develop a plan to answer this or other questions you may have.

Self-Assessment

- I followed instructions to **measure** my resting heart rate and my exercising heart rate.
- I **collected data** by recording **measurements** in a chart.
- I described how my heart rate changed after exercise.
- I made an **inference** about why my heart rate changed when I exercised.
- I **communicated** by discussing possible reasons for variations in resting heart rates and exercising heart rates.

Chapter 2 Review

Chapter Main Ideas

Lesson 1

• Communicable diseases are caused by pathogens such as bacteria and viruses.

• Communicable diseases can be spread by sneezes, coughs, animal bites, and contaminated food and water.

• The body defends against pathogens by keeping them out, destroying them, or making them harmless.

• Taking vaccines, covering sneezes and coughs, and washing hands help prevent communicable diseases. Taking medicine, resting, and drinking fluids help treat them.

Lesson 2

• Heredity, surroundings, and behavior can cause noncommunicable diseases.

• Noncommunicable diseases may be treated and controlled by medicine, surgery, radiation, or changes in lifestyle.

Lesson 3

• Ways to prevent injuries include wearing a safety belt and protective equipment, exercising safely, and obeying traffic signs.

• The Food Guide Pyramid can help people get enough nutrients.

• Alcohol, tobacco, and other drugs--except medicine—can harm health and cause dependence.

• Rest can help the body recover from work or play, relieve stress, and make energy available for cell growth and repair. Exercise helps keep arteries clear of fatty substances and strengthens muscles.

Reviewing Science Words and Concepts

Write the letter of the word or phrase that best completes each sentence.

a. allergy
b. antibiotic
c. antibody
d. asthma
e. athero-sclerosis
f. cancer
g. cardiovascular disease
h. communicable disease
i. dependence
j. drug abuse
k. emphysema
l. immunity
m. noncommuni-cable disease
n. pathogen

1. Any illness that can spread from one person to another is a ___.

2. An agent, such as a virus, that causes communicable disease is a ___.

3. A substance that makes a pathogen harmless is an ___.

4. Resistance to disease through the presence of antibodies is called ___.

5. A medicine that kills bacteria is an ___.

6. Hay fever is an example of a reaction to certain substances, otherwise known as an ___.

7. Any illness that cannot spread and is not caused by a pathogen is a ___.

8. An allergy that may result in breathing difficulty and wheezing is ___.

9. A disease of the lungs in which air sacs are damaged is ___.

10. Any disease of the heart or blood vessels is called ___.

11. A disease in which fatty substances build up on the inside walls of arteries is ___.

12. The uncontrolled growth of abnormal cells is called ___.

13. A physical or mental need for a drug is ___.

14. The intentional use of drugs for reasons other than health is called ___.

Explaining Science

Write a paragraph to answer these questions.

1. If someone with a cold sneezes nearby, how will your body try to defend itself?

2. How do allergies develop, and how can a person with an allergy deal with the disease?

3. What might a seven-day, healthy-lifestyle plan include?

Using Skills

1. Based on the graph on page D 33, how many more students like individual activities than team sports? Follow these steps to **solve** the **word problem:**

a. Tell what information you need.

b. Tell what operations you will use.

c. Answer this question: How many students like to do individual activities?

d. Answer this question: How many like to do team sports?

e. Solve the problem: How many more students like to do individual activities than team sports?

2. For the next fifteen minutes, observe your classmates for practices that could spread communicable diseases or prevent diseases from spreading. Record your observations, without naming names. **Communicate** your observations to the class and discuss how you all might prevent the spread of disease.

3. Many daily activities, such as crossing the street, can involve risks. **Infer** what precautions you could take to make such an activity safer.

Critical Thinking

1. You are going to the beach. **Apply** what you learned about reducing the risk of skin cancer. List items you would take with you.

2. Yesterday your friend Michael told you he has started smoking. Write a letter to persuade him to make a better **decision.**

3. You learned a neighbor has atherosclerosis. **Evaluate** whether it will be safe for you to visit her home and join her for a meal. Explain your reasoning.

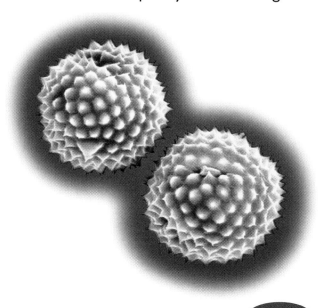

Unit D Review

Reviewing Words and Concepts

Choose at least three words from the **Chapter 1** list below.
Use the words to write a paragraph about how these concepts
are related. Do the same for **Chapter 2**.

Chapter 1
air sac
bronchial tube
diaphragm
exhale
inhale
trachea

Chapter 2
antibiotic
antibody
communicable
  disease
immunity
noncommunicable
  disease
pathogen

Reviewing Main Ideas

Each of the statements below is false. Change the underlined
word or words to make each statement true.

1. The lining of the nose makes a sticky liquid called <u>tissue</u>, which adds moisture to the air breathed in.

2. Gases and nutrients can pass through the thin walls of blood vessels known as <u>arteries</u>.

3. Energy is released when body cells combine <u>water</u> and sugar.

4. The fist-sized <u>lungs</u> are the main organs of the excretory system.

5. As the urinary bladder fills with <u>nitrogen</u>, nerve cells send a message to the brain.

6. <u>Asthma</u> is one of the body's defenses against pathogens.

7. The allergy known as <u>emphysema</u> can result in breathing difficulty and wheezing.

8. Although it affects various parts of the body, <u>atherosclerosis</u> always involves the uncontrolled growth of abnormal cells.

9. The six kinds of nutrients that the body needs are carbohydrates, fats, <u>oils</u>, vitamins, minerals, and water.

10. Both nicotine and alcohol can cause <u>alcoholism</u>, which is the mental or physical need for a drug.

Interpreting Data

Use the Food Guide Pyramid to answer the questions below.

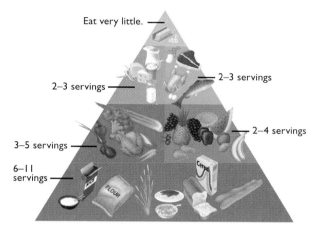

Eat very little.

2–3 servings

2–3 servings

2–4 servings

3–5 servings

6–11 servings

1. How many servings of foods such as carrots and broccoli should people eat each day?

2. How many servings of foods such as candy and soft drinks should people eat each day?

3. What are some fun and healthy foods and drinks that you could serve at a class party? List at least three foods and two drinks that your classmates would enjoy and that fit with the Food Guide Pyramid.

Communicating Science

1. Draw and label a diagram that shows the order in which the following body parts are used when you inhale: trachea, nostrils, air sacs, nose, bronchial tubes. Add a caption that summarizes what happens to inhaled air as it moves through each of those body parts.

2. The walls of air sacs, and of capillaries throughout the body, are very thin. Write a paragraph that explains why this is important.

3. Write a paragraph or draw a diagram to explain the body's three lines of defense against pathogens.

4. Make a chart to summarize what you have learned about the causes and prevention of allergies, emphysema, atherosclerosis, and cancer.

Applying Science

1. How much control do you have over your breathing? List situations in which you can change your breathing in some way. Then write about what you cannot change. What do you conclude?

2. About two-thirds of your body weight is water. Use that amazing fact to make a poster that could be placed near a drinking fountain in your school or community. Your poster should encourage people to drink lots of water.

3. You're thirsty, and that juice your best friend is drinking looks awfully good. Should you accept a sip from your friend's juice container? Why or why not? Write a few sentences to explain.

4. Make a list of safety rules for your favorite sport or other physical activity, or for a typical day in your life. Plan to post the list where you will see it often.

Unit D
Performance Review

"Your Body and You" Television Special

Using what you learned in this unit, prepare a television special about the human body and how to keep it healthy. Complete one or more of the following activities to be included in the TV special. You may work by yourself or in a group.

Animal Systems

Choose an animal group other than mammals. Use books, videos, or on-line sources to learn about the animals' respiratory and excretory systems. Prepare a display of your findings. You might draw pictures, or you might make models with materials such as balloons, clay, and drinking straws. As you present your display, explain how the animal systems are similar to and different from the human systems.

Hiccups Survey

Normally, the diaphragm contracts and relaxes in a gentle rhythm. Sometimes, however, the diaphragm becomes irritated and contracts suddenly. A hiccup results. Conduct a survey to determine the popularity of various hiccup cures. How many people hold their breath, or breathe into a paper bag, or drink a large glass of water, for example? Use paper or a sound recorder to collect and analyze your survey information. Use the data you collect to create a bar graph, and present your graph to viewers of the television special.

Cooking for Health

Plan a meal with at least one serving from each food group (except Fats, Oils, and Sweets) in the Food Guide Pyramid. Act out how to prepare the meal. Instead of real food, use pictures you have drawn or photo collages you have put together. Talk about what makes your meal a healthy one.

Disease Time Line

Do some research about the history of disease prevention and treatment. You might focus on communicable diseases, noncommunicable diseases, or a specific disease that interests you. Prepare a time line showing some highlights in the fight against the disease or diseases you have chosen. Present your time line as part of the television special.

Public Service Announcement

Write a script for a public service announcement about drugs. The announcement might be about tobacco, alcohol, another specific drug, or drug abuse in general. Your goal is to discourage young people from using the drug or drugs. Include a catchy slogan, snappy dialogue, a surprise ending, or something else to grab viewers' attention.

Summarizing Ideas and Writing a Persuasive Letter

Outlining a Report or Letter

An outline can help you organize your thoughts before you write. An outline lists the main ideas and supporting details for the different parts of a report or letter.

Each main idea on an outline is listed next to a Roman numeral, such as I, II, and III. The supporting details listed below a main idea are listed next to a letter, such as A, B, and C.

The sample below shows an outline that someone might make for Chapter 1 of this unit.

Chapter 1 Respiration and Excretion

I. **Taking Oxygen into the Body**
   A. How the Nose Prepares Air for the Lungs
   B. How Gases are Exchanged in the Lungs
   C. How Muscles Help the Lungs

II. **Using Oxygen**
   A. Getting Oxygen to Body Cells
   B. How Cells Use Oxygen

III. **Getting Rid of Cell Wastes**
   A. How Cells Make and Get Rid of Wastes
   B. How Blood Removes Cell Wastes
   C. How the Body Excretes Water

Make an Outline

Use this model to make an outline for Chapter 2 of this unit. Use the lesson titles and the main ideas from each lesson to complete your outline.

Write a Persuasive Letter

Use your outline to write a persuasive letter that states what you and your friend can do to make your lifestyles more healthful. Write one sentence for each main idea in your outline. Then write one sentence for each of your supporting details. Use transition words such as first, next, then, because, and however to shape your ideas into three paragraphs. Remember to add a brief introduction and closing for your letter.

Remember to:

1. **Prewrite** Organize your thoughts.

2. **Draft** Write your persuasive letter.

3. **Revise** Share your work and then make changes.

4. **Edit** Proofread for mistakes and fix them.

5. **Publish** Share your letter with your class.

Your Science Handbook

1

Safety in Science

Scientists know they must work safely when doing experiments. You need to be careful when doing experiments too. The next page shows some safety tips to remember.

Safety Tips

- Read each experiment carefully.

- Wear safety goggles when needed.

- Clean up spills right away.

- Never taste or smell substances unless directed to do so by your teacher.

- Handle sharp items carefully.

- Tape sharp edges of materials.

- Handle thermometers carefully.

- Use chemicals carefully.

- Dispose of chemicals properly.

- Put materials away when you finish an experiment.

- Wash your hands after each experiment.

Using the Metric System

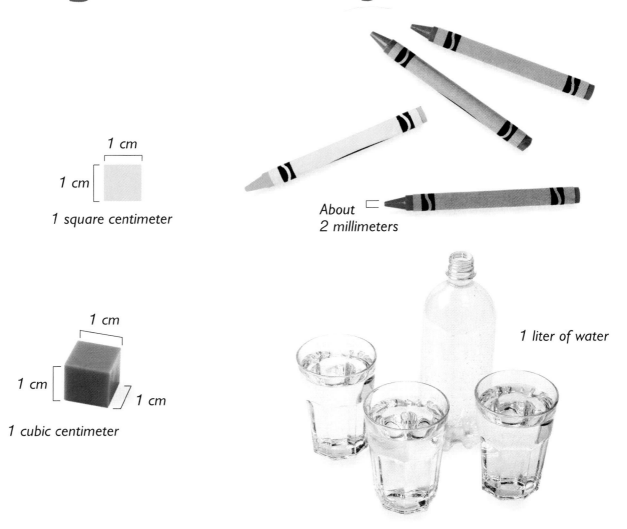

1 cm
1 cm
1 square centimeter

About 2 millimeters

1 cm
1 cm
1 cm
1 cubic centimeter

1 liter of water

11 football fields end to end is about 1 kilometer.

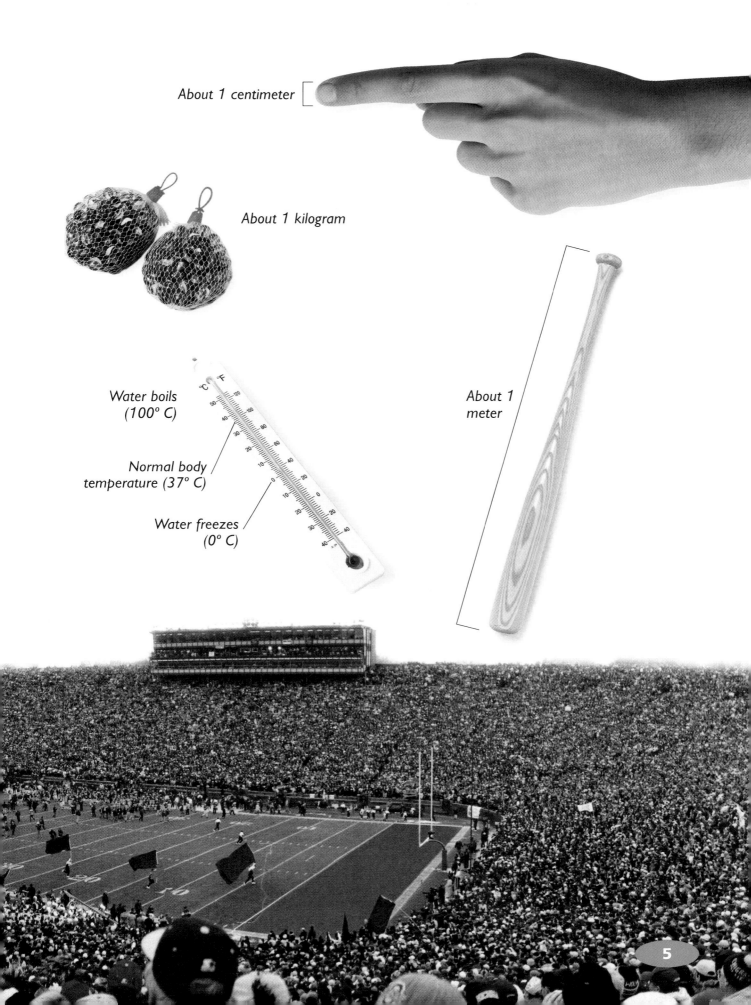

About 1 centimeter

About 1 kilogram

Water boils
(100° C)

Normal body
temperature (37° C)

Water freezes
(0° C)

About 1
meter

5

Observing

How can you refine your observations?

In the critical process of observation, your five special senses—sight, hearing, touch, smell, and taste—can provide you with information.

While observing an object or activity, your senses may focus on some of the available details more closely than on others.

Your observations may be refined, or made more complete, by repetition. Repetition can help your senses provide you with additional information.

Practice Observing

Materials

- journal
- hand lens
- pen or pencil
- tape measure

Follow This Procedure

1. Observe three trees on the way to school. Record what you see in your journal.

2. Make up questions about what you observed. Did the trees have leaves? What were their shapes? What color were they? Answer your questions based on your observations.

3. What other information did your senses provide about the trees?

4. Write about what you observed as a journal entry.

5. Repeat your observations the following day. Refine your observations by noticing what was there that you hadn't seen the day before.

6. Observe how many trees you see on the way to school. If there are too many, count the number on one block or along one mile.

7. Refine your observations by counting them a second time.

Thinking About Your Thinking

Which observations did you refine through repetition? Compare notes with your classmates. Did they improve their observations by repeating them? Which ones did they refine?

Communicating

How can you make your communication effective?

Effective communication uses words, pictures, charts, and graphs to share ideas and information.

The use of simple comparisons can help to communicate information that would otherwise be difficult to get across.

The use of data such as size, color, shape, and hardness, can enhance your descriptions and make your communication even more effective.

Practice Communicating

Materials

- pad
- pen or pencil
- 3 different rocks
- crayons or colored pencils

Follow This Procedure

1. Observe some rocks on your way to school. Without naming them, describe the different types of rocks you observed by their sizes, shapes, and colors. How many types did you observe?

2. Look closely at three different types of rocks. Use comparisons to describe them.

3. Describe their size, color, shape, and hardness.

4. If several colors are present, describe the most common color.

5. Describe how the rocks that you have vary. Describe similarities and differences.

6. Make a chart of the qualities of your rocks. Draw the rocks according to your observations. Color your drawings to look like your rocks.

Thinking About Your Thinking

Compare your chart to your classmates'. How were the rocks alike and different?

How would the rocks be different in an environment unlike the one you live in? Why do you think this is so?

Classifying

How can you classify living things and objects?

Living things and objects are classified according to their common properties. Scientists group organisms by their similarities and differences. They group minerals by their color, streak, hardness, and luster. There are several minerals shown on this page. Can you tell them apart?

Practice Classifying

Materials

- quartz
- pyrite
- graphite
- unglazed piece of tile
- coin
- scissors

Follow This Procedure

1. Make a chart like the one below.

2. Look at each mineral and fill in the information in the "color" column.

3. Test the "streak" of each mineral. The streak is the color the mineral leaves behind when you scratch it on your tile. Complete the "streak" portion of your chart for each mineral.

4. Each mineral reflects light in a certain way. Luster is the way the mineral reflects light. Some minerals are shiny and some are dull. Hold each mineral up to a light source and observe the way light is reflected. Fill in the "luster" part of your chart.

5. Hardness can be determined by completing a few simple tests. If you can scratch the mineral with your fingernail, the mineral is very soft. If you can scratch it with a coin, it is soft. If you can scratch it with a pair of scissors, it is medium hard. If the scissors don't scratch the mineral, it is hard. Using the results of these tests, fill in the "hardness" part of your chart.

Thinking About Your Thinking

Use the information in your chart to compare and contrast how these three minerals are alike and different. Do any of these minerals have the same characteristics? What uses do you think these minerals have? Use your classification chart to help you answer these questions.

Name	Quartz	Pyrite	Graphite
Color			
Streak			
Luster			
Hardness			

Estimating and Measuring

How can you estimate and measure with centimeters?

Scientists use the metric system of measurement. A meter is about the distance from a doorknob to the floor. A meter is 100 centimeters. Look at your little finger. Your nail on that finger is about 1 centimeter in width.

Look at the pictures of balloons on this page. Estimate how long each balloon is in centimeters using your fingernail as a measuring tool. Measure the balloons using a metric ruler. How accurate were your estimates?

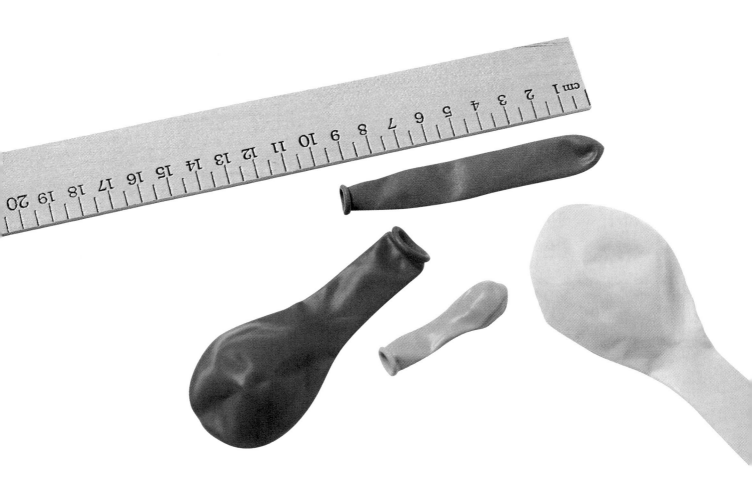

Practice Estimating and Measuring

Materials

- metric ruler
- classroom objects (pencils, erasers, paper clips, crayons, books)

Follow This Procedure

1 Make a chart like the one below.

Object	Estimate	Actual measurement

2 Gather several classroom objects and put them on a table or your desk. Work with a partner.

3 Using your fingernail as a measuring tool, estimate how long each object is. Write your estimates on your chart.

4 Check with your partner and see if he or she got the same estimate.

5 Use the ruler to measure the length of each object in centimeters. Write your measurements in the chart.

6 Check with your partner to see if he or she got the same measurements.

Thinking About Your Thinking

Suppose you wanted to estimate and measure the length of your school hallway. Would you use your fingernail and metric ruler as your measuring tools? Why or why not? What measuring tools might be more accurate?

Inferring

How can you make inferences?

You infer when you make a reasonable conclusion based on what you observe or on your past experience. To make an intelligent inference you must carefully observe everything around you.

Combining what you observe in the present with what you have learned from your past experience can also help you make better inferences.

Look at the rainbow on this page. Based on your observations and past experiences, when and where do you usually see rainbows?

Practice Inferring

Materials

- bowl of water
- mirror (small enough to fit into bowl)
- white paper

Follow This Procedure

1 Fill the bowl with water.

2 Place the small mirror in the bowl, reflecting side upward.

3 Turn the mirror so that it faces the sun, preferably near a window.

4 Move a piece of paper in front of the bowl until you see colors on the paper.

5 Have you ever seen a rainbow? Did it seem similar to what you have just observed?

6 Based on your current observation and past experience, what can you infer about sunlight? Is it made of only one color? Is it a mixture of colors?

Thinking About Your Thinking

List the steps you used to make an inference about the color spectrum of sunlight.

How did combining past experience with current observations help you make the correct inference?

Predicting

How can you make accurate predictions?

When you predict, you try to form an idea about what will happen to an object based on evidence you have studied or observed.

Suppose someone asks you to make a prediction and you have no idea what a good answer might be. What should you do then? If you have no past experience to draw on, do a small test. The results will give you information to draw on so you can make a prediction.

Practice Predicting

Materials

- penny
- paper towel
- cup of water
- dropper

Follow This Procedure

1. Place the penny on the paper towel with the head side up.

2. Put some water in the dropper. Practice putting a few drops of water from the dropper onto the penny.

3. Predict how many drops of water will fit on the head of the penny.

4. Wipe the water off the penny and begin dropping water on the penny again. Count the number of drops. Continue to add water drops to the penny until the water slips over the edge of the penny onto the paper towel.

5. Turn the penny over to the tails side. Predict how many drops of water will fit on this side of the penny.

6. Repeat the experiment.

Thinking About Your Thinking

Did you make an accurate prediction at Step 3 of how many drops of water would fit on the penny? How about after you made some observations? How did additional information give you a better chance to make an accurate prediction? Was your prediction for the tails side more accurate than the heads side? Why do you think so?

Making Operational Definitions

How do you make an operational definition?

An operational definition is a definition or description of an object or an event based on your experience with it. There are four basic steps in writing an operational definition.

1. Observe an object or event.

2. Think about these observations.

3. Describe what the object can do, what happens during the event, and what you can observe.

4. Write a definition that communicates what the object does or what happens during the event.

Practice Making Operational Definitions

Materials

- bottle with water
- balloon
- whistle
- straw with one end up
- kazoo (comb with waxed paper)

Follow This Procedure

1. Pick an object that produces sound.

2. Draw and diagram the object on your own paper. Show how the sound from the object is produced.

3. Write an operational definition for the object. What does it do?

Thinking About Your Thinking

Choose another object and repeat the activity. Compare and contrast the two sound-producing objects. How are they alike and different?

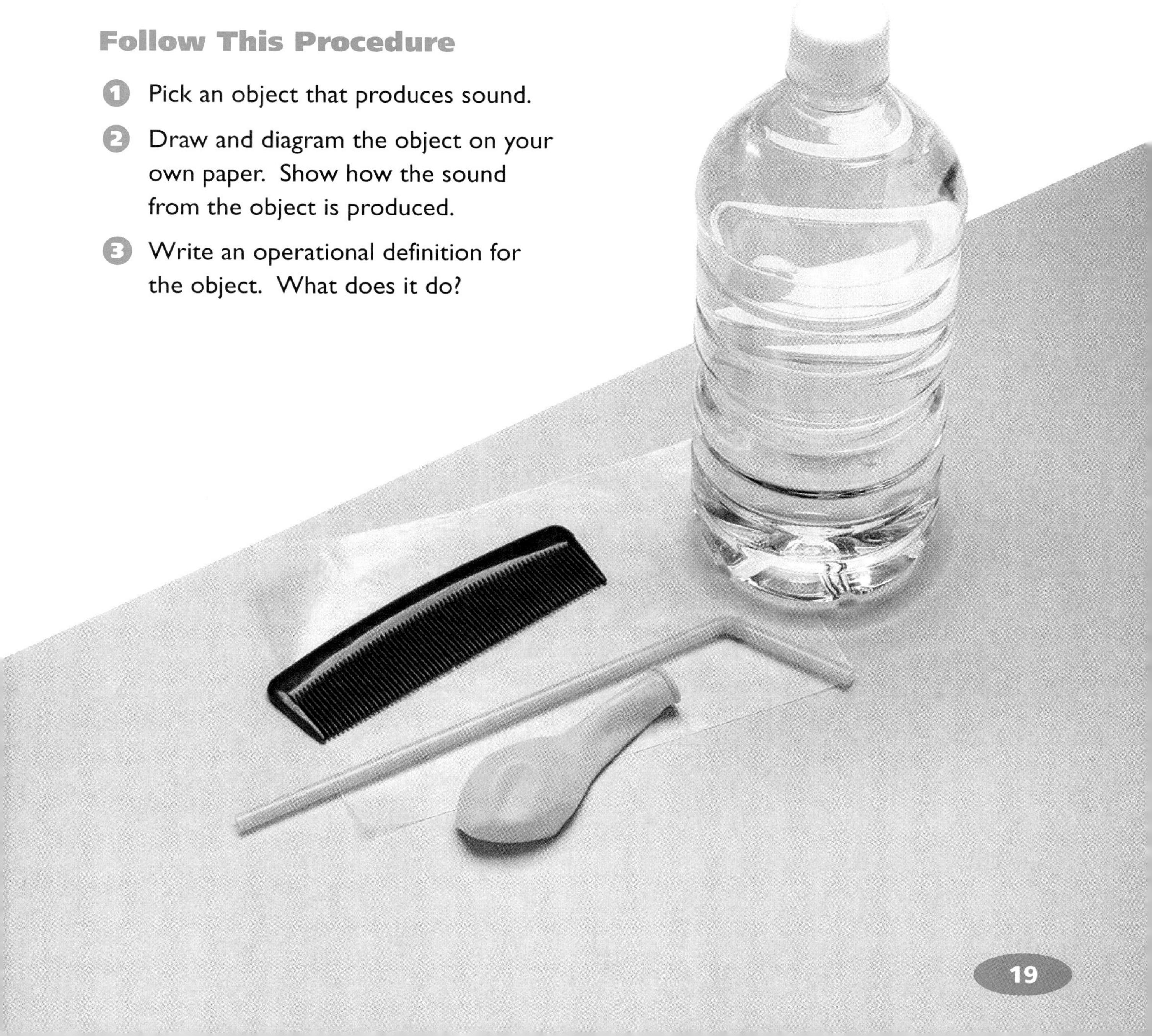

Making and Using Models

How can building a model make a concept clear?

Making a model of an idea in science is one way to better understand the idea. For example, you cannot observe the difference between the way air particles move in warm air and cold air.

Making a model of how air particles react to temperature changes can help you learn about this complicated idea. All you need is a balloon and a marker. And a good set of lungs!

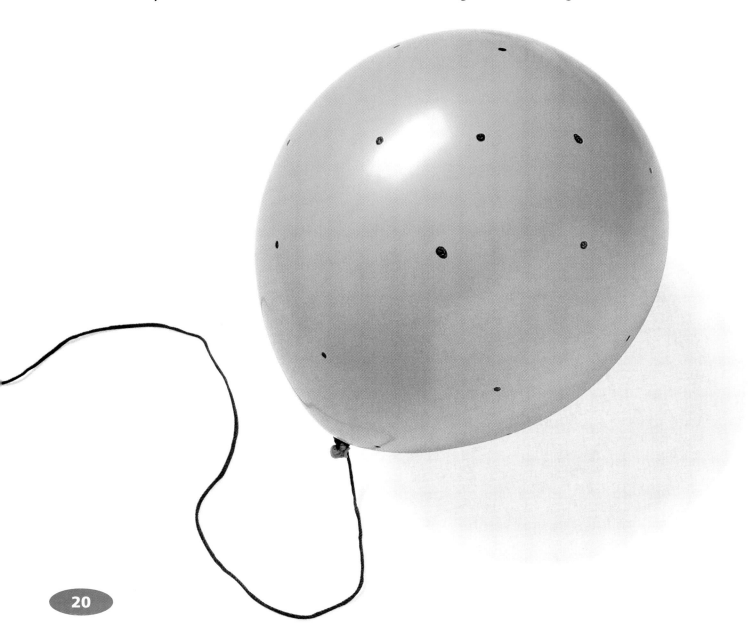

Practice Making and Using Models

Materials

- light-colored balloon
- black marker

Follow This Procedure

1. In this activity, you will make a model with your balloon to show how air particles move as air is heated and cooled.

2. Draw dots on the balloon with the marker.

3. Blow up the balloon and hold the end closed. Describe what happens to the dots as the balloon inflates.

4. Slowly let the air out of the balloon. Describe what happens to the dots as the balloon deflates.

5. If this model shows air particles move as air is heated and cooled, what do the dots represent?

6. What does the process of blowing up the balloon represent?

7. What does the process of letting air out of the balloon represent?

Thinking About Your Thinking

Explain how this balloon model acts like the particles in air being heated and cooled. Does air expand when it is heated or when it is cooled?

Formulating Questions and Hypotheses

How do you formulate questions and hypotheses?

Asking questions is the beginning of the scientific process. Formulating hypotheses that can be tested is the next important step.

Hunches, careful observation, and past experience, may lead you to ask questions and formulate hypotheses.

Although it is a good idea to keep your questions and hypotheses as specific as possible, it is also important to keep the BIG picture in mind. Isaac Newton observed apples falling from a tree. But his work with gravity explains what keeps Earth in orbit around the sun.

Practice Formulating Questions and Hypotheses

Materials

- 6 small objects
  - 2 different-sized balls
  - 2 different-sized wooden cubes
  - 1 key
  - 1 pencil
- tall clear plastic glass
- water
- marker
- stop watch
- paper towels

Follow This Procedure

1. **Question**: How do the properties of an object (size, shape, volume, density, and weight) affect how fast it will fall through a liquid?

2. Make a chart like the one below.

3. Write the name of each object on your chart. List as many of its properties as you can.

4. Write a hypothesis about the objects and their drop time. Which properties will the object with the shortest drop time have? the one with the longest drop time?

5. Fill the plastic glass about three-fourths full of water. Mark the level of the water with your marker.

6. Drop each object into the cylinder of water from just above the lip of the glass. Time how long it takes the object to reach the bottom. Record your measurement on the chart. Refill the glass with water to the mark after you test each object.

7. Which properties contributed to a fast drop time?

Thinking About Your Thinking

State the relationship between properties of an object and drop time. Was your hypothesis correct? Why or why not?

Object Name	Drop Time	Properties

Collecting and Interpreting Data

How do you collect and interpret data in an organized, efficient manner?

You collect and interpret data whenever you gather observations and measurements into graphs, tables, charts, or diagrams, then use the information to solve problems or answer questions.

A well thought-out plan and an organized way of recording will help you collect your data.

Choosing the best method for showing your data will help you interpret it correctly.

Time Spent Indoors/Outdoors

	Hours Indoors	Hours Outdoors
Monday		
Tuesday		
Wednesday		
Thursday		
Friday		
Saturday		
Sunday		
Total		

Practice Collecting and Interpreting Data

Materials

- journal
- pencil
- colored pencils

Follow This Procedure

① Have you ever compared how much of your time you spend indoors and how much time you spend outdoors? In order to find out, you'll have to collect and interpret data. In your journal prepare a chart like the one shown on page 24.

② For the next seven days collect data on all of your indoor and outdoor time. Carefully check every change in your location. Record how much time you spend outdoors and how much you spend indoors.

③ Take the data from your chart and reorganize it into a bar graph. Use different colors for indoor or outdoor time. Show how many hours you spent indoors and outdoors each day.

④ Interpret the data in your chart or graph to answer the following questions: Do you spend the most time indoors or outdoors? Do you and your classmates spend the same amount of time indoors during weekdays and weekends?

Thinking About Your Thinking

Could you make an accurate interpretation of your data if you had only collected data for one day? Would your data and interpretations vary if you collected it in the summer or the winter? on a holiday? How can you adjust your data to account for these changes?

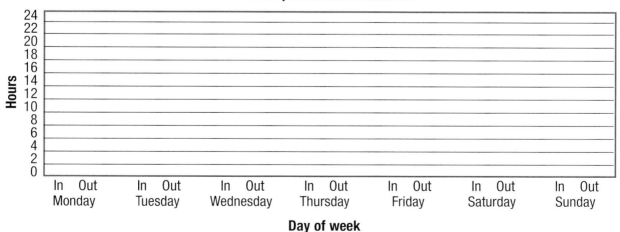

Time Spent Indoors/Outdoors

Identifying and Controlling Variables

How do you identify and control variables accurately?

A variable is anything that can change in an experiment. You identify and control variables when you change one factor that may affect the outcome of an event while all other factors are kept constant.

Using precise methods will help you identify the variables correctly and control them effectively. For example, do you know how long it takes salt to dissolve in water? By changing one variable and controlling all the others, you can find out!

Practice Identifying and Controlling Variables

Materials

- salt
- teaspoon
- 250 mL of clear water
- clear container
- stirring stick
- timer or watch with second hand

Follow This Procedure

1. Make a chart like the one below.

Amount of Salt	Length of Time for Salt to Dissolve
1 teaspoon	
2 teaspoons	
3 teaspoons	
4 teaspoons	
5 teaspoons	

2. Add 1 teaspoon (5 mL) of salt to the 250-mL container of water. Stir until the salt is completely dissolved.

3. In the chart record the length of time required for the salt to dissolve.

4. Repeat this procedure using 2 teaspoons, 3 teaspoons, 4 teaspoons, and 5 teaspoons of salt. Important: Always start with plain water before adding any salt.

Thinking About Your Thinking

What variable did you change? What is being tested? (Hint: What did you time?) Which variables were kept constant? What did you find out about how the amount of salt affects the length of time it takes the salt to dissolve?

Experimenting

How can you improve your experimenting skills?

Scientific experimenting involves the design of an investigation to test a hypothesis in order to solve a problem. When you consider a problem, state it first in general terms. After the experiment is completed, a conclusion is drawn based on the results of the experiment.

When you design your investigation, give careful consideration to the one variable you wish to change and to how you can accomplish that. Be certain that you keep all the other variables constant.

In any experiment, record your data so that it correctly reflects what happened in your investigation. Finally, only state conclusions that can be reached from analysis of your data.

Practice Experimenting

Materials

- 4 rubber bands of equal lengths but of varying widths
- pencil with an eraser
- masking tape
- jumbo paper clip
- container of objects equal to a total of 500 grams
- metric ruler

Follow This Procedure

1. State the problem. Which rubber band will stretch the most when a weight is added? Design and conduct an investigation to help you find out.

2. Write a hypothesis to state which rubber band you think will stretch the most.

3. Design your experiment. Tape the pencil to a table with the eraser extending over the edge of the table. Use the rubber band, jumbo clip, and weight to test your hypothesis. Keep all the variables but one the same to be sure the experiment is a fair one.

4. Construct a chart like the one below. Record your data in millimeters.

Rubber band width	Length before weight	Length after weight	Difference

5. Do the experiment.

6. Graph the results listed in your chart. Use the graph below as a model.

7. State your conclusion.

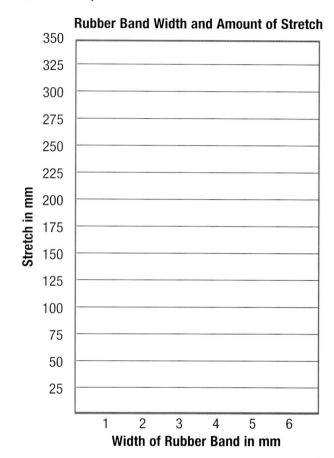

Rubber Band Width and Amount of Stretch

Stretch in mm
350 325 300 275 250 225 200 175 150 125 100 75 50 25

Width of Rubber Band in mm
1 2 3 4 5 6

Thinking About Your Thinking

What did you learn from this investigation? How can having a too-specific hypothesis in the experimental process cause a problem? Can too broad a focus in later steps create a problem as well? Explain.

Tools

Tools can make objects appear larger. They can help you measure volume, temperature, length, distance, and mass. Tools can help you figure out amounts and analyze your data. Tools can also provide you with the latest scientific information.

▲ *Computers are used by scientists in many ways, such as collecting, recording, and analyzing data.*

▲ *Safety goggles are worn by scientists whenever they are working with materials that might damage the eyes.*

▲ *Calculators make analyzing data easier and faster.*

▲ *Hot plates are often used by scientists as a heat source in experiments.*

◀ *Microscopes make objects look larger, so you can see more detail.*

Metric rulers and meter sticks are used by scientists to measure length and distance. ▶

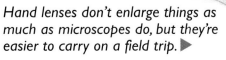

Hand lenses don't enlarge things as much as microscopes do, but they're easier to carry on a field trip. ▶

Thermometers are tools that measure temperature. ▶

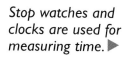

Stop watches and clocks are used for measuring time. ▶

▲ Tape recorders are used by scientists to record and learn about sounds made by organisms or objects.

▲ Compasses are used to indicate direction. The directions on a compass include north, south, east, and west.

▲ Balances are used to measure mass.

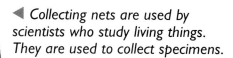

◀ Collecting nets are used by scientists who study living things. They are used to collect specimens.

▲ Cameras can be used to take pictures of what something looks like. Pictures help you record and compare objects.

▶ Magnets can be used to test if an object is made of certain metals such as iron.

Life Cycles

A life cycle describes how an organism grows, matures, and reproduces. The life cycle of each species is somewhat different. These two pages show the life cycle of four typical organisms: a single-celled organism, a flowering plant, an insect, and an amphibian.

Life Cycle of a Single-Celled Organism

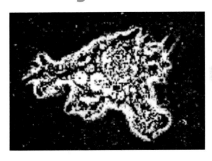

"Parent"
Organisms like this ameba reproduce by simple cell division.

Division
This one ameba cell is dividing into two cells. The parts of the cell have already been copied.

"Offspring"
The two halves have separated into two cells. The cells will grow. In time each can become a "parent" and divide to form two more amebas.

Life Cycle of a Flowering Plant

Germination
When the tiny plant inside a seed begins to grow, the seed germinates. A root grows out of the seed and down into the soil. A stem begins to grow upward through the soil.

Seeds
Seeds grow in the center of the pollinated flower. Eventually the seeds are scattered or fall to the ground.

Seedlings
When the stem of a young plant grows up out of the ground into the light, the plant is called a seedling.

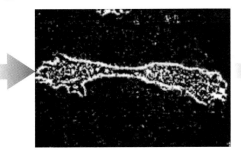
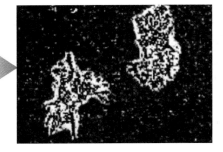

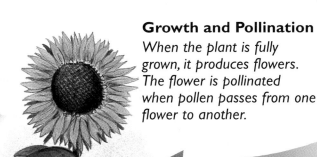

Growth and Pollination
When the plant is fully grown, it produces flowers. The flower is pollinated when pollen passes from one flower to another.

Life Cycle of a Butterfly

Eggs
A female butterfly lays her eggs, usually on leaves.

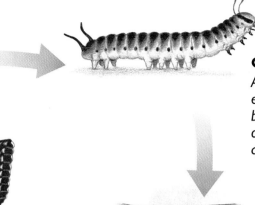

Caterpillar
After a caterpillar emerges from its egg, it begins eating leaves and other plants. It grows quickly.

Change
A caterpillar spins a silk thread around its body, and a hard cover forms. Inside, the caterpillar's body slowly changes to a butterfly.

Butterfly
In time the covering splits open and an adult butterfly comes out. Soon the female butterfly is ready to lay eggs.

Life Cycle of a Frog

Eggs
A female frog lays many eggs into a stream or lake.

Young Tadpole
The egg hatches. When the tadpole comes out, it has gills.

Older Tadpole
Slowly a tadpole changes into a frog. Its legs grow and its tail becomes smaller. Its lungs develop.

Adult Frog
When the frog is fully grown, it breathes with its lungs. It also gets oxygen through its skin.

Simple Systems

In a simple system, a few parts work together to function as a whole. A bicycle is one kind of simple system. All the parts work together to let you move, change directions, and stop when you wish.

Bicycle System

Structural System
The frame and handlebars make up the structural system of a bicycle. All other systems attach to this system.

Seat System
The seat is a system made of the seat, the seat springs, and a seat height adjustment mechanism.

Gear System
The gear system is made up of many parts. It is used to control how much force is needed to turn the pedals.

Gear shifters
Handlebars
Seat height adjustment mechanism
Metal seat with pad
Brake levers
Brake cable
Gear cable
Gears on rear wheel
Rear reflector
Frame
Front reflector
Brake caliper
Brake pad
Pedals
Spoke
Crank
Air valve
Chain
Axle
Axle
Front wheel reflector
Rear wheel reflector
Gears attached to pedals
Tire
Wheel

Wheel System
The tire, the air valve, the wheel, the spokes, and the axles are all parts of the wheel system.

Brake System
The brake levers, brake cables, brake calipers, and brake pads work together to help a rider stop the bicycle.

Visibility System
The front reflector, rear reflector, and wheel reflectors are part of the visibility system. The system makes the bicycle more visible in the dark.

Weather Systems

You learned how the parts of a bicycle work together to make up a simple system. Now you will find out how different parts of the earth work with the sun to make up a system. The sun's energy enables water from the hydrosphere to evaporate and condense in the water cycle. Water moves between the oceans and other bodies of water, the air in the atmosphere, and the land. Winds moving over the earth can be dry or humid. They can be warm or cold. The humidity and temperature of the moving air affects the water and the land beneath it. The earth's movement around the sun and its position in the sky affect the way the winds blow above the land and the way the waters move through the oceans. These and many other interactions among the many parts of the system determine the weather tomorrow where you live and all over the earth.

An example of how this complex system affects the earth's weather is the way one kind of major storm, a hurricane, forms. All the forces work together to form the most destructive kind of storm in the world, like the one below.

Weather

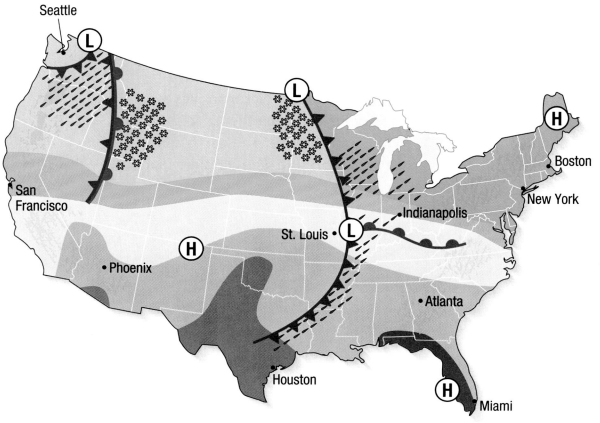

Map Key

Conditions		Fronts			Pressure systems		High temp
Rain	Snow	Warm	Cold	Stationary	High	Low	°F

Temperature zones

Below 10	10s	20s	30s	40s	50s	60s	70s	80s	90s	100s

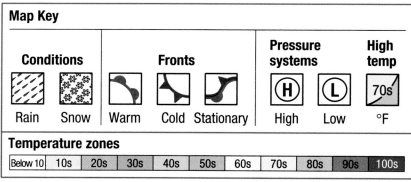

Hawaii

A weather map can tell you about weather conditions in many places. Colored bands indicate temperature zones. Other symbols tell the location of fronts and precipitation such as rain and snow. High pressure and low pressure systems are indicated by letters.

Alaska
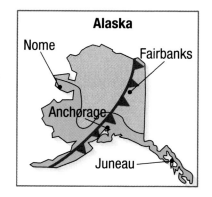

Weather balloon

Weather balloons are used by scientists to send instruments high into the atmosphere to collect information about weather. ▶

▲ Rain guage

Rain guages measure how much rain or other precipitation has fallen.

▲ Barometer

Barometers measure air pressure and can help predict changes in weather.

◀ Weather vane

Weather vanes show the direction the wind is blowing. An arrow points in the direction from which the wind is coming.

◀ Wind sock

Wind socks show the direction that the wind is blowing. They point in the direction that the wind is blowing.

Anemometer

Anemometers measure wind speed. ▼

Rock Cycle

All rocks, both above and below the surface of the earth, are slowly changing. Several factors cause these changes. These factors include heat, pressure, chemical reactions, and the forces that wear away, move, and deposit materials. The rock cycle in the diagram below shows the ways that rocks change.

Notice that the diagram shows the three types of rocks: igneous rocks, sedimentary rocks, and metamorphic rocks. Igneous rocks are rocks formed from melted mantle, called magma, that comes from deep within the earth. Sedimentary rocks are formed when layers of sediments, such as sand, are pressed or cemented together. Metamorphic rocks are igneous or sedimentary rocks that have been changed by heat or pressure. Along with the three types of rock, the diagram also shows magma and sediments. These change too.

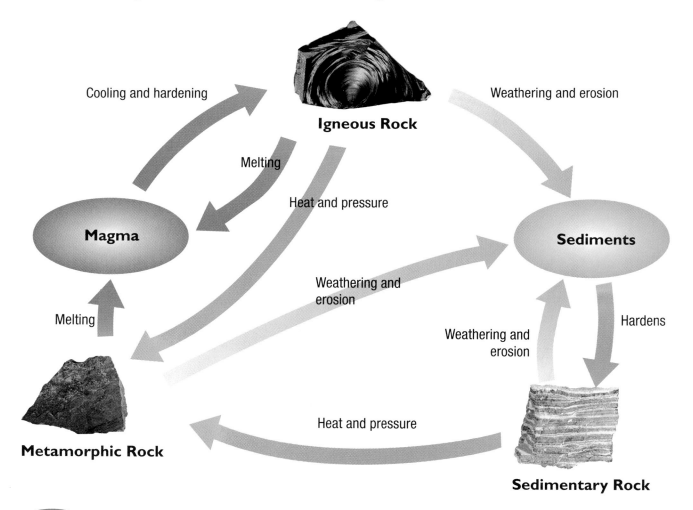

Cooling and hardening

Igneous Rock

Weathering and erosion

Melting

Heat and pressure

Magma

Sediments

Melting

Weathering and erosion

Hardens

Weathering and erosion

Metamorphic Rock

Heat and pressure

Sedimentary Rock

Fossil Fuels

Fossil fuels form when the remains of living organisms are buried deep under layers of sediment. Bacteria break down the organisms and produce energy-rich compounds of carbon and hydrogen. After millions of years under great pressure, coal or oil can form.

Forest plants die and form peat

Under pressure, peat becomes lignite

More pressure and more time results in soft coal

After enormous pressure and still more time, hard coal that is almost pure carbon forms

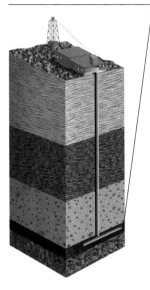

Marine organisms die and decay

Heat and pressure change them into oil and natural gas

Oil and gas move upward toward the surface

Pools of oil and gas are trapped beneath non-porous rock

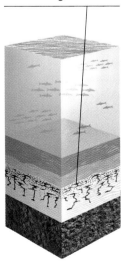

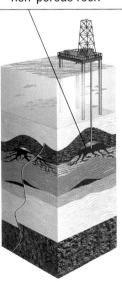

Mineral Identification and Classification

To identify and classify minerals, scientists observe several physical properties, including color, streak, hardness, and luster. Each property is explained in the table below. Often these properties alone are enough to identify a mineral.

Mineral Key					
Name	Graphite	Halite	Pyrite	Hematite	Quartz
Color simply means what color the mineral is. When used with other properties, color is helpful in identifying a mineral.	dark gray to black	clear; white, pink or blue tint	brassy yellow	reddish gray to black	clear, milky white, yellow, pink, or brown
Streak refers to the color of powder a mineral leaves behind when it is rubbed against a hard, rough, white surface.	black	white	greenish black	reddish brown	white
Luster refers to how a mineral reflects light. Lusters include metallic, glassy, waxy, pearly, and dull.	dull metallic	glassy	metallic	metallic	glassy
Hardness describes how easily a mineral can scratch another mineral. Hardness is measured by the Mohs hardness scale shown on the next page. A mineral with a higher number can scratch a mineral with a lower number.	1.5	2.5	6.5	6.5	7

Sometimes a mineral cannot be identified using just those properties. Fortunately there are a number of other physical properties that can be useful. These include texture, heft, magnetism, fracture, and cleavage. *Texture* is a property that describes the way a mineral feels. For example, a mineral may feel powdery, rough (like sand paper), or greasy. Graphite feels greasy. *Heft* refers to how heavy a mineral feels compared to other minerals of the same size. *Magnetism* is a simple property to test. If a mineral is attracted to a strong magnet, it is magnetic. If not, it is nonmagnetic. *Fracture* and *cleavage* are properties that describe how a mineral breaks and the shapes it forms when it breaks. The Mohs scale of hardness helps identify minerals by their hardness.

Mohs Hardness Scale

Talc 1

Gypsum 2

Calcite 3

Fluorite 4

Apatite 5

Orthoclase 6

Quartz 7

Topaz 8

Corundum 9

Diamond 10

The Geologic Time Scale

Most scientists think that the earth is about 4.6 billion years old. Scientists call the time the earth has existed geologic time. Geologic time is divided into large units of time called eras. The eras are shown in the chart below.

Geologic Time Scale				
Name	Began (millions of years ago)	Ended (millions of years ago)	Duration (millions of years)	Additional Information
Precambrian	4,600	600	4,000	The oldest time shown is the Precambrian. The oldest fossils are from the Precambrian.
Paleozoic	600	225	375	The Paleozoic Era followed the Precambrian and lasted 375 million years.
Mesozoic	225	65	160	The Mesozoic Era is sometimes called the "Age of the Dinosaurs."
Cenozoic	65	—	65	The current geological era is the Cenozoic Era. It began 65 million years ago. You live in the Cenozoic Era.

Fossil Hunters

The scientific name for a fossil-hunting scientist is paleontologist. Paleontologists search for, identify, and study fossils to learn about life in prehistoric times. The pictures on this page show two paleontologists who make a living by combining science, art, travel, and adventure.

In South America Sereno's team found a small skeleton from an undiscovered dinosaur they named Eoraptor ("dawn raptor"). About one meter long, this predator used its razor-sharp teeth and long claws to capture prey. In this picture Sereno is working on the fossil jaw of an Eoraptor.▼

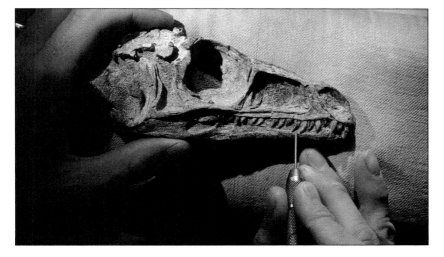

▲ *Paul Sereno, shown in the picture, has led expeditions to China, the Sahara Desert in Africa, and the Andes Mountains in South America.*

◄ *John Horner is a paleontologist who has changed many people's opinions of how dinosaurs lived. Before Horner's discoveries, many scientists thought that dinosaurs did not live in large groups. When Horner discovered Maiasaura ("good mother lizard"), he found many Maiasaura nests in one place. This indicated that at least some dinosaurs nested and lived together. Horner also has found evidence that Tyrannosaurus ("terrible lizard") was closer to a scavenger than a mighty predator. Behind Horner you can see where a Tyrannosaurus was discovered.*

Body Systems

The different organs in your body make up organ systems. The parts of a simple system work together to perform a function. In a similar way, the organs in a system in your body work together to perform a function. All the systems work together to make your body work.

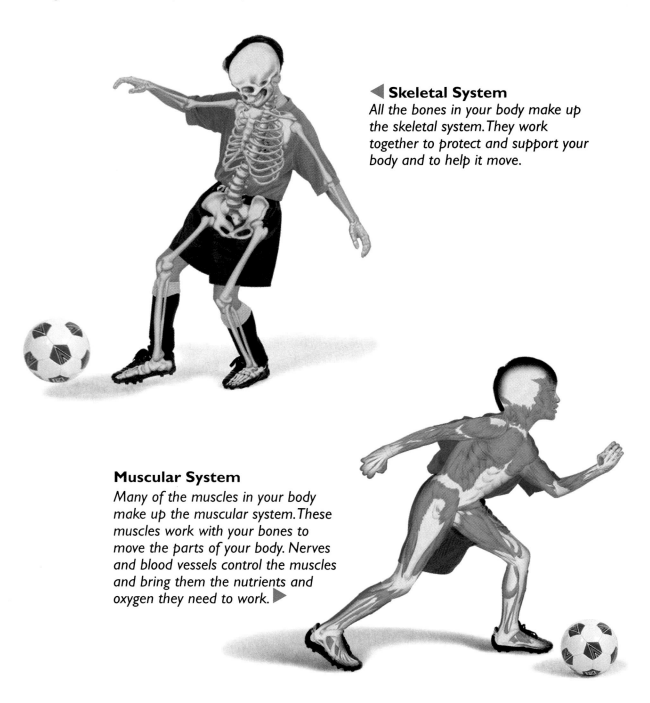

◄ Skeletal System
All the bones in your body make up the skeletal system. They work together to protect and support your body and to help it move.

Muscular System
Many of the muscles in your body make up the muscular system. These muscles work with your bones to move the parts of your body. Nerves and blood vessels control the muscles and bring them the nutrients and oxygen they need to work. ▶

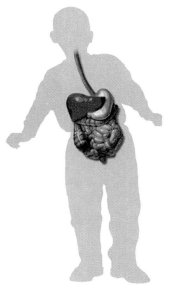

▲ Digestive System
Organs in your digestive system break down food into nutrients that your cells can use. Then blood vessels carry the nutrients to all the cells of your body.

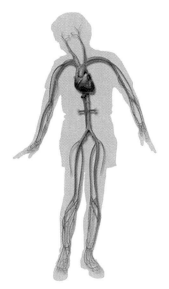

▲ Circulatory System
Your heart, blood, and blood vessels make up your circulatory system. This system carries nutrients from your digestive system, oxygen brought in by your respiratory system, and wastes from both systems to and from your body cells.

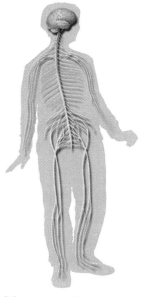

▲ Nervous System
Your nervous system includes your brain, spinal cord, and nerves. It gathers information from your environment, passes information to different parts of your body, and helps you interpret and use the information. Your brain sends signals to your muscles and organs so they function properly.

Respiratory System
Your respiratory system helps bring oxygen to the cells of your body and removes carbon dioxide and other wastes from cells. Air you breathe enters your lungs and passes into blood vessels that take it to all your cells. ▼

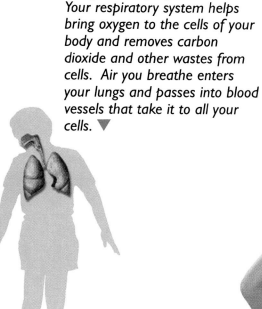

◀ Excretory System
Your excretory system removes certain kinds of wastes from your body. This system includes your kidneys and urinary bladder. The kidneys remove waste from your blood and pass it to the bladder. Then the wastes leave the body.

8000 B.C.   **6000 B.C.**   **4000 B.C**   **2000 B.C.**

Life Science

Physical Science

● **3000 B.C.**
The Egyptians develop geometry. They use it to re-measure their farmlands after floods of the Nile River.

Earth Science

● **8000 B.C.** Farming communities start as people use the plow for farming.

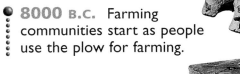

Human Body

4th century B.C.
Aristotle classifies
plants and animals.

3rd century B.C.
Aristarchus proposes that the
earth revolves around the sun.

4th century B.C.
Aristotle describes the
motions of falling
bodies. He believes that
heavier things fall faster
than lighter things.

260 B.C. Archimedes
discovers the principles of
buoyancy and the lever.

4th century B.C. Aristotle
describes the motions
of the planets.

200 B.C. Eratosthenes
calculates the size of the earth.
His result is very close to the
earth's actual size.

87 B.C.
Chinese report observing
an object in the sky that
later became known as
Halley's comet.

5th and 4th centuries B.C.
Hippocrates and other Greek
doctors record the symptoms of
many diseases. They also urge
people to eat a well-balanced diet.

Life Science

Physical Science

83 A.D.
Chinese travelers use the compass for navigation.

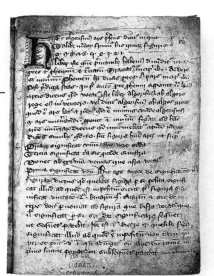

About 750–1250
Islamic scholars get scientific books from Europe. They translate them into Arabic and add more information.

Earth Science

140 Claudius Ptolemy draws a complete picture of an earth-centered universe.

132 The Chinese make the first seismograph, a device that measures the strength of earthquakes.

Human Body

2nd century
Galen writes about anatomy and the causes of diseases.

1100s
Animal guide books begin to appear. They describe what animals look like and give facts about them.

1250
Albert the Great describes plants and animals in his book *On Vegetables and On Animals*.

1555
Pierre Belon finds similarities between the skeletons of humans and birds.

9th century
The Chinese invent block printing. By the 11th century, they had movable type.

1019
Abu Arrayhan Muhammad ibn Ahmad al'Biruni observed both a solar and lunar eclipse within a few months of each other.

1543
Nikolaus Copernicus publishes his book *On The Revolutions of the Celestial Orbs*. It says that the sun remains still and the earth moves in a circle around it.

1265
Nasir al-Din al-Tusi gets his own observatory. His ideas about how the planets move will influence Nikolaus Copernicus.

About 1000
Ibn Sina writes an encyclopedia of medical knowledge. For many years, doctors will use this as their main source of medical knowledge. Arab scientist Ibn Al-Haytham gives the first detailed explanation of how we see and how light forms images in our eyes.

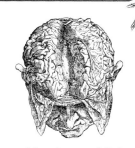

1543
Andreas Vesalius publishes *On the Makeup of the Human Body*. In this book he gives very detailed pictures of human anatomy.

1600	1620	1640	1660	1680

Life Science

1663 Robert Hooke first sees the cells of living organisms through a microscope. Antoni van Leeuwenhoek discovers bacteria with the microscope in 1674.

1679
Maria Sibylla Merian paints the first detailed pictures of a caterpillar turning into a butterfly. She also develops new techniques for printing pictures.

Physical Science

1600
William Gilbert describes the behavior of magnets. He also shows that the attraction of a compass needle toward North is due to the earth's magnetic pole.

1632 Galileo Galilei shows that all objects fall at the same speed. Galileo also shows that all matter has inertia.

1687
Isaac Newton introduces his three laws of motion.

Earth Science

1609–1619
Johannes Kepler introduces the three laws of planetary motion.

1610 Galileo uses a telescope to see the rings around the planet Saturn and the moons of Jupiter.

1669
Nicolaus Steno sets forth the basic principles of how to date rock layers.

1650
Maria Cunitz publishes a new set of tables to help astronomers find the positions of the planets and stars.

1693–1698
Maria Eimmart draws 250 pictures depicting the phases of the moon. She also paints flowers and insects.

1687
Isaac Newton introduces the concept of gravity.

Human Body

1628 William Harvey shows how the heart circulates blood through the blood vessels.

1700   **1720**   **1740**   **1760**   **1780**   **1800**

1735 Carolus Linnaeus devises the modern system of naming living things.

1759 Emile du Châtelet translates Isaac Newton's work into French. Her work still remains the only French translation.

1789 Antoine-Laurent Lavoisier claims that certain substances, such as oxygen, hydrogen, and nitrogen, cannot be broken down into anything simpler. He calls these substances "elements."

1704 Isaac Newton publishes his views on optics. He shows that white light contains many colors.

1729 Stephen Gray shows that electricity flows in a straight path from one place to another.

1781 Caroline and William Herschel (sister and brother) discover the planet Uranus.

1784 French chemist Antoine-Laurent Lavoisier does the first extensive study of respiration.

1798 Edward Jenner reports the first successful vaccination for smallpox.

1721 Onesimus introduces to America the African method for inoculation against smallpox.

1805   1810   1815   1820   1825   1830   1835

Life Science

1808 French naturalist Georges Cuvier describes some fossilized bones as belonging to a giant, extinct marine lizard.

1838–1839 Matthias Schleiden and Theodor Schwann describe the cell as the basic unit of a living organism.

Physical Science

1800 Alessandro Volta makes the first dry cell (battery).

1820 H.C. Oersted discovers that a wire with electric current running through it will deflect a compass needle. This showed that electricity and magnetism were related.

1808 John Dalton proposes that all matter is made of atoms.

Earth Science

1830 Charles Lyell writes *Principles of Geology*. This is the first modern geology textbook.

1803 Luke Howard assigns to clouds the basic names that we still use today—cumulus, stratus, and cirrus.

Human Body

1842 Richard Owen gives the name "dinosaurs" to the extinct giant lizards.

1859 Charles Darwin proposes the theory of evolution by natural selection.

1863 Gregor Mendel shows that certain traits in peas are passed to succeeding generations in a regular fashion. He outlines the methods of heredity.

1847 Hermann Helmholtz states the law of conservation of energy. This law holds that energy cannot be created or destroyed. Energy only can be changed from one form to another.

1842 Christian Doppler explains why a car, train, plane, or any quickly moving object sounds higher pitched as it approaches and lower pitched as it moves away.

1866 Ernst Haeckel proposes the term "ecology" for the study of the environment.

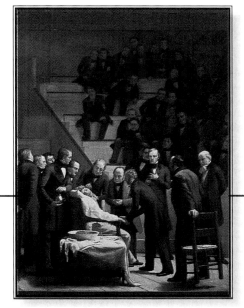

Early 1860s Louis Pasteur realizes that tiny organisms cause wine and milk to turn sour. He shows that heating the liquids kills these germs. This process is called pasteurization.

1840s Doctors use anesthetic drugs to put their patients to sleep.

1850s and 1860s Ignaz P. Semmelweis and Sir Joseph Lister pioneer the use of antiseptics in medicine.

| 1875 | 1885 | 1895 | 1905 |

Life Science

● **1900–1910** George Washington Carver, the son of slave parents, develops many new uses for old crops. He finds a way to make soybeans into rubber, cotton into road-paving material, and peanuts into paper.

Physical Science

● **1897** J. J. Thomson discovers the electron.

● **1905** Albert Einstein introduces the theory of relativity.

1895 Wilhelm Roentgen discovers X rays. ●

1896 Henri Becquerel discovers radioactivity. ●

Earth Science

1907 ● Bertram Boltwood introduces the idea of "radioactive" dating. This allows geologists to accurately measure the age of a fossil.

1912 ● Alfred Wegener proposes the theory of continental drift. This theory says that all land on the earth was once a single mass. It eventually broke apart and the continents slowly drifted away from each other.

Human Body

● **1885** Louis Pasteur gives the first vaccination for rabies. Pasteur thought that tiny organisms caused most diseases.

1920s Ernest Everett Just performs important research into how cells metabolize food.

1947 Archaeologist Mary Leakey unearths the skull of a *Proconsul africanus,* an example of a fossilized ape.

1913 Danish physicist Niels Bohr presents the modern theory of the atom.

1911 Ernst Rutherford discovers that atoms have a nucleus, or center.

1911 Marie Curie wins the Nobel Prize for chemistry. This makes her the first person ever to win two Nobel Prizes, the highest award a scientist can receive.

1938 Otto Hahn and Fritz Straussman split the uranium atom. This marks the beginning of the nuclear age.

1942 Enrico Fermi and Leo Szilard produce the first nuclear chain reaction.

1945 The first atomic bomb is exploded in the desert at Alamogordo, New Mexico.

1938 Lise Meitner and Otto Frisch explain how an atom can split in two.

1946 Vincent Schaefer and Irving Langmuir use dry ice to produce the first artificial rain.

1933 Meteorologist Tor Bergeron explains how raindrops form in clouds.

1917 Florence Sabin becomes the first woman professor at an American medical college.

1928 Alexander Fleming notices that the molds in his petri dish produced a substance, later called an antibiotic, that killed bacteria. He calls this substance penicillin.

1935 Chemist Percy Julian develops physostigmine, a drug used to fight the eye disease glaucoma.

1922 Doctors inject the first diabetes patient with insulin.

| 1950 | 1955 | 1960 | 1965 | 1970 |

Life Science

1951 Barbara McClintock discovers that genes can move to different places on a chromosome.

1953 The collective work of James D. Watson, Francis Crick, Maurice Wilkins, and Rosalind Franklin leads to the discovery of the structure of the DNA molecule.

1972 Researchers find human DNA to be 99% similar to that of chimpanzees.

Physical Science

1969 UCLA is host to the first computer node of ARPANET, the forerunner of the internet.

1974 Opening of TRIUMF, the world's largest particle accelerator, at the University of British Columbia.

Earth Science

1957 The first human-made object goes into orbit when the Soviet Union launches *Sputnik I.*

1969 Neil Armstrong is the first person to walk on the moon.

1972 Cygnus X-1 is first identified as a blackhole.

1967 Geophysicists introduce the theory of plate tectonics.

1962 John Glenn is the first American to orbit the earth.

Human Body

1954–1962 In 1954, Jonas Salk introduced the first vaccine for polio. In 1962, most doctors and hospitals substituted Albert Sabin's orally administered vaccine.

1967 Dr. Christiaan Barnard performs the first successful human heart transplant operation.

1964 The surgeon general's report on the hazards of smoking is released.

NO SMOKING
American Cancer Society

1975	1980	1985	1990	1995	2000

1988
Congress approves funding for the Human Genome Project. This project will map and sequence the human genetic code.

1997
Scientists in Edinburgh, Scotland, successfully clone a sheep, Dolly.

1975 People are able to buy the first personal computer, called the Altair.

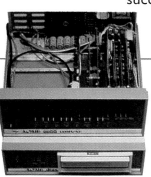

1996 Scientists make "element 112" in the laboratory. This is the heaviest element yet created.

1979 A near meltdown occurs at the Three Mile Island nuclear power plant in Pennsylvania. This alerts the nation to the dangers of nuclear power.

1976 National Academy of Sciences reports on the dangers of chlorofluorocarbons (CFCs) for the earth's ozone layer.

1995 The first "extra-solar" planet is discovered.

Early 1990s The National Severe Storms Laboratory develops NEXRAD, the national network of Doppler weather radar stations for early severe storm warnings.

1981 The first commercial Magnetic Resonance Imaging scanners are available. Doctors use MRI scanners to look at the non-bony parts of the body.

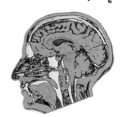

1982 Dr. Stanley Prusiner identifies a new kind of disease-causing agent—prions. Prions are responsible for many brain disorders.

1998 John Glenn, age 77, orbits the earth aboard the space shuttle *Discovery*. Glenn is the oldest person to fly in space.

Glossary

Full Pronunciation Key

The pronunciation of each word is shown just after the word, in this way: **ab·bre·vi·ate** (ə brē′ vē āt).

The letters and signs used are pronounced as in the words below.

The mark ′ is placed after a syllable with primary or heavy accent, as in the example above.

The mark ′ after a syllable shows a secondary or lighter accent, as in **ab·bre·vi·a·tion** (ə bre′ vē a′ shən).

a	hat, cap	g	go, bag	ō	open, go	ᴛʜ	then, smooth	zh	measure, seizure
ā	age, face	h	he, how	ò	all, caught	u	cup, butter		
â	care, fair	i	it, pin	ô	order	ù	full, put	ə	represents:
ä	father, far	ī	ice, five	oi	oil, voice	ü	rule, move		a in about
b	bad, rob	j	jam, enjoy	ou	house, out	v	very, save		e in taken
ch	child, much	k	kind, seek	p	paper, cup	w	will, woman		i in pencil
d	did, red	l	land, coal	r	run, try				o in lemon
e	let, best	m	me, am	s	say, yes	y	young, yet		u in circus
ē	equal, be	n	no, in	sh	she, rush	z	zero, breeze		
ėr	term, learn	ng	long, bring	t	tell, it				
f	fat, if	o	hot, rock	th	thin, both				

A

acceleration (ak sel′ə rā′shən), rate of change in speed or direction of movement.

acid (as′id) **rain,** rain containing acids formed when air pollutants react with water vapor.

air pollution (pə lü′shən), the addition of any unwanted substance into the air.

air resistance (ri zis′təns), friction caused by gas molecules in the air hitting an object and slowing it down.

air sac (sak), one of the tiny pouches in the lungs in which the exchange of oxygen and carbon dioxide takes place.

allergy (al′ər jē), a harmful reaction to certain substances.

antibiotic (an′ti bī ot′ik), a medicine that kills bacteria.

antibody (an′ti bod′ē), a substance made by certain white blood cells that attaches to a pathogen and makes it harmless.

asteroid (as′tə roid′), a rocky object that revolves around the sun.

asthma (az′mə), an allergy that affects the respiratory system and may result in breathing difficulty and wheezing.

atherosclerosis (ath′ər ō sklə rō′sis), a disease in which fatty substances build up on the inside walls of arteries.

atmosphere (at′mə sfir), the layer of gases that surrounds the earth and contains the clouds.

atom (at′əm), the smallest particle of an element that has the properties of the element.

B

bacteria (bak tir′ē ə), tiny, one-celled organisms, some of which can cause diseases. (singular: bacterium)

bar graph (graf), a graph that uses vertical or horizontal bars to show data.

behavioral adaptation (bi hā′vyər əl ad′ap tā′shən), an inherited behavior that helps an organism survive.

bronchial tube (brong′kē əl tüb), one of the pair of tubes that branch off from the trachea and go into the lungs.

C

cancer (kan′sər), the uncontrolled growth of abnormal cells.

capillary (kap′ə ler′ē), a tiny blood vessel with thin walls through which oxygen, nutrients, and wastes pass.

carbon monoxide (kär′bən mo nok′sīd), a colorless, odorless, poisonous gas made up of carbon and oxygen.

cardiovascular (kär′dē ō vas′kyə lər) **disease**, a disease of the heart or blood vessels.

cast (kast), a fossil formed by sediments filling up a mold.

cause (koz), a person, thing, or event that makes something happen.

cell (sel), the basic unit of a living organism.

cell membrane (mem′brān), a thin layer that makes up the outside of the cell and controls what enters and leaves it.

cell wall, a stiff outer layer that helps keep plant cells firm.

Celsius (sel′sē əs) **(°C),** a temperature scale in which water boils at 100°C and freezes at 0°C.

chemical (kem′ə kəl) **change,** a change that produces new substances with new properties.

chemical (kem′ə kəl) **energy,** energy stored in the way atoms are connected to each other.

chemical property (kem′ə kəl prop′ər tē), describes the way a substance reacts with other substances.

chemical reaction (kem′ə kəl rē ak′shən), a process that produces one or more substances that are different from the original substances.

chloroplast (klôr′ə plast), the green cell part in plant cells that traps and uses light energy.

chromosomes (krō′mə sōmz), structures in the nucleus of a cell that control the cell's activities.

classify (klas′ə fī), to arrange in groups using a system.

climate (klī′mit), the average weather conditions in an area over many years.

comet (kom′it), a ball of ice, dust, and gases that travels through space and orbits the sun.

communicable disease (kə myü′nə kə bəl də zēz′), an illness that can spread and is caused by a pathogen.

community (kə myü′nə tē), all the populations living together in one area.

compare (kəm pâr′), to point out how things are alike and how they are different.

compound (kom′pound), a substance made up of atoms of more than one element.

conclusion (kən klü′zhən), a decision or opinion based on the evidence and reasoning.

condensation (kon′den sā′shən), the process of changing from a gas to a liquid.

condense (kən dens′), to change from a gas to a liquid.

constellation (kon′stə lā′shən), stars that appear to be in a group when viewed from Earth.

consumer (kən sü′mər), an organism that consumes other organisms for food.

contrast (kən trast′), to show differences.

core, the center part of the earth, beneath the mantle.

crust, the top layer of the earth, above the mantle.

cytoplasm (sī′tə plaz′əm), jellylike material that fills most of a cell.

D

decomposer (dē′kəm pō′zər), an organism that helps to break down and decay dead organisms and the wastes of living organisms.

denominator (di nom′ə nā′tər), the number below the line in a fraction; the number of equal parts in the whole.

dependence (di pen′dəns), the need for a drug, which may be a mental need, a physical need, or both.

deposition (dep′ə zish′ən), the dropping of materials moved by erosion.

diaphragm (dī′ə fram), the large muscle below the lungs that helps you breathe.

digit (dij′it), a symbol used to write numbers: 0, 1, 2, 3, 4, 5, 6, 7, 8, 9.

dominant (dom′ə nənt) **gene**, a gene that can prevent the expression of another gene.

draw a conclusion (kən klü′zhən), reach a decision or opinion based on evidence or reasoning.

drug abuse (ə byüs′), the intentional use of drugs for reasons other than health.

E

ecology (ē kol′ə jē), the study of the relationships among the living and nonliving parts of an area.

ecosystem (ē′ kō sis′təm), all the living and nonliving parts in an area.

effect (ə fekt′), whatever is produced by a cause; a result.

egg cell, a cell that can join with a sperm cell to form a new individual.

electric current (i lek′trik kėr′ənt), the steady flow of electrical charges, usually in a wire.

electrical (i lek′trə kel) **energy,** energy carried by electricity.

electron (i lek′tron), particle in an atom that has a negative electrical charge.

element (el′ə mənt), a substance that cannot be broken down into other substances by heat, light, or electricity.

elliptical (i lip′tə kəl), oval-shaped, like a flattened circle.

emphysema (em′fə sē′mə), a disease of the lungs in which air sacs are damaged.

energy pyramid (en′ər jē pir′ə mid), a diagram that compares the amount of energy available at each position, or level, in the feeding order.

erosion (i rō′shən), the moving of weathered rock and soil.

evaporate (i vap′ə rāt′), to change from a liquid to a gas.

excretory system (ek′skrə tôr′ē sis′təm), the group of organs that get rid of cell wastes.

exhale (eks hāl′), to breathe out.

F

fertilization (fėr′tl ə zā′shən), the joining of a sperm cell and an egg cell.

fertilized (fėr′tl īzd) **egg,** the cell that results when an egg cell and a sperm cell unite.

food chain, the path of energy and matter in a community.

food web, a combination of all the food chains in a community.

fossil (fos′əl), any remains or trace of an organism that was once alive.

fossil fuel (fos′əl fyü′əl), a fuel that formed over many years from the remains of living organisms.

frequency (frē′kwən sē), the number of waves passing a point in one second.

friction (frik′shən), a force that resists the movement of one surface past another surface.

G

galaxy (gal′ək sē), a group of billions of stars, dust, and gases in a space held together by gravity.

gene (jēn), the section of a chromosome that controls a trait.

generator (jen′ə rā′tər), a device that uses a magnet to change mechanical energy into electrical energy.

genus (jē′nəs), a group of similar species.

geologic (jē′ə loj′ik) **time,** the time the earth has existed, expressed in eras or long periods of time, rather than in years.

GFCI outlet, a special outlet with a safety switch that instantly switches off in some dangerous situations to help prevent a shock.

global (glō′bəl) **warming,** an increase in the earth's temperature.

graphic source (graf′ik sôrs), a drawing, photograph, table, chart, or diagram that shows information visually.

gravity (grav′ə tē), a force that acts to pull pairs of objects together.

greenhouse effect, the process by which gases in the atmosphere absorb heat and keep the earth warm.

greenhouse gases, carbon dioxide, water vapor, and other gases in the atmosphere that absorb infrared radiation from the earth's surface.

groundwater, water from rain or snow that sinks into the earth and is stored there.

H

habitat (hab′ə tat), the place where a species lives.

humidity (hyü mid′ə tē), the amount of water vapor in the air.

hybrid (hī′brid), an individual that has a dominant and a recessive gene for a trait.

hydrosphere (hī′drə sfir), the water part of the earth's surface.

I

igneous (ig′nē əs) **rock,** rock formed from melted rock that comes from deep within the earth.

immunity (i myü′nə tē), the body's resistance to a disease through the presence of antibodies.

inertia (in ėr′shə), the tendency of an object to stay at rest or to remain in motion unless an outside force causes a change.

infrared radiation (in′frə red′ rā′dē ā′shən), energy with a wavelength longer than the wavelength of light.

inhale (in hāl′), to breathe in.

inherited (in her′it id), passed to offspring from parents.

invertebrate (in vėr′tə brit), an animal that has no backbone.

K

kidney (kid′nē), one of the pair of organs of the excretory system that filter cell wastes from blood.

kilometers (kə lom′ə tərz) **per hour,** the number of kilometers something can travel in one hour.

kilowatt (kil′ə wot), a unit used to measure how fast electricity is used; 1,000 watts.

kilowatt-hour (kil′ə wot our), a unit used to measure the amount of electrical energy.

kinetic (ki net′ik) **energy,** the energy of motion.

kingdom (king′dəm), the largest group into which an organism is classified.

L

lightning, a giant spark of electric charges moving between a cloud and the ground, between a cloud and another cloud, or within the cloud.

light year, the distance light travels in one year.

liter (lē′tər), a metric unit of capacity or volume equivalent to 1,000 milliliters.

lithosphere (lith′ə sfir), the shell of the earth, made up of the crust and the rigid, outer part of the mantle.

M

mammal (mam′əl), an animal that has hair or fur and feeds its young with milk produced by the mother.

mantle (man′tl), the middle layer of the earth, between the crust and the core.

mass, the amount of matter in an object.

mechanical (mə kan′ə kəl) **energy,** energy an object has due to its motion, position, or condition.

metamorphic (met′ə môr′fik) **rock,** rock formed when igneous or sedimentary rock is changed by heat or pressure.

meteor (mē′tē ər), a bright streak of light that passes through Earth's atmosphere.

meteorite (mē′tē ə rīt′), a piece of a meteoroid that lands on Earth after passing through the atmosphere.

meteoroid (mē′tē ə roid′), a small piece of rock or metal that travels in space around the sun.

milliliter (mil′ə lē′tər), a metric unit of capacity or volume equivalent to 0.001 liters.

mimicry (mim′ik rē), an adaptation in which one species resembles another.

mineral (min′ə rəl), a natural, nonliving solid with a definite chemical structure.

mixture (miks′chər), two or more substances that are mixed together but can be separated out because their atoms are not combined.

model (mod′l), a representation of how something looks or works.

mold (mōld), a fossil that is a hollow place shaped like an organism.

molecule (mol′ə kyül), two or more atoms joined together; the smallest unit of many substances.

mucus (myü′kəs), a sticky liquid produced by the linings of the nose and other body parts that open to the outside.

mutation (myü tā′shən), a permanent change in the structure of a gene or chromosome.

N

neutron (nü′tron), particle in an atom that has no charge.

niche (nich), the role of a species in an ecosystem.

noncommunicable disease, (non′kə myü′nə kə bəl də zēz′) an illness that cannot spread and is not caused by a pathogen.

nonrenewable resource (non′ri nü′ə bəl rē′sôrs), a resource that cannot be replaced after it is used.

nuclear (nü′klē ər) **energy,** energy produced when an atom splits apart or when two atoms join to form one atom.

nucleus (nü′klē əs), the cell part that controls the cell's activities; the center of an atom, where protons and neutrons are located.

numerator (nü′mə rā′tər), the number above the line in a fraction; the number of equal parts in a fractional amount.

O

ozone (ō′zōn), a molecule of oxygen that contains three atoms of oxygen.

P

paleontologist (pā/lē on tol/ə jist), a scientist that searches for, identifies, and studies fossils to learn about life in prehistoric times.

pathogen (path/ə jən), an agent that causes disease.

period (pir/ē əd), a three-digit group of numbers, separated from other groups by a comma.

periodic (pir/ē od/ik) **table,** a chart that classifies elements by their properties.

petrified fossil (pet/rə fīd fos/əl), a fossil formed when minerals slowly replace some or all of an organism, turning it to stone.

photosynthesis (fō/tō sin/thə sis), the process by which plants use sunlight to make sugar from water and carbon dioxide.

physical (fiz/ ə kəl) **change,** a change in one or more physical properties.

physical property (fiz/ə kəl prop/ər tē), a way of describing an object using traits that can be observed or measured without changing the substance into something else.

plate, a large section of the earth's surface made of the crust and the rigid, top part of the mantle.

plate tectonics (tek ton/iks), a theory stating that the earth's surface is broken into plates that move.

pollination (pol/ə nā/shən), the movement of pollen from a stamen to a pistil.

pollutant (pə lüt/nt), an unwanted substance added to the air, water, or land.

population (pop/yə lā/shən), all of the members of one species that live in the same area.

potential (pə ten/shəl) **energy,** stored energy or energy that an object has due to its position.

precipitation (pri sip/ə tā/shən), any form of water that falls to the earth from a cloud.

producer (prə dü/sər), an organism that uses sunlight to make sugar from water and carbon dioxide.

proton (prō/ton), particle in an atom that has a positive electrical charge.

R

radiant (rā/dē ənt) **energy,** energy that travels as waves and can move through empty space.

recessive (ri ses/iv) **gene,** a gene whose expression is hidden by a dominant gene.

reflection (ri flek/shən), the bouncing of light off a surface; a way to gather and focus light.

refraction (ri frak′shən), the bending of light as it passes from one material to another; a way to gather and focus light.

renewable resource (ri nü′ə bəl rē′sôrs), a resource that can be replaced within a reasonably short time.

respiratory system (res′pər ə tôr′ē sis′təm), the group of organs that take oxygen from the air and remove carbon dioxide from the body.

rock cycle, the ways that rocks change from one form to another.

runoff, water that falls onto land and drains off the surface.

S

scavenger (skav′ən jər), an animal that feeds on the bodies of dead organisms.

sedimentary (sed′ə men′tər ē) **rock,** rock formed when sediments are pressed or cemented together.

selective breeding (si lek′tiv brē′ding), breeding plants or animals with certain traits to produce offspring with those traits.

sequencing (sē′kwəns ing), putting in the correct order.

solution (sə lü′shən), a mixture in which a substance breaks up into its most basic particles, which are too small to be seen, and spreads evenly through another substance.

sound energy, energy of vibrations carried by air, water, or other matter.

species (spē′shēz), a group of organisms of only one kind that can interbreed in nature.

spectroscope (spek′trə skōp), an instrument that separates light into a pattern of lines of different colors.

speed, a measure of how far something travels in a certain period of time.

sperm (spėrm) **cell,** a cell that can join with an egg cell to form a new individual.

streamline, to design smooth, rounded surfaces on an object so it slips through the air with the least resistance.

structural adaptation (struk′chər əl ad′ap tā′shən), an adaptation of an organism's body parts or its coloring.

switch, that part of a circuit that closes the circuit and allows electricity to flow or opens the circuit and prevents the flow of electricity.

T

thermal (thėr′məl) **energy,** energy of the movement of atoms and molecules.

trachea (trā′kē ə), the tube that leads from the throat toward the lungs, also called the windpipe.

U

urinary bladder (yur′ə nâr′ē blad′ər), a muscular, baglike organ that stores urine until it leaves the body.

urine (yur′ən), a liquid formed in the kidneys consisting of nitrogen wastes, some salts, and extra water.

V

vascular (vas′kyə lər) **plant,** a plant with long tubes inside that carry food and water to all the parts of the plant.

velocity (və los′ə tē), a measure of speed in a certain direction.

vertebrate (vėr′tə brit), an animal with a backbone.

vibration (vī brā′shən), rapid back and forth motion of air or other matter.

virus (vī′rəs), a tiny particle that can reproduce only inside the cells of living things.

volt (vōlt), a unit used to measure how strongly the electrons in a wire are pushed.

W

water vapor (vā′pər), water in the form of an invisible gas.

watt (wot), a unit used to measure how fast electrical energy is used.

wavelength (wāv′lengkth′), the distance from a point on one wave to the same point on the next wave.

weathering (weŦH′ər ing), the process that breaks down and changes rocks.

weight, the force gravity exerts on an object's mass.

Index

Acknowledgments

Illustration

Borders Patti Green
Icons Precison Graphics

Unit A
9 Carla Kiwior; 11, 12, 13, 15, 17, 19j, 33, 110, 112, 114, 119, 124, 125, 126, 128, 130, 133, 134 J.B. Woolsey; 16 John Zielinski; 30, 31 Richard Stergulz; 47, 54 Precision Graphics

Unit B
11, 12, 13, 14, 15, 16, 17, 18, 19, 37, 113 Eric Ovresat; 30, 100, 101, 121, 133 John Massie; 31 Doug Knutson; 46 Mike Dammer; 49 Annie Bissett; 52d, 91, 92, 94, 98, 114, 115, 124, 125, 127 J.B. Woolsey; 65 Jerry Tiritilli; 78, 80, 82, 88, 89, 134 Dave Merrill; 117 Precision Graphics; 121 John Massie

Unit C
10, 15, 16, 17, 18, 20, 77, 85, 86, 87, 91, 92, 94, 96, 97, 99, 102, 111, 115, 117, 118, 119, 124, 129a, 129b, 130 J.B. Woolsey; 33, 34 Precision Graphics; 48, 51, 52, 58, 59, 60 John Massie; 66 Tim Huhn

Unit D
9, 10, 11, 23 Christine D. Young; 12, 13, 17, 21 Nadine Sokol; 37, 48, 55 Tim Huhn; 39 J.B. Woolsey; 51 Precision Graphics;

End Matter 39 William Graham

Photography

Unless otherwise credited, all photographs are the property of Scott Foresman, a division of Pearson Education. Page abbreviations are as follows: (T) top, (C) center, (B) bottom, (L) left, (R) right, (INS) inset.

COVER:
D. Cavagnaro/Visuals Unlimited

Front Matter
i T Bob Daemmrich Photography; iv T PhotoDisc, Inc.; iv B E. R. Degginger/Bruce Coleman Inc.; v T Zig Leszcynski/Animals Animals/Earth Scenes; vi B PhotoDisc, Inc.; vi T Jose Fuste Raga/Stock Market

Unit A
1 Mitsuaki Iwago/Minden Pictures; 2 T Vincent OBryne/Panoramic Image; 2 C Dennis Kunkel/MicroVision; 2 B-Inset Saola/Philippe Hurlin/Liaison Agency; 3 C Raphael Gaillarde/Liaison Agency; 3 T NASA; 3 B ZEFA/Stock Market; 10 T Alfred Pasieka/SPL/Photo Researchers; 10 C CNRI/SPL/Photo Researchers; 10 BL Dr. Tony Brain & David Parker/SPL/Photo Researchers; 10 BC Dr. Tony Brain & David Parker/SPL/Photo Researchers; 10 BR Dr. Tony Brain & David Parker/SPL/Photo Researchers; 11 B Kevin Schafer; 11 T Mike Abbey/Visuals Unlimited; 14 T Secchi-Lecaque/Rousel-UCLAF/CNRI/SPL//Photo Researchers; 14 CR David Phillips/Photo Researchers; 14 CL Ray Simmons/Photo Researchers; 14 BR Alfred Pasieka/SPL/Photo Researchers; 14 BL Biophoto Associates/Photo Researchers; 15 L SPL/Photo Researchers; 17 L CDC/SS/Photo Researchers; 17 R Mike Abbey/Visuals Unlimited; 18 T Gary W. Carter/Visuals Unlimited; 18 C John Burnley/NASC/Photo Researchers; 18 BL G. I. Bernard/Animals Animals/Earth Scenes; 18 BR Stuart Westmorland/Tony Stone Images; 19 B PhotoDisc, Inc.; 19 T PhotoDisc, Inc.; 20 R Gerard Lacz/Animals Animals/Earth Scenes; 20 L Richard Day/Animals Animals/Earth Scenes; 21 David Young/TOM STACK & ASSOCIATES; 24 T OSF/Animals Animals/Earth Scenes; 24 B Carl Roessler/Animals Animals/Earth Scenes; 25 B George Harrison/Bruce Coleman Inc.; 25 T Breck P. Kent/Animals Animals/Earth Scenes; 25 CR PhotoDisc, Inc.; 25 CL William J. Weber/Visuals Unlimited; 26 TL David B. Fleetham/OSF/Animals Animals/Earth Scenes; 26 TR Rod Planck/Photo Researchers; 26 B PhotoDisc, Inc.; 27 L Maslowski/Visuals Unlimited; 27 R Tony Dawson/Tony Stone Images; 29 Darrell Gulin/Dembinsky Photo Assoc. Inc.; 31 William Grenfell/Visuals Unlimited; 32 T Virginia P. Weinland/Photo Researchers; 35 Kevin Schafer; 41 TL Carolina Biological Supply/Phototake; 41 TR Carolina Biological Supply/Phototake; 41 BL Carolina Biological Supply/Phototake; 41 BR Carolina Biological Supply/Phototake; 42 L M. Abbey/Photo Researchers; 42 C M. Abbey/Photo Researchers; 42 R M. Abbey/Photo Researchers; 43 Fred Bavendam/Minden Pictures; 44 B Brian Parker/TOM STACK & ASSOCIATES; 44 T Jean Claude Revy/Phototake; 44 TC Jean Claude Revy/Phototake; 44 BC Jean Claude Revy/Phototake; 44 B-inset Jean Claude Revy/Phototake; 45 Barry L. Runk/Grant Heilman Photography; 46 Tom Evans/Photo Researchers; 51 T Michael Newman/PhotoEdit; 51 B E. R. Degginger/Bruce Coleman Inc.; 55 T Ron Kimball; 55 B W. Layer/OKAPIA/Photo Researchers; 56 C Richard Thom/Visuals Unlimited; 56 T Betsy R. Strasser/Visuals Unlimited; 56 B Herb Gehr/Life Magazine, © Time Inc.; 57 Armine M. Sefton, Outsmarted by Bugs, SCIENCE SPECTRA, Issue 10, 1997, p 34; 60 Moravian Museum, Brno, Czechoslovakia; 62 BL Dennis Kunkel/MicroVision; 62 BR Oliver Meckes/Photo Researchers; 62 T SPL/Photo Researchers; 63 B Superstock, Inc.; 63 T BBC Photo; 64 Granger Collection; 65 TL Jim Steinberg/Photo Researchers; 65 TR John A. Anderson/Animals Animals/Earth Scenes; 65 BR Robert S. Peabody Museum of Archaeology, Andover; 65 BL Robert S. Peabody Museum of Archaeology, Andover; 66 B Larry Lefever/Grant Heilman Photography; 68 Frank Siteman/PhotoEdit; 71 Brian Parker/TOM STACK & ASSOCIATES; 76 Superstock, Inc.; 77 Ted Levin/Animals Animals/Earth Scenes; 78 TL Fletcher & Baylis/Photo Researchers; 78 TR Fritz Prenzel/Animals Animals/Earth Scenes; 78 BL Michael Fogden/Animals Animals/Earth Scenes; 78 BR Suzanne L. & Joseph T. Collins/Photo Researchers; 78 C Zig Leszcynski/Animals Animals/Earth Scenes; 79 C Robert Maier/Animals Animals/Earth Scenes; 79 TR Danny Brass/Photo Researchers; 79 B Doug Locke/Dembinsky Photo Assoc. Inc.; 79 TL Runk/Schoenberger/Grant Heilman Photography; 79 TC Runk/Schoenberger/Grant Heilman Photography; 80 B Walter Chandoha; 80 T Stephen Dalton/Animals Animals/Earth Scenes; 81 C M. Fogden/Bruce Coleman Inc.; 81 B G. I. Bernard/OSF/Animals Animals/Earth Scenes; 81 TL Joe McDonald/Visuals Unlimited; 82 T Tony Stone Images; 83 Phil Degginger/Color-Pic, Inc.; 84 T Mickey Gibson/Animals Animals/Earth Scenes; 84 B Runk/Schoenberger/Grant Heilman Photography; 85 T Chris McLaughlin/Animals Animals/Earth Scenes; 85 BL Zig Leszcynski/Animals Animals/Earth Scenes; 85 BR Runk/Schoenberger/Grant Heilman Photography; 86 John Serrao/Photo Researchers; 87 T Hal H. Harrison/Photo Researchers; 87 C Gijsbert van Frankenhuyzen/Dembinsky Photo Assoc. Inc.; 87 B Thomas Kitchin/TOM STACK & ASSOCIATES; 90 Ron Kimball; 91 B Gary Schultz/Wildlife Collection; 91 T Jim Brandenburg/Minden Pictures; 92 T Jen & Des Bartlett/Bruce Coleman Inc.; 92 B Joe McDonald/Animals Animals/Earth Scenes; 93 T Doug Sokell/TOM STACK & ASSOCIATES; 93 C Tom Bean/Tony Stone Images; 94 CR Jim Steinberg/Photo Researchers; 94 BR Thomas Kitchin/TOM STACK & ASSOCIATES; 94 BL E. R. Degginger/Photo Researchers; 94 T Laurence Pringle/NAS/Photo Researchers; 94 CL Michael P. Gadomski/Photo Researchers; 95 T Jeff Lepore/Photo Researchers; 95 B John Serrao/Visuals Unlimited; 98 C Ron Kimball; 98 R Ron Kimball; 98 L Walter Chandoha; 99 Images reproduced from EYEWITNESS NATURAL WORLD by Steve Parker with permission of DK Publishing, Inc.; 100 T Breck P. Kent; 100 B Breck P. Kent; 101 T Science VU/Visuals Unlimited; 101 B Erwin & Peggy Bauer/Bruce Coleman Inc.; 102 T J. Beckett/American Museum of Natural History/Department of Library Services, Neg. No. 5758(6); 102 B Runk/Schoenberger/Grant Heilman Photography; 103 TR Francois Gohier/Photo Researchers; 103 B Larry Magino/Image Works; 103 TL Staffan Widstrand/Wildlife Collection; 105 Doug Locke/Dembinsky Photo Assoc. Inc.; 106 T Raphael Gaillarde/Liaison Agency; 114 T Michael Fogden/DRK Photo; 114 BR Francois Gohier/Photo Researchers; 114 BL Mark W. Moffett/Minden Pictures; 119 Francis/Donna Caldwell/Visuals Unlimited; 120 B Gail Shumway/FPG International Corp.; 120 T Jeanne Drake/Tony Stone Images; 121 B Luiz C. Marigo/Peter Arnold, Inc.; 121 T Alan & Sandy Carey/Photo Researchers; 122 T Jany Sauvanet/Photo Researchers; 122 BL David M. Phillips/Visuals Unlimited; 122 BR Kjell B. Sandved/Visuals Unlimited; 123 R Robert A. Lubeck/Animals Animals/Earth Scenes; 123 L Frans Lanting/Minden Pictures; 127 David M. Phillips/Visuals Unlimited; 139 Luiz C. Marigo/Peter Arnold, Inc.; 141 VU/Steve Maslowski/Visuals Unlimited

Unit B
1 Lester Lefkowitz/Stock Market; 2 T Vincent OBryne/Panoramic Image; 2 C Arie deZanger for Scott Foresman; 2 B Apollo/PhotoEdit; 3 CL Courtesy of Six Flags, California; 3 CR Courtesy of Six Flags, California; 3 B Mark E. Gibson/Gibson Color Photography; 9 T Erich Lessing/Art Resource, NY; 9 B The Granger Collection, New York; 12 CR Charles D. Winters/Photo Researchers; 13 CR Charles D. Winters/Photo Researchers; 13 T John D. Cunningham/Visuals Unlimited; 16 PhotoDisc, Inc.; 18 T Bruce Iverson; 20 Brent. R. Constantz, Ph.D., Norian Corporation; 29 TR John Paul Endress/Stock Market; 33 Inset Tony Freeman/PhotoEdit; 33 Alan Oddie/PhotoEdit; 34 Brown Brothers; 52 L James Balog/Tony Stone Images; 52 R James Balog/Tony Stone Images; 53 L James Balog/Tony Stone Images; 53 R James Balog/Tony Stone Images; 57 NASA; 58 T NASA; 58 B NASA; 59 Harold Edgerton Photos/Palm Press; 62 Barbara Stitzer/PhotoEdit; 66 T Yerkes Observatory; 67 T Superstock, Inc.; 67 C Jose Fuste Raga/Stock Market; 67 B Mark Richards/PhotoEdit; 73 Barbara Stitzer/PhotoEdit; 74 Roger Tully/Tony Stone Images; 77 Dennis Kitchen/Tony Stone Images; 79 Dennis Kitchen/Tony Stone Images; 81 Cary Wolinsky/Stock Boston; 82 Jose Carrillo/PhotoEdit; 86 R Jeff Greenberg/PhotoEdit; 87 C Dan Dempster/Dembinsky Photo Assoc. Inc.; 87 R M. Long/Visuals Unlimited; 88 BR Joyce Photographics/Photo Researchers; 88 T E. R. Degginger/Bruce Coleman Inc.; 88 BL Stu Rosner/Stock Boston; 92 CL; 92 R Pat OHara/Tony Stone Images; 93 L VANSCAN" Thermogram by Daedalus Enterprises, Inc.; 94 David Parker/SPL/Photo Researchers; 99 Spencer Grant/PhotoEdit; 115 Kent Wood/Photo Researchers; 132 L. S. Stepanowicz/Visuals Unlimited; 135 Chromosohm/Sohm/Stock Boston; 141 B Globus, Holway & Lobel/Stock Market